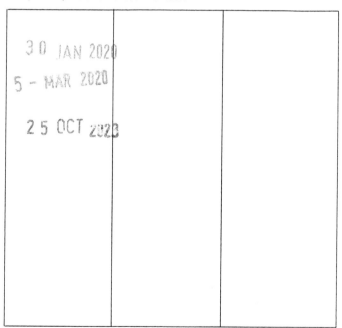

Battles of the Jacobite Rebellions

Battles of the Jacobite Rebellions

Killiecrankie to Culloden

Jonathan Oates

Pen & Sword
MILITARY

First published in Great Britain in 2019 by
PEN & SWORD MILITARY
An imprint of
Pen & Sword Books Ltd
Yorkshire – Philadelphia

Copyright © Jonathan Oates 2019

ISBN 978-1-52673-551-5

Typeset in 11/13 point MinionPro

Printed and bound by TJ International

Pen & Sword Books Ltd incorporates the Imprints of Aviation, Atlas, Family History, Fiction, Maritime, Military, Discovery, Politics, History, Archaeology, Select, Wharncliffe Local History, Wharncliffe True Crime, Military Classics, Wharncliffe Transport, Leo Cooper, The Praetorian Press, Remember When, White Owl, Seaforth Publishing and Frontline Publishing.

For a complete list of Pen & Sword titles please contact
PEN & SWORD BOOKS LIMITED
47 Church Street, Barnsley, South Yorkshire, S70 2AS, England
E-mail: enquiries@pen-and-sword.co.uk
Website: www.pen-and-sword.co.uk

Contents

List of Illustrations

Preface

The battles of the Jacobite campaigns (also known as the Jacobite rebellions and the Jacobite risings depending on whether the writer is hostile or sympathetic towards them) were part of the last military campaigns in Britain in which formed armies confronted one another. Much has been written about this aspect of British history ever since the eighteenth century and there is no sign, at the beginning of the twenty-first century, of such a trend abating. However, most studies focus on a particular campaign, usually the last struggle of 1745 which was led by Charles Edward Stuart, popularly known as Bonnie Prince Charlie or the Young Pretender, especially on the man himself and on the last battle, Culloden. In recent years there have been some very illuminating works produced which have done much to extend our understanding of the period, especially from the military point of view.[1] There are a few books about the conflict thirty years earlier and these have multiplied in the present century.[2] Focus on the other Jacobite attempts are even more limited, being chiefly restricted to biographies of the first principal leader, Viscount Dundee.[3] That said, there have been two recent books on the less well-known invasion attempts of 1708 and 1719.[4] Like all great historical topics, this is encrusted with a great deal of mythology in the popular mind, perpetuated by film, TV, songs and ballads.

This book aims to provide a concise account of all the campaigns, focusing on the battles which helped decide their outcome. There have been single-volume accounts previously, but they are either very limited in scope, concentrate on non-military matters or are very restricted in their source material.[5] Single-volume works about particular battles, especially Culloden, have been published.[6] There have also been books about battles in Scotland and Britain which usually include accounts of some of the battles of this era. This work details the battles and has interlinking chapters to explain the campaigns that led up to them and which followed them. These latter chapters will be fairly brief in order to give more space to the actual combat; they do not pretend to provide a detailed account of the events in these periods.

Rather it is the chapters on the battles which are given the most weight, as the title would suggest. Each of these will provide the same range of information. They will begin with a brief summary of the forces involved on both sides; wherever possible unit by unit, with strength of each where known. Wherever possible, contemporary estimates of numbers will be given. Sometimes, for the regular forces, these are based on muster rolls made before the battle. In many cases, exact and undisputed figures are unavailable, so a range will be provided; often only total figures for an army can be stated, as in the instance of General Wills's troops at Preston and in this case it is only an estimate.

We will then proceed to the initial deployment and aims of each commander, before progressing to the mechanics of the battle; what happened, why and with what results. Quotations from the letters, diaries and memoirs of those present will be used, as will any archaeological evidence available. Finally there will be a discussion of the battle's results and casualty figures, sometimes on a unit-by-unit basis or a range of estimates given by contemporaries where official figures (often disputed) are lacking.

The years 1689–1746 cover over five decades of warfare. In the late seventeenth century, the infantry of most armies in western Europe still employed the pike and matchlock musket. By the onset of the following century these had been swept away by flintlock muskets and bayonets, though cavalry and artillery were very similar. Yet Highland Scottish warfare, though not preserved in aspic, had changed but little except for the final demise of the bow, and prioritized melee over firefights. Warfare was essentially a case of regular versus irregular, but it was never a foregone conclusion that the former style of modern fighting would crush that of the 'backward' latter.

As with conflict on the European Continent, this was warfare which involved numerous nationalities. Despite the continued notion in popular fiction (for instance, the characters in the television series *Outlander* constantly referring to the English army and featuring, with one exception, only English soldiers among the redcoats) and the media (broadsheets noting that Culloden being a defeat for the Scots), this was nothing as simple as a war between the Scots and the English. In fact in 1689–90 both armies were overwhelmingly Scottish. In the following century, both nationalities fought on both sides; as well as Spanish, French and Irish troops fighting with the Jacobites and Dutch and Hessians and even some expatriate Irish and French being allied to their opponents. Multinational forces were the norm on the Continent; the Duke of Marlborough led Dutch and Germans as well as British troops in the War of Spanish Succession as the Duke of Cumberland was to do thirty years later in the War of the Austrian Succession. There is insufficient space in this book to discuss the officers and men of the armies which fought in these battles, but analysis can be found, for the Forty-Five, in books by Reid and Duffy; for the Fifteen and Eighty-Nine in those by Oates and Reid (see Bibliography).

This book, therefore, will use published and manuscript primary sources from record offices and libraries throughout England and Scotland to tell the story in the words of the participants from both sides of the battles of the Jacobite campaigns. It does not intend to discuss the details of the campaigns which they form an important part of except to give context and meaning to the fighting. Nor does it set out to offer the arguments of previous historians, though it is informed by former writings.

Dates will be in the Gregorian Old Style calendar in use in Britain until 1752 unless otherwise noted. Measurements will be in miles, feet and inches and money is pre-decimal (12 pence equals 1 shilling and 20 shillings to the pound). It should also be noted that given casualty figures often include numbers of wounded and missing; many of those in these categories either died of wounds or were actually dead.

Acknowledgements

Many people over the years have contributed, not always wittingly, to this book. The member of Keighley Public Library staff who issued me in the summer of 1982 with a book about the Jacobites, for one. Then there were my parents, who in 1985–6 took me around a number of sites in Scotland associated with various places mentioned herein. More recently I have been guided around the battlefields of Killiecrankie by Rulzion Rattray and of Prestonpans by Arran Johnstone, both experts in these struggles. My brother has unfailingly provided hospitality on my research trips to Scotland as well as taking me around Sheriffmuir. Help from archive and library staff at numerous places, but notably The National Archives, the National Records of Scotland, the National Library of Scotland, the Royal Archives and the British Library, to name the most prominent, was crucial. Finally I should like to recall that this book would never have been written had it not bene for the suggestion made by my former tutor, Professor Brian Kemp, and also my colleague since 2012, Dr Piotr Stolarski, who suggested I write this. I would like to dedicate this book to military history enthusiast (inter alia), Piotr Stolarski.

Maps

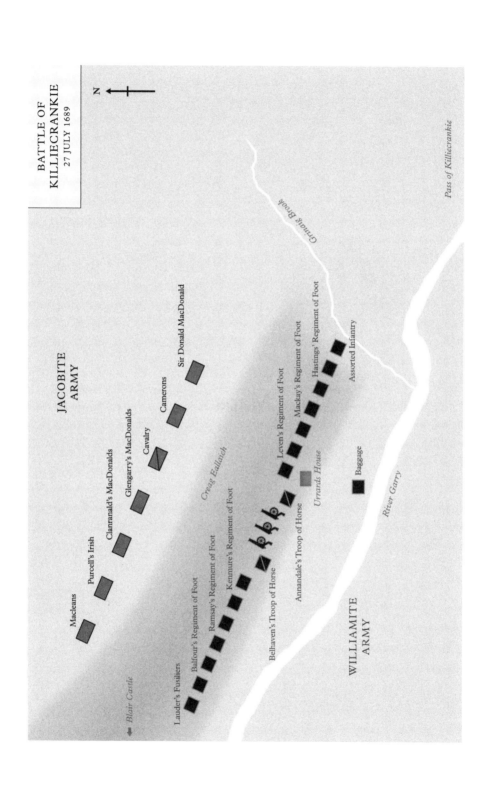

BATTLE OF
KILLIECRANKIE
27 JULY 1689

N

JACOBITE
ARMY

Macleans

Purcell's Irish

Clanranald's MacDonalds

Glengarry's MacDonalds

Cavalry

Camerons

Sir Donald MacDonald

Blair Castle

Lauder's Fusiliers

Balfour's Regiment of Foot

Ramsay's Regiment of Foot

Kenmure's Regiment of Foot

Belhaven's Troop of Horse

Annandale's Troop of Horse

Creag Eallaich

Leven's Regiment of Foot

Mackay's Regiment of Foot

Hastings' Regiment of Foot

Assorted Infantry

Urrards House

Grange Brook

Baggage

WILLIAMITE
ARMY

River Garry

Pass of Killiecrankie

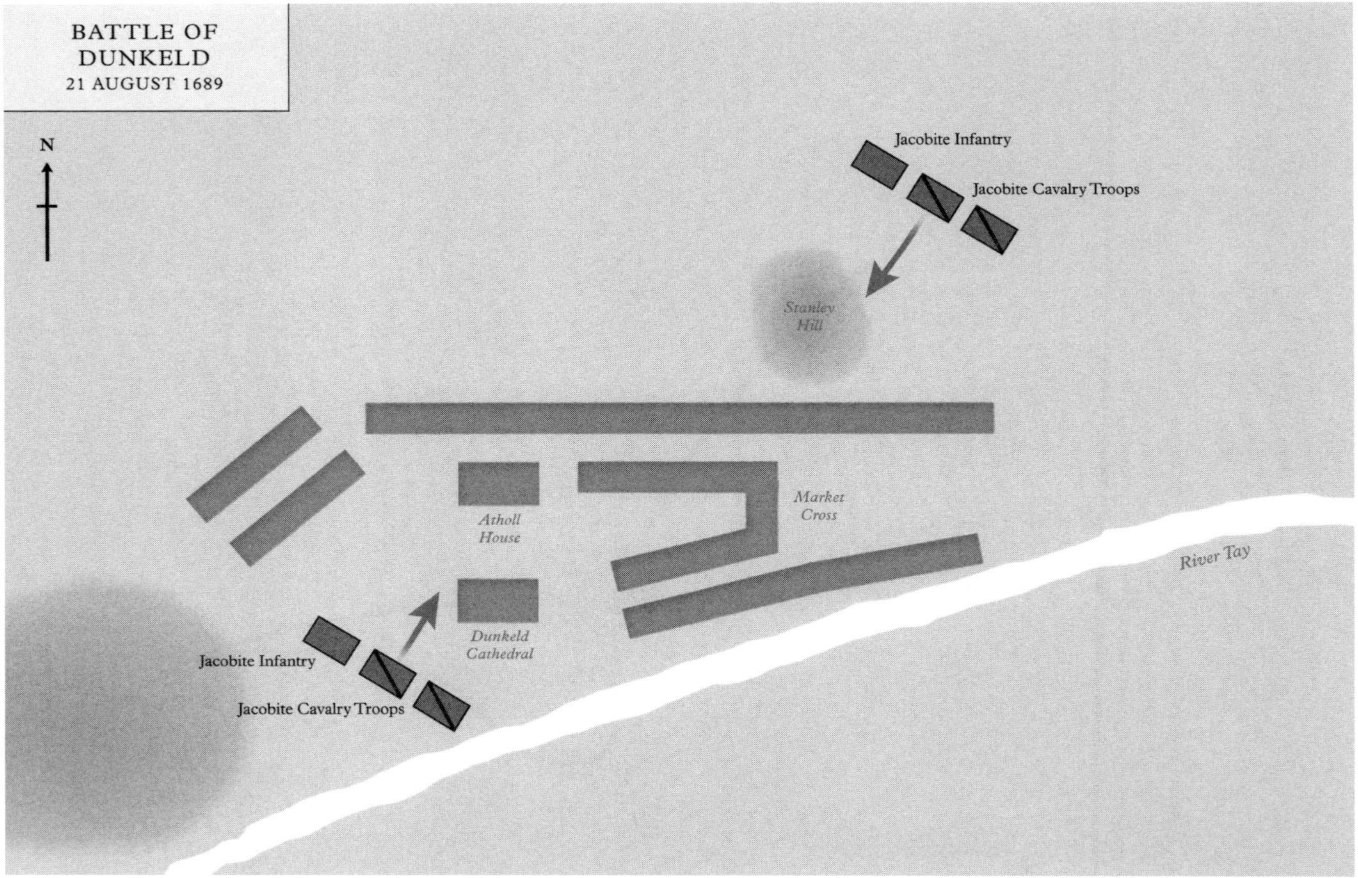

BATTLE OF
DUNKELD
21 AUGUST 1689

N

River Tay

Jacobite Cavalry Troops
Jacobite Infantry

Stanley
Hill

Market
Cross

Atholl
House

Dunkeld
Cathedral

Jacobite Infantry
Jacobite Cavalry Troops

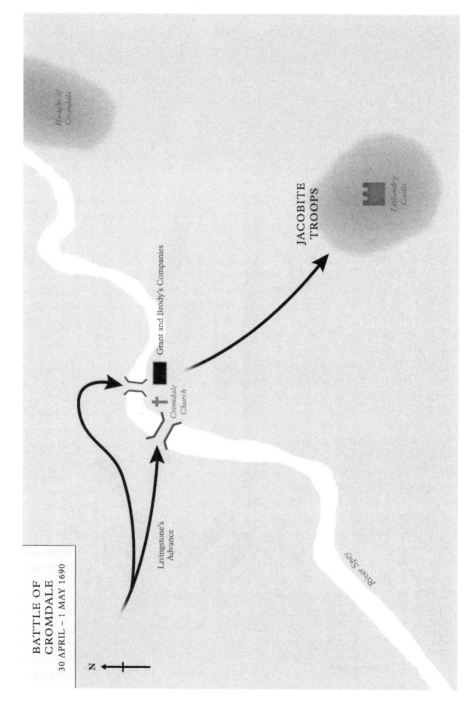

BATTLE OF
CROMDALE
30 APRIL – 1 MAY 1690

N

Haughs of
Cromdale

Grant and Brody's Companies

Cromdale
Church

Livingstone's Advance

JACOBITE
TROOPS

Leithentry
Castle

River Spey

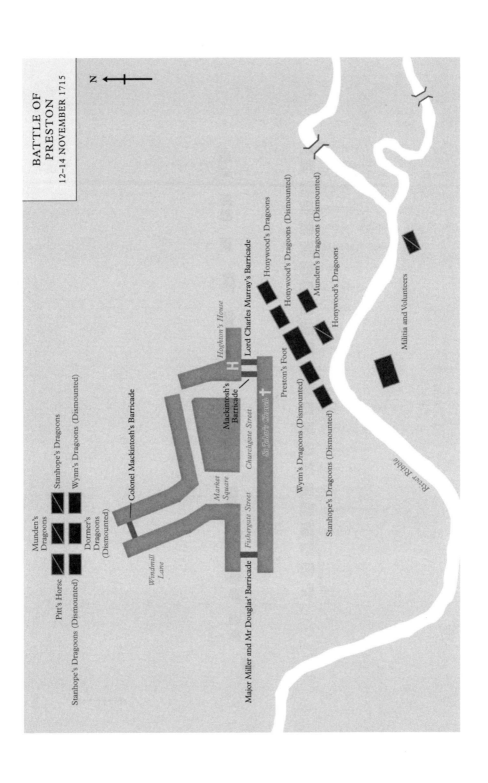

BATTLE OF
PRESTON
12–14 NOVEMBER 1715

N

Munden's
Dragoons

Stanhope's Dragoons

Pitt's Horse

Wynn's Dragoons (Dismounted)

Stanhope's Dragoons (Dismounted)

Dormer's
Dragoons
(Dismounted)

Colonel Mackintosh's Barricade

Windmill
Lane

Market
Square

Fishergate Street

Churchgate Street

Hoghton's House

Mackintosh's
Barricade

St John's Church

Lord Charles Murray's Barricade

Honywood's Dragoons

Honywood's Dragoons (Dismounted)

Preston's Foot

Munden's Dragoons (Dismounted)

Honywood's Dragoons

Wynn's Dragoons (Dismounted)

Stanhope's Dragoons (Dismounted)

Major Miller and Mr Douglas' Barricade

River Ribble

Militia and Volunteers

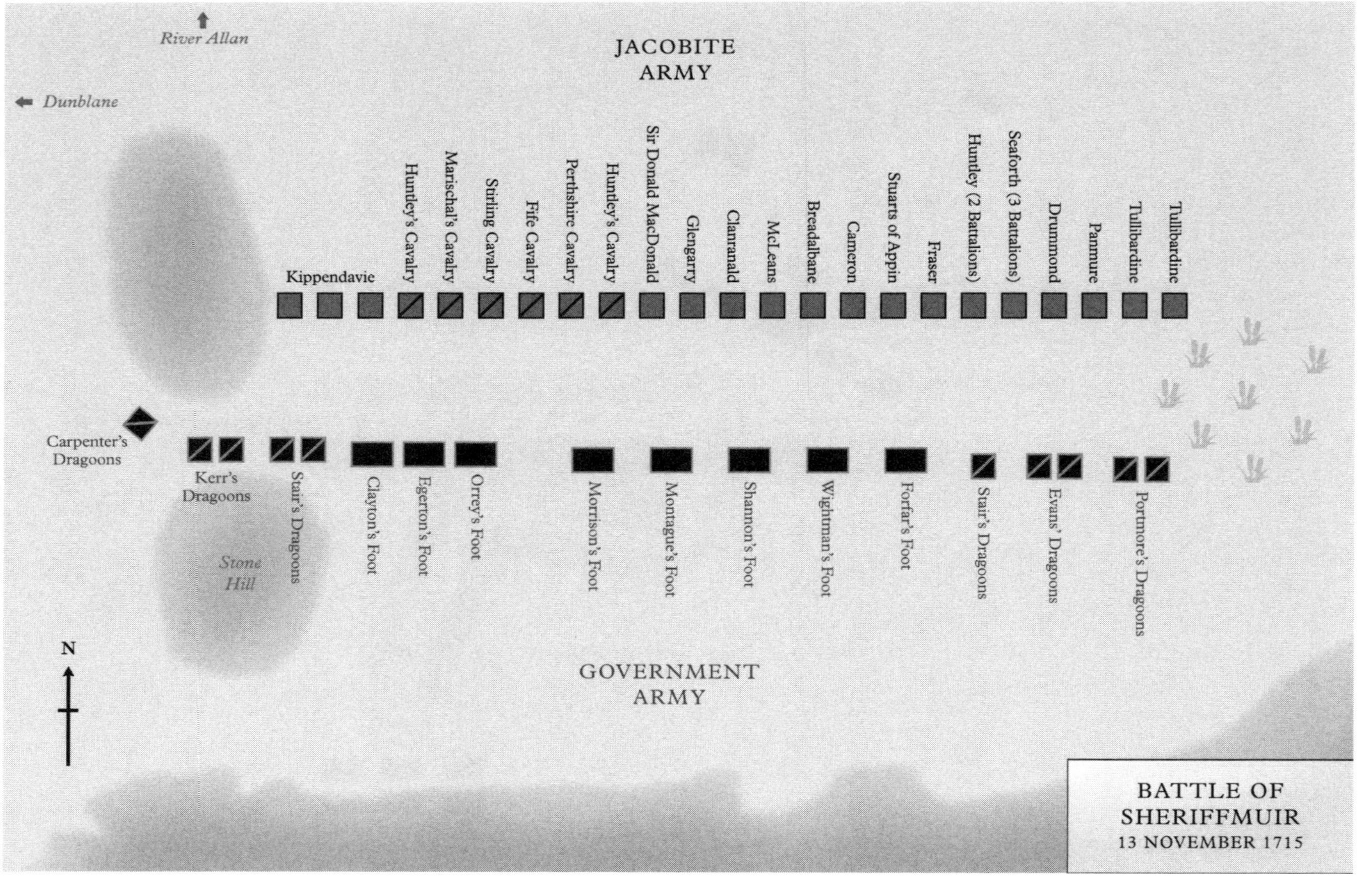

BATTLE OF SHERIFFMUIR
13 NOVEMBER 1715
JACOBITE ARMY
GOVERNMENT ARMY
River Allan
Dunblane
Kippendavie
Huntley's Cavalry
Marischal's Cavalry
Stirling Cavalry
Fife Cavalry
Perthshire Cavalry
Huntley's Cavalry
Sir Donald MacDonald
Glengarry
Clanranald
McLeans
Breadalbane
Cameron
Stuarts of Appin
Fraser
Huntley (2 Battalions)
Seaforth (3 Battalions)
Drummond
Panmure
Tullibardine
Tullibardine
Carpenter's Dragoons
Kerr's Dragoons
Stair's Dragoons
Clayton's Foot
Egerton's Foot
Orrey's Foot
Morrison's Foot
Montague's Foot
Shannon's Foot
Wightman's Foot
Forfar's Foot
Stair's Dragoons
Evans' Dragoons
Portmore's Dragoons
Stone Hill
N

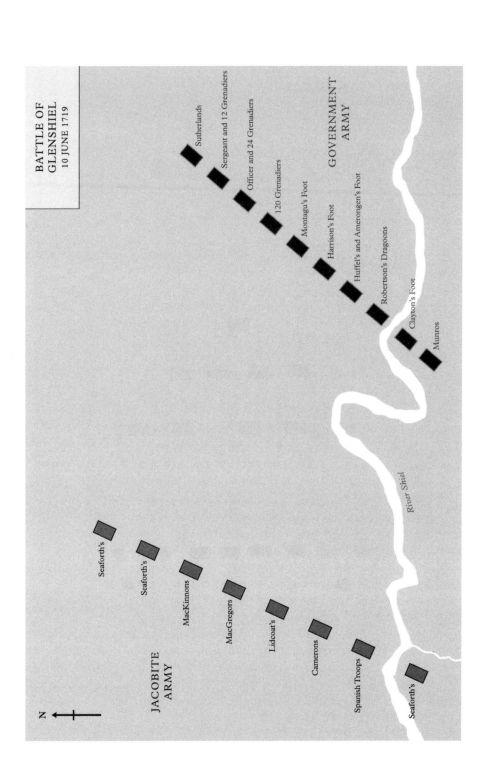

BATTLE OF
GLENSHIEL
10 JUNE 1719

N

JACOBITE
ARMY

Seaforth's

Seaforth's

MacKinnons

MacGregors

Lidcoat's

Camerons

Spanish Troops

Seaforth's

River Shiel

GOVERNMENT
ARMY

Sutherlands

Sergeant and 12 Grenadiers

Officer and 24 Grenadiers

120 Grenadiers

Montagu's Foot

Harrison's Foot

Huffel's and Amerongen's Foot

Robertson's Dragoons

Clayton's Foot

Munros

N

Firth of Forth

Cockenzie

Seton

JACOBITE ARMY

MacDonals of Clanranald

MacDonals of Glengarry

MacDonals of Keppoch & Glencoe

Camerons

Stuarts of Appin

Atholl Men

Menzies

Viscount Strathallan's Cavalry

MacLauchlans

Duke of Perth's Men

GOVERNMENT ARMY

Hamilton's Dragoons

Murray's Foot

Lascelles' Foot

Lee's Foot

Guises' Foot

Artillery Guard

Gardiner's Dragoons

Preston House

Long Ditch

Preston

BATTLE OF PRESTONPANS
21 SEPTEMBER 1745

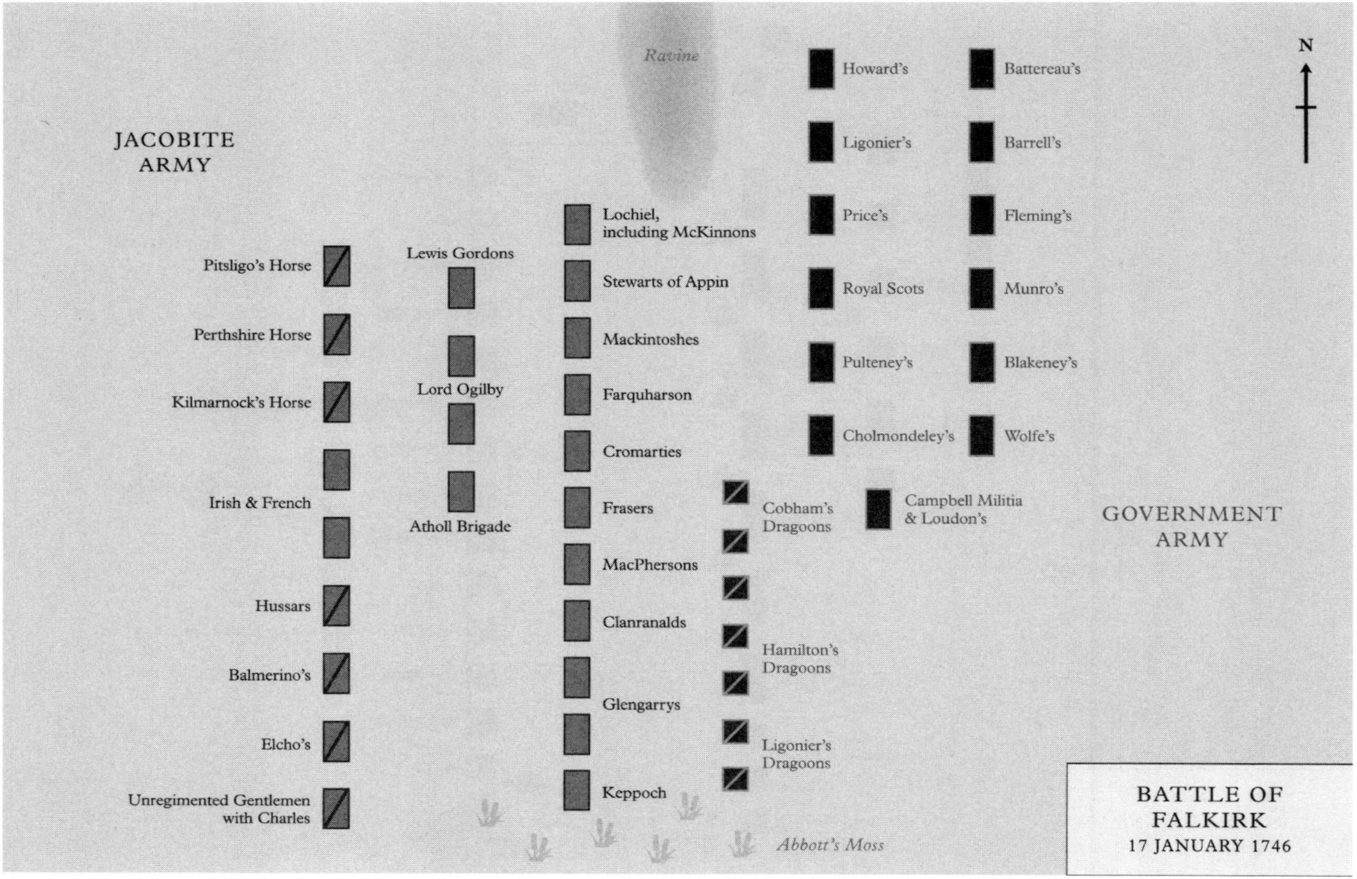

N

JACOBITE ARMY

Battereau's Howard's

Barrell's Ligonier's

Fleming's Price's

Munro's Royal Scots

Blakeney's Pulteney's

Wolfe's Cholmondeley's

Campbell Militia & Loudon's

Cobham's Dragoons

Hamilton's Dragoons

Ligonier's Dragoons

GOVERNMENT ARMY

Raine

Lochiel, including McKinnons

Stewarts of Appin

Mackintoshes

Farquharson

Cromarties

Frasers

MacPhersons

Clanranalds

Glengarrys

Keppoch

Abbott's Moss

Lewis Gordons

Lord Ogilby

Atholl Brigade

Pitsligo's Horse

Perthshire Horse

Kilmarnock's Horse

Irish & French

Hussars

Balmerino's

Elcho's

Unregimented Gentlemen with Charles

BATTLE OF FALKIRK
17 JANUARY 1746

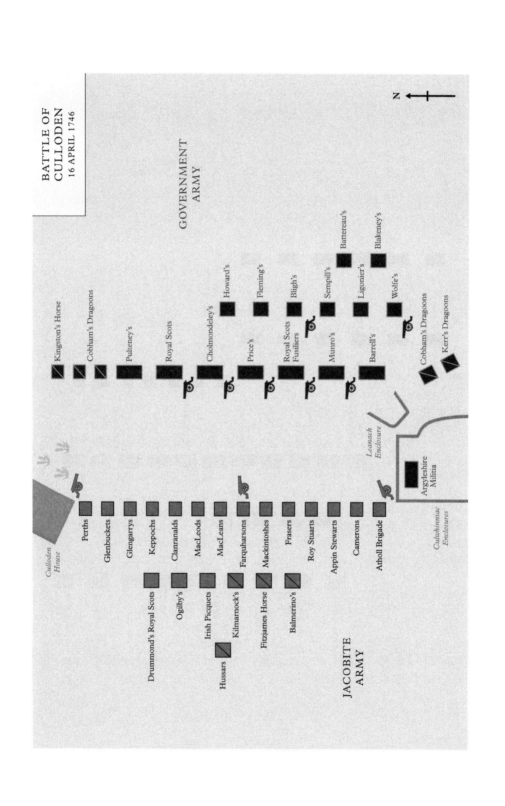

BATTLE OF
CULLODEN
16 APRIL 1746

N

GOVERNMENT
ARMY

Kingston's Horse

Cobham's Dragoons

Pulteney's

Royal Scots

Cholmondeley's

Price's

Royal Scots
Fusiliers

Munro's

Barrell's

Howard's

Fleming's

Bligh's

Sempill's

Ligonier's

Wolfe's

Battereau's

Blakeney's

Cobham's Dragoons

Kerr's Dragoons

Argyleshire
Militia

Leanach
Enclosure

Culchinniac
Enclosures

Culloden
House

Perths

Glenbuckets

Glengarrys

Keppochs

Clanranalds

MacLeods

MacLeans

Farquharsons

Mackintoshes

Frasers

Roy Stuarts

Appin Stewarts

Camerons

Atholl Brigade

Drummond's Royal Scots

Ogilby's

Irish Picquets

Kilmarnock's

Fitzjames Horse

Balmerino's

Hussars

JACOBITE
ARMY

Chapter 1

The Origins of the Jacobite Campaigns, 1688–1689

Britain's last phase of internal warfare came about because of the conflict set in motion by James II of England and VII of Scotland (1633–1701) and many of his subjects in both kingdoms. He had succeeded his charming and politically astute brother, Charles II, on the latter's death in February 1685. Charles had ruled in alliance with the Anglican and Episcopalian Protestant elites supported by the mass of society under them, and had done so in his final years without Parliament. Opposition was limited and became increasingly marginalized. His brother lacked Charles's skills and was an open Catholic, unlike the great majority of his subjects who hated and feared Catholicism, if not individual Catholics. Defeating two rebellions in 1685 with relative ease, James was confident that he could push forward with his policies designed to promote Catholics in state and society. Essentially he used his controversial prerogative powers as monarch to waive Parliamentary legislation barring Catholics from positions in the armed forces (which he greatly expanded in peacetime; another unpopular move), the universities and other institutions, and promised religious toleration for all Christians. In doing so he managed to alienate many of his natural supporters.

Parliaments in both England and Scotland refused to comply with his wishes, so were prorogued. James hoped to recall them in order that they would agree to his wishes, but never got the chance. In 1688, a son was born to his queen. This was James Francis Stuart (1688–1766), known to friends as James III and VIII and to enemies as the (Old) Pretender. The prospect of a future line of Catholic monarchs appalled many in Britain and the usual celebrations for the royal birth were muted. This birth also thwarted William of Orange (1650–1702), Stadtholder of the Dutch Republic who was married to James' eldest and Protestant daughter, Mary (1662–94), for had James died without male issue he would have been Britain's next ruler. Seven disgruntled English lords contacted William to persuade him that he should come to Britain and rid them of their Catholic king.

On 5 November, William's armada arrived at Torbay. He had a large multinational army with him, including Dutch, Danes, Germans, English and Scots. Yet James had a larger army, reinforced from Scotland, assembling on Salisbury Plain. Although most had never fired a shot in anger, it would seem on paper to have been a formidable force. The weakness was that a number of senior officers including John Churchill (1650–1722), later Duke of Marlborough, and Lord Cornbury, men who James should have been able to trust, deserted to William, taking a minority of the troops with him. James still had enough men to deal with William but his nerve broke and, feeling betrayed, he left the country, escaping on the second attempt to France by the year's end. Meanwhile anti-Catholic mobs destroyed Catholic properties.

In both England and Scotland there was much discussion as to Britain's political and constitutional future. Even some who detested James and his policies were concerned to see him dethroned and the succession broken. Yet eventually the crowns were offered to William and Mary, who succeeded in February 1689 in England and April in Scotland. There was really no alternative, and William was *in situ* with sizeable armed forces.

James was in France in exile, but his brother monarch and co-religionist Louis XIV (1638–1715) of France wished to see him enthroned again, if only to weaken William III who was Louis's arch enemy in the Nine Years War (1688–97) which had just begun. One reason why William was keen to take the British throne was that he could then combine British resources with those of the Dutch Republic in his struggle against the French. James arrived in Ireland in March 1689 with French troops and quickly gained the support of much of the population because, unlike in mainland Britain, most were Catholic and thus sympathetic towards his policies. With Ireland as a base he could then attempt to retake the rest of his kingdoms. However, the English and Scottish settlers in Ulster were Protestant and so unwilling to acquiesce without a struggle and thus their strongholds in Inniskillen and Londonderry had to be first subdued and this was to prove no easy task.

In Scotland a convention of representatives of the nation was summoned in Edinburgh in March 1689 to decide the country's future although William had already been accepted as a protector. The convention was divided over who to accept as King, but James's letter to them was as undiplomatic as William's was not. Some representatives left the convention and prominent among these was John Claverhouse, Viscount Dundee (1648–89), a Lowlander and a professional soldier. He was a strong supporter of James. The Duke of Gordon held Edinburgh Castle for James, but isolated as he was, he was unable to actively assist his monarch.

There was also concern in the Scottish capital about the lack of troops, the small Scottish army having been disbanded. William agreed to despatch a regiment of Scottish cavalry and three weak regiments of the Anglo-Dutch Brigade (about 1,100 men) under Major General Hugh Mackay (1640–92). Before they could arrive, Dundee, allegedly fearful of being murdered, left Edinburgh with a troop of cavalry from the regiment he was once colonel of. The convention wrote to him at his home near the city of Dundee, requiring him to return to the Scottish capital. He did not do so and in April gathered his men and raised the standard of James II. Evading arrest, he and his men went to the Highlands to gather support.

The Scottish convention believed they needed to create an army and gave commissions for ten regiments of infantry and twelve troops of cavalry to be raised by noblemen believed loyal to the new monarchs, who had now been recognized as rightful rulers of Scotland as well as England. Mackay was concerned that Dundee might raise men to fight for James. Followers of James were known as Jacobites after the Latin for James (Jacobus). Termed rebels by the government and its supporters, they will be referred to as Jacobites from now on.

By the end of April, Mackay marched north with 200 of the Anglo-Dutch troops and two regiments of cavalry in order to apprehend Dundee. The latter's faster-moving forces eluded Mackay and in the following month were able to take tax revenues from Perth and Dunkeld, seize a few of the Scottish government's officers and even threaten the city of Dundee. There were others in the Highlands who supported James and at the end of May there was a gathering in Lochaber of these men, which included the clans of the Camerons, the MacDonalds, the Macleans and the Stewarts of Appin. There were other successes for the Jacobites at this time. Ruthven barracks was garrisoned by a newly-raised company of Scottish government infantry and was called upon to surrender. Lacking supplies and, after three days, no prospect of relief, Captain Grant surrendered it at discretion and marched off.

Mackay, now at Inverness, had sent messages to Brigadier Barthold Balfour in Edinburgh to despatch Colonel George Ramsay with 600 of the Anglo-Dutch infantry and a regiment of English cavalry to reinforce him. However, Mackay's correspondence was intercepted by his enemies and Ramsay, marching north from Perth, was confronted by the Marquis of Atholl's numerous tenants and felt it was too dangerous to progress and so retreated. Dundee also learnt that a number of officers in one of Mackay's regiments of horse were Jacobites and so might be able to bring their men to his side.

Although Mackay's troops were well entrenched, their supplies were limited, they were outnumbered and he was lacking the reinforcements he desired. After having encountered a scouting party of Jacobites he withdrew his men. There then followed a three-day pursuit, in which on at least one occasion the Jacobites prepared for battle, but eventually Mackay was succoured by two regiments from Edinburgh. It was then Dundee's turn to flee. Before he did so, the Macleans fought a regiment or two of English cavalry. Contemporaries differed over the results of the skirmish, with each side presenting it as a victory for themselves. Mackay did not think he could pursue Dundee for he believed his cavalry would be unable to subsist in the mountainous terrain. Mackay learnt of the plotters amongst his cavalry and had them sent as prisoners to Edinburgh.

Dundee and his command were safe enough, but most had to be disbanded because of the lack of supplies. He spent much of June and July writing to potential supporters, such as Cluny of MacPherson and Lord Murray, Atholl's son. He emphasised that the king's cause was enjoying success in Ireland, with Londonderry's fall being imminent, and that substantial support from Ireland was on its way. Neither was correct.

Mackay felt that he needed to secure the Highlands and especially Scotland's towns and cities to deny the supplies they potentially offered to the Jacobites. He left a strong garrison in Inverness, whilst the newly-raised Scottish regiments garrisoned other places. At Edinburgh the castle surrendered due to lack of supplies to Sir John Lanier, who had brought some English forces to Scotland. Currently both sides were at stalemate, unable and unwilling to engage on potentially disadvantageous terms. However, steps were afoot that would lead to a major confrontation.

Dundee tried to raise more men to the Jacobite cause; on 10 July he ordered the Athollmen to meet him at Blair in arms. To encourage them, he assured them he had 4,000 men and would tell James of their actions. There was also a threat, letting them know that any who refused the call would be deemed traitors.[1] He wrote on 18 July to Cluny of MacPherson, 'tis high time for you to draw to armes, which I desire you to do with all your men and followers'. Four days later he wrote again, referring to Irish support having arrived and that French help was soon anticipated.[2] Likewise on 10 July he implored that the Robertsons of Strachloch and Bleaktoune 'rise in arms and come to Blair of Atholl'.[3]

Meanwhile, George, first Earl of Melville (1636–1707) and Secretary of State for Scotland, wrote to Mackay on 4 June to state that he had been told by William to return to the Lowlands to secure Edinburgh and Glasgow 'for the safety if the country rather than goe in pursuit of Dundee through the Highlands which would render the horse unserviceable through want of forrage travelling in bad wayes'.[4] There were also fears of an incursion from Ireland, though Mackay wrote that the Earl of Portland assured him that there was 'no thing to feare from that parte' or he would have marched southwards immediately.[5] By 13 June he had despatched Colchester's cavalry southwards, in order to assuage the politicians' fears.[6]

On 20 June, Mackay decided to march more of his forces, principally 500 men from the Anglo-Dutch regiments, towards Edinburgh. He reasoned that he could not pursue his enemy into difficult terrain and he would be unable to subsist his forces there. Furthermore, his illness of earlier in the year had returned and so he was unable to ride a horse, a key ingredient for an active commander in the field. He told the Duke of Hamilton, 'I will nevertheless leave this country as well provided as I can'.[7] In order to keep a grip on the north he left Sir Thomas Livingstone (c.1652–1711) with his own cavalry regiment, Leslie's regiment, 200 men from Leven's regiment and 100 from Hastings's, in all about 1,000 men. Berkeley's cavalry garrisoned Aberdeen.[8]

On 12 July, Mackay was back in Edinburgh, discussing the possibility of having a fortress built in the west Highlands. During this time, Dundee secured Atholl and Badenoch.[9] Mackay was still in the capital on 20 July. However, two days later, he was preparing to leave to confront Dundee, by marching to Stirling and then to Perth. He was confident of the result, 'it seems they will have a last pull for it, for in their own mynds I doe believe that this small succour will more discouradge sort of them, more then it will raise their hops'.[10]

Mackay took six regiments of foot 'making at most 3000 men' and four troops of both horse and dragoons. He intended to meet the Earl of Argyle with the forces at his command. What determined him to march was a letter from Lord Murray telling him that his father's castle at Blair had been taken for the Jacobites by the steward there. Murray told him he had no hopes of persuading his father's tenants of switching their allegiance to William. He would therefore go to Atholl and gather the tenants and retake the castle. Mackay replied that all he wanted was that Murray try to keep the men from joining the Jacobites.[11]

Although Mackay was eager to march towards Atholl to prevent Dundee from marching to Lochaber, delays in the government's provision of meal and horses to transport it, meant eight or ten days passed before Mackay could follow Murray into Perthshire. Eventually Mackay 'prest with all earnestness his dispatch to secure at least the country of Athole with others adjacent, from casting themselves headlong in the adverse party'. As part of this he intended to retake Blair Castle and so took four petards with him to destroy its gates, and then leave a strong garrison there.[12]

Two days later after leaving Edinburgh, he was at Stirling. He felt himself 'to be straitned for provisions in this expedition'. It was here that he ordered the majority of the cavalry to march to Perth to rendezvous with him there.[13] Mackay told Hamilton, 'coming here to Stirling I find what wherewith be great deficiencie in the fournishing of the hors for the transport of meal.

I am affrayed of the inevitable evill which will follow if the forces should want subsistence.' There were provisions arriving for two weeks, but he needed them for four weeks, and that they were at Perth. Without such a supply he would have to retire from the theatre of operations without any opportunity to engage the enemy.[14]

It was when he was at Stirling that a letter from Murray arrived, telling him that Dundee was in Badenoch and was marching to Atholl. If Mackay did not arrive there first, he could not promise him that the 1,500 Atholl men would not join Dundee. Because of this, and the fear that men from the Isles, Badenoch, Monteith and Marr might join Dundee, Mackay realized he could not halt his command's march at Perth to await the cavalry he had ordered to rendezvous with him there. Anything that looked like faintheartedness in his forces might encourage other Jacobites to rise for James II. Possession of the castle at Blair would stem Jacobite recruits from Atholl.[15]

Mackay was also confident in his own forces. This was despite the fact that 'all of them [were] almost new raised levies'. He thought that the Jacobites had 'shewed nothing that looked like briskness' in the opening stages of the campaign. So because of his confidence and the need to secure the castle, Mackay eschewed the additional four troops of dragoons and two of horse that he would otherwise have had in his little army.[16]

Dundee learnt of his enemy's advance towards Blair Atholl and began to summon his forces there on 21 July. If the castle fell, it could cut his communications between northern and western Scotland. He was impressed by the loyalty of the Athollmen and marched the men he had at his immediate command, 1,800 in all, towards Blair. Orders were given for the rest of his army to follow him. There were only 240 Camerons with him, so John, the eldest son, was sent with messengers to bring up the rest of the clansmen.[17]

Dundee marched to Atholl with all speed. En route he was joined by Major General Alexander Cannon and Colonel Nicholas Purcell from Ireland with 300 men, a far cry from the numbers requested and promised, and the Highlanders were 'miserably dissapoynted'. Dundee was not outwardly dismayed and his men, though half starved, had faith in him and were in good spirits as a serious military confrontation loomed.[18]

Mackay was certainly eager for battle but was unsure as late as 26 July whether Dundee would oblige him, writing then to the Lord of Weemys, 'I doe not believe that Dundee is so neare, though I wish he were, let his forces be what they will'.[19] Meanwhile, he marched from Perth to Dunkeld, where he told Hamilton, that he must take the castle 'for is impossible an army can passe without som prejudice particularly to the corns where grass is wanting . . . I shall doe all the diligence I can towards the reduction of Blair Castle and the settling a garrison in it to serve us as a magazine', though it would need to be made stronger by the employment of pioneers.[20]

At midnight on 26 July Mackay had a letter from Murray. This told him that he had lost the race. Dundee was in Atholl and Murray had left Blair and travelled through the pass of Killiecrankie, southbound. Murray told Mackay that he had left men to secure the near side of the pass for Mackay's benefit.[21] The first major clash of arms was now imminent as the armies were to fight over Blair Castle. Battles over the possession of a fortress were not uncommon as they represented a tangible gain.

Chapter 2

The Battle of Killiecrankie, 27 July 1689

It was a 'good' day to fight a battle. It was the height of summer, which meant that there were many hours of daylight and an absence of rain which would otherwise make musketry and cannon useless. Visibility was good. Yet for the uniformed regular troops, the heat would be an added strain on a day that would be difficult enough, physically and emotionally.

Dundee arrived at Blair Castle on the morning of Saturday, 27 July and learnt that Mackay's force was at Dunkeld, 16 miles away to the south, and on their march to Blair. They would have to march through the Pass of Killiecrankie. This was a narrow path at the foot of a steep hill, where only three men could pass at a time. Although a handful of resolute men could have held up a far larger force there, there was no one to oppose him, at least not at that point.[1] According to the Jacobite Colonel Hector Macneill, there was initially a Jacobite plan to march immediately towards the enemy with 400–500 men to attack them in the pass. Many officers supported this idea as they believed the army was not strong enough to defeat Mackay's complete army on other terrain. Yet this would take too much time and there was too little to authorize it. The troops were too far distant and so an order was given 'to our little army to come up att all expedition imaginable'.[2]

That morning, at daybreak, Mackay sent despatches to Perth to hurry up the six troops of dragoons and horse which were part of his command, though they were never to arrive, leaving his force pitifully short of cavalry. Lieutenant Colonel George Lauder was sent ahead with '200 choice fusiliers', to secure the pass ahead of the main force 'and to send back what advertisement they could have of the enemy'. They left Dunkeld at four in the morning. He then marched his main body of troops towards them. It was accomplished by ten that morning. The troops were then allowed two hours to refresh themselves. Mackay met Murray before the pass, and it was ascertained that there were 200–300 Atholl men with him, most having left to save their cattle. Mackay thought that this was 'reasonable as well as customary'.[3]

Lauder sent his force through the pass and found that it was clear. The rest of the army marched through it in the following order: Balfour's, Ramsay's and Kenmure's infantry regiments, then Belhaven's troop, followed by Leven's and Mackay's infantry. The baggage train of 1,200 horses was next. Hastings's regiment and Annandale's troop brought up the rear. This latter infantry regiment was then assigned to guard the baggage for Mackay believed that the Jacobites might detach men to attack it or that the country people, seeing it was undefended, might plunder it.[4] The baggage was also guarded by 100 men sent from the laird of Weemys.[5]

Meanwhile, a few miles to the north-west, Dundee called a council of war as to whether to fight or not. Those with military experience suggested that they should delay until the units expected had got there, to maximize their strength. Clan chiefs argued for an immediate attack whilst morale was high. Dundee agreed, but was told that he should not lead from the front. He told them that was exactly where he would be and this proved to be a fateful decision.[6]

The Jacobite army marched towards the Pass of Killiecrankie and formed up on 'a rugged uneven, but not very high mountain'. Mackay's force had already cleared the pass and were forming up on the plain which extends along the river. Sir Ewan Cameron of Lochiel believed that Mackay wished to use his superior numbers to outflank Dundee, so he drew up his men in just one line, without any reserve. Mackay's men stood in ranks of three. Since they were tired by their rapid march in order to get through the pass without being attacked, they were allowed to sit on the ground where they would otherwise have stood.[7]

Once Mackay's first five regiments and Belhaven's troop had reached the other side of the pass, they halted in a cornfield on the banks of the River Garry in order to allow the slower-moving rearguard to catch up. Mackay ordered Lauder to advance with 200 fusiliers and a troop of horse, presumably Belhaven's, in order to locate the Jacobite army. They advanced some hundreds of paces up the hill. Advance parties of the Jacobite army came into view. Mackay galloped to where the viewpoint was. He ordered Balfour to have the ammunition distributed and to put the soldiers under arms.[8]

Mackay could see some small groups of Jacobites about a mile away. They were marching slowly along the foot of a hill near Blair, the Creag Eallaich, towards where his army was. Before refreshing himself, he sent orders to Balfour to march towards where he was, with all the infantry. Yet ahead was 'an eminence just above the ground . . . of a steep and difficult ascent, full of trees and shrubs, and within a carbine shot' of where his men were. Mackay believed that this terrain would be advantageous to his enemy, reasoning that from it 'they could undoubtedly force us with their fire in confusion over the river'.[9]

In order to counter this, he had each regiment form by a Quart de Conversion (a 90-degree turn in the line) to the right of the ground on which they stood, so that they were all facing the slopes. They then marched up the hill and avoided the difficulty just foreseen. Their new location meant that they 'got a ground fair enough to receive the enemy', but were not in a position to attack them, for within musket shot there was another contour before them. His army, therefore, were on the lowest contour whereas the Jacobites were above them, with their backs to the very high hill. This, Mackay believed, was the natural position of the Highlanders, who preferred to have a sure retreat behind them, especially if their enemy included cavalry.[10]

By now the five regiments of infantry and one troop of horse were in position. Hastings's regiment was still marching through the pass. The Jacobites were visible on the slopes above them. Mackay resolved to have his troops remain where they were, rather than 'to put his men out of breath and in disorder by attacking the enemy against the hill'. He had his regiments move in order that only a little distance remained between each one. The 200 fusiliers that Lauder had led through the pass remained together (thus denuding the regiments the benefit of these elite troops), 'posted advantageously upon the left of all, on a little hill wreathed with trees'. Each of the regiments was then divided into two and then each arranged so that it was three men deep. In the middle of the battle line there was a great opening and it was here that he placed his two troops of horse. By now both were together and Hastings's regiment had arrived as well and the latter were now on the right of his line. Mackay also placed a 'detachment of firelocks from each battalion to the right hand to fortify Hastings' [under-strength] regiment'. It is not known how large this collection of men was, nor who led it. To their immediate right was a small brook running off the Garry. Mackay intended, when the Jacobites attacked and after his infantry had fired, to have the cavalry flank the enemy on either side, as he did not want to expose his cavalry to the enemy's, believing the latter's to be superior in quality, composed as they were largely of veteran troops against Mackay's newly-raised horsemen.[11]

We now turn to the composition of each army, beginning with the Jacobites. There are varying figures given by contemporaries. One was that Dundee had 2,500 infantry and a troop of cavalry.[12] Another stated there were but 1,800 infantry and 45 cavalry.[13] Macneill gave the figure of but 1,600 and also one of 1,900.[14] Captain Creighton, who was not present, states that there were 1,700 infantry, including 300 Irish, and 45 cavalry.[15] The total number was under 2,000 men according to Cameron.[16]

Individual unit strengths given by contemporaries are as follows:

> Order of battle from right to left:
> Macleans under Sir John Mclean, 200 or 500
> Irish battalion under Colonel Nicholas Purcell, 300 men
> Clanranalds, 400 or 600
> Glengarrys, 300
> Cavalry Troop, 40–50 men (initially on the left flank)

> Camerons, 240 strong, but 40 detached as advance guard
> Sir Donald MacDonald's battalion, 500 or 700.[17]

At a minimum, there were about 1,980 Jacobites, at a maximum, 2,680, but the true figure probably lies somewhere in between. There was no artillery and cavalry formed a mere 2 per cent of the army.

It is generally agreed that Mackay had a numerical advantage. As to contemporaries, Sir Ewan Cameron of Lochiel believed that Mackay had 3,500 infantry and two troops of horse.[18] Another Jacobite source listed him as having eight regiments of foot, totalling 4,500, with two troops of horse.[19] Highest is Creighton's estimate of 5,000 men.[20] Hamilton put his numbers at 4,000 infantry and thought he had four troops of horse.[21] Mackay wrote that he had 3,000 infantry at most and the cavalry.[22] As he was in actual command of these troops it would seem that he was probably best placed to know the most accurate figure. Sir John Lanier wrote a few days later that Mackay had 3,000 men, too.[23] An anonymous contemporary source agrees with Mackay that he had 3,000 foot and two troops of horse.[24] There were also three 'leather guns' (cannon with long, thin barrels wrapped in leather for lightness), in the charge of Master Gunner James Smith and Second Lieutenant Theodore Drury.[25]

It is impossible to be sure of the numbers of each unit, for there are no surviving muster rolls or lists of numbers. In theory each infantry regiment should have been 780 men strong, but the reality is likely to have been far different. The total strength of Dutch-Scottish regiments, Ramsay's, Mackay's and Balfour's, was 1,960 in 1688, but this had plummeted to 1,100 in March 1689 as William had creamed off the best men for service elsewhere, and though more may have been recruited thereafter as ordered, there may also have been losses due to illness, desertion, wounds and death. In May there is a reference to Balfour's regiment being supplied with 400 pikes and 400 muskets (suggesting a strength of 800, perhaps) and later that month that Ramsay's having 600 veterans. Ramsay's had 624 men in April 1689 judging by its order for uniforms.[26] One contemporary source noted that in sum these three regiments consisted at the battle of 1,500 men in total.[27]

Leven's regiment began its existence in March with 800 men, and by July had a depleted strength due to 200 men being at Inverness and similarly Hastings's regiment, having 500 men in 1688, then 780 men in early 1689 (in 1690 it is cited as being 606 strong), lacked 100 men who were at Inverness.[28] The contemporary source just mentioned has Leven with 600 men at least and Hastings with 500.[29] Annandale's Troop and Belhaven's Troop numbered 'about a hundert hors' in total.[30] There were also 100 Highlanders led by Lord Weemys' son, as baggage guards.[31]

What was perhaps significant about the army's composition was its lack of cavalry; whereas conventionally cavalry might make up a quarter to a third of an army, as had been the case at Sedgemoor, here, with only about 100 cavalrymen and 3,000 infantry, the proportion was a thirtieth. If Mackay had been facing a regular army he would have had serious problems as his cavalry would not have been able to prevent the enemy's from combining attacks with their infantry on his infantry. As it was, the Jacobite cavalry was even fewer than his and formed an even smaller proportion of their army. Yet a more substantial cavalry force could have given the advantage to him. He thus went into battle lacking such; perhaps he believed that he could win without them.

It is also worth noting that this was largely an inexperienced army whose training was limited. Leven's and Kenmure's regiments and the two troops of horse had only been in existence for four months. Hastings's had been formed four years ago but had probably not heard a shot fired in anger. Although the three Dutch regiments had been in existence far longer, the majority of the men in these units had limited experience of war. The troops had a mixture of weapons; mostly matchlocks, but some with flintlocks, some with bayonets but many not, and some had pikes not firearms. Apparently on 20 July all of Kenmure's musketeers, perhaps 450, were provided with bayonets, but the regiment's pikemen retained their unwieldly weapons.[32] Leven's musketeers were all matchlock-armed.[33]

They were arrayed from left to right as follows:

> Lauder's detachment of 200 fusiliers
> Balfour's (Anglo-Dutch)
> Kenmure's (Scottish)
> Ramsay's (Anglo-Dutch)
> Annandale's (Scottish)
> Belhaven's (Scottish)
> Leven's (Scottish)
> Mackay's (Anglo-Dutch)
> Hastings's (English)
> Assorted troops from all regiments.

Mackay's forces were strung out in a thin line to maximize firepower at the expense of reducing their morale and melee value. Placing the elite infantry at the left risked reducing the morale and strength of the other regiments. Whilst it was understandable that the best troops be pushed forward through the pass, not returning these men to their units thereafter was taking a risk.

Dundee had sent out advance guards to find out where his enemy was, but they could not initially see their seated enemies. It was only when they moved nearer and Mackay's men rose to their feet to await attack, that they were seen. Dundee had his men stand on the brow of the hill opposite to them. Having seen Mackay's order of battle, he chose to counter any possible outflanking by extending the gaps between his own units. It was late afternoon when this manoeuvre had been completed, as both sides extended their lines which 'consumed a good part of the afternoon'.[34] James Seton, the Earl of Dunfermline, later wrote that they 'possessed themselves on a strong ground'.[35]

The Jacobites extended their line of battle towards their left wing. Mackay was concerned that this might be an attempt to outflank his force to its own right. It might even be an effort to get between his army and the pass, 'which would be a very advantageous post for them, whereby they could cut all communication betwixt us and Perth'. This was worrying because Mackay expected six troops of horse and dragoons, as well as additional supplies. Furthermore, any Jacobites who did so, might be able to raise the Atholl men to their cause. This manoeuvre 'brought the enemy, whatever his design might have been, to a stand, and so we lookt upon one another for at least two hours'.[36]

According to Cameron, the first shots of the battle were fired by Mackay's men, whilst Dundee was altering his army's dispositions. Yet Mackay thought otherwise. He claimed that because he was so obvious a target and the Jacobites were so close, they fired at him 'all over where he moved'. Firing at a single individual at long range with notoriously unreliable muskets led not to Mackay being hit, but rather several of his men being wounded at the very onset of the battle. Meanwhile, Balfour's regiment had advanced too rapidly and were out of line. The Jacobites made no attempt to attack them, so Mackay, fearing that they might be outflanked, had them retire to be in alignment with the other regiments.[37]

As was not unusual in warfare at this time, Mackay made a short speech to the men nearest to him. He told them that their cause was just, that they were fighting for Protestantism, not only in Britain, but in the world. The happiness of their country and the maintenance of their laws, depended on their successful defence of them on that day. They must not betray such by any faintheartedness on their part. He also reminded them of their own safety:

> assuring them that if they kept firm and close they should quickly see their enemy's take the hills for their refuge . . . but on the other hand, if they happened to give way (as he should not expect) before that rabble of the Highlanders, they might freely conclude few or none of them should escape those naked pursuers far speedier of foot than they . . . stand to it like men fighting for their religion and liberty against the invaders of both.[38]

According to him, it had a positive effect for the men 'all answered with the greatest chearfullnesse imaginable, that none of them, should abandon me'.[39]

Mackay had no desire to attack, for reasons already explained. He feared that the Jacobites might attack and this could unsettle his men, unaccustomed to their way of fighting. Yet he could not pass the river with his enemy in such close proximity. Therefore, 'He resolved then to stand it out, tho' with great impatience, to see the enemie come to a resolution, either of attacking or retiring, whereof they had more choice than he'. This was to pass the initiative to the Jacobites. However, the government army did possess artillery and so Mackay ordered that the three guns, which had been carried on horseback, to open fire, in order to provoke an attack.[40]

They continued to do so, according to one eyewitness, for an hour, presumably ceasing when their ammunition was expended.[41] Likewise, Private Donald McBane wrote 'when they Advanc'd we played our Cannon for an Hour on them'.[42] Yet, according to Mackay, 'they [the guns] broke with the third firing' and proved of little use.[43] However, the damage caused by the guns was very slight indeed.

Perhaps to counter this, there was more Jacobite musketry aimed at Mackay as he stood or rode in front of his army. A few of his men were wounded, though the firers missed their principal target. In order to facilitate their aim, some Jacobites stationed themselves in the few houses which stood on the slope, or possibly in the one house with walls and sheds as described by Macneill. Annoyed by this, Mackay ordered his brother, Lieutenant Colonel James Mackay, to send a captain and some musketeers out of his own regiment to dislodge them. He hoped that this skirmish might lead to a more general battle which he was wanting before night fell. The party (presumably a company) of fifty men, led by Captain Angus Mackay, went to the houses and chased the Jacobites there away, having caused them a few casualties.[44] According to one source, the skirmishers were from Maclean's, and they lost five men but inflicted higher casualties on their enemy.[45] Another source states that the Jacobites fled to another house and then Mackay went to dislodge them from there as well, but never returned. This suggests that the main action took place shortly afterwards and the combatants in this skirmish were enveloped in the larger battle.[46] Mackay wrote that half an hour after this skirmish the battle began in earnest.[47]

McBane described the scene thus: 'we then gave a shout, Daring them as it were to advance, which they quickly did to our great loss'.[48] The fire was annoying but only occasionally deadly as Cameron wrote, 'The continual fire of the enemy from the lower ground covered them, by a thick cloud of smoke, from the view of the Highlanders, whereof several dropping from time to time, and many being wounded'.[49]

Such firing led to some of the Jacobites demanding that they attack, but with the sun beating down in their faces, Dundee urged patience until the sun began to set and was no longer an impediment to their sight. Cameron realized that the men needed something to divert them from being immobile targets. He commanded his men to shout and this was echoed by the remainder of the army; by those adjacent and then extending throughout the whole. There was also the sound of musketry, cannon and the enemy's shouts, echoing along the hills, rocks and caverns. Apparently the 'Highlanders fancy that their shouts were much brisker and louder than that of the enemy'.[50]

Cameron then gave his men a speech, complimenting them on their noise and declaring that their vigorous shouting was a good omen, in contrast to that of their enemy, which he told them was 'low, lifeless and dead'. He claimed that his words spread through the army and 'how wounderfully they were incouraged and animated by them'.[51]

It was about a half-hour before sunset when the attack came; Dunfermline put it at seven in the evening. Mackay had already commanded the regimental officers to begin their regiments' fire when the Jacobites were about a hundred paces away. They would fire by platoon 'to discourage the Highlanders meeting with continual fire'.[52] According to McBane, 'the sun going down caused the Highlandmen to Advance on us like Mad Men, without shoe or stocking, covering themselves from our Fire with their Targes'.[53] An anonymous Jacobite officer claimed the Highlanders threw away their plaids, haversacks and other 'utensils' to fight in shirts and doublets only.[54] Cameron wrote, 'Dundee gave orders for the attack, and commanded, that so soon as the Macleans began to move from the right, that the whole body should, att the same instant of time, advance upon the Enemy. It is incredible with what intrepidity the Highlanders endured the Enemy's fire; and though it grew more terrible upon their nearer approach, yet they, with a wonderful resolution, kept up their own, as they were commanded'.[55]

It is unclear how much fire the Jacobites received from their opponents, as one eyewitness puts it that they engaged in melee 'before we could fire three shots apiece'.[56] Yet McBane wrote 'we could [only] Fire three shots a-piece'.[57] Musket fire was the crux of the battle. If Mackay's musketeers could inflict sufficient casualties on the charging Jacobites, they could either stop them or kill/wound sufficient that those who reached their ranks would be inadequate in number or/and dispirited to win a hand-to-hand fight. The cavalry could then attack the Jacobites in the flank and rear and so complete the victory. Dundee had no reserves and so a reverse would leave him with no second chance to change the battle's course. To maximize his firepower Mackay had deployed his battalions in three ranks rather than the conventional six, so doubling his firepower. This meant that all the men in all three ranks could fire. Men fired by platoon, one at a time, so volleys were continual; men not firing would be reloading.[58] The weakness in Mackay's disposition was that the lines were thin and thus vulnerable to an enemy that was able to charge home; secondly he had no reserve, so any breakthrough would be fatal. As with Dundee, he was taking a risk that line would defeat charging column. Dundee had his troops in small compact units, 'separate bans like wedges condensed and firm'.[59] As with the column tactics employed by the French in the Revolutionary and Napoleonic battles over a century later, this was ideal for little-trained and inexperienced troops, as it did not require drill and exercise by experienced NCOs or any tactical finesse. It needed speed and bravery; troops in column moving rapidly forward, especially downhill, can cut through thin lines of the enemy, especially those unaccustomed to such aggression; casualties caused by defensive musketry can be ignored by their fast-moving colleagues.

Mackay lost his gamble. Musketry on this occasion, though deadly, was insufficient to stop their advance. If Mackay had 2,000 musket-armed troops, then that would mean 4,000–6,000 musket balls at most being fired at the charging men. Assuming one volley was fired at long range, then most of the first would have been ineffectual. Firing at close range would be deadly, but possibly only a third did so, and there are other factors which would lead to it being less so. Firstly, about half of the infantry were relatively inexperienced, two regiments having only been raised earlier that year and another only in 1685 and had no experience of battle. Secondly, the troops were firing uphill and would be less accurate as shots would naturally be too high. Thirdly, the Jacobites were advancing down terraces which meant that some would be out of view for part of the time that they were charging. We could also add that the three guns were now of no use, either, so there was no canister to be used against the massed chargers.[60]

The extent and effectiveness of the musketry was variable, too. Mackay wrote 'that of my regiment, my Lord Levens, and Kenmore with the half of Ramsay's battalion made pretty good fire'. Mackay claimed that his own regiment 'made great fire . . . being well exercised thereto by my brother', and though this made 'execution' among the Jacobites, it was not enough. However, on the left wing 'the other half of Ramsays, with Balfours whole regiment, and Lauder's detachment of 200 men gave ground, or rather fled without any firing'.[61]

Lauder's 200 men on the far left of Mackay's army, though he had '200 of the choice of our army, but did as little as the rest of that hand', but Mackay had no clear view of them, so could have been mistaken.[62] Archaeological evidence indicates that the weight of fire from these regiments on the left was less than elsewhere (32 per cent of projectiles found here compared to 58 per cent in the centre), though was still not wholly insignificant.[63] Recent archaeological evidence suggests that one grenadier in Mackay's army threw a grenade at the attackers. This is the first time that such a weapon was used on a British battlefield. No contemporary makes a note of this, which suggests its value was limited.[64]

Yet the Jacobites would have presented an easy target, being twelve to fourteen men deep according to General Hawley, writing years later.[65] The musketry had not been ineffectual, as Cameron later noted, 'the greatest part of them [the Jacobites] fell within a few paces of their enemy when they received their last fire'.[66] But it was, overall, insufficient to prevent the Jacobite advance. Cameron's son, present at the battle, later wrote, 'Other neighbours suffered a great deal in that engagement, but my father's loss was the more, because he was obliged to attack an entire regiment with less than half of his clan, and was at the same time flanked by another regiment'. Overall, though, the Jacobite losses were severe, as we shall later see, but they were not enough.[67]

The Jacobites also fired at close range, too, 'like one great Clapp of thunder'.[68] Of Mackay's regiment, Captains Lamy and Angus Mackay were shot as was their lieutenant colonel, though none fatally.[69] Yet Macneill wrote of there 'being a perpetuall running fyre till we came to their very breast'.[70] However, Mackay stated that the Jacobite fire was 'ragged'.[71] Macneill later wrote that there was 'but smale loss on their syde'.[72] It is possible that there may have been some archery on the Jacobites' part; bows were mentioned as being carried by some and another poet noted that on the battlefield, 'And not an arrow was discharged that day needlessly'.[73]

According to McBane, 'At last they threw away their Musquetts, drew their Broad Swords advanced furiously upon us, and were in the middle of us'.[74] The Jacobites 'fell in pell-mell among the thick of them with the broad swords. After this the noise seem'd hushed; and the fireing ceasing on both sides, nothing was heard for some moments but the sullen and hollow clashes of broadswords, with the dismall groans and crys of dyeing and wounded men'.[75]

Macleans fought Mackays and routed them.[76] Lieutenant Colonel Mackay, already injured, was killed, fighting among a handful of his veteran pikemen. Captains Lamy and Angus Mackay, having being already wounded by musket balls, were killed by broadsword-wielding Highlanders, having been abandoned by most of their men; the musketeers were the first to flee. Apparently Angus Mackay 'fought stoutly for his lfy', and disingadged himself, having received four considerable wounds of broadswords in his head and body'. Lord Leven saw him and gave him his own horse to carry him away. Captain-Lieutenant Mackenzie was left mortally wounded among the dead. Five lieutenants were killed; another two captains were left wounded, so, 'all the captains of the battalion . . . were either killed or doe bear the marks of their good behaviour'. According to Mackay, it was this regiment on which 'the greatest force of that side was poured upon'. He thought that this was because some of the Jacobite officers had served in it when on the Continent and 'were of the opinion if it were beat that it would facilitate the rest of the work'.[77]

There was 'a hideous noise which made Kenmure's whole regiment run and they being placed in the middle the Highlanders came upon the middle', presumably attacking other regiments in the flanks.[78] However, Kenmure's regiment also took severe losses. The captain of the company in which Lieutenant David Stewart served was killed and he was taken prisoner. Captain James Donaldson received seven wounds, though he lived and was taken prisoner, losing £100 to his captors.[79] The regiment's lieutenant colonel, John Ferguson, was also killed.[80]

It has also been suggested that there was another reason why the line collapsed so quickly. Atholl men began to fall on the baggage in the rear and men in Mackay's regiment 'cryed treachery and ran'. This had potentially crucial results as it was claimed 'Dundee would certainly have been routed if the Atholl men had lyen by and Mackay's men had stood to it'.[81]

Lieutenant Chambers, 'a resolute man according to the testimony of his officers', was cut down. Lauder tried to rally his men, but without success. Ramsay also failed in rallying his men.[82] That there was some fighting on Mackay's left is further evidenced by the fact that a Jacobite officer's target shield was found there, damaged in melee, but the fewer musket balls found there does suggest that firing by the regiments on the left wing was limited compared to the fire elsewhere in the battlefield.[83]

Seeing the Jacobite attack, and now the firing on both sides was over, Mackay called on Belhaven's troop to ride forward to attack the right flank of the enemy, with Annandale's, 'ordering him to flank to the left hand the enemy'. This could have 'been of such effect had they the resolution to obey their orders, and wold have so encouraged the foot that in all appearance the Highlanders would have soon run for it'. Belhaven's did not move forward, so Mackay led them himself and once Belhaven 'commanded them did behave vey honestly'. They were now to the right of Kenmure's infantry and disordered some of them, 'and so began the first break so neere as I can remarque'.[84] This was countered by the Jacobites. Dundee was with his few cavalry in the centre of his army. The cavalry had been led by Dunfermline, but that morning he had been superseded by Sir William Wallace of Craigie, to Dundee's displeasure. When the cavalry advanced, with Dundee at their head, Wallace 'either his courage failing him, or some accident interposing', ordered the horsemen to wheel to the left. This halted the cavalry and brought them into confusion.

Unaware of this, Dundee continued to ride forwards towards Mackay's two troops of cavalry, stationed at the centre, near to the artillery. He rode into the smoke. Following him were Dunfermline and sixteen cavalrymen. Despite Wallace's orders, the men followed Dundee. He raised himself on his stirrups, waving his hat to urge his followers on. Mackay's cavalry 'made but little resistance. They were routed and warmly pursued by those few gentlemen.' Wallace and those with him took no further part in the action.[85]

However, another claim is that Belhaven's stood one fire, suggesting the Jacobite cavalry fired their pistols and then making as if to go in with the sword, before their opponents fled, 'but could not be persuaded to return', whilst Annandale's stayed and fought, at least for a while.[86] A number of carbine and pistol balls were found by a recent archaeological survey, though these may have been fired at both Mackay's infantry or his cavalry.[87] The Jacobite cavalry pushed back their opposite numbers, 'who, in fleeing in the confusion they were in some of them brock in upon their left wing of their own foot'.[88]

Incidentally, there is a claim that the guns which had long been silent, fired on Dundee's cavalry, presumably to little or no effect, however.[89] This could account for the Jacobite cavalry turning on them after having seen off Mackay's cavalry. Wallace was opposed to this but Dunfermline attacked the men with the guns with sixteen horsemen and 'beat the enemies from their cannon and took them before the rest of the horse came up'.[90] James Smith, master gunner in charge of the artillery, 'received many wounds in his head and body'.[91]

Mackay was unaware that his cavalry were not following him against the Jacobites. Calling their officers to follow him, 'he spurr'd his horse through the enemy'. He was shocked to find 'no body nevertheless followed him, but one of his servants, whose horse was shot in passing'. Alone, Mackay wished that he had had fifty reliable troopers with him, for he believed that if this had been so, 'he had certainly, by all human appearance recovered all'.[92]

In the confusion of battle, Mackay was able to pass through a crowd of advancing Jacobites. After having done so, he viewed the battlefield. He saw that 'all his left had given way and got down the hill . . . so that in the twinkling of an eye in a manner, our men, as well as the enemy were out of sight, being got doun pall mall to the river where our baggage stood'. He found this a sad spectacle and was initially surprised to see himself alone on the field.[93] He wrote, two days later, 'there was no regiment or troop with me, but behaved lyck the vilest coward in nature [except two]'.[94]

Meanwhile, the Jacobites were getting the best of the melee. Their casualties here were light, 'few or none of them were killed after they drew their swords'.[95] According to the Jacobite Earl of Balcarres, 'they [Mackay's men] defended themselves but faintly'.[96] A Jacobite officer claimed 'the enemy . . . did not maintain their grounds two minutes after the Highlanders were amongst them'. It seems to have been a one-sided fight. The same officer wrote, 'Many of General Mackay's officers and soldiers were cut down through the skull and necks to the very breasts; others had skulls cut off above their ears like night caps, some soldiers had both their bodies and cross belts cut through at one blow; pikes and small swords were cut like willows'.[97] The melee was over quickly and the redcoats soon broke off, according to Macneill.[98]

The retreat was startling, the Jacobites having 'oblig'd us to Retreat, some fled to the water, and some another way, (We were for the most part New Men)'.[99] According to Cameron, 'The Highlanders had ane absolute and compleat victory. The pursute was so warm that few of the enemy escaped.'[100] There was another Jacobite account of those, 'who followed the slaughter for a good way'.[101] One report was that 'the slaughter in the battle was equall but after the battle most of Mackay's men were killed by the Atholl men and by the country men and such as they killed not they robbed ym of their money and stript them to the shirt'.[102]

The shock of troops charging against foes who are unaccustomed to that method of warfare also contributed to the defeat. Similar results were to occur at Prestonpans in 1745 and to a lesser extent at Sheriffmuir in 1715 and at Falkirk in 1746. A rout was fatal to the defeated troops, as Richard Kane, a contemporary military theorist, noted, 'if they are broke, not a man in 10 escapes . . . for, upon all warm Pursuits, there is but little quarter to be expected'.[103]

McBane was trying to escape. According to him:

> I fled to the Baggage and took a horse, in order to Ride the water. There followed me a Highlandman with sword and targe, in order to take the horse and kill myself, you'd laugh to see how he and I scampered about; I kept always the horse between him and me. At length he drew his Pistol and I fled, he fired after me; I went above the Pass, where I met with another water, very deep, it was about eighteen feet over betwixt two Rocks, I resolved to jump it, so I laid down my Gun and hat, and jumped and lost one of my shoes on the jump [this was the Soldier's Leap] . . . The Enemy pursuing hard I made the best of my way to Dunkeld, where I stayed till what of our men was left came up.[104]

Many were lost in the rout; McBane recalling, 'many of our men was lost in that water and at the Pass'.[105] Some of the Atholl men 'after the fight they fell upon our men that were scattered, and killed droves of them'.[106]

Many of those who had fled were in a wretched state. When Mackay joined 'about two hundred of his broken troops', they were 'in such a miserable plight, and so gashed and deformed with their wounds that they moved the compassion of their greatest enemys. So great, however, was the fright of these wretches, that they travelled all that night, some of them bound with ropes, or supported by their comrades on their horses, and others trailing their limbs after them, and crying out with the smart of their wounds.'[107]

According to Cameron, Mackay's actions after his men were in rout were those of shock and despair: 'when he saw his army intearly broken and dispersed, he was in such a consternatioun that for some moments he remained, as it were, stupid and undetermined what to doe; but being afraid of falling into the enemy's hands, he made off with whip and spur, and never halted until he arrived at the Laird of Weems his house in Apnadow, and the next night he came to Drummond Castle'.[108] Yet Mackay's own account is rather different, as we shall see.

The Jacobite attack was not universally successful, however. This was because Dundee's line was shorter than Mackay's due to the former being outnumbered. There were no Jacobites in front of Leven's regiment. Thus this newly-raised Scottish regiment fired at Cameron's men in the flank; the latter lost 120 men 'which was just one half of his number, and was occasioned by a furious fire that he received in the flank'. Mackay put this down to 'the diligence and firmity of the said Earle and his lieutenant colonel, major and other officers'. Even so, the Camerons' target, Mackay's regiment, were 'routed and destroyed in a manner that few of them ever returned to their colours'.[109]

Mackay later wrote that Leven's regiment did so well firstly because they were not so strenuously attacked. Secondly. there was a greater proportion of officers to men than in the other regiments. He added that they were 'very good brisk gentlemen'. He considered that Hastings's regiment had the same advantages.[110] Lanier praised the latter thus, 'behaved themselves well that they were not broken'.[111] Another account stated that 150 of the Scottish soldiers rallied because they 'had been in service abroad and remembered the ill consequences of such a flight would expose 'em to the swords of persons nimbler than themselves'.[112]

Sir Donald MacDonald's attack also faltered; again they were on the Jacobite army's left flank. His flank was exposed to the fire of Hastings's regiment. Several of the Highlanders began to fall under their musketry. Sir Donald, noticing both this and that there were houses and dykes which might provide his men with cover, had them take shelter there, seeking the safest option. Orders were sent to them, that they were needed to support Cameron's attack, but these were slow to be carried out because the men were scattered behind a variety of forms of cover and doubtless reluctant to emerge from it and risk their lives again.[113]

However, Hastings's regiment suffered casualties and was pushed back. Major Jacobs was wounded.[114] An anonymous report claimed 'Coll Hastings behaved himself well but was beat off his ground and upon that retiring till he knew that Leven's men had stood'.[115] Likewise Major Robert Bruce of Leven's was killed along with several lieutenants.[116] It would seem that, contrary to the statements often made about both these units standing entirely firm, one-half of both fled after taking casualties in hand-to-hand fighting; Mackay had divided each regiment into two, after all, and as we shall note, the men from these two regiments who left the battlefield in good order amounted to only about 400.

Mackay, thinking he was alone on the battlefield, 'looking further to the right he espied a small hep of red coats'. He galloped over to them and found that it was part of Leven's regiment. Yet another version states that 'the General Mackay was missing till after ye business was over and they say was found in a thicket'.[117] Leven (now remounted by his servant bringing up another horse) and most of his officers were there. Mackay praised them for their valour. According to one account, Leven had recovered the colours of Mackay's regiment and when the two met, 'Mackay lighted and embraced him, and kissed him many times, saying he had saved his honour, his life and the kingdome. He would never forgett it and he would represent it fully to the King.'[118] One account claimed 'The first officer that left his post from Mackay's army, was the Lord Leven; the glistening and clashing of the Highlanders' swords and targets scared his horse so much, that he ran six miles before he could draw back'.[119] Yet this seems unlikely; not only does Mackay contradict it but elsewhere in the same account there are known inaccuracies.

However, Leven's men were in a confused state because there were men from other regiments with them. Mackay asked Leven and his officers to put the men in 'condition to receive the enemy, whom he minutely expected'. Mackay then rode off to see Hastings's regiment. The commanding officer there had been able to repel and pursue some of their enemy and was returning his men to their original position. His pikemen had deterred another attack. The Jacobites' plundering of the baggage allowed the remnant of his army some respite. Mackay sent a captain from his own regiment, who was on horseback, to find any officers or men from the same regiment and to urge them 'back to joyn him, in which case he assured them of advantage'.[120]

Dundee's sixteen cavalrymen, having chased Mackay's cavalry off the field, returned to the battlefield. They were surprised to find some of Leven's regiment and Hastings', still there and formed. Dunfermline wanted to attack, and so suggested gathering about fifty to sixty Highland infantry. These men were currently looking after the corpses of their dead comrades. Language differences were problematic as the Highlanders could only speak Gaelic. However, Drummond of Balhaldys, Cameron's son in law, began to gather some of the men together. They began to march against Hastings's regiment.[121]

What was left of Hastings's regiment were not wholly isolated. Seeing the Jacobites moving towards them, Leven's regiment advanced to their aid. The Jacobites refused to engage, partly because some of their number were 'rather followers of the army than souldiers'. Their officers decided they should retreat and in doing so came across, what was to them, a shocking and terrible sight. They 'discovered the body of their noble General, who was just breathing out his last'. Dundee had been shot and the fatal ball had entered his body on the lower part of his left side. They carried him off, possibly just about still living, but in doing so received fire from Leven's regiment. Another casualty was Haliburton of Pitcurr, who was shot and died two days later.[122]

Apparently when Dundee was shot, he was caught from falling off his horse by one Johnston. Then, 'the viscount then asking the said Johnston how the day went, and that he answered the day went well for the king (meaning king James), but that he was sorry for his lord: and that the viscount replied it was the less matter for him seeing that the day went well for his master'. His body was wrapped in highland plaids after the battle and was buried at Blair on the next day.[123]

Once they had got out of the range of their enemy's musketry, they began to be tearful. Some other Jacobites began to gather with them. Drummond found others. There was a desire to return to the fight against Leven's regiment. A total of sixty men agreed to do so. They marched ahead but found that the enemy were in possession of a large house, possibly Urrards, and it would be an insurmountable task to have dislodged them from it. Although more Jacobites returned to the field by midnight, the would-be defenders had already taken the opportunity to retreat under cover of darkness.[124]

According to Balcarres, Mackay's remaining men missed their opportunity to reverse the day's outcome. He was of the opinion that they were only partly involved in the fighting and 'if these had had resolution they might easily fall upon the Highlanders whilst they were indeed about the spoil and so quite changed the fate of the day but neglected this opportunity . . . were in such a consternation they knew what to do'.[125]

Mackay expected that his men might be attacked at any moment. He had decided against stationing his men in the house and grounds because he thought that if he was not relieved, then 'there was no hope of escaping out of the enemy's hands by defending an inclosure so far from new relief'. The return of his nephew brought no new hope that anything had gone well for him on the left. The nephew explained that he had seen twenty men formed at the edge of the wood where Lauder had initially been posted. He thought that these might be men of his own regiment. So he decided to exhort them to make at least one discharge if they were attacked. Galloping over, he discovered that these were Jacobites. At this point he had some men with him, and being that they were apparently resolved to fight, the Jacobites there, unable to see their numbers due to dusk falling, allowed them to withdraw unmolested.[126]

A few men of Mackay's regiment, finding the injured Captain Mackenzie, carried him with them and joined those troops remaining on the stricken field. Mackay led the remnant of his forces from the field, about 400 men (Lanier claimed there were 500 men, drawn from Hastings's and Leven's regiments), after taking one last look at the Jacobites to see whether they were going to approach the river after him. He was joined by a few men from Annandale's horse; two officers and four or five men, as well as Belhaven. These troopers then acted as scouts during the retreat. They crossed the Garry unmolested. There was no sign of any Jacobites in pursuit, so Mackay had to decide where they should retreat to. Some of his officers suggested that they should go to Dunkeld and thence to Perth, retracing the route that they had taken towards Killiecrankie earlier in the day. Instead, Mackay resolved to march several miles into the Highlands, then crossing the Strathspey, over to Castle Drummond, which was garrisoned, and then to Stirling. There he hoped to 'make all the speed possible to fall upon some present measures'.[127]

This course of action was still opposed by some of his officers. They told him that some of the men under their command were so demoralized that they would make no resistance if the Jacobites attacked. Mackay was 'very well satisfied of the truth of what they alledged'. Yet he was unbending because he thought that Dundee, who he believed was still alive, would pursue with his cavalry, leaving the infantry to carry on with their plunder of the baggage. Therefore, he wanted to put his men in territory that would be unsuitable for cavalry to fight in. He also chose that route because it would mean they would not fall prey to the Athollmen who might otherwise 'run the whole night and next day upon the runnaways'. Two miles from the battlefield, he met Ramsay with 150–200 men, mostly men who had thrown away their weapons in flight. They joined forces and now there were 600–700.[128]

Continuing by a little river, the men came to some houses, part of the estate of Lord Weemys, whose son was a captain who had served against the Jacobites. Travelling over hills and bogs, the men did not stop during the night. At daybreak they found themselves in Strathspey. However, the countrymen thought that they were Jacobites come to plunder, perhaps because of their less-than-regular appearance, and 'did raise a great noise and shout'. This alarmed Mackay's men, most of whom scattered to the hilly ground. Mackay and some of his mounted officers rode among them and with the aid of their pistols threatened them back again. About 100 men, however, did not rejoin their comrades. Their fate was to be 'knockt in the head and stript, or taken prisoners'. The others continued without much halt, even though it was Sunday, arriving late that night at Castle Drummond. They reached Stirling on 29 July, allegedly, but improbably, 1,500 strong.[129]

Yet, even for the victors, losses were serious. Despite routing their enemy, the Jacobites did not have 'it cheap bought . . . for they lossed very near a third of their number [about 600]'.[130] Apart from Dundee, a number of lesser officers were also slain; the laird of Largo, a MacDonald chieftain and several other MacDonald gentlemen, a brother of Glengarry's, several relatives of Sir Donald MacDonald, a number of Macleans 'and a multitude of others whom it were tedious to recount'.[131] Mackay agreed with Cameron that, apart from Dundee, 'several gentlemen of quality of the countys of Angus and Perth, but also many of the best gentlemen among the Highlanders, particularly among the MacDonalds of the Isles and Glengarie, were killed'.[132] A letter allegedly written by Dundee after the battle gives Jacobite losses as 900.[133] These had been caused by the lethal musketry that could have denied them the victory had they been equally deadly all along Mackay's line.

Mackay's army suffered the higher casualties. Murray wrote on the day after the battle, 'I have no particular account yet of the losses, but sertenlay ye losses is grat'.[134] According to Cameron, 'No less than eighteen hundred of them were computed to fall upon the field of battle' and he thought that this was a sixth of the total.[135] MacPherson put losses at between 1,500–2,000, with 500 prisoners taken.[136] Macneill wrote of 2,000 dead and 500 prisoners; as did Balcarres.[137] Dunfermline wrote, 'I does believe there was never a greater victory in soe short a time they left 1200 [dead] on the spot and I doubt not but there was as many in the flight we have about 400 prisoners and many of their officers are killed and we have 10 or 12 of their best officers prisoners'.[138]

Contemporary letters were concerned about officers who had died. The dead included Lieutenant Beverley Newcomen, son of Sir Thomas Newcomen, and Captain Tom Stanley of Hastings's battalion.[139] Although many men from Leven's regiment had survived, on 17 August the unit was clearly depleted, with Mackay writing to Leven 'your Lordship's regiment is render'd incapable to serve in haste'.[140] Lieutenant Ferguson's death left his family of a young widow and two children aged under five in dire straits. Apparently they were unable to access his estate worth £300 annually. There were debts to pay and she petitioned for immediate possession, invoking a custom dating back to James IV, stating that if a man died in battle, this would be granted.[141]

Since no official casualty rolls were compiled, it is impossible to know the scale of Mackay's losses. He claimed that he brought between 600–700 men away from the stricken field, and as the man on the spot it is not unreasonable to suppose that this is probably the most accurate estimate. There were 500 prisoners. If we accept that Mackay had about 3,000 soldiers at the day's start, then the difference between the survivors under Mackay and the prisoners taken equates to 1,800–1,900 dead, but the true figure is probably a little less because some fugitives, such as McBane, did not join Mackay and fled straight to Edinburgh via Dunkeld. Even so, we are probably looking at perhaps 1,600 dead, or just over 50 per cent of the entire force, many of whom would have been killed in the pursuit following the collapse of the formed units of Mackay's, Balfour's, Kenmure's and Ramsay's. Individual unit casualties are unknown, and the two cavalry troops clearly had losses for there is a reference for them having to recruit in September, as had Leven's in August. By November some of the officer prisoners taken were exchanged.[142] It is probable that the men from the four regiments which fled took more casualties than Hastings's and Leven's, and that the cavalry took least as they could outpace their pursuers.

These were serious casualties indeed by contemporary standards. At the Boyne in the next year, the defeated Jacobites lost about 2,000 men or about 10 per cent of their total and at Waldeck about 5,040 of 24,000 Frenchmen were lost. Mackay's losses outweighed in percentage terms the Jacobite dead at Culloden and that battle is often termed a massacre and Jacobite casualties are stressed. However, in Montrose's victories at Inverlochy, Auldearn and Kilsyth in 1645 the defeated Covenanters had lost over half their men due to the bloody routs.[143] Overall, given the heavy losses on both sides, this was the bloodiest battle in the whole of the campaigns, because of the effective musketry on the Williamites' side and then the numbers they lost in the brief melee and the rout.

Mackay had lost so heavily because many of his soldiers routed and were pursued by a faster-moving enemy who attacked them whilst they were virtually defenceless and in many cases unarmed. When an army can conduct an orderly retreat and/or has friendly forces nearby who can deter a vigorous pursuit this can be avoided, as occurred for the Allies at Fontenoy in 1745. Such was not the fortunate lot of some of Cope's troops at Prestonpans in 1745, of Mar's at Sheriffmuir in 1715 and of the Jacobites at Culloden in 1746, where the luckless fugitives were cut down in hundreds by their pursuers, whether lightly-clad Highlanders or mounted dragoons. In the latter case alone this has been termed a war crime, though it was a commonplace if undoubtedly bloody part of battle.

There were many wounded as well as dead. Corporal Richard Robertson of Kenmure's regiment, sustained twenty-two wounds in his body and head, yet survived. Hugh Ross of Mackay's received two musket balls in his legs and was unable to walk thereafter without stilts. Captain James Donaldson of Kenmure's received seven wounds and was robbed of £100.[144]

Care for the wounded was limited. Hospital and medical care on a large scale for soldiers was poor, as the campaign in Ireland also showed. Apparently there were no army surgeons present with Mackay's men at Stirling, though there was meant to be one per regiment. However, David Mure or Muir, a Stirling surgeon who had been employed at the castle for four years, was on hand to assist. He tended to the wounded from the regiments of Leven, Mackay, Hastings and Kenmure; in all about 250 men. He sent to Edinburgh for medicine and used claret to bathe and forment wounds. On January 1691 he had to apply to the Privy Council for reimbursement.[145] It seems this plea fell on deaf ears for in a letter of 1708 he wrote of his services, adding, 'for all of which I have never yet received anything'.[146]

It would be a mistake to assume that the pursuing Jacobites were all wholly consumed by bloodlust. Many prisoners, doubtless many of whom were wounded, were taken by the Jacobites. Several of them were officers; Captain Van Best of Ramsay's, Captain Donaldson and Lieutenant John Nisbet of Kenmure's, Lieutenant Finch of Hastings's and Lieutenant John Hay.[147] Prisoners were initially taken to a lower room in Blair Castle where they were questioned by Dunfermline and Cannon, now the senior Jacobite officer. Those taken were led away, but as Nisbet recorded, Colin Mackenzie 'was very kind to the witness and had twice given him money and some other necessaries' on the march along Loch Rannoch. Their eventual destination was Mull, though many did not reach there until the end of August.[148] As for the men in the ranks, it was difficult for the Jacobites to hold their 500 prisoners, due to want of provisions, so after having them swear that they would not bear arms against James II, they were released.[149]

The loss of baggage was also substantial. This should be unsurprising as one of the motives of some in the Jacobite army was loot. Officers were robbed of gold and clothing 'which was considerable'. Major Simekell lost 200 guineas and was stripped of his clothes.[150] According to Lanier, 500–600 horses were taken as well as a whole month's pay for the whole army.[151] Lieutenant Ferguson lost £400 worth of gold, money, horses and other equipage.[152] All the army's tents, baggage and provisions were taken, along with the king's standard carried by Mackay's regiment.[153] The cannon and copious quantities of ammunition were lost.[154] Dunfermline wrote, 'We got their cannon and such a plunder that I never thought a Scots army could have had the like for there was a great deal of silver work and money in abundance'.[155] Horses were also taken; John Grant of Ballindoch rode a bay horse taken from one of the prisoners.[156]

On the following day, the surviving Jacobites viewed the field of battle. It was a grim sight:

> The dreadfull effects of their fury appeared in many horrible figures. The enemy lay in heaps almost in the order they were posted; but so disfigured with wounds, and so hashed and mangled, that even the victors could not look upon the amazeing proofs of their own agility and strength without surprise and horror. Many had their heads divided into two halves by one blow; others had their sculls cut off above the eares by a backstrock, like a night-cap. Their thick buff-belts were not sufficient to defend their shoulders from such deep gashes as almost disclosed their entrails. Several picks, small swords and the like weapons, were cut quite through, and some that had scull-capes had them so beat into their brains that they died on the spott.[157]

The first knowledge of the battle came to the government on the day afterwards when a number of junior officers, the most senior being Lauder, and men engaged in the battle arrived in Edinburgh on the evening of 28 July. One was from a lieutenant Harrison, 'coming it seems so early away'. His relatives differed as to his behaviour with some believing he left the field too soon 'and has done him no good heer'.[158] Another report was from a lieutenant in Mackay's regiment. Hamilton wrote on 29 July that there were various accounts of the battle, 'but to tell true, they all differ in particulars'. He added that only 'inferior officers and souldiers come' and 'none of ym van give certain accounts of the loss'.[159]

Hamilton, understandably put the blame on Mackay, writing: 'it seems Mackay has been too forward that after a march of 16 miles should engadge the enemie when his men were weary and the nixt day there was 4 troops of Horse and 2 of Dragoons to have joined him and I fear his foot did not stand to it and they should but run after some firing when the Highlanders came to a close fight with ym.'[160]

On 29 July, Mackay started to put the case for his defence. He assessed what had happened, writing, 'there was no regiment or troop with me, but behaved lyck the vilest cowards in nature, except Hastings and my Lord Levens, whom I praise at such a degree, as I cannot but blame others, of whom I expected more'. His troops and he were now clearly exhausted after having marched 'without halt or rest for two days and two nights' and Mackay himself wrote that he was 'now so overtaken with sleep that I can say no more'.[161]

Mackay also promoted his own position to Murray shortly afterwards:

> What men may speak to my disadvantage I doe not much care, for I dessyre them to get a man more zealous and upright for the cause; and if they attack mee in point of conduct, they must know the trade better than I, to condemne me withal. When the King thinks he can be better served of another in Scotland, no man shall be more read to resign the charge in anothers hand then myself, to serve His Majesty's interest elsewhere, if he has occasione for me, so that those men who will charge me with any blame, will lose their aime, for I am prepared for those recontres, having no other interest in this whole matter but that of conscience for my religion and affection to my souveraigne and the country wherein I was born, for whose peace and settlement I shall not only pray, but with God's assistance, willingly fight.[162]

What was needed next 'is, that men goe quickly to work to stop the consternation of our friends, as well as the hops and pryde of our enemys'. He told Hamilton that Lanier's and Colchester's cavalry should be sent to Stirling and that Bargany's infantry march to Dundee until he could gather the troops he needed to 'chasse those highland barbarians again'.[163]

When news of Killiecrankie arrived in Edinburgh there was anxiety. Balcarres, who was there under arrest, later stated, 'Never were men in such a consternation as Duke Hamilton and the rest of the Parliament at Edinburgh, when they knew from those that fled of the defeat of Mackay'. Some thought of leaving the city to seek safety in England or in the West. There was discussion whether the Jacobite prisoners should be released or guarded more closely, though the latter was what happened. There were visits by those who had supported the Revolution to Jacobite prisoners assuring them of their continued support for James. Despite Lauder telling that all was lost, they decided to await further news.[164]

Melville wrote that 'I have done all I can to represent the present nakedness of the country as to arms and ammunition and otherwise . . . the said party of our forces under the command of Major General Mackay by which the said party did sustaine considerable loss, which perhaps may animate and encourage any who are disaffected to joyne with the rebels against us'.[165]

Hamilton wrote from Edinburgh to tell Melville that 'after a sharp ingadgement Dundie being much stronger, the Major General was quiet defeat'. Lauder had managed to get to Perth and told Lord Ruthven that the army had 'being wholly routed'. Detailed accounts of the battle were lacking, however. It was not known that Dundee was dead and it was believed that Mackay was killed or captured.[166]

It was thought that the defeat at Killiecrankie would have far-reaching consequences for William's entire campaign against James. Hamilton wrote, 'my humble opinion is, that his Majestie must first beat Dundie and secuir this kingdom [bef]or[e] he attempt any other thing'. He thought that, as Dundee was now master of all Scotland north of the Forth 'great numbers of disaffected' would join him 'so the King must make hast to assist us to reduce him, for I fear wee shall not be able to defend this side of the Forth long'.[167] He feared that Perthshire and Angus would rise for the Jacobites.[168] Hamilton wrote on 1 August, 'by which the said party did sustain considerable loss, which may perhaps animate and encourage any who are disaffected to join the rebels'.[169]

Panic was not the only response in Edinburgh. On hearing of the military defeat, Hamilton called a meeting of the Privy Council. There it was decided that all regular troops should be concentrated at Stirling. Currently these were the infantry regiments of Mar, Blantyre and Bargany, whilst Argyll with his own regiment, Glencairnes's and Angus's, were summoned. Messages were sent to the West to summon all the militia there. Lanier wrote to summon the English forces in Northumberland, specifically instructing Heyford's Horse to Glasgow, but he did not think they could arrive until 6 August. Meanwhile, he went to Stirling to take command there, 'to put the troops yr in as good condition as he can', though there was a shortage of general officers in Scotland. Lanier feared that Leslie's and Berkeley's units in the north and would be cut off by the Jacobite army between them and Stirling.[170] Hamilton wrote, 'if we not able to defend Stirling this place we cannot stay in but must returne to England'. Parliament was not, however, adjourned on that day as to do so might discourage the populace.[171]

Mackay thought that Dundee's death was critical: 'he now looked upon his defeat to be of greater consequence, and more beneficial to his master's interest than the most absolute victory could have been'. This was because 'the Highlanders will allow none of their own chiefs to command as General; and they have no other officer that either can conduct them, or that so much as knows how to make proper use of so important a victory'.[172] Melville wrote on 5 August, 'I apprehend Dundee's death will bridle a little his party's joy and retard their progress'.[173] Likewise, Lockhart wrote on 30 July, 'Dundee and Colonel Canon [!] are both killed for sertin and so I hope tho we have lost the field we have wine the day for I know not any who can take it'.[174] Creighton noted that William said 'He knew Lord Dundee so well that he must have been either killed or mortally wounded, otherwise before that time, he would have been in Edinburgh'.[175]

If this was a Jacobite victory, it appears not to have felt like one, as Cameron described the victorious army's condition on 28 July:

> The death of their brave Generall, and the loss of so many of their friends, were inexhaustible fountains of grief and sorrow. They closed the last scene of this mournfull tragedy in obsequys of their lamented General and other Gentlemen who fell with him, and interred them in the church of Blair Atholl with a real funeral solemnity, there not being present one single person who did not participate in the general affliction.[176]

Murray agreed, writing, 'I have heard ye neus of Lord Dundee bean killed, wch is a gretter loss then all their vicktory will gane them. It will hinder people from going to that party.'[177] On the other hand, Dunfermline, writing on 29 July to Breadalbane, wrote, 'My lord, seeing all things I is going soe well with the King . . . have what men you can at this place on Saturday next for all the countys hear about are rising if Your lordship doe not joyn I am afraid it will make people have a bad opinion of you.'[178] Yet he was encouraging Breadalbane to join the Jacobite cause, so such an optimistic spin is understandable.

Dundee was as dead as Charles II and it remained to be seen how this would affect his master's cause in Scotland. His death was without a doubt, though, a blow to the Jacobite cause. Killiecrankie was thus a pyrrhic victory for the Jacobite cause and had been purchased at far too high a price. Strategically it was to prove indecisive.

Chapter 3

The Battles of Dunkeld and Cromdale, 1689–1690

After the battle of Killiecrankie, command of the Jacobite army passed to Major General Alexander Cannon, as senior regular officer there, and numbers increased to about 5,000 men, due in part to the recent victory. Mackay was eager to regain the initiative, however, and routed a small party of Jacobites at Perth. Cannon withdrew his men into the Highlands in a controversial move to avoid conflict rather than exploit the victory. Yet as Mackay's army and that of Sir John Lanier advanced northwards, Cannon's was able to slip southwards and take advantage of an isolated regiment of newly-levied Scottish infantry at Dunkeld.

A contemporary publication described Dunkeld thus:

> A Town on the north of the Tay, at the foot of the Grampian Hills being surrounded by pleasant woods . . . chief market town of the Highland . . . The Ruin of the cathedral church are yet to be seen, but that which chiefly adjoins it, are the stately buildings, lately erected by the Marquis of Athole, father of the present Duke.

Most of the cathedral's walls still stood, as did its tower. It was located just to the west of the town, overlooking it, whilst Athole's manse was to its centre and the town spread itself out in a line to the north of the river.[1]

Meanwhile, Lanier was currently at Forfar to the east with two regiments, Colonel Ramsay was at Perth to the south with three regiments of Anglo-Dutch infantry who had not been at Killiecrankie and Mackay was to the north-east. On 19 August 1689 an order was issued to Lanier to take Blair Castle by force. He was supplied with four 6-pounder guns and Second Lieutenant Drury, who had survived the debacle at Killiecrankie, with fifteen men to handle them. Lanier had marched with his men to Brechin and there was a skirmish on 15 August near there with the advance party of the Jacobite army. A few men on both sides were killed, but then the Jacobites returned. This may have been because Cannon received news that there was an isolated Scottish regiment at Dunkeld and so there was an opportunity to cut it off. Lanier knew nothing about this. He retired to Forfar, where he received orders from the council to march to Atholl in order to garrison Blair House and Finlarig House. Next day he marched to Coupar, within 10 miles of both Dunkeld and Perth.[2] Similar behaviour occurred next year, when he was serving in Ireland. Lanier made many unnecessary delays on his march to Cullen to guard the artillery camp and in doing so allowed Sarsfield's cavalry to destroy it.[3]

The Privy Council, 'without the consideratiuoin of the insuffiicencie of the place for defence', ordered the newly-raised Earle of Angus's regiment, led by Lieutenant Colonel William Cleland (c.1661–89), to Dunkeld, ten miles above Perth, 'separate from all speedy succour, and exposed to be carried by insult, without the least prospect of advancement to the service by their being posted there'.[4] Following instructions from the Privy Council, Colonel Ramsay ordered the regiment from Perth to Dunkeld at the beginning of August, in order to observe the enemy and to secure the town from them.[5]

They had been paid on 6 August and had been at Doune and Dunblane until 12 August when the momentous decision was made, though when they arrived there Cleland was told to contact Lanier and the commanding officer at Perth of this and then to obey their orders from that point on.[6] A trooper in Eglington's troop of horse later wrote, 'The toun heiring of yr coming all the men went out of it . . . marching into Cannon's army'. They told him that there would only be one regiment there.[7] Cannon learnt that Angus's regiment was stationed in Dunkeld, apparently with 'a designe to destroy the country of Atholl'.[8] The Jacobites 'had not such prejudice at any of the forces at this regiment, whom they called the Cameronian Regiment, whose oppression against all such as were not of their own sentiment made them generally hated and feared in the northern counties'.[9] The Cameronians had been virulent enemies of the Episcopalians following their persecution in the 1670s and 1680s.

On Saturday, 17 August, Angus's regiment arrived at Dunkeld.[10] Concerned that the Jacobites might be close at hand, they stood to their arms that night, being within the walls near to the cathedral and at the large house nearby belonging to the Marquis of Atholl, but their night was undisturbed.[11]

Next day, Sunday the 18th, the Jacobites began to appear on the hills around the town. As yet they were only in relatively small numbers. Lieutenant John Blackader of Angus's regiment, stated that there were only groups of twenty to thirty men in sight. Angus's men were busy that day in defending the town by constructing entrenchments in Atholl's property. Where there were breaches in the walls, loose stones were placed there. Dykes were scaffolded. In all this they were undisturbed.[12]

The Jacobites who were sighted were probably scouting parties who noted the presence of the regiment in the town and reported this news back to Cannon.

Cameron later wrote that the latter 'had intelligence that the Cameronian Regiment, so called from their following one Cameron, ane extravagant Fanatick Preacher . . . commanded by Lieutenant Colonel Cleland, had taken possession of Dunkeld, with a design to destroy the country of Atholl. To prevent this, he resolved to dislodge them, and might have easily affected it.'[13]

That afternoon, the Jacobites had been building up their strength near to Dunkeld. According to Blackader, 60 or 80 men were now visible at a distance on the hill, but another account puts their numbers at 300 and they were on the hills to the north of Dunkeld. It was customary in siege warfare for the besiegers to offer parley to the defenders as a prelude to any armed confrontation and this convention was followed here. A Jacobite fixed a white cloth to the top of a halberd (he may have been a sergeant and this weapon may have been taken from the field of Killiecrankie), and also brought a letter for the commanding officer with him.[14]

Cleland received the man and read the letter. It claimed that the Jacobites asked 'Whether ye come for Peace or War, and do certifie you, that if ye burn anyone's house there, will we destroy you'. Blackader stated that the letter was 'full of great threatening and boastings' and that his commander answered it 'briskly'. In detail, Cleland stated, 'We are faithfull subjects to King William and Queen Mary . . . if you who send these threats, shall make any hostile appearance, we will burn all that belongs to you and otherwise chastise you as you deserve'. Cleland also had the government's Act of Indemnity, offering pardon to anyone submitting to its authority, read out at the market cross, though the intended audience for this is unclear, unless the messenger was still there and it was for his benefit and those who he might later relay it to.[15]

More practically, Cleland must have realized that by his act of defiance, an attack on the town would probably not be long delayed. Without knowing what numbers would be opposed to his single regiment, he may have feared the worst. At some point in that day he sent a messenger, almost certainly on horseback, to Perth, about 10 miles to the south-east, to ask Ramsay for reinforcements, stating that the Jacobites were 'coming down upon him'.[16]

On the next morning, that is to say, Monday, 19 August, there was good news for Cleland and his men. Ramsay, in charge of the troops at Perth, had sent cavalry (for speed) to Cleland's aid. Or had he? According to a trooper in the force, they 'marched without orders of the comidant' and did so at night time. Once they were within two miles of Dunkeld, they halted to refresh the horses and set sentries to watch until daylight. The force was led by Lord Cardross and consisted of the troop of Grubbit's Horse, a troop of Eglington's Horse (on 3–4 June Grubbit's had apparently 50 men and Eglington's 41) and three troops of Cardross's dragoons; a total of five troops of cavalrymen, possibly numbering 500 men in all, but more likely only about 200. One estimate of the government's complete strength at Dunkeld was between 1,400–1,500, though this is almost certainly an exaggeration. The cavalry marched that morning to the town and drew up at its rear in a barley field. Cleland and his officers showed the newly-arrived officers where the Jacobites were, on the hills above the town. Apparently there were 400 Jacobites within a quarter of a mile of the town and more in the hills; some of the former were allegedly 'so neare as they wer heard to call us traitors and rebells'. Meanwhile the troopers entered the town and took refreshment, though were told to be ready for action at the sound of a trumpet.[17]

The trumpet call came and two troops of Cardross's cavalry, Bennet's and Agnew's, rode out of town towards the Jacobites. They reconnoitred the fields near to the town and marched towards the hills. According to a trooper of Agnew's, 'So soon as they noticing us advancing towards ym retired, all in throw a wood, we persewing ym'. They seized four or six Jacobites. Seven or eight horses were also taken, but they could see no one else, so returned to the town that night. At that time, Cleland learnt that the fiery cross was being used to summon Jacobite supporters to their cause. Combat could not be long delayed.[18]

That afternoon, Ramsay wrote from Perth the following letter to Cardross:

> My Lord,
>
> I was uneasie till I heard from yow, but knowing of yow being there and of your good conducke, it quieted me much. I think these dragoons and Horse can be of little use in these grounds, so I thincke yow lordship may come back here with them. Lieutenant Colonel Cleland says he wold be able to maintain his poste if he got provisions and ammunition. He will be able, I hope, to do it, for I have sent him part of bothe this day with yowr captain-lieutenant, and shall send him more the morrow.
>
> I am, your lordship . . .
>
> My lord, stay not on that side of the water the toune is on, but stay a mile on the other side of the water till day and then come to this toune tomorrow.[19]

It is not certain when this letter arrived, perhaps on the morning of the 20th. There is no suggestion as to how Cardross responded to it. Nor is there any evidence that the ammunition promised by Ramsay ever arrived, but the letter suggests it was at a low level.

Ramsay also wrote to Lanier, who was now at Coupar, letting him know of the Jacobite advance towards Dunkeld and where they could defeat Angus's regiment there.[20] Ramsay believed that Angus's would be defeated and asked Lanier what his orders were. Lanier did not know the country and delayed acting until he had reached Perth.[21]

Jacobite strength near Dunkeld had been building up. Apparently on Tuesday morning 'many people appeared upon the tops of the hills' and in the woods; variously estimated at between 500–600 to 1,000. These were 600 Athollmen, two companies of Strathsay's infantry and some horse. Jacobite camp fires were visible. The Jacobite began firing on their enemies. At eight in the morning, Cleland's force marched out of the town to engage them, and Jacobite numbers were thought to number about the same as his own. A small number of Eglington's Horse under a lieutenant acted as scouts. They had some infantry with them to cover their retreat if needed. Captain George Monroe, with forty fusiliers, fifteen halberdiers and thirty horse, spearheaded the force. Then there was Sir James Agnew with twenty dragoons. Then more of Angus's regiment; Ensign Lockhart with yet another thirty halberdiers. Apparently 'the halberds were excellent weapons against Highlanders' swords and targets in case they should rush upon the shot, with their accustomed fury'. Captains John Campbell and Robert Hume, 'two brave young gentlemen', then led 100 fusiliers. Captains Borthwick and Harries with 200 musketeers followed them. An unspecified number of pikemen made up the rear. Left in the town, manning the dykes, were 150 men. These may have included Blackader for he only stated about the ensuing action that there was some skirmishing between small parties of each side. Either he had no experience or knowledge of these encounters or deemed them to be insubstantial.[22]

It must have been a leisurely march because the same account which cited eight o'clock as the time of their marching out claimed that it was not until six hours later that the Jacobites were found. According to the trooper in Agnew's troop, the vanguard was fourteen men from that troop and fourteen from Livingstone's. Two or three hundred Jacobites were concealed in a glen in ambush. They opened fire at long range. Cornet Livingstone of Grubbit's Horse was unfortunate to be wounded in the knee, and between two and four of his troopers were shot, but none fatally. The cavalry then may have retired or held their ground, accounts differing, and Monroe advanced with his company of forty fusiliers and sent a volley of musket balls towards the Jacobites, several of whom fell; perhaps as many as 21 being killed (a large number if true), which led to the latter retreating to join their main party of about 600 men. They rallied on the next hill, however. The wounded cavalrymen returned to Dunkeld to have their injuries dressed.[23]

These were not the only Jacobites in view. They also included cavalry as well as infantry. The main body of the troops advanced against them and the anonymous trooper, whose wound had been seen to and returned for more, wrote, 'We lying clos ower against other, skirmishing and fyring all yt day with little loss'. Cleland ordered Monroe to send a sergeant and six men to a house near the wood to dislodge the twenty Jacobites who he had seen there. This feat accomplished, albeit with three men wounded, one of whom later died, the little army then retired in good order to Dunkeld. This was probably because night was falling. The cavalry had apparently been eager for a fight but could not do so as the enemy had withdrawn. Retreat was also imperative because the cavalry left first, followed by the infantry, though Blackader claimed the horsemen came away after only one or two hours in the field and 'our lieutenant colonel did the like'. Losing so many men made their continuance in the open dangerous. Young William Sandilands had been particularly active, firing his gun eleven times. Apparently thirty Jacobites had become casualties, according a Jacobite prisoner on the following day.[24] A few prisoners were taken, 'who denied their being concerned with them, though I doubt not but they were'. They also informed Cardross that the Athollmen and Strathspey men would arrive on the next today and then on that day after Cannon and others.[25]

Cleland received the second of two messages sent by Ramsay for Cardross. These were that the cavalry led by Cardross were to return to Perth as soon as possible. Ramsay wrote that afternoon:

> My Lord,
> I desir'd yowr lordship last night to retire the Horse and Dragoons under your Command. Except yow have orders from some generall person to the Contrarie yow must do soe yet or be answerable for what shal fall out. Major General Lanier knows of Angus Regiment being there. I had a letter from him last night which acquaints me of the bodie of the enemy moving towards Atholl, one letts me know he intends to move this way, yet I thincke it fits yow yet retire, this is from my lord, yow lordships most humble servant . . .
>
> My lord, take such measures that the enemy come not betwixt us and yow and so stop your passadge.[26]

Mackay thought that Ramsay did not think that the cavalry he had sent would be of use in defending the town. Yet Mackay later wrote that Ramsay should either have marched all his forces from Perth to Dunkeld 'to maintain the post if he thought it of consequence'. Or he should have given Cleland orders, 'if he found not the place tenable against such numbers as he could expect against him', to retreat up the river.[27]

On receipt of the first, Cleland had informed Ramsay that he had been 'engaged with the Enemy, and it was necessary he should stay'. The second message could not be resisted, however, and so by the day's end the five troops of cavalry departed for Perth. Cardross wrote, 'I came unwillingly away but behaved to obey my reiterated orders'. The trooper wrote, 'he would not allow of yt, but ordrd us in all haist to return wt the king's standart'. Blackader stated, 'Our men were mightily discourag'd to hear this'. Cleland considered that the cavalry were too few against the numerous enemy. Once the cavalry had gone, some of the officers and men of the remaining battalion suggested that they should follow suit, on the basis that they were in an 'open, useless, place, ill provided of all things and in the midst of Enemies growing still to greater numbers'. This latter they knew because the vanguard of Cannon's main force had been sighted that afternoon, just before light faded.[28]

Initially, Cleland 'charged those retreating dragoons with the loss of his regiment'. To combat the wish for departure, Cleland 'compelled them and told them, that tho every man went away, he resolved to stay himself alone'. Apart from this moral blackmail, some of his officers used 'Arguments of Honour' that every soldier, but especially the officers, were deemed to hold. The officers then assembled their horses and shot them in order that their men not doubt their staying and that 'they would run all hazards with them'. These actions and words were effective. The troops stood at their arms that night in Atholl's house and gardens.[29]

The battle was to be soon at hand, so we shall now examine those forces participating in it.

Lord Angus's Regiment

Officer commanding (Captain unless otherwise stated)	Lieutenant	Ensign	NCOs and drummers	Privates
Colonel the Earl of Angus (absentee)	-Walsh	Robert Crichton	7	57
Lieutenant Colonel William Cleland	Andrew Gilchrist	John Pringle	7	54
Major James Henderson	Henry Stuart	John Boyd	7	61
Ker of Kersland	William Oliphant	Hugh Ferguson	7	61
George Monroe	Charles Dalzell	William Campbell	6	57
Roy Campbell	-Hutchinson	James Campbell	7	59
William Hay	John Forester	Francis Nasmith	6	57

Officer commanding (Captain unless otherwise stated)	Lieutenant	Ensign	NCOs and drummers	Privates
Dhu Campbell	William Cathcart		7	57
William Borthwick	Nathaniel Johnston		7	47
Robert Hume	William Campbell		6	57
-Ballantine	James Cranston	John Lang	6	57
John Haldane	-Veitch	John Cleghorn	7	57
William Herries	Robert Tait	Andrew Derriston	4	61
James Lindsay	James Ballantyne	John Wilson	4	60
Ninian Steel	John Blackader	John Kirkland	6	57
James Gilchrist	-Calder	Archibald Wilson	7	57
John Mathison	William Clarke	Francis Hislop	7	60
John Caldwell	Adam Hackness	-McCulloch	7	57
John Stephenson	John Stewart	John Hay	6	62
William Grieve	James Aikeman	-Stephenson	7	59

Gideon Elliott was the surgeon and Alexander Shields the chaplain.[30]
Total strength at muster on 10 July 1689 was 61 officers and 1,281 men, the latter including 39 sergeants, 51 corporals and 37 drummers with 1,154 privates.[31]

Unusually, the regiment had twenty companies rather than the standard twelve. Its strength at Dunkeld has been variously estimated. Cameron stated it was 1,200 men strong.[32] The contemporary history, written by the victors stated there were between 700 and 800 men who arrived in the battalion at Dunkeld on 17 August 1689.[33] On 6 July the Privy Council noted that they had 1,140 men, but this may well have been reduced in the subsequent seven weeks due to illness and desertion.[34]

A victorious army often downplays its strength to inflate its victory whilst a defeated one inflates it to downplay its own defeat. However there is another possibility; as we have seen, reinforcements arrived – and then departed after briefly seeing action – and it may well be that the higher number as stated by Cameron refers to his enemies' strength when at their temporary numerical height.

Allegations were made against Cleland's running of the regiment. He was alleged to have had the men train with insufficient ammunition, made to march on the Sabbath day and to have made them sleep in fields rather than in proper quarters. He was accused of pocketing the money he should have used to pay for the men's hats and stockings and kept them short of food and ammunition, all of which 'are very discouraging to many of ye officers and soldiers and my Lord Angus.'[35] How true these are is another question, for Cleland was never in a position to counter them.

As to the strength of the Jacobites, Blackader believed they were between 3,000–4,000, and claimed a prisoner stated it was the latter number.[36] Another estimate was 4,000.[37] The anonymous account stated the Jacobites were 'repute in all above 5,000'.[38] Cameron has the lowest number, 'now declined to about three thousand men'.[39]

The units in the Jacobite army at this point in the campaign were as follows, but the numbers cited below had declined prior to the battle.

Unit	Strength
Stewarts of Appin	200
MacGregors	Not given
Camerons	620
McPhersons	250
MacDonalds of Glencoe	Not given
Athollmen	600
Fergusons	Not given
Frasers	120
Gordons of Strathdown and Glenlivet	Not given
Macleans	200–500
Irish regiment	300*
MacDonalds of Glengarry	400
MacDonalds of Clanranalds	400
Sir Donald MacDonald	500
Four cavalry troops	300

Strengths given are the numbers stated just after Killiecrankie; that of the Irish and the cavalry troops are the numbers given at the previous battle and are probably not those they enjoyed at Dunkeld; that for the Irish perhaps lower as the latter is not known to have taken any casualties at Killiecrankie whereas the infantry may well have done.[40]

The Jacobites, unlike their enemies, also had artillery. Cameron refers to their having 'several cannons and field pieces which had been taken from the enemy'. These were presumably the three guns from Mackay's army at Killiecrankie. However, as Cameron quickly added, 'he had not so many balls as he had guns'. It is not known whether he had any men who knew how to fire these guns, either.[41]

Cleland's men were outnumbered by at least four to one and quite possibly more. It may have looked hopeless and in the open field would have been. Yet small numbers could prevail against larger in defensive positions; the defence of Glasgow in 1679 and Bristol in 1685 had shown that and as we shall see the attack on Preston in 1715 was no pushover. At least they had adequate time to make what defensive preparations they could. According to Black-ader, he was not dismayed. He posted his men behind the ditches and dykes that he had had erected previously. Others were posted in the cathedral and Atholl's house. Some soldiers were posted in forward positions from which had escape routes. Captain Hay and Ensign Lockhart went to Stanley Hill, just to the north edge of the town. An officer and twenty-eight men advanced to a stone dyke at the foot of the said hill.[42] Another contemporary noted that the defenders had 'advantages of walls, hedges, ditches, houses'.[43] Yet the defences were far from adequate, Mackay writing, 'all their defence was but low gardens, in most places not above four feet high'.[44]

Cannon's plan was to launch a frontal attack on the town. This was criticised in retrospect by Sir Ewan Cameron, admittedly a critic of his, writing 'he resolved to dislodge them, and might have easily effected it, had he used a little policy, and sent a small party of five or six hundred men to have trained them out of the town, where they were strongly fortified, and kept the army att a short distance, as he could easily have done, without the enemy's getting any intelligence, the people thereabouts being all his friends'.[45]

At dawn on that day, Wednesday, 21 August, the Jacobite army appeared on the hills above the town. Their baggage was in the hills to the west, en route to Atholl. Apparently they had a train of 1,000 horses, taken from Mackay's army at Killiecrankie. Before seven in the morning, the Jacobite artillery was moved down the hills and towards the town. It was accompanied by 100 armoured soldiers, and a regiment of infantry. Two troops of horse marched around the town and took up a position to the south-west, between the ford and the cathedral. Another two troops of horse stood to the north-east of the town. Apparently they 'shewed much eagerness to encourage and push on the Foot' into action; possibly there may have been a reluctance among some of the infantry for the fight.[46] Blackader believed that the Jacobite cavalry was also posted so as to cut off any retreat that they might make, 'which they nothing doubted of'.[47] According to one source two guns employed by the Jacobites made a breach in one of the town's defences. Afterwards they fell silent.[48]

The attack, when it came, was unsubtle. Blackader wrote 'the enemy approached very fast, the Highlanders came running on like desperate

Villains, firing only once, and then came on with Sword and Target'. Cameron wrote, 'he . . . marched his army . . . in a full body towards their trenches'.[49] John Cameron, the chief's son, later recalled, 'I had the honour to attack at the head of my ffather's men'.[50] Such a charge had been successful at Killiecrankie, but against resolute troops under cover, behind defensive works, these tactics were inappropriate. Fighting in a built-up area was unusual.

As the Jacobites approached, there were exchanges of musketry. Hay's men, who had been defending part of the town, fired on the attackers but were driven back, 'not being able to sustain their great number and fierceness'. Hay was the only casualty among his company, however. At another point, the Jacobites in armour and another battalion were attacking elsewhere, but 'after they had entertain'd them briskly with their fire, from a pretty space, the Rebels forc'd the Dyke and obliging them to retire, firing from one little dyke to another, and at length to betake themselves to the House and Yard dykes'.[51] Maclean's men had been the first Jacobite unit to attack, and once they had beaten the defenders from the walls, helped each other over them.[52]

Elsewhere, a lieutenant and his eighteen men at the eastern end of the town advanced three men to fire on the Jacobites and then retreated. The lieutenant burnt some houses and then joined his men as they withdrew. Lieutenant Stewart was defending a barricade near to the market cross and saw some of his comrades retreating. He had his men follow suit. In doing so, he was killed as 'a multitude of the Rebels [came] upon them'. Blackader wrote they were 'pressing in upon us to the very cross in the middle of the town, where another party of our men fired on them, and then retired in order'.[53] The defenders were being pushed back, but were able to do so in good order whilst inflicting casualties on their enemies.

Cameron described the battle rather differently and, from the Jacobite viewpoint, more positively as they 'beat the enemy's out-guards, and entering the town in the very face of their fire, without any thing to cover them, brock through all opposition, and rushed in upon such of them as were posted in the lesser houses, where they putt all thy found to the sword without any mercy'.[54]

At the west end of the town, Lieutenant Forrester and Ensign Campbell's twenty-four men fired sharply on the Jacobites who had by then taken possession of a house. Large numbers of Jacobites attacked them and forced them back. All the outer posts had now fallen. Cameron later wrote: 'Never was there, on any occasion, more resolution and less conduct shown than in this; and so surprizeing was their boldness, that they stood naked in the open streets exposed to the enemy's fire, and killed them in the windows, till they cleared the town of them.'[55]

There was desperate fighting in several places in the town. One was at Atholl's house. Cameron recalled, we 'drove them into the Marquess of Athol's house, which being a strong place, they were not to be beaten from that post so easily'.[56] Blackader also described a successful stand of his men as the Jacobites 'came swarming in on all heads, and gave a desperate assault in four places all at once, first firing their Guns, and then running in on us with their swords and targets; but it pleased God they were also bravely repulsed, our men still firing on them, where they came on thickest'.[57]

There was also fighting close to the river. Muskets were fired at point-blank range, 'the shot liberally pour'd in their Faces'. Melee took place as well, with the Jacobites attacking sword in hand and their enemies resisting with pikes and halberds and so 'returned their Blows with interest'.[58] Blackader commended the men's courage, stating that veteran soldiers there claimed 'They never saw men fight better; for there was not the least sign of fear to be seen on any of them; everyone performing his part gallantly'. He ascribed this to 'the Lord wonderfully assisting our men with courage'.[59]

One of the defenders' greatest losses, as had been the case with the Jacobites at Killiecrankie, was that of their leader. At the beginning of the battle, Cleland had been 'going up and down encouraging his men'. The Jacobites were using their muskets as well as swords as some fired from houses as well as from the hills. According to one account, 'And by two shots at once, through the head and another through the liver, the brave lieutenant colonel was kill'd; while he was visiting and exhorting the officers and souldiers at their several posts. He attempted to get into the house that the soldiers might not be discouraged at the sight of his dead body: but fell by the way'.[60] Blackader stated that this death 'which is never enough to be lamented'.[61] Cameron referred to him as being a brave man.[62]

This took place only an hour into the battle. The second-in-command, Major Henderson, was also struck down by Jacobite gunfire. Wounded by several musket balls, he was incapacitated and died four days later. Other officers also became casualties. Captain Caldwell was shot in the breast and was unlikely to recover. Captain Borthwick was shot in the arm, and whilst fellow captain, Steel, was wounded, he was patched up and returned to his post. Captain Monroe, in the meantime, took command.[63] Possibly he was the senior captain, and was ranked second on the list of the regimental captains.

Monroe left his own post to the care of Lieutenant Stewart. Finding his men being galled by musketry from Jacobites located in houses, he had his pikemen assemble in small parties with burning faggots 'on pike ends to fire their houses, and where keys were found locked and burnt all within: which raised a hideous noise from these wretches and the fire'. Sixteen Jacobites perished thus. The inhabitants had long fled, either to the surrounding fields or sheltered in the cathedral.[64]

Yet it is possible that the Jacobites may have been on the point of victory, despite the undoubted strength of Atholl's house. According to Cameron, 'their ammunition was all spent to a shott, and they upon the very point of surrendering att discretion, when the General commanded his men, even against their own inclinations, to retire'.[65] Another account noted that the powder was almost exhausted and bullets were long gone, too. But instead of contemplating surrender, to deal with this crisis, men cut lead off the house roofs, melted it down in furrows on the ground and cut it into bullets for instant use.[66] This is possible, for this account states that the battle continued until 11 o' clock. There had been 'continual thundering of shot from both sides and flames and smoak, and hideous cryes filling the air'.[67] The wind was clearly blowing through the town because apparently all but three houses, ironically close to the cathedral, were damaged by fire.[68]

MacPherson's account has the Jacobites retreating due to their ammunition being exhausted.[69] Another account suggests an alternative, or at least an equal possibility for the battle's ending with the attackers withdrawal: 'At length the Rebels, wearied with so many fruitless and expensive Assaults; and finding no abatement of the Courage or Diligence of their Adversaries who treated them with continual shot from all their posts, they gave over and fell back and ran to the hills in great confusion.'[70] Blackader stated that the attackers 'found themselves necessitate to flee back on all hands, leaving a number of dead carcasses behind'. He also recorded that some fled into houses 'to fire upon us, our Men went to set fire to the houses and burnt many of them'.[71]

There appear to have been attempts by some of the Jacobite officers to recommence the attack, according to prisoners taken afterwards. The men refused because of the ferocity of their opponents, 'they could fight against men, but it was not fit to fight against devils' or as Blackader wrote, 'they said we were mad and desperate men'.[72]

It was not absolutely certain that there would not be another attack. The defences were repaired and seats from the church were used to plug any gaps that could be found. Trees from a small hill, which in the battle had provided some Jacobites with cover, were cut down and pressed into service too. It was only after these precautions had been taken was there the luxury of celebration. News of the fighting was despatched to Perth.[73]

The defenders rejoiced. They beat their drums, flourished their flags and shouted their contempt for their enemies. God was praised for their deliverance, too, as Blackader stated, 'Our men gave a great shout and threw their caps in the air, and then all joined in offering up praises to God for a considerable time for so miraculous a victory'. Psalms were sung. He added 'It was not by might, or Power, nor by Conduct, (our best officers being killed) . . .' The men's courage was also stressed.[74]

In repulsing the attack, several officers were killed; Cleland, Henderson and Captain Wall. Captains Hay, Caldwick, Steel and Borthwick were wounded. About eight to ten privates were killed.[75] A newspaper reported furthermore that fourteen men had been wounded.[76] Cameron thought that the government forces had been severely mauled; 'There were above three hundred of them killed, and a great many more wounded . . . the greatest part of the slaughter was of those who were slain att first in the little and less tenable houses of the toun.'[77] Another Jacobite account claimed 120–200 dead.[78] The regimental muster roll noted that one man from Ker's company had been killed in the battle and that one man from Campbell's company had been killed and another wounded.[79] Clearly more were slain than these two, but it would seem that numbers were remarkably low.

There is a great deal of variance with the losses suffered by the Jacobite army. The government's newspaper stated that 150 had been killed and several wounded.[80] Higher estimates were also given; about 300 slain, claimed a contemporary account of the battle.[81] Cameron dismissed such high figures: 'Many of the Highlanders were wounded, but not above eighteen or twenty of them killed, which looked like a miracle.' According to him, the reason was their enemies' faulty marksmanship, 'the enemy's shott somewhat resembled thunder, in this, that it had more noise than effect; for, observing that the Highlanders put their guns to their eye, and that they seldome missed their mark, they had not courage to expose themselves, but shott at random, whereby they did little execution'. Yet his son wrote that casualties among the clan were heavy, as they had been at Killiecrankie.[82] MacPherson states that two captains, a captain-lieutenant and other officers of Maclean's regiment were dead and their colonel had had his leg broken by a musket ball.[83] Government horse and dragoons from Perth scoured the countryside after the battle and found more Jacobite corpses, presumably men who had died from their wounds.[84]

The Jacobites had been defeated but their forces had not been routed. The battle served to blunt their offensive yet again, following Cannon's previous refusal to engage Mackay, and further weakened his leadership. Admittedly a unimaginative frontal assault on a defended place against resolute defenders was never going to be easy. Cannon took that chance, though, and in doing so failed. Yet it was not wholly successful for the government either. More could have been made of this battle had Lanier and Ramsay marched towards Dunkeld in order to turn a Jacobite setback into a rout. Neither of them had Mackay's confidence and so missed a chance to end the campaign there and then.

Cardross and his cavalry returned to Dunkeld on the day after the battle, arriving in the afternoon. He saw that the Jacobites had retired a little to the north of the town. When Jacobite scouts noted his arrival, they left and the main body retreated to Atholl thereafter. On that Thursday morning, 100 infantrymen from Perth arrived to reinforce the Dunkeld garrison.[85]

The first news that the government had about the battle was revealed in a letter from Sir William Lockhart to Melville two days later. He had heard from Ramsay, who told of the attack on Dunkeld, the death of Cleland and other officers, as well as 'cutt of a grate part of the Regiment'. There was no news from the town itself at this point. Lockhart wrote, 'We wait ane express with grat impatience'. News varied as to whether the whole Jacobite army had attacked the town or merely the Atholl men.[86]

Given the disparity of forces involved and the lack of support given to Angus's regiment, controversy arose. The complaints were 'that that regiment without Horse should have been sent to such an advanced post' and 'why Colonel Ramsay, the very day befor the action, should have called them to Perth'. One other criticism was that 'it was generally thought that Cardross, notwithstanding Ramsay's order, should not have marched [away]'. He had skirmished with the Jacobites and had seen their cavalry and what Ramsay had not.[87]

There was an inquisition into the Privy Council's decision to send the regiment to Dunkeld. Leven had opposed the move, 'and told as plainly as if he had seen it, what would be their fatte'. In a letter from three of the regiment's captains 'they complain more of their being ill used, their giving any account of the action, such as Cardross leaving them, the want of pouder and ball'.[88]

Mackay also surmised that a major defeat could have been inflicted on the Jacobite army at this time had Lanier better knowledge of the country or had Ramsay acted differently. As soon as Lanier was at Coupar, the forces at Perth could have crossed the Tay and linked up with Lanier's men. United, they could then have marched to Dunkeld. It was not only Mackay who complained but apparently Ramsay did so, too, alleging 'that Sir John Lanier's delaying his resolution too long after he had given his account of the pressing danger of the post of Dunkeld', thus excusing his own inaction.[89]

Although there were attempts by the Jacobites to portray the battle as a 'near miss', it resulted in the end of the Jacobite campaign for the year 1689 even though it was not quite autumn yet (when the Jacobite campaigns of 1715 and 1745 were just about to begin). Cameron wrote:

> By this weak conduct, Canon suffered so extreamly in his reputation
> and his men were so dispirited by his misimploying their valour,

that, the winter now approaching, they dropt away, and he in the end obliged to retreat to Lochaber, where the remainder were dismissed, excepting the few Irishmen . . . and the Lowland officers who were dispersed into such quarters as the country afforded.

The Lowlanders had lost all hope of a successful outcome unless they 'gott a general that was capable to conduct them'.[90] There was some additional fighting; Lanier clashed with sixty Jacobites on 24 August near Fettercairn, killing twenty-four and capturing thirty, while six escaped.[91] Lord Murray also noted the Jacobite dissension after the battle, but also put it down to their reaction to the arrival in Scotland of additional forces from England in response to the Killiecrankie debacle.[92] Yet by the following month two cavalry regiments; Colchester's and Berkeley's, were ordered southwards, though the former only as far south as Carlisle.[93]

The Jacobites retired to Blair Atholl for six days after the battle, but had not given up and on 24 August entered into a bond to provide men for the next campaign, numbering 1,810 men. Sir John Maclean, Sir Donald MacDonald, Sir Ewan Cameron, Glengarry and Benbecula all promised 200 men each; Sir Alexander Maclean, the Stewarts of Appin, Keppoch, MacGregor, Enverary all promised 100 men, Callochele, Largo, McNaughton, Bara and Glencoe 50 men and Struan 60.[94]

By the end of 1689 Mackay's troop numbers in Scotland were being reduced due to a lack of money in the Scottish treasury. There was also despondency in the Jacobite camp in the new year with some calling for peace feelers to be explored and bemoaning the lack of any promised help from Ireland or France. Yet others were determined to maintain the struggle. Mackay focussed on building a fortress in the western Highlands but had placed a strong garrison in and around Inverness commanded by Major General Livingstone. Naval vessels were sent to harry the Highlanders on the Western Isles.

Meanwhile, in the north of Scotland, on 22 April 1690 Livingstone heard that there were Jacobites at Mackintosh's house at Aberarder, Strathern, which was 15 miles from Inverness. With 1,000 infantry, four troops of horse and some dragoons, and with artillery, he moved to attack them. The Jacobites retreated when they were within six miles of them. Ramsay's and Angus's regiments were to march to join Livingstone, but on hearing there was a Jacobite threat to Montrose, returned there.[95]

Mackay's plans were known about by the Jacobites and apparently, 'the very noise of it occasioned such alarm among the rebels'. The newly-arrived Major General Thomas Buchan (c.1641–1724), as the senior major general to Cannon, took over command of the Jacobite army. According to Balcarres, the plan was for him 'to go down to the borders of the low country, to amuse the enemy and fatigue their troops by allaruming them in severall of their quarters'.[96] He asked the clans to supply him with 100 men each and had 1,500 men with him. He hoped to collect more supporters. At the end of March they marched from Keppoch to Kilwinny at the end of Loch Ness. By the middle of April, they were in Strathspey and remained on the north bank for ten days, Balcarres writing that instead of taking action as discussed, he 'continued there without doing anything'. He was to quarter his men in the woods of Glenlochy 'where they could not be attacked but under great disadvantage, yet he would not hearken to this advice'. Instead he put his men in the villages near Cromdale, 'though all the clans positively protested against that march'. Two hundred men led by Grant and Brody were sent to guard the fords over the Spey, and apparently they 'were so well posted that they might have stopt the enemy from crossing that great river'.[97]

Mackay learnt that Buchan was 'taking the field' and ordered Livingstone to monitor his progress. His command, based in Inverness, consisted of three regiments of infantry, his own regiment of horse and an unquantifiable number of dragoons. He was also instructed to 'labour, by a detachment of the best of his men, to get a catch of them, or at least to hinder the grouth of their number'. However, although Livingstone was able to learn of their whereabouts (apparently by threatening to torture a captured Jacobite agent, which then in Scotland was a legitimate tactic) and to march to that vicinity, his problem being that of supplies. It was only with 'great difficulty' that the cavalry could find forage and the infantry their victuals. As soon as Buchan retired to the hills, he was obliged to return to Inverness. He gave Mackay 'nothing but Ill News'.[98]

Upon hearing this news, Mackay gathered 3,000 troops from Stirling, Dundee and Glasgow, to march to Perth. This was so that they could then march to counter any further Jacobite support that might accrue to Cannon and Buchan.[99] Livingstone discovered that despite the difficulties of coming to blows, that he must act as soon as possible. Many of those who appeared to be supportive of the government were now intimating that they intended to join the Jacobites. Livingstone wrote, that the Jacobite march 'increased as a snow ball daily . . . affrighted and discouraged the country'.[100] He wrote to Mackay to tell him what his plan was and that many in the north were planning to join the Jacobites.[101]

Livingstone's field forces consisted of the following:
Leslie's Infantry regiment, 400 men:

Captain	Lieutenant	Ensign
John Fowke		John Meres
Tankard	George Villars Carleton	
Sir James Leslie		Edward Juckes
John Price		William Kerr
Major Tankred		George Morris
William Rugeley	Clifford Lowther	
	James Baker	
John Price		

Six companies of Grant's infantry regiment, perhaps 300–350 men:

Rank	Names
Field officers	Colonel Laird of Grant, Lieutenant Colonel Patrick Grant, Major Hugh Mackay
Captains	Alexander Grant, John Grant, John Forbes, Laird John Burgiss, George Gordon, Robert Grant, Robert Ross[102]

One company of Mackay's Highlanders, 100 men.
Three troops of Livingstone's Dragoons, 300 men:

Colonel Thomas Livingstone		Cornet Williams
Sir William Douglas	Lieutenant Robert Preston	Cornet Patrick Gray
Major Aeneas Mackay	Lieutenant Lewis Lawder	Cornet John McDuigall
Captain Henry Balfour	Lieutenant William Murray	Cornet David Crichton
Captain John Islay	Lieutenant Andrew Agnew	Cornet George Boswall
Captain Sir William Douglas	Lieutenant David Beaton	Cornet Cavillie

Minister, Alexander Sutherland, ADC James Afleth.[103]
One or two Troops of Lord Tester's Horse, perhaps 50–100 men.
Total: c.1,200 men.[104]

Jacobite officers claimed their force numbered between 1,400–1,500 men; Mackay that they had 'much the same' as Livingstone. Mackay also wrote that they had '800 of their worst men' and had been reinforced by 'some Badenoch men'.[105] The force included several companies of Macleans, judging by later lists of prisoners.[106] It also numbered many Camerons, too.[107] The two forces were roughly the same number. Neither possessed any artillery to slow them down. This was to be the smallest battle of all in these campaigns.

Livingstone marched his men eight miles from Inverness in search of the Jacobites. They reached Brodie and remained there for two days, waiting for the slow-moving baggage trains carrying crucial supplies. They also waited for an additional three troops of dragoons and Captain Burnet's troop of horse. Patience was also necessary to gain additional intelligence.[108]

The Jacobite forces were in Strathspey, 'threatening to slay and Burn all that would not joyn', according to Livingstone. On 30 April he learnt where they were; eight miles from Strathspey. This was in the land of the laird of Grant, a supporter of William III and a Scottish Privy Councillor. A captain of a company of Grant's regiment held a castle in Strathspey had reported that the Jacobite force had left Badenoch to Strathspey and had marched to within two miles of the castle.[109]

On the night of 30 April the Jacobite encampment was visible by its camp fires. Scouts discovered the lie of the land, how deep the river was and that 'the Ground was somewhat boggish'. Livingstone's force was two miles from his enemy and had been marching through the evening and night. Livingstone wrote, 'I form'd a Design to attack them by surprise, for they did not know of our being arrived, but my Men and Horse being so extremely wearied, I gave them about half an hour to refresh themselves'.[110]

Captain Grant at the castle knew of Livingstone's advance and kept the castle gates locked in order to prevent any of those who had taken shelter there from leaving it and letting the Jacobites know of their peril. Livingstone's forces were ready at two in the morning of the first day of May. Captain Grant met him and showed him where the Jacobites were. He offered to guide him there himself.[111]

A council of war was held for Livingstone to brief his officers prior to the attack. He was still not certain whether an attack should take place. He asked his subordinates to see to the condition of their men to ascertain 'if they were able to do it'. The officers declared 'they would stand by me to the last man and desired earnestly to go on'. Fortunately for them, the Jacobite camp was on the plain, a mile and a half from any strong ground, for they did not know that their enemies were so close. Mackay later wrote, it was 'just as if they had been led thither by the hand, as an ox to the slaughter'.[112]

A night attack is extremely risky, as would have been well known to soldiers in 1690. Only five years previously, Monmouth's forces had marched through the night to surprise James II's army at Sedgemoor. It was a bold plan and a necessary one so that irregular troops had a chance of defeating regulars. The attack failed because the attackers were unable to achieve the crucial surprise necessary for success. Monmouth's army was decisively defeated on the following morning.

The force marched by a covered way to conceal their approach until the last moment and arrived by the river. There was a ford on the Spey, near to a church, guarded by two companies of 200 Jacobites led by Captains Grant and Brody. It was now three in the morning. Livingstone had some infantry and dragoons skirmish with them, to distract their attention from the main assault, whilst the bulk of his forces marched another quarter of a mile towards another ford, guided by the knowledgeable Captain Grant. This thrust was spearheaded by two or three troops of Livingstone's dragoons, a troop of Tester's horse and Captain Mackay's Highlanders.[113]

This force was able to cross the river before they were noticed. The Jacobites were asleep in tents and houses. Livingstone later wrote, 'and then we do see them run in parties up and down, not knowing which way to turn themselves, being surprised'. The Jacobites 'take the alarm as moving confusedly as irresolute men'. He then 'commanded all the Horse and Dragoons to joyn, and pursued hem, which affrighted them so'.[114] Apparently 100 Jacobites were killed 'in the first hurry'.[115]

The Jacobite account of the battle has it that 'as soon as they recovered themselves, they formed into partys, made head against the enemy, and fought with that desperate resolution in their shirts' with their swords and shields. Therefore, there was no pursuit, 'Sir Thomas was glade to allow them to retreat without attempting to pursue them'.[116]

However, Livingstone wrote that 'they took themselves to the hills, at the foot of Combrel we overtook them, attacked them, killing betwixt three and four hundred upon the place and took about one hundred prisoners, the greater part of them officers'. Livingstone stated that the Jacobites only escaped because mist descended 'so we could scarcely see one another, otherways the slaughter should have been greater'. The retreat was successful for the pursuers' horses were ready to collapse and the force was drawn up on low ground.[117]

The Jacobite leaders had been caught napping. On the first alarm Buchan sent away his nephew and some officers and men, though they later surrendered. Buchan escaped, though, he 'got of, without hat, coat or sword'. He was later seen, in a state of exhaustion, at a cousin's house in Glenlivet. Cannon also escaped, in a nightgown. Dunfermline had, providentially, left the day before the fighting. Buchan and Cannon fled in different directions, the former looking for Cannon's men. Livingstone had nothing but praise for his men, 'The resolution and forwardness of the Troops was admirable' and though most of the fighting had been by the cavalry, the infantry unable to get to the front line, yet they 'marched after us with as great Diligence as possible'.[118]

About fifty of the Jacobites, mostly gentlemen, went to the nearby Lethendry Castle with the intention of holding it to the last. Livingstone sent a messenger to them to offer them mercy if they surrendered. The Jacobites opened fire during this attempt at parley. Two grenadiers were shot dead and another was wounded. Lieutenant George Carleton had experience of using grenades from campaigning abroad, or so he claimed. Putting four into a bag he crept towards the castle by using an old ditch to reach an old house near to it. He intended to be close enough in order to throw his missiles into the castle itself.[119]

He threw the first, which 'put the enemy immediately into confusion'. The second grenade fell short. The third one exploded just after it had been thrown and so likewise was ineffectual. The fourth went through a window in the castle 'so it increased the confusion, which the first had put them into; that they immediately called out to me, upon their parole of safety, to come to them'. Carleton went to the barricaded main door, which had been reinforced by great stones. The Jacobites inside were now ready to surrender if mercy would be granted.[120]

Carleton returned to Livingstone to relate his account and pass him the news of the wish for a conditional surrender. Livingstone told Carleton to return to inform them that 'He would cut them all to pieces, for their murder of two of his grenadiers, after his proffer of quarter'. Carleton left, 'full of these melancholy tidings', but as he did, his commander came towards him. He said, 'Hark ye sir, I believe there may be among them some of our old acquaintances (from the Dutch service). Therefore, tell them, they shall have good quarter'. Carleton 'very willingly' took this news back and delivered it. The Jacobites immediately threw down their barricade and one Brody, who had earlier fought at the ford, came out from the main door. Apparently he had been wounded by having part of his nose blown off by one of the grenades Carleton had thrown. The two men went to Livingstone, who confirmed Carleton's message and then all the Jacobites surrendered. Carleton wrote, 'the Highlanders never held up their heads so high after this'.[121]

Cameron stated that 'the loss on both sides was pretty equall'.[122] However, Livingstone stated that between 300 and 400 Jacobites had been killed, including 20 officers and 400 others.[123] A government report claimed that 900 were dead and 100 captured; surely an exaggeration.[124] Another account states there were 400 Jacobite dead and 200 prisoners.[125] John Cameron wrote that 'Our Clan had a considerable loss at that unhappy business of Crombdale'.[126] The prisoners had been sent to Inverness by 17 May, with the rank and file being accommodated in the castle and the officers allowed their liberty in the town but under guard. Yet there was not accommodation for them there. Most of the latter were soon sent to Edinburgh, guarded by ninety dragoons. By 26 May, fifty-four prisoners were there, including Sir David Ogilby and Archibald Kennedy.[127] Their lot was not a happy one, as one Francis Beatton, in Edinburgh's Tolbooth, complained to Argyle, 'being taken at Crombdaill and ever since kept upon a very small allowance (2d per diem) which we could not subsist upon had it not been supplied by the charity of some tender hearted Christians'.[128]

The Jacobites also lost all their baggage, provisions, 1,000 arms and ammunition. The standards of King James and Queen Mary were captured. There was plunder for the victors, too, as Livingstone noted. Healths were drunk with wines taken from the Jacobite camp. Livingstone believed that he had had three men wounded, but none seriously, as well as having had a dozen horses killed and a greater number disabled.[129] This ignores the two grenadiers killed at the castle.

A government report was that this was the 'Entire Defeat of the most considerable Force of the Highland Rebels'.[130] Mackay wrote, 'the news whereof did very much good to the King's affairs both in Scotland and England, by abating the confidence of their Majesties' enemies in both Parliaments'.[131] It had been the Jacobites' costliest defeat of the campaign, much of it caused by carelessness.

Mackay concluded that the victory had been due to numerous reasons. Firstly, Livingstone had procured intelligence that the Jacobites were in close proximity to him, secondly that his troops were led in silence towards the enemy, thirdly that the inexperienced captain of the troops in the castle concealed his march, and fourthly that Buchan camped his men in a vulnerable position contrary to usual Jacobite procedure. Lastly, Mackay wrote 'tho' Sir Thomas Livingstone did all that could be expected of a carefull diligent officer, the captain of the castle, altogether a novice, seemed to have had the greatest share in this favourable success'.[132]

The Jacobites dispersed: they had been on campaign for six weeks, had been defeated, scattered and had lost their supplies. They also wanted to see their families again.[133] A government newssheet from Edinburgh, published a week later told that the Jacobites had told James that they could not hold out any longer, that they were in a starving condition and how 'the rebels are in a great consternation, faring they shall have no relief from Ireland and doubts not but the common people will yield at the first approach of any of the King's forces'.[134]

As with the fighting at Dunkeld, the results were as much moral than physical. Cameron wrote, 'the ill conduct of General Buchan so discouraged the Lowland gentlemen, that not a man of them thought fit to joyn with him'. Some Highland chiefs began to submit to the government; MacDonald of Largo and McAlastair of Loup did so on 16 June.[135] As with Dunkeld, this had been another victory for the Scottish government's forces, but as with Dunkeld it was not decisive in itself. Rather, both served to dent and depress the Jacobite cause, which was becoming increasingly unattractive as an option to the uncommitted and those Jacobites already in arms. However, the fighting was not at an end.

There were numerous skirmishes and small sieges in the Highlands throughout the remainder of the year, though none were conclusive, as the Jacobites avoided another battle. Mackay was ordered to go to Ireland where the tide was turning against the Jacobites; William's forces had won the Battle of the Boyne in July and James had fled to France thereafter. In 1691 fighting in Scotland was at an even lower ebb, with neither side able to deliver a decisive blow. Peace of a sort was made at Achallader in the summer, with the Jacobites promising to swear allegiance to William and Mary once James had given them dispensation to do so, in return for substantial cash payments and a promise of no reprisals. This was the first and last time that such a compromise treaty with made with 'rebels', but was indicative of the government's wish to bring the conflict to an end, given that their priority was the war with France. William gave his enemies a deadline of 1 January 1692, though James was slow in responding to his supporters' urgent needs, as they needed his authority to yield. The war in Ireland ended with the Treaty of Limerick in October 1691 and effective resistance to William's rule was now at an end.

Chapter 4

Peace and Storm, 1692–1715

The Jacobite campaigns were not one uninterrupted period of warfare of just over half a century. As with the fifteenth-century 'Wars of the Roses', there were several periods of internal peace. In our case there were two such lengthy phases, due to the international environment and the capability and willingness of the Stuart claimant to attempt to assert their rights.

After the battle of Cromdale it was twenty-five years before there was another battle in Britain. The Treaty of Achallader in the summer of 1691 had promised an end to the struggle and monetary compensation to the Jacobite leaders provided they swore allegiance to William by the end of the year or they would face 'fire and sword'. However, they sought James's permission to end their fealty to him, and he was slow in granting that. It was only in the last week of December 1691 that they were released from their former ties and there was a rush to take the oaths before a civil magistrate.

Not all were able to do so, the Glengarrys and the MacDonalds of Glencoe being amongst them. Sir John Dalrymple, the new Secretary of State for Scotland, was determined to make an example and had the king's authority to act against any recalcitrant clans. The Glengarrys were the first choice but they were relatively strong in comparison to the depleted military resources of the Scottish army, now led by Livingstone. The more vulnerable and smaller MacDonalds of Glencoe were the targets instead. On 13 February 1692, two companies of Argyle's regiment, after accepting hospitality from the MacDonalds, received orders to kill all the clansmen there. The massacre was not competently carried out, but thirty-eight people, including the chief, were killed.

In the short term, the killings encouraged others to come forward to take the oath of loyalty. Although there was an official enquiry, no one was prosecuted for their part in the massacre. William's rule in Scotland was marred by events not wholly under his control, such as years of famine and the failure of the Scottish colonial expedition at Darrien. However, the defeat of the French fleet at La Hogue in 1692 ended any possibility of a French invasion. Attempts to assassinate him failed and on the Continent William and his allies were able to frustrate Louis XIV's expansionist ambitions, Louis recognized the British succession, and a truce was arranged at Ryswick in 1697. For four years in western Europe there was peace.

At home the question of the succession was rearing its head. Mary had died in 1694. William had no heirs and his successor, his sister-in-law Anne, had seen all her children die, the last being the 13-year-old Duke of Gloucester in 1700. The English Parliament had to decide who would become king after Anne's death. Over the Channel, James II had died in 1701, but his son, James Francis Stuart, now 13, was recognized by Louis XIV as rightful King of Britain, James III and VIII.

Parliament passed the Act of Settlement in 1701. This gave the throne, after Anne's death, to the next Protestant in line. This was a grandson of James I and VI, George Lewis (1660–1727), Elector of the small north German state of Hanover. Crucially he was a Protestant. Yet Scotland, an independent state with a shared monarch, had not been consulted and would not necessarily fall in behind its southern neighbour.

The English government insisted that the solution was a union between the two kingdoms. Many in Scotland were averse to surrendering their proud independence, but some were in favour of it on economic grounds. Scotland was a poor country and had suffered much in the previous decade. Negotiations on union were the prime domestic concern over the next few years. In 1702 William died and was succeeded uncontroversially by Anne, whose government proceeded with the plan for unification. By a mixture of compromise and bribery, the Scottish Parliament agreed to its own demise. Scotland lost its political identity by this Act of Union of 1707, though sent members to the Parliament in London, retained its legal and religious settlement and was able to participate commercially with England and its colonies. The economic benefits were not immediate, however.

Unpopularity of the Union and the ongoing War of the Spanish Succession (1701–13), in which Britain and France were on opposing sides, gave the Jacobites another major opportunity. The war was going badly for the French, who suffered unprecedented major defeats at the hands of the allies, led by the Duke of Marlborough. Scotland presented Louis XIV with the possibility of striking back at his island enemy. A French fleet of twenty-one transport ships carrying 5,000 troops on board and seven escort ships was assembled at Dunkirk in February 1708 and with them sailed James Francis Stuart, a young man of 19. The plan was to disembark the troops in Scotland and link up with Scots disaffected with the Union and so susceptible towards Jacobitism. With the bulk of the country's armed forces fighting abroad, Britain was particularly vulnerable.

However, neither of the two French commanders who sailed with James were enthusiastic about the project. The Comte de Gace, commander of the troops, had to be offered military and political preferments before he agreed to take part. Admiral Comte Claude de Forbin, in charge of the fleet, had told Louis XIV that success was impossible and went along believing it a mere forlorn hope. News that part of the French fleet was preparing to sail towards Britain was known of in London and on 19 February orders were given to despatch Admiral George Byng (1663–1733) to the fleet at Spithead, though it was unknown whether their destination was merely to bombard 'sea port towns' or was a feint or something more serious. On 26 February Byng put out to sea with eleven ships.

Preparations were not amiss on land, either. Major General William Cadogan (1671–1726) had ten battalions of infantry embark from Ostend on 5 March. Other troops were marched north towards Scotland, including regiments of Foot and Horse Guards, along with two of dragoons. Troops from Ireland were also put on call, but even so it was estimated that it would not be until 1 May that a significant force would be assembled together in the north of England. Meanwhile, investors took fright and the value of stocks tumbled.

The French fleet set sail in March 1708 and managed to reach the Firth of Forth relatively unscathed, though battered by the elements. They were off the Fifeshire coastline, between Crail and Pittenweem. James was eager to disembark, armed with his proclamation as King of Scots and with a call for a new Parliament. Yet although there was support in Scotland for him, none of these men were at the right place at the right time. There was no one awaiting the French armada when it arrived.

The window of opportunity was short lived. When Admiral Byng and his Royal Navy squadron were sighted on 15 March, for Forbin the game was up. He would not even land James and his handful of followers ashore, despite their pleas. His concern was for his ships, and though he lost one to Byng, the remainder escaped and sailed round the north of Scotland, outsailing their pursuers. There was the possibility of landing at Inverness, but bad weather persuaded Forbin not to and so the fleet eventually arrived back in France, having lost many ships and men as had the Spanish Armada in 1588.

The Duke of Berwick, an illegitimate son of James II and VII, later wrote that this was a missed opportunity, writing of the admirals' decision not to let James land:

> This consideration ought not to have prevented him, for the material point was, that the troops should land with the Young Pretender; all Scotland expected him with impatience and was ready to take arms in his favour; what is more, England was at that time entirely unprovided with troops, so that he might have advanced, without resistance, into the north, where numbered of considerable persons had promised to join him.[1]

It is hard to know what would have happened had the French troops landed. It would have been the most serious invasion since 1688 and there was little in the way of troops in Scotland to have opposed them. The Earl of Leven, commander of the few troops in Scotland, later said that he would have had to have retreated to Berwick. However, support in Scotland might not have been significant had only James and his entourage arrived. As it was, there was now no need to withdraw forces from the Continent to deal with the issue and the Allied armies won another major victory over the French at Oudenarde later in the year.

Fighting on the Continent continued despite Marlborough's victories. In Britain discontent at this seemingly endless and expensive war led to a change in government in 1710 and the Tories returned to power, seeking to bring Britain's involvement in it to an end. The Peace of Utrecht in 1713 led to France rescinding her claim to the Spanish throne and Spain making territorial concessions to both Britain (Gibraltar and Minorca) and Austria (in the Low Countries and in Italy). France had to recognize the Hanoverian succession as being legitimate and to expel James from the chateau of St-Germain-en-Laye, where the Jacobite court had been since 1689.

The question of succession to the British thrones reared its head once more, as Anne died on 1 August 1714 and the Tory government sent for George in Hanover, who arrived six weeks later, when he was proclaimed King. Some Tories were in favour of James, but their rivals, the Whigs, were supportive of George I. The Jacobites had made few preparations for this event, though it had been clear that the Queen had been in poor health for some time. James made a protest about his rival being crowned, but it had little immediate effect in Britain. He and his supporters began to make plans and sent supporters to France, Spain and Sweden to seek aid.

However, it soon became clear that George, crowned as King George I on 20 October, did not enjoy universal popularity in his new realm. There were a number of riots on his coronation day, chiefly in the south of England. His political partiality soon became obvious for he began to offer the chief positions in the civil state and the army to known Whigs. This was because he trusted this party which had opposed Britain's unilateral departure from the recent war and universally supported the Hanoverian succession. That said, he did offer some posts to the Tories but few accepted. The general election next year saw a Tory majority in the Commons fall and a Whig majority replace them. This was due to the power of the Crown being in support of them and because there was a suspicion among some that the Tories favoured Jacobitism and Catholicism.

There was a fresh round of protests in May and June 1715, centred on three dates in the political calendar; 28 May being George's birthday, 29 May being the anniversary of the Stuart restoration of 1660 and 10 June being the birthday of James Stuart. Throughout many English towns and cities, supporters of both James and George took to the street to protest their loyalties. Yet this was not a prelude to a major uprising in England and by the summer of that year these protests had died down. Yet it was a different story in Scotland, with antagonism over the Union still prevalent. It would only need a spark to set the heather on fire and that was provided by a recently-ejected politician with a grievance.

Chapter 5

The Campaign of 1715

Although plans had been made to attempt a Jacobite restoration earlier in the year, the initiative was seized by John Erskine, the sixth Earl of Mar (1675–1732), until the previous year Secretary of State for Scotland, after having travelled from London to Scotland in August. He was motivated by hopes of a return to power and the wealth that went with it, and in Scotland he knew had an aggrieved constituency with nationalistic and religious woes who were looking for a lead. Under the pretence of holding a hunt, he was able to meet numerous Scottish nobility and gentry who assured him of support before the Jacobite banner was unfurled in public on 6 September 1715 at Braemar.

Fears among others of a Jacobite insurrection were rife that summer. They led to new regiments being raised in England and to calls for the Dutch to supply 6,000 troops as stipulated by treaty. Yet the number of troops in Scotland was, as in 1708, minimal. There were initially orders to seize men suspected of Jacobitism, but there were insufficient soldiers to do this. Four battalions of infantry and one dragoon regiment were gathered at Stirling, rightly seen as the place to hold in order to prevent a Jacobite advance into the Lowlands and then England. Unlike in 1689 there was no march against the Jacobites. In London, George I appointed John Campbell (1680–1743), the Duke of Argyle, as commander of his forces in Scotland, and, after authorizing £10,000 to pay the troops, Argyle rode northwards. Unlike Mar, Argyle was an experienced soldier.

Perth was deemed the gateway to the Highlands. It was ungarrisoned except for a number of armed townsmen. Seizing the initiative and arriving ahead of reinforcements, the Jacobites took the city on 14 September without any blood being spilt. It became the Jacobites' centre of operations for the remainder of the campaign and Mar made it his headquarters. He used his political and administrative skills in ordering the newly-arrived recruits into the semblance of an army and in this had the assistance of some experienced soldiers, though the expected support from abroad never arrived.

In Edinburgh, and quite independently of Mar, there had been an attempt to take the castle by a number of local Jacobites. They had bribed a sergeant and two soldiers of the garrison to assist them with throwing a ladder over the walls at night. Yet they talked too much in advance of their *coup de main* and the civil and military authorities were alerted. When the attempt was made, on 8 September, the conspirators were detected and the rope ladder thrown back. The three men in the castle were arrested, as were a few others. Had they succeeded, the Jacobites would have secured valuable stores of military equipment as well as a major propaganda coup.

Shortly afterwards, Argyle arrived in Edinburgh before travelling to Stirling. He was dismayed with what he saw and what he learnt. In his correspondence with his political masters in London he constantly stated that, in the face of overwhelming odds against him, he needed additional troops or he would be defeated or have to retreat out of Scotland. He was told that he would receive battalions from Ireland and, eventually, troops from the Dutch Republic. Argyle was unimpressed and complained that there were more soldiers in England than in Scotland and it was in the latter not the former that there was a Jacobite army in being.

This was because the government feared that there was a greater danger of a Jacobite insurrection in England. Troops were sent to garrison towns and cities which might harbour Jacobite sympathies. These included towns in the West Country, Oxford and London. Only when it was certain that there would be no rising in England could substantial forces be directed to the northern kingdom. This did nothing to assuage Argyle's fears and he threatened to resign at least once.

And eventually, the English Jacobites did rise in revolt. Following attempts to seize Thomas Forster (1683–1738), an MP for Northumberland, and James Radcliffe, the third Earl of Derwentwater (1689–1716) in Northumberland, these two brought their servants, friends and tenants together at Corbridge on 6 October, before moving to Rothbury and then to Warkworth, hoping for succour from France. Forster also wrote to Mar to request help from Scotland. Forster only had about 300 horsemen, but he was soon joined by Viscount Kenmure and about 100–200 horsemen from the Scottish Lowlands. The English Jacobites hoped that Newcastle, the foremost city in the north-east, would have welcomed them, but their opponents closed the gates and raised the militia and posse to resist them and the Jacobites shied away from confrontation.

Pleas for help from the government were answered and Lieutenant General George Carpenter (1657–1734) was sent with a command of three regiments of dragoons and a battalion of infantry to Newcastle. Learning of their approach, Forster withdrew to Kelso. There he had arranged to meet with the troops sent from Mar.

Mar decided to split his forces by sending Forster Brigadier William Mackintosh (c.1657–1743) of Borlum with about 2,000 men, taken from several infantry battalions. They crossed the Firth of Forth under the cover of darkness on the night of 10/11 October, losing several hundred men who were forced by Royal Navy vessels to withdraw. With Jacobites now to his north at Perth and to the east of Edinburgh, which was undefended by regular troops, Argyle was caught in a quandary. Taking some dragoons and mounted infantry he rode to Edinburgh in order to deter an attack there. Although he was too weak to attack Mackintosh, he did threaten him with the result that the latter retreated and marched to England. Meanwhile Mar marched his depleted forces towards Stirling. Argyle quickly returned and on doing so deterred Mar who, supplies running short, went back to his base.

The Jacobites met at Kelso and Kenmure was to lead them when in Scotland and Forster in England. They were unable to decide on their strategy; whether to advance into England and engage Carpenter's outnumbered forces or to menace Edinburgh or Stirling. Deciding on the line of least resistance, they marched along the Scottish borders, with Carpenter's men in pursuit. The latter eventually desisted, but the Jacobites had another difficult choice; take Dumfries, defended only by militia, or march into north-west England, where mass support from the English Jacobites was promised. Despite dissension and widespread desertion from the Scots, the decision to re-enter England was taken on 1 November.

Mar awaited the Jacobite clans from the West who had been involved in a bloodless confrontation with Argyle's brother, the Earl of Islay, at Inveraray. They were also concerned that the garrison at Fort William might attack their homes when they left to join Mar. This led to Mar's inactivity at Perth, except for the despatch of patrols to numerous towns in Scotland to gather tax revenues, arms and ammunition, all of which his forces were in need of. Men and horses were also been trained, drilled and learning to stand gunfire, though Mar's critics accused him of inaction.

The Jacobite cause also underwent a minor setback in terms of morale when a money-gathering expedition to Dunfermline on 23 October went wrong. The troops sent there were lax in posting sentries. This was unfortunate because Argyle had learnt of their being in the town. He sent Portmore's dragoons. They scouted the Jacobite positions and attacked at night, killing several and taking a number of prisoners whilst suffering no fatalities themselves.

Both sides were gathering additional strength as time passed. Argyle received men from Ireland, taking his forces up to eight battalions of infantry and five of dragoons, as well as the Glasgow militia and a troop of volunteer cavalrymen. He also cobbled together a number of small-calibre guns and crews. He eagerly anticipated the arrival of the Dutch troops who were on their way, following negotiations at the Hague. Mar, in the other hand, heard that the western clans were on the march and they numbered about the same as Argyle's entire command. He also anticipated the coming of James Stuart.

However, internationally speaking, support for the Jacobite cause was minimal. Overtures were made to Sweden, an enemy to George I in his role of Elector of Hanover, but these were rebuffed. The death of Louis XIV in 1715 did not spell an end to hopes from France, but British diplomacy stopped any active French assistance. The Spanish did offer discreet financial aid, but when it arrived, it was too late.

In early November, with the arrival of the western clans, Mar, with vastly stronger forces at his back, decided to march towards Stirling, though planned to outflank castle and town in order to avoid battle by having a subsidiary force pinning Argyle's little army down. En route he would meet up with the clans and then hopefully march to Edinburgh without any serious military encounter.

His plans had been learnt of by Argyle. He was determined to be proactive and march to the north-east to confront Mar near to Dunblane, in order to avoid being outflanked at Stirling. The Glasgow militia were left at Stirling under the command of Lieutenant Colonel Blackader, who had seen service as a lieutenant at Dunkeld a quarter of a century ago. Argyle reached Dunblane on 12 November and his enemies were but a few miles away. Little did he know but on that day fighting had begun at Preston. Argyle's men camped between Dunblane and the hamlet of Newtoun, whilst Mar's were just south of the river Allan, a few miles northward.

Meanwhile, the Anglo-Scots Jacobite army in England bypassed the border fortress of Carlisle and then routed the county forces of the Cumberland posse and militia at Penrith. Marching southwards through Appleby and Kendal they attracted a few followers, but no opposition. Lancashire, with its significant Catholic minority, especially among the gentry, seemed more promising, especially as both a regiment of dragoons and the county militia departed as the Jacobites advanced. Although in both Lancaster and then Preston (reached on 9 and 10 November) the Jacobites were welcomed and James proclaimed as rightful king, numbers joining were far less than the 20,000 once promised. The plan was to then march south to Manchester, scene of noisy Jacobite protests in the June of that year, then to the rich port of Liverpool.

Unfortunately, Jacobite intelligence was poor. Forster had been told by his allies in Lancashire that they would be able to let him know if any of the Government army arrived within 40 miles of Preston. Since he heard nothing he felt safe and confident. Unbeknown to him, Carpenter's forces, having returned to Newcastle after the fruitless pursuit, rested and then, leaving the battalion of infantry in the town, rode through Durham and Yorkshire with the three regiments of dragoons, collecting militia and volunteer cavalry from Yorkshire en route. More dangerous was the force led by Major General

Charles Wills (1666–1741) which had been gathering in the Midlands before marching to Manchester, then Wigan. This was composed of five regiments of dragoons, one of horse and a battalion of infantry. There were other forces, but Wills left one regiment of dragoons to garrison Manchester and another two units were left in his wake. At Wigan on 11 November, he was met by the Lancashire militia under Sir Henry Hoghton MP, and several hundred armed Dissenters. Battle loomed.

Chapter 6

The Battle of Preston, 12–14 November 1715

The first battle of the campaign was also to be the last ever fought on English soil, and as with Dunkeld a quarter of a century before, it was to be fought in a town. Preston was built on rising ground and its principal street, running west to east, was Fisher Gate Street. To the south-east the street led to the road to Wigan, to the west to Liverpool. Friar Gate Street was the main road leading northwards, towards Lancaster. The first mile of the road to Wigan was a hedge-lined lane which ended with the Ribble Bridge and a little more to the south-east Darwen Bridge. To the west of Fishergate was a marsh bordering on the river. Surrounding the town were enclosed fields, perhaps market gardens. To the south and west of the town was the River Ribble, flowing westwards from Yorkshire and reaching the Irish Sea just to the west of Preston.

General Wills was aware of the location of his enemy and had gathered his troops at Wigan on 11 November. Although Forster was informed of Carpenter's movements to his north, he may have been in the dark about those of Wills. As his chaplain, the Rev. Robert Patten, wrote 'All this while they had not the least Intimation of the Forces that were preparing to oppose them, much less of the Approach of the King's army'. This was because Forster relied on the promises made by the Lancashire Jacobites, who were in sole charge of providing him with local intelligence. They assured him that they would let him know when any enemy was within 40 miles of him. However, Forster was let down.[1]

Derwentwater learnt about their enemies' proximity very late on 11 November. According to one unnamed officer:

> When this letter was communicated to General Forster, he appeared dispirited, and then, as at all other times, very unfit for such an important command. He had nothing to say, but sent the letter to my Lord Kenmure. His lordship upon reading it, going with other persons of note to Mr Forster's quarters, found himself in bed without the least concern. A council being called, it was thought convenient to detach a party of Horse towards Wigan, as an advance guard, and another party of Foot to Darwin and Ribble Bridges, and

the whole army had orders to be in readiness to take the field. But to our great surprise, these orders were countermanded by Forster.[2]

The Jacobites took no positive action on the day prior to the battle, though since the foot soldiers had only arrived on the previous day, a day's rest was not unreasonable. The Jacobite leadership was not enthusiastic for an immediate battle; heightened perhaps, by the hope that they could have benefitted from support from Manchester and the resources of Liverpool before such a contest would be joined, perhaps hoping that it would be unnecessary, as in 1660.

It is difficult to ascertain numbers involved in the battle.

Regular Forces under General Wills

Cavalry
Brigade 1 – Brigadier Honywood
Honywood's dragoons.
Wynn's dragoons.
Brigade 2 – Brigadier Munden
Munden's dragoons.
Stanhope's dragoons.
Brigade 3 – Brigadier Dormer
Dormer's dragoons.
Pitt's horse.
Infantry
Preston's foot.
Artillery
None.
Auxiliary Forces
Lancashire Militia, under Hoghton (560 strong).
'A considerable party' of armed Dissenters under James Wood and Mr Walker (300 strong).[3]

Ironically, Preston's battalion was the very same unit that had successfully defended Dunkeld a quarter of a century previously, but probably very few men saw both battles. Only Pitt's and Preston's were veteran regiments; the other five had only been raised as recently as July 1715 and so contained many inexperienced and barely-trained officers and men, though some had served in the army previously.

John Clerk of Penicuik erroneously claimed Wills led 1,000 cavalrymen and a company of infantry.[4] One source claims that the combined forces of Wills and Carpenter (who had three cavalry regiments) numbered 2,500.[5] This would make each of the above units about 250 strong. Allowing for the cavalry units to be weaker – Carpenter's force of three dragoon regiments was probably only about 600 – so, allowing 220 men per cavalry regiment, Preston's foot may have numbered as many as 700 men. Numbers could have been lower. Argyle's regiments of cavalry numbered between 166–174 men each, excluding officers, and the infantry battalions were between 238 and 369 men strong, again excluding officers.[6] It is also worth noting that of Wills's dragoon regiments, all were newly raised; only Pitt's horse and Preston's foot were veteran units. Wills's force probably numbered between 1,400 and 1,800. As will be seen, the militia and volunteers did not take part in assaults on the town.

Wills's whole command did not take part in the action. He had an additional two veteran battalions of infantry, Fane's and Sabine's, but did not wait for them to arrive before attacking. Ensign Charles Colville (1691–1775) of the grenadier company of Preston's foot, wrote, 'indeed I have heard him blamed for not waiting for two old regiments on infantry which he knew well were within a few days march of him'.[7] However, it is uncertain where these were; on 3 November Fane's was at Litchfield and on 12 January Sabine's was at Hereford.[8] Yet a newspaper reported they were two days' march away.[9]

Jacobite Forces under Thomas Forster

Scottish Forces
Lowland Horse
Hamilton's troop – 4 men.
Hume's troop – 20 men.
Lockhart's troop – 14 men.
Carnwath's troop – 19 men.
Wintoun's troop – 15 men.
Scottish Infantry
Mackintosh's battalion – 295 men.
Lord Charles Murray's regiment – 137 men.
Mar's battalion – 36 men.
Strathmore's regiment – 158 men.
Nairn's regiment – 122 men.

Unregimented (or in single-figure commands) Scots infantry – 328 men.
It is important to note that the Scots included men from both the Highlands and the Lowlands.
English Forces
English Cavalry
Douglas' Troop – 15 men.
Shaftoe's Troop – 16 men.
Hunter's Troop – 14 men.
Organized into tiny commands – 150 men.
Unregimented (mainly Lancastrians) – 549 men.
N.B. Some of the above would have had horses, especially if part of a gentleman's command from Northumberland or Lancashire, but some would have been on foot.
Artillery
Six cannons of uncertain calibre (probably small) taken from Lancaster with untrained gunners; a sailor in the force, who, according to Patten 'did not know much how to use them' was in charge.
Totals: 1,026 Scots, 744 English, 12 Irish and one Dutchman. Furthermore, 17 men were thought to be killed in the battle. Grand total of 1,800.[10]
N.B. All numbers above are of those who were made prisoner and some were taken after the battle but had not participated in it. The actual force would have been numerically stronger.

Again, as with Wills's force, total numbers are impossible to ascertain. Patten did not even try. The lowest estimate was 1,400 and as noted above, this was utterly erroneous.[11] A press report alleged it was between 2,000–3,000.[12] The Rev. Peter Rae estimated them at above 4,000.[13] The highest number was quoted in the press and in correspondence between Viscount Townshend and James Craggs as between 4,000 and 5,000.[14] And a reference in the West Riding Sessions refers to 1,500 men escaping the battle, which if added to the above would make 3,300.[15]

The complete number is the sum of the prisoners taken on 14 November, those killed and those who escaped. Although the first number is approximately 1,783 (based on TNA, KB8/66 and various contemporary published sources), those killed amounted to about 17 and the number of those who escaped the final debacle is impossible to know. Various figures were put forward, as we shall see, but it is impossible to know how accurate these are.

Certainly, it would have not been too difficult for numbers of Lancastrians to have either escaped on the night of 12 November when not all escape routes were blocked, or to have melted back into the civil population with the connivance of friends and relatives. But as to the number who did, no answer can be given. Perhaps the true figure might have been about 2,500 – if the Jacobites had about 1,500 when entering England, and almost 500 Englishmen from the north-western counties joined, then 2,000 must surely be an absolute minimum number. But we cannot know how many fled before the surrender. Perhaps about 2,500 is a reasonable estimate. However, not all may have been combatants. Many were servants, possibly unarmed.

Even so, with the two armies roughly evenly matched in numbers, or perhaps a slight superiority in numbers for the Jacobites, the advantage lay with the latter, because they were defending positions. Conventionally, a 3:1 superiority over the defenders is needed for a successful assault. The odds seemed to be stacked in their favour, if they stood.

At last the two sides were about to fight one another. For the Jacobites, this was involuntarily. After avoiding combat for the past weeks, they now had no alternative but to do so. Retreat against a faster-moving army would result in the loss of most if not all of their force as infantry would be caught in the open. Wills, on the other hand, was enthusiastic for a trial of strength, as per his orders. With instructions to attack as soon as possible, he did not feel it necessary to await Carpenter's regiments. Furthermore, ambitious for a promotion to lieutenant general, he probably wished to take all the credit for what he may have assumed would be an easy victory over what he imagined, not without some justification, were poorly-armed and indifferently-led amateurs. Colville stated the reason as follows:

> I must do that justice to our General, who as I observed before has been blamed for not waiting for more troops, that being posted on the Grenadier Company and having thereby an opportunity of hearing the General's orders and remarks, that when we came to the Ribble Bridge and found the bridge and hollow way not defended, he said that people must surely be in a confusion else they would surely have defended their strong post, and therefore I will attack them and not give them time to think.[16]

The battle took place over three days. The first was Saturday, 12 November. It is possible that some Jacobites planned to march from Preston on 11 November towards Manchester, but did not do so. However, this was only postponed until the following day. As preparations were underway on this subsequent day, reports began to come through that Wills's forces were marching towards them. Forster did not believe these at first, but such was their number that he was forced to acknowledge their truth in the end. Already the Rev. Paul, carrying messages to allies in Staffordshire and Leicestershire, had travelled southward and had been stopped by Wills's troopers, but had been allowed to pass.[17]

Once Wills knew that the Jacobites were still at Preston, he gave the order to march at daybreak, perhaps at about seven in the morning. He arranged his men prior to the march in the following fashion. A captain and fifty of Preston's foot and the same number of an unspecified cavalry regiment formed the vanguard. Following them were the remainder of Preston's foot. Next were Honywood's brigade, then Dormer's and then Munden's at the rear. The baggage wagons followed on afterwards. After a few miles, Wills was approached by James Wood and Mr Walker, two dissenting ministers, and their armed congregations. They offered to help and Wills agreed to let them accompany his men and that he would allot them a place when they had arrived at Preston.[18]

By the time the Jacobites were certain of the danger they were in, a body of infantry had already marched as far as the Ribble Bridge. Forster, with some cavalry, rode south and saw the vanguard of the regular army. Patten was sent back with this news to the forces in the town while Forster's men reconnoitred a ford across the Ribble in case it could be used as a means of making a flank attack against the regulars. In the sixteenth century, the bridge was described as being 'a great stone bridge of Ribble, having a very great arches'.[19] Lieutenant Colonel John Farquharson of Invercall had command of the 100 'choice, stout and well-armed Men' of Mackintosh's battalion to hold the bridge. They were ordered back into the town.[20] However, according to Peter Clarke, these forces were 300 cavalrymen despatched by Derwentwater.[21] Apparently this nobleman, on seeing Wills's vanguard, believed that they were on the Jacobite side, shouting 'they are all for us'.[22]

The order to withdraw was criticised by Patten, who remarked 'This Retreat was another wrong step, and has been condemned on all hands as one of the greatest oversights they could have been guilty of'. He stated that there were no fords nearby and that the bridge could be barricaded and made impregnable to assault.[23] However, Mackintosh later remarked that the bridge was untenable because Wills's men could have crossed the river by the fords, those two at Penwrotham and one at Walton-Le-Dale, presumably.[24] If Wills did not know where the other crossing points were, he had enough Lancashire loyalists who would have been able to tell him.

Yet the alternate plan, to fight in the town itself, was also criticised, as being 'the maddest resolution that ever man could be capable of, to pretend to keep one open [i.e. unwalled] place without provisions or ammunition'.[25] Indeed, one Jacobite later claimed, 'At first it was resolved to fight them in the fair fields, which . . . probably would have ended gloriously, for us, for we were all hearty, and well inclined, to the work and the enemy were mostly raw green men and much fatigued . . . For was it not plain madness for more or equall a number to the enemy and of as good hearts, if not better, to coop themselves up.[26]

Inside the town, 'the Rebels were not idle . . . nor did they appear in the least discouraged, but applied themselves resolutely to their Business' and barricades had been erected at the main streets. There were two on Church Gate to the east of the town. The most easterly, just within the outer limits of the town, was manned by troops led by Lord Charles Murray. In support of him, near to St. John's Church, was a barricade under Brigadier Mackintosh's command. In reserve were the gentlemen volunteers under the direction of Derwentwater and Viscounts Kenmure, Wintoun and Nithsdale. They were near to the church as well. Others were stationed centrally in the market place. The third main barrier was to the north of the town, on Windmill Lane, and was under the direction of Colonel Mackintosh. The final barricade was posted on the westerly end of Fishergate and the men there were under the command of Major Miller and Mr Douglas. As well as these four main entry routes into Preston, the by lanes were also manned.[27] Troops also secured the houses near to the barricades, and stood ready in cellars and at windows to receive the enemy.[28] One Captain Innes, with fifty men, was posted in Hoghton's town house 'which was of great service'.[29] Meanwhile, only Carnwath's horsemen and some of the English were mounted, most fought on foot.[30]

Cannon were also placed at these barricades. There were two at the Churchgate barricade, 'charged with small bullets', presumably as a form of canister.[31] Perhaps the others were at Windmill Lane and at Fishergate. Four of these cannons were described as 'good' and the other two were of very small calibre. They had been mounted on carriages found at Hoghton's house.[32] Richard Shuttleworth encouraged his men by 'giving directions how to make the Trenches' and 'pull'd off his coat & work'd amongst the men himself', claiming the guns would be loaded with eighty bullets and would do great execution. Derwentwater offered money to his men to raise their spirits.[33]

Not all believed the defence was efficient. One officer wrote 'our army was scarcely modelled when the enemy was upon us'.[34] A Lowlander noted that they had managed to 'coop themselves up in a town, which had no wall, and where there was no provisions . . . But we were no better used in the defence of the town'.[35] Even more fatally, there was also no overall command or co-ordination of the Jacobite army; as was said in the following year at the trials, 'no orders at all was given but everybody did as he pleased'.[36]

Wills's men arrived at Ribble Bridge at one o'clock. Patten claimed that Wills 'did indeed expect some Difficulty and Opposition at this Place'. He was doubly certain that an ambush was in the offing once he was aware that the bridge had been abandoned. Therefore, 'he proceeded with Caution, and caused the Hedges and Fields to be view'd and the ways Laid open for his Cavalry to enter'. The infantry drew up in platoons ready for firing upon their enemies prior to crossing the bridge.[37] Finding none were awaiting his troops here, caution turned to optimism and he expected that the Jacobites must have left Preston and were in full retreat to Scotland.[38]

However, he was soon disabused of such notions and prepared for battle. Wills surveyed the town and noted the barricades flung up there, as well as the cannon which had been posted to reinforce these positions. He then made his own dispositions. There was to be a two-pronged attack to storm the barricades and thus take the town. To the south-east of the town, Honywood was to command Preston's regiment and fifty men (dismounted) from each of the five dragoon regiments, supported by the remainder of Honywood's dragoons (mounted), in case the Jacobites tried to break out. To the north of the town, Dormer was in charge. Under him were the dismounted dragoons of Dormer's and Wynn's regiments, and a dismounted squadron of Stanhope's dragoons. In order to support this attack were Pitt's horse and the remaining squadrons of Munden's and Stanhope's dragoons. The auxiliary forces were placed to the south of the town, to prevent any Jacobites escaping in that direction and to prevent any aid coming from Manchester.[39] There was to be no attack on the barrier on Fishergate Street, probably because Wills lacked the men to adequately attack three entrances to the town at once and also because of the marshy ground there would make it difficult for troops to form up. Some of the troops probably used grenades in the assault, but these were probably of little use; one which had failed to explode was uncovered in the nineteenth century.[40]

After the troops had got themselves into position, the assault commenced at about two in the afternoon.[41] Honywood's attack on Brigadier Mackintosh's barrier was met with a murderous fire, not only from behind the barricades but from the cellars and windows of nearby houses. According to Patten, one Hunter 'behav'd with great Vigour and obstinacy at Preston, where he took possession of some Houses during the Attack, and galled that brave Regiment . . . making a great Slaughter out of the windows'. Likewise, that of Douglas was 'very vigorous at the Action at Preston; where he and his men were possess'd of several Houses, and did a great deal of Harm to His Majesty's Forces from the Windows'.[42] So devastating was this musketry that within ten minutes, according to Peter Clarke, 120 of the attackers had been killed and the remainder obliged to retreat.[43] Another source gives 180 as the casualty figure, including several officers.[44] These figures should be taken as being impressionistic. The very real fog of war caused by the abundance of musket smoke in confined spaces made accuracy impossible, even without any exaggeration. Yet according to Colville, those Jacobites firing out of houses 'did not hurt us as they durst not look out of the windows to take their aim'.[45]

Many of those struck by musket balls were not killed. The rank and file among the attackers were wounded. Edward Cavin, a 21-year-old of Wynn's Dragoons, with four months service had been 'shot in the head and left thigh'. Adam Cadwell, from the same regiment and three years his senior was 'shot through ye body'. Another was Guy Cerlton, aged 28, 'his breast bone broke at Preston his right leg disabled by a sword'. Henry Pawley, 30 years old, of Stanhope's Dragoons, was 'wounded at Preston wholly disabled in his left thigh'. Preston's battalion took most casualties. Three suffered eye wounds, one was wounded in both legs, another lost part of his right shoulder to a cannon ball. There were also arm and hand wounds.[46]

There were many instances of individual bravery on both sides. Regular officers led from the front. Brigadier Honywood was wounded in the assault.[47] Among those who could not retreat was his fellow, Major John Preston, adjutant of Preston's foot, who had been wounded and would have been killed had not the Jacobite Captain Nicholas Wogan risked his own life to try and save him. Although Preston died soon after, he acknowledged his enemy's gallantry and subsequent kindness and hoped Wogan would be civilly used after the surrender.[48] Another instance of bravery on the Jacobite side was when a man carrying a gunpowder cask to supply his compatriots at the barrier was told he risked death in taking it there. He still agreed to do so, and was killed in the attempt.[49] It was said, 'During the whole Action Mr Radcliffe was in the midst of the Fire, and expos'd to so much Danger as the meanest soldier then upon Duty'.[50] The Hon. Basil Hamilton, a Jacobite captain, 'behaved himself with a great deal of Courage in the Action'.[51]

Forster allegedly appeared at this barrier – the only positive action that anyone accredits him with during the fighting – and exposed himself to hostile fire and ordered Macintosh to sally out against the retreating regulars. When Mackintosh refused to do so, Forster threatened him with a court martial for disobeying his commanding officer. Mackintosh explained his reasoning:

> That if his Foot had sallied out, they might by that means been parted from the Horse, and so left naked to have been cut off: Besides, nothing more frightens the Highlanders than Horse and Cannon. As for obeying Mr Forster, in letting the Horse sally out, he said, if the Horse had attempted any such Thing, they would have gone through the fire of his men; for they were afraid the Horse

design'd such a Thing, and would have been made able to have made a Retreat and left them pent up in the Town.[52]

Some of the officers of Preston's battalion learnt that there was an unbarricaded lane in which the adjacent houses were unmanned. They met some resistance there, but pushed it aside. Apparently the Jacobites there had been given orders to withdraw. Captain Innes with fifty Highlanders had garrisoned Hoghton's house, which was nearby, but were told to withdraw by Forster, though they could have probably have held out. This house was a key strategic point as it was noted that, 'it did command the head of the Hollow Way that leads from the bridge to the town, and the street in the Mercat Place, and a great part of the neighbouring fields'.[53] Innes, 'at first he refused to obey without a written order'.[54] Even so, in their bid to take possession of it, some of Preston's regiment were killed by musketry from Jacobites in nearby houses. The regulars also secured possession of a house opposite to Hoghton's. The troops in these two houses accounted for 'almost all the Loss the Rebels sustained during the action'. As Colville explained, 'from which we had a full view of the rebels and soon made them quit their post and retire into the church'.[55] Patten blamed Mackintosh for such inept orders to withdraw in his bid to clear Forster of any blame.[56]

Others of Preston's battalion then progressed through the streets and came up against Mackintosh's barrier. Lord Forrester, showing great bravery, scouted the position in order to note where the Jacobites were posted. He was fired upon, but remained unscathed and, returning to his men, led them against the barrier. A terrible fire from the barricade and adjacent houses caused 'a great many of that old and gallant Regiment' to be killed or wounded. John Hunter's men made 'a great Slaughter' by firing from house windows. Forrester himself was hit several times, though none proved mortal. When his men returned fire, they could do little damage to their opponents who were at least partially concealed by the available cover, and who could fire their well-aimed shots at the attackers with ease. A few defenders were struck and at least three Jacobite officers there later died of their wounds.[57]

There was some artillery fire directed against the attackers, too. It was not terribly effective. Some of it resulted in only bullets hitting the sides of houses 'so that no execution was done thereby'.[58] The seaman in charge of the two guns facing Preston's regiment 'acted so madly, whether it was that he had too little Judgement, or too much Ale, or perhaps both'. His first shot knocked a chimney down. The second was better, doing 'execution, and oblig'd the Regiment to halt'. And that is all that is known of the cannon fire.[59]

Murray's barrier was also attacked, but despite being hard pressed, he and his men made a gallant defence. Patten refers to Murray thus: 'his Courage and Behaviour at a Barrier, where His Majesty's Forces made a bold attack, was singularly brave'. According to one source, 'My Lord Charles Murray . . . showed undaunted Courage and killed severall with his own hand'.[60] Others were involved in hand to hand fighting, 'close work with sword and pistol . . . our gentry attacked the enemy bravely with their broadswords. The dispute lasted a long time'.[61] Murray called for Patten to summon assistance from the reserves under Derwentwater. Patten returned with fifty men. The clergyman was then asked to stand atop the barrier and to view the situation. He was wearing his clergyman's robes and was not suspected of being a Jacobite and so no one fired at him. He then reported back to Murray. There was then a renewed assault, presumably by the elements of the dismounted regiments of dragoons, for Patten writes that they were 'for the most part, raw, new-listed Men and seemed unwilling to fight, yet the Bravery and good Conduct of experienced Officers, supplied very much that Defect'.[62]

Forrester's men were also fired upon by a flank attack by Derwentwater's volunteers, 'and received the enemy with a very brisk and successful fire'. One officer suggested that artillery be placed in the churchyard to demolish Hoghton's house and for Derwentwater (described as 'brave and undaunted') and Murray to attack. Forster vetoed it, arguing 'the body of the town was the security of the army'.[63] Yet eventually, after suffering losses, the troops were reluctant to renew the assault, one source claiming 'they never durst approach for the dragoons were all raw men and those that came within shott never returned'.[64]

There had been another attack on the south side of the town at four. Here, 300 regulars entered a back street which abutted Churchgate Street. Again, accurate fire on the part of the defenders, who lined gardens, walls and hedges, resulted in, allegedly, 140 regulars being killed, though this must be an exaggeration.[65]

Although most of the action occurred in the eastern part of the town, there was also fighting elsewhere. Colonel Mackintosh's barrier on the north side of Preston was attacked by Dormer's troops. Mackintosh had nearly 300 men under his command. Again, his men 'made a dreadful Fire upon the King's Forces, killing many on the spot' and once again, the attackers had 'to make a Retreat'. Dormer received a shot in his leg. Once again, Patten alleges that such a retreat was due to the troops being but newly-raised men.[66]

As night drew on, one tactic employed by both sides was to burn property near to the Jacobite barriers. Dormer had Captain James Gardiner, Sergeant Johnstoun, Corporal John Marlow and a dozen troopers of Stanhope's, to burn houses up to the barricade they had recently attacked.[67] Apparently eyewitnesses observed that Gardiner, 'signalized himself very particularly: for he headed a little body of men . . . about twelve, and set fire to a barricado of the rebels, in the face of their whole army while they were pouring in their shot, by which eight of the twelve that attended him fell'.[68]

Some houses and barns were burnt near to the entrance of Churchgate Street, thus forcing the Jacobites nearby to retreat. According to Colville, some Jacobites were taken prisoner and passed back to the dragoons.[69] The smoke caused by the burning buildings enabled troops to move without being fired upon or to dislodge enemies from their positions. Wills's men were ordered to light up the houses in which they occupied. This enabled them to see their targets, but also let the Jacobites to see them. The ensuing exchanges of musketry thus killed and wounded several on both sides. Orders were then given to extinguish these lights, but these were interpreted as instructions to put more candles in the windows.[70] Trenches were also dug to help keep the regulars' two wings in communication in case of attack and these were supervised by one Lieutenant Robinson.[71] Meanwhile, both armies lay on their arms and there was sporadic fire.[72]

At the end of the day, some properties to the north of the town were also burnt. Had the wind not being blowing northwards, most of the town might have burnt.[73] A total of twenty-nine houses, two cottages, ten barns, four outbuildings, two stables and one mill were destroyed; of these, six were on Churchgate and nine on Friargate.[74] This was fortunately far less than had burnt at Dunkeld in 1689.

Despite being generally victorious by the day's end, many among the Jacobite command came in for censure. One source claimed 'our commanding officers, when there was Use for them, either could not be found, or when got, could not command'.[75] Lord Widdrington later confessed the reason for his inaction was because he was confined indoors due to an attack of gout. According to Patten, 'I could never discover any thing like Boldness or Bravery in him, especially after His Majesty's Forces came before Preston'.[76] Forster was similarly confined: 'The maids of Generall Forster's Lodgings will take their Oaths out that he was in Bedd with a sack possett in the hottest time of ye action.'[77] Others among the Jacobite leadership were less than active; Patten asserting that unspecified individuals 'kept themselves warm in a chimney corner during the heat of the Action'.[78] However, not all were useless. It was said 'No man of Distinction behaved better than my Lord Derwentwater' by exposing himself to hostile fire, encouraging the men by gifts of money and helping throw up entrenchments for the artillery.[79]

Meanwhile, Mackintosh began to write to Mar, letting him know of the army's success.[80] Not all shared his feelings, however, some Jacobites taking the opportunity provided by nightfall to escape. According to Rae 'a great many made their Escape through the secret Passages and By-Lanes into the

Country'. Some had escaped via Fishergate, where no troops had been posted. This was despite the diligence of other soldiers surrounding the town.[81] The militia, too, were said to be 'very serviceable in guarding the Passes and several parties attempting to force their way through them, were either killed, taken or beat back'.[82] It is impossible to know how many escaped. The West Riding Quarter Sessions thought 1,500 had done so, and searches for escaped Jacobites were also ordered by the Northumberland Quarter Sessions.[83]

Yet why was this so? The Jacobites had repelled most of their enemies' attacks, but at least some were aware that Carpenter's men were expected. It seems probable that this civilian army (at least as far as most of the Englishmen were concerned) had been shocked at their first experience of the bloody reality of a battle. They may have expected a peaceful restoration as in 1660, and certainly nothing in the campaign hitherto would have prepared them for such a rude awakening. After all, the army had met no physical resistance hitherto – the posse had fled at Penrith and the militia and Stanhope's dragoons had not contested their progress at Lancaster.

There were many wounded after the battle. It might have been thought that, in the light of there being thirty surgeons, doctors and physicians among the Jacobite army, that the wounded men would have been well treated.[84] The White Bull Inn on the Market Square seems to have been appointed for use as a makeshift field hospital, but treatment was variable. The Jacobite Captain Peter Farquharson, being shot through a leg bone, 'endured a great deal of Torture in the Operation of the Surgeon . . . His Leg was cut off by an unskilled Butcher, rather than a Surgeon, and he presently died'. However, several of the regulars who had been wounded and then taken prisoner seemed to be in good spirits, assuring Patten that 'not one Man belonging to the King's Forces but would not die in their Country's Cause'.[85] Others, though, claimed 'all the prisoners lookt upon the affair as lost'.[86] At least fifty officers and men were taken prisoner following the fighting at Murray's barrier and 'owed the day was lost to them'.[87]

Wills's conduct on the first day's fighting later came in for heavy censure by Carpenter, who claimed that Wills 'made a rash attack, highly blameable, by loosing so many men to no purpose, before I came up'.[88] Certainly, at the end of the first day's fighting, most of the casualties were from the Government army. Patten remarked 'Hitherto the Rebels seem'd to have had some Advantage, having repulsed the King's forces in all their Attacks, and maintained all their Posts'.[89]

Some Jacobites thought that an opportunity for a vigorous counter-attack had been lost. Captain Murray advocated such, as did Derwentwater in one account. As a Lowlander noted, this 'could not have failed of success, for we were uppish and had lost six men, whereas many of the enemy were killed and wounded and were much fatigued, dispirited being mostly raw and new levied troops. But our generals [one account pins this on Forster] positively refused.'[90] This could have been because the troops were tired and low on ammunition. There would have been little daylight left and that to leave the security if the town may have been seen as taking an undue risk when they had hitherto done so well. The Jacobite leaders were known for their caution so these reasons would have seen very valid to them.

Another source elaborates on this theme, claiming that at 11 o' clock, with Murray's men being short of ammunition, a deputation arrived at Forster's quarters, but they found him 'lying in his naked bed, with a sack possett, and some confections by him: which I humbly judge was not a very becoming posture at this time for a general . . . everyone is convinced that he failed in almost every point of his prudentials, if not worse'.[91]

Why should Wills have instigated frontal attacks on defensive positions? He wrote on the following evening 'I made such attacks as were necessary to convince the rebels of my being in a condition to reduce them by force'.[92] This sounds like post facto justification, and the following alternative hypotheses are also worth pondering. As a professional soldier he may well have felt his enemies were amateurs who would not stand against a determined assault (certainly, a lack of offensive spirit on the part of the Jacobites in the campaign to date had been evident). He may also have been ambitious and determined to score off his rival, Carpenter, by gaining a victory without his help. Or he may simply have been zealously carrying out his orders to engage and defeat the enemy as soon as possible. Finally we might ask whether there was an alternative. Since, lacking artillery and sufficient supplies (which would have taken time to procure), a lengthy siege was out of the question, the only way to attack the enemy was the assault which was so apparently unsuccessful and undoubtedly costly, and thus was criticised, but his critics had no other suggestions to offer. And, costly though it was, it did have the effect of reducing the morale of some of the defenders, including, crucially, Forster and his coterie. The *coup de grâce* was, though, to come on the following day.

Those who argue that Wills should have waited for reinforcements should bear the following in mind, however. Firstly, Wills did not know how long he would have had to wait for them and then wait for them to become battleworthy. Secondly, the time spent waiting would enable the Jacobites to have strengthened their defences. Thirdly, morale of his waiting troops might have fallen and that of the Jacobites might have risen, believing their enemies were afraid to attack them.

On Sunday, 13 November, General Carpenter arrived to the north of Preston with his three regiments of dragoons (Cobham's, Churchill's and Molesworth's; only the first was a veteran regiment) and a number of volunteer and militia cavalry at either nine or ten in the morning.[93] Carpenter's men were probably of limited immediate use, because they had marched from Newcastle in but six days, without any of the usual stopping days, and had been in the saddle since early October before that.[94] In the following year, one of his regimental officers, Colonel Molesworth, was reimbursed £600 by the Treasury in account of 'the losses sustained by his regiment by horses killed and disabled and other extraordinary expenses in the long and continued marches in a very rigorous season in pursuit of the rebels'.[95] On arrival, Wills and Carpenter conferred. Wills, as junior officer to Carpenter, offered to relinquish overall command to his colleague. Carpenter remarked, perhaps sarcastically, 'he had begun the Affair so well, that he ought to have the Glory of finishing it'. He approved of some of Wills's troop dispositions, but, having inspected them, was disconcerted to find that no one was guarding the road from Preston which led to Liverpool. He could see Jacobites leaving by that route. Therefore, he ordered Pitt's horse to be stationed there in order to stop them. One of the cavalry's first acts was to cut down a number of fleeing Jacobites. Cornet Shuttleworth was slain. He had a green taffeta banner with a buff silk fringe and the sign of a pelican feeding her young. The banner read 'Tantum Valet amor Regis and Patria' ('So prevalent is the love of our King and Country'). Carpenter also established a system of communications between the disparate parts of the army so that if an attempt to break out was made, those attacked could be reinforced.[96] Cobham's and Churchill's dragoons were posted on the north side of the town and Molesworth's to the south. Wills had established his command post near to the road to Lancaster.[97]

There was some fighting in the morning as a party of dragoons was beaten back and, 'Some few men on both sides were killed this forenoone'. However, this was the last attack. A cease fire was soon agreed on thereafter, at Wills's instigation in order that they might bury their dead.[98] The arrival of Carpenter's forces may have been decisive. Widdrington later stated that when they had been seen, he 'said very loud before their men that they were all undone, and upon that they consulted to ask termes'.[99] Likewise, according to Patten, 'And now our People began to open their Eyes, and to see that there was nothing but present Death before them if they held out longer and that there was no Remedy, but, if possible, to make Terms'.[100]

Matters were looking black for the Jacobites. Ammunition, which had ever been a problem, was running very low, especially after so much had been expended in the successful defence of the previous day. Provisions, too, were becoming scarce. The Jacobites were divided as to their best course of action. The Highlanders 'were for sallying out against the King's Forces, and dying, as they called it, like Men of Honour, with their Swords in their Hands'. Charles Radcliffe alleged 'he had rather die with his sword in his hand, like a man of honour, than be dragged like a felon to the scaffold'.[101] This was because, with supplies running low, and with the danger that the enemy might be reinforced, especially with artillery, to be cooped up in a town was to be in a very grave situation indeed. It was also suggested that houses near the church be burnt and another idea was to drive the regulars from Hoghton's house.[102] Not all agreed. Forster was persuaded by Henry Oxburgh and Widdrington to parley, convincing their leader that terms would be granted. Presumably they hoped that they would be treated as prisoners of war, rather than traitors. Their plan was not made known to most of the army until the afternoon.[103]

The mental and psychological states of Forster and his coterie are crucial at this point. At best, he had played little part in the proceedings of the previous day. Having no experience of soldering, his first experience of wholesale death and destruction probably shattered his nerve. He did not like the current situation and wanted to escape it by any means he could. There may have been an element of cowardice here, or at least human weakness. Apparently, the sight of Carpenter's force was decisive: 'the chief prisoners assur'd me [Carpenter] and others that as soon as they saw my detachment from the steeple the Lord Widdrington who was in the churchyard said very loud before their men that they were all undone, and upon that they consulted to ask termes'.[104] Colville agreed with this assessment, writing, that Carpenter's arrival, 'which might have added to their panic and confusion, which we afterwards learnt from themselves had seized them from the beginning'.[105]

Widdrington and Derwentwater, 'solicitous to prevent any further Destruction' were 'instrumental to induce all in arms to submit'. They were confident in obtaining mercy.[106] Henry Oxburgh, accompanied only by a trumpeter, was according despatched at either one or two o'clock to treat with Wills. He was chosen because of his having served in the army fifteen years ago, and claimed that he had acquaintances there who would be sympathetic.[107] The Jacobite rank and file had been told that honourable terms were to be sought and so they remained quiet. Had they known Oxburgh's true mission, they would have shot him as he left Preston.[108] Wills told him that no terms would be forthcoming as he did not have the power to negotiate with them (they were classed as rebels and so could not expect anything more; in any case, when Argyle requested such plenipotentiary powers he was denied them) and that they must surrender at discretion, which only guaranteed that they would not be put to the sword straight away. Oxburgh argued, but Wills was adamant. If the Jacobites did not surrender in an hour, they would be attacked again. Captain Dalzell was sent to Wills in order to seek terms for the Scots, but received the same answer as Oxburgh.[109]

At his trial, Wintoun claimed that promises had been made by Wills. He said that he had been 'encouraged by His Majesty's officers to depend on His Majesty's mercy'. Yet the counterclaim was made that 'this deponent gave them no hope of mercy'.[110] A contemporary account stated that Wills 'desir'd them to surrender to the King's mercy and he would represent their case in the most favourable Manner'.[111] Lieutenant Colonel Stanhope Cotton, Wills's ADC, told a Jacobite who asked about this subject while in Preston 'Sir, that I cannot assure you of, but I know the King to be a very merciful Prince'.[112] Possibly such promises gave Wintoun and others hopes for mercy. Yet the Jacobites, in the eyes of the law, were deemed rebels and traitors and could expect trial and punishment. Carpenter later said that such hope 'was very unanswerable by the Rules and Discipline of War'.[113]

Derwentwater and Mackintosh also went individually to parley with Wills. According to one source, Wills was threatening and abusive towards them. Derwentwater allegedly said that if there was no help within 12 days they would surrender.

> Upon this Wills swore a great oath and pulls his watch out of his pocket and swore that if they did not surrender within twelve hours' time he would cut every man of them in pieces and swore he would not given them a moment's time longer. This he confirmed by the most bitter oaths, curses and execrations in the world, that lord Derwentwater was perfectly terrified that his very lips trembled.

Wills allowed the peer to return to Preston 'for he had a mind he should spread the terror among the rest'. Although Mackintosh could match the soldier in oaths, each claiming to beat the others' forces with a fraction of their own men, even he seems to have been impressed by Wills's 'terrible air'.[114] Wills wrote that evening, 'nor shall I give him any other terms than relying on the King's mercy, to which I imagine they will submit, being sufficiently convinced I have them in my power'.[115]

At three or five o'clock, Wills sent Cotton to Preston to receive the Jacobites' answer. Cotton was told that the English and Scots Jacobites were, as ever, in dispute, and that they asked Wills to wait until seven on the following morning. Wills accepted these terms on three conditions; that the Jacobites did not throw up new defences, that they did not allow any of the men to escape and that they offered up hostages.[116] The latter was insisted upon by Carpenter.

These terms were eventually agreed to, though at first neither Derwentwater nor Widdrington could be found and Mackintosh was in bed. Carpenter told Dalzell that he wanted two hostages; Kenmure and Derwentwater. Dalzell told him Kenmure would not agree to this, and when Carpenter suggested Mackintosh as an alternative, was refused again. Carpenter recalled, 'I was unwilling to make great Difficulties, it growing towards night'. They agreed on Colonel Mackintosh. The hostages went out at eight.[117]

This was shocking news to some of the men as a Lowlander noted, 'the first knowledge we had of it was when wee saw Colonel Cotton'.[118] Meanwhile, Cotton sent a drummer to all the houses held by the regulars in Preston to let them know that a cease fire had been arranged and that no more firing was to occur until ordered otherwise. Unfortunately, whilst Cotton was on this mission, the drummer was shot dead, probably by a Jacobite who was hostile to the idea of surrender; it was only at this time that the army knew what its leaders had been planning for it.[119]

Inside Preston, the disputes between the Jacobites turned violent: 'it was astonishing to see the Confusion the Town was in, threatening, yea, killing one another.' One man was shot and several wounded. Forster was blamed by some and one Mr Murray fired his pistol at him, only to miss as Patten deflected his aim. Some Scots still wished to fight their way out, to escape or die in the attempt.[120] This seemed a positive step, as one man later wrote, 'if this had been done, we had made a very good Account of them, most of their dragoons being but new levied men'. The bitterness towards officers among the rankers was caught by the same man who later wrote, 'there were never a handful of men of all occasions, more ready to fight, and never commanding officers as it appear'd, less forward'.[121] Apparently 'some were for bringing out Forrester like a publick sacrifice'.[122] Others reproached Forster, 'to his face and all he could answer was, that he was sensible of the Incapacity he had for his office, cryed like a child, was sorry for what he had done'.[123]

There was yet another difference of opinion among the Jacobite leadership. The anonymous Lowlander reported, 'yet Witherington pretended by arguments to defend the reasonableness of the capitulation, in fact Mr Bazill Hamiltown with tears declared already we were betrayed'. Lord Murray, Major Nairn, Philip Lockhart, Captain Straiton, Derwentwater and Winton 'shewed a great resentment agt the cessation, saying it was downright treacherous', but Earls Nithsdale and Carnwath and Captain Dalziell supported Forster and Widdrington. They alleged the capitulation 'would be fair and honourable' and that terms would be given to the surrendered.[124]

It seems that some of the English and Scots horsemen, including Derwentwater and his brother Charles, were intending to fight their way out by leaving Preston to the north. They mounted their horses with their men and assembled at the marketplace. Winton, Lockhart, Nairn and Shafto agreed, suggesting that Macintosh's infantry flank the hedges on the Lancaster road and the Scots gentry force their way through the enemy. One account stated Mackintosh agreed to march his men to join them at the barrier. However, Mackintosh never arrived and without his men, the force felt they were incapable of a successful escape. Another version claimed Mackintosh said 'it was too late to make such an attempt as after hostages were given upon our side'. Carnwath agreed with Mackintosh, claiming the surrender was honourable and necessary. Morale was so low that that night, despite suggestions to the contrary, all the Jacobite sentries were withdrawn from their posts, except those under Captain Lockhart's command. The regulars saw this as their opportunity to take these and make the Jacobite position even more hopeless.[125] One anonymous Jacobite stated, 'This was very choking to us all, but no helping of it, for no sooner had we left our posts than they made themselves masters of them, and of our cannon'.[126] Some were resigned to their fates, 'to it by promises of a fair and honourable capitulation'. They were 'so much surprised by grief they would take notice of nothing'.[127] A bitter Jacobite noted, 'I believe this is the first instance of a victorious army after action, yielding themselves prisoners to the vanquished' and Englishman Gabriel Hesketh said 'he was made a prisoner without cause'.[128] Patten, who was always his master's advocate, explained why a breakout was not countenanced: 'It is true this might have been attempted, and perhaps many would have escap'd; but it could not have been perform'd without the Loss of a great deal of Blood, and that on both Sides; and it was told them that it would be so, and that if they did get out, they would be cut off by the Country People'.[129]

On 13 November the Jacobites had three options. Firstly, they could stand their ground and hope to defeat further attacks by their enemy, as on the previous day. Yet with ammunition virtually exhausted this was only to invite defeat. This option was never considered. Secondly, they could have tried to fight their way out. It is impossible to say what the outcome would have been. Some would have escaped, some would have fallen or have been captured. It was a risk and as seen the Jacobite leaders were risk averse. So option three, surrender, seemed best. It was certainly safest in the short term; they would not be killed on the spot. There was no best option, but a choice between three poor ones.

It is hard to assess the results of the second option because it was never attempted. Much would depend on the morale of men on both sides. Despite their exhaustion, a sizable proportion of the Jacobite rank and file felt confident, some of those who did not had fled after the first day's fighting; it is difficult to be certain about that of their opponents who had been bloodily repulsed, but who had received reinforcements. Yet the Jacobites were predominantly an army of infantrymen; their cavalry was inferior to that of their enemies. Infantry lacking adequate firepower and discipline are vulnerable to cavalry in the open. A successful escape would require, to have any chance of success, a determined and united leadership. This it lacked and therefore it did not happen.

When the allotted hour of seven arrived on Monday, 14 November, Forster told Wills that the Jacobites were ready to surrender. Even at this late hour, Mackintosh was of a different view. He told Wills that, as a soldier, he knew that to surrender at discretion was the worst fate of all, and would not do it. He was told that the alternative was for the town to be stormed and for all the defenders to be put to the sword. Kenmure informed him that he and the other Lowland nobles agreed with Forster. Presumably Mackintosh then realized, with almost half of the Jacobites surrendering, his Highlanders were too few to continue to effectually resist and that he had to face the unpalatable prospect of surrender. Hostilities were at an end.[130]

Forster was much criticised for the surrender. He was commander-in-chief and so the responsibility was his. Two published accounts by Jacobites lay the blame on his shoulders, as do two manuscript accounts (all by Scots). Some even wondered where his true loyalties lay. Chester diarist Henry Prescott wrote 'tis from probable reasons suspected that Gen. Forster betray'd his own party'.[131] However, Thomas Hearne (1678–1735), an Oxford Jacobite, was told by one of the Scots officers at Preston, that 'there was no Treachery in General Foster, or any of the rest, but Cowardice, Foster being a timorous Man, and unwilling to fight, or the shew the least part of a General, and so surrendered his Men, whereas had he been all at courageous, the Business had been certainly done for the King.'[132] James Stuart, whom he met in the following year, did not blame him, and indeed appointed him Steward of the exiled Jacobite court household at Urbino, later Palazzo Mutti.[133] Forster appears to have been weak and incompetent but not a traitor. Patten laid the blame for the defeat on Mackintosh, 'The Brigadier has got the character of Brave and Bold . . . but we all must say, we saw little of it at Preston' and blamed 'a Party' for attacking Forster.[134]

In January 1717 there was further discussion about the Jacobite leadership at Preston. The Jacobite Dr Patrick Abercomby informed Mar:

> The avarice, roguery, insufficiency and cowardice of the command-
> ers and others of our people at Preston are perpetually talked of,
> and asserted with great oaths by not a few here and at St. Germaine.
> The persons they chiefly exclaim against are the Brigadier, his two

brothers and bastard son, Capt. Dalziel etc. The particulars related of them are so infamous that one cannot prevail with oneself to believe them.[135]

There was also dissension among their enemies. Just before they mounted to enter Preston, Carpenter and Wills fell out. Wills took 'on him great command' and so Carpenter, his senior officer 'us'd him very freely'. Apparently, he was even considering placing Wills under arrest, but Lords Carlisle and Lumley prevailed upon him not to do so. If this had occurred, 'itt might have proved fatall to His Majesty's Service', for the Jacobites were still armed and Carpenter even thought that Wills might have ordered the troops under his command to have assisted him against Carpenter. 'So I did not do itt' wrote Carpenter.[136]

Cotton and a number of regular troops then disarmed the Jacobites. Carpenter and Wills then rode in in state, with the majority of their forces behind them. Honywood, with other troops, entered from the opposite end of Preston and they met at the market place, where the defeated Jacobites were drawn up. The gentlemen prisoners were placed in the town's inns; The Mitre, The White Bull and The Windmill, whilst the rank and file were herded into the town's largest public building, the parish church, though 300 of them were housed in the property of Robert Boyes for two weeks, where they caused £30 worth of damage. Apparently, 'several of the country people were in the disorder and confusion hurried into the church, with the rebells'. In the church, 'they took what care of themselves as they could, ripping all the linings from the seats or pews, and making thereof Breeches and Hose to defend themselves from the extremity of the weather'.[137] According to Lieutenant Colonel Forrester, the prisoners were 'under closer confinement than the general intended'.[138]

However, even at this late stage, a few escaped. One Littleton, a priest, evaded capture by disguising himself as an apothecary.[139] Francis Legh was concealed by one Mrs Whitehead.[140] One Mr Dickenson also escaped.[141] Simon Fraser had been wounded in the leg and was in bed so evaded capture.[142] Some men had tried to join the Jacobites but luckily for themselves did not arrive in time; a Mr Gamul was one, apparently, so he returned to Chorley instead.[143] Not all were so fortunate in their escape attempts, for Thomas Sydall, a Manchester blacksmith, was taken by dragoons, 'who were, with great Difficulty, dissuaded from hanging him by the way' and was returned to Preston with his neck in a halter.[144]

Lord Carlisle talked with the English Jacobite peers, 'they being at this time under great dejection of mind'. He suggested that if they gave information about other Jacobites, mercy might be shown. He also recommended to Wills that all the tax money taken by the Jacobites along the route of the Jacobite march be returned. He also 'desired him to take particular care, that no innocent person be carryd away when the prisoners are removed, for some townsmen had ended up in the church along with the majority of the Jacobite prisoners, that being the one place where they are at present secured'.[145]

Because there were insufficient quarters in Preston for all the troops, Carpenter's men rode to Wigan to refresh themselves. After all, they had 'chac't the rebels a month', with unusuall difficultys and fatigue' and were in need of good quarters. However, as Carpenter wrote, this made it impossible for him to have arrested Wills, 'tho he deserved it'.[146]

Casualty figures were disputed, especially among the regular army. Official figures, as published in the contemporary press and laid down by Rae, recorded that four officers and fifty-three men of other ranks had been killed and a further ninety-two of all ranks were wounded.[147] Most were from Preston's infantry battalion, with forty dead and fifty-two wounded. Pitt's, Honywood's and Munden's suffered least, with none dead and only a total of six wounded. Wynn's suffered thirty casualties and the other two regiments eighteen in total. It is also worth observing that seventy-two horses were killed in the combat, roughly equally shared between the five dragoon regiments, and Pitt's horse suffered none.[148]

The Jacobites estimated that losses were far higher. Patten claimed that five officers and over 200 private men ('how many, it is hard to determine') were killed.[149] Clarke gives a higher figure; 270.[150] An even higher figure was given by one officer; 335 killed and wounded.[151] It was certainly high, with Forrester writing on 16 November, 'We have had our share of it, all the officers that were along with me were either kill'd or wounded save two, with very near 100 of our best men, soe you may believe the loss of soe many brave gentlemen, takes off a good dale of the joy I should have had, in gaining so considerable ane affair . . . I escap'd very well myself having only received two slight wounds, one in the face and the other in the hand'.[152] A newspaper reported that 150 of Preston's had been killed and wounded.[153] Carpenter later wrote that Wills had 'made a rash attack, highly blameable, by loosing so many men to no purpose'.[154] That casualties should have been high is explained thus by Patten, that the attackers were made 'under the greatest Disadvantage imaginable . . . being all the time naked, and expos'd to the Fire of the Rebels from Windows, Barriers and Entrenchments'.[155]

How can such differences be squared? We should remember that the official figures would probably have been compiled under Wills's auspices and it is commonplace for victorious generals to underestimate their casualties – and for the opposing side to exaggerate those of their opponents. Carpenter, who was a professional rival of Wills, can also be assumed to be prejudiced, for some townsmen had ended up in the church along with the majority of the

Jacobite prisoners, against Wills. On the other hand, Patten, who dedicated his *History* to Wills and Carpenter, had no obvious reason to exaggerate casualty figures; and Forrester's bias is unknown. The official figures are probably too low, but do indicate that Preston's regiment was in the thick of the fighting, whereas Pitt's horse were kept in reserve and merely had one man wounded and no deaths among horses and men.

As to the Jacobites, the figure was remarkably low. Patten's estimate is of seventeen killed and twenty-five wounded and Rae agreed with this.[156] Clarke's figure of eighteen or nineteen dead is similar.[157] The Merse officer gives thirty-five killed and wounded.[158] The discrepancy in casualty figures should not be surprising. Troops under cover always have less killed and wounded than those in the open attacking them, especially when both sides have roughly equal numbers to begin with. Those killed included one Mr Clifton, dying a few hours after being shot in the knee, Thomas Brereton, dying from a 'Vast Flux of Blood' due to a number of wounds and Peter Farquharson, shot through the leg and dying at an unskilled surgeon's hands. Rank and file killed are not mentioned by name.[159]

News of the victory soon reached London; on 15 November in fact. Wills had sent Colonel Maurice Nassau of Grant's foot (presumably a staff officer) to relay the news to the court; he received £500 for having done so.[160] The reaction was wholehearted. Henry Liddell wrote on 17 November, 'You see a joy through out the City which can't be well parallel'd and the court shew no less satisfaction. This noble action has nipp'd the designs off our enemys in the budd so they can't expect a plentiful cropp.'[161] Lady Cowper, wife of the Lord Chancellor, wrote, 'The Surrender of these Prisoners filled the Town with Joy'.[162]

William Pulteney (1684–1764), Secretary of State at War, wrote on 16 November to Carpenter:

> I write this letter with a very good deal of pleasure because it gives me an occasion to express to you the Joy which I have upon you and Mr Wills success against the King's enemys. I never did question but His Majesty's Forces would be victorious under such commands, and there is not a person in the world takes a greater share in your success than myself.[163]

It also meant that the Dutch battalions which had been to march to Lancashire, could be diverted towards Hull and thence to Scotland. Other troops could also be sent to Scotland. Confidence in the regime rose with victory over the Jacobites at Preston and Sheriffmuir, too. On 2 November, with undefeated Jacobite forces in both countries, South Sea stock stood at 90 5/8 – 89 and

Bank Stock at 118 ¾ – 119. By 19 November, with the government looking far more secure, these figures stood at 94 ½ – ¾ and 124 ¼ – ½.[164]

The extent of the victory was not exaggerated, by Argyle, never optimistic, who wrote to Viscount Townshend on 19 November:

> I received last night a letter from Mr Carpenter with the good news of the Rebells at Preston being all Prisoners but he makes a Reflection at the end of his letter wch is a very wrong one, he imagines those at Perth may upon this news desire to capitulate. I hope His Majesty's ministers have not been of this opinion, because it would literally very greatly endanger the whole.[165]

More moderately, the Lord Justice Clerk wrote, 'this will putt ane end I hope to the rebellion in England, and must have good consequences as to us'.[166]

Battles are rarely decisive; Marlborough's great victories in 1702–8 are undoubted but they did not result in the capitulation of France; there were another twelve years of warfare between Sweden and her enemies after her major defeat at Poltava in 1709. Though the battle of Preston did not end the campaign nationally, its significance is that it ended any hope that the Jacobites might make any military headway in the Hanoverian heartland of England. It also strengthened the government's position in Scotland by allowing all the Dutch troops brought over to be sent there, as well as Newton's and Stanhope's dragoons to be sent northwards, too. This was a severe blow to the Jacobite cause and a great bolster to that of the government. In fact, the battle of Preston was the most decisive battle in the entire Jacobite campaigns, more so than the bloodier Killiecrankie or Culloden; an entire army had been lost; not killed, but captured. The Jacobite defeat here had been absolute. This was never to happen again.

Chapter 7

The Battle of Sheriffmuir, 13 November 1715

Whilst hostilities were cooling off at Preston, on 13 November 1715 they were just about to begin on the moorland to the east of Dunblane. Argyle's forces were outnumbered by their opponents, but numbers are stated variously. The best method is to examine the figures given in the Scottish State Papers of 1715 compiled by the army for the government's benefit. These figures below are those for 29 October (for the first five battalions, then stationed at Stirling) and for 24–31 December 1715 (for those who did not arrive until after that time) and so are those nearest the date of the battle. Casualties taken at Sheriffmuir, based on newspaper reports, which may be incorrect, have been added to the last three battalions. These figures below, then, must be taken as approximate.

Infantry

Unit	Sergeants	Drummers	Rank and file	Total
Forfar	18	18	295	331
Montague	18	12	222	252
Wightman	20	10	253	283
Orrery	22	18	329	369
Shannon	20	10	332	362
Morrison	28	14	323	365
Clayton	20	20	239	279
Egerton	20	20	266	306
Totals	166	122	2,259	2,547

Add 5.5 per cent for officers as per Culloden below, which gives an additional 143, so total of 2,799 infantry (officers and men).

Dragoons

Unit	Sergeants	Drummers	Corporals and privates
Portmore	6	6	171
Carpenter	6	6	165
Evans	6	6	170
Stair	6	6	151
Kerr	6	6	153
Total	30	30	810

Add 8 per cent for officers as Culloden below which gives an additional 62, so total of 872 cavalry.

Based on figures of 29 October 1715, except for Evans's and these are for 24–31 December 1715, plus the 22 men of Evans's killed and captured at Sheriffmuir.[1]

Artillery

6 x 3-pounders

18 gunners

Rothes' mounted volunteers: 60 or about 150.[2] The Laird of Gorthie wrote 'For want of troops the Duke of Argyle was obliged to make up his line with them, doing just the same service that the dragoons did'.[3]

Total strength: 3,749 plus 60–150 volunteer cavalry.

The army was divided into three brigades; that on the left was led by Major General Thomas Whetham and Brigadier Grant, that in the centre by Major General Joseph Wightman (d.1722) and Brigadier Clayton and that on the right by Brigadiers Evans and Forfar.

We now turn to the army led by Mar. There is a 'List of the King's Army', compiled at Perth on 5 November, so just a few days before Mar's march south-wards. It would appear to be the most reliable account of the Jacobite army at that time.

The final battlefield disposition, based on the only known contemporary map, and from left to right, was as follows:

Infantry

Marquis of Tullibardine's battalion: number unknown.

Struan of Robertson's battalion: 223 men.

Earl of Panmure's battalion: 475 men.

Drummond's battalions: 623 commanded by the Viscount Strathallan, 257 and Logie Almond: 366.

Marquis of Seaforth's Foot (three battalions): 1,100, made up of the following Applecross: 350, Fairburn: 400, Ballmackie and McKeddin: 350.

Lord Huntley's Foot (four battalions) 1,162, made up of the following, Gordon of Glenbucket's: 330, Leith's 303, Innes' 322, Cluny McPherson's, 207.

Frazerdale and Chisholm: 500.

Stewarts of Appin: 263.

Camerons: 611.

Breadalbane's three battalions: no numbers given.

MacLeans: 327.

Clanranald: 528.

MacDonalds, 566 in all: Glengarry: 461, Glencoe: 105.

Sir Donald MacDonald: 650.

Position unknown

MacKenzies, 700?.

Campbell of Glenlyon: no numbers given.

Lord Ogilvie's: 352.

Envery's: 240.

Total infantry: 8,270 plus others; perhaps a total of about 9,000 infantry.

Cavalry

Marquis of Huntley's first squadron: 132.

Rollo's Perthshire squadron: 70.

Sinclair's Fife squadron: 80.

Linlithgow's Stirling squadrons: 108.

Earl Marischal's squadrons: 120.

Marquis of Huntley's second squadron: 132.

Position unknown

Earl of Southesk's squadron: 74.

Marquis of Seaforth's: 50.

Total strength of cavalry: 766.[4]

Artillery

Eleven guns, six brass and five iron. Calibre unknown, probably small; no powder or ball.[5]

No known gunners.

It is therefore impossible to ascertain a figure, but it would seem that Mar had just under 10,000 men under his command, with perhaps just over 9,000 infantry and 766 cavalry. This was the largest army that the Jacobites were ever able to put together in the field; for the first and last time they had a decisive advantage in numbers when faced with an enemy in the open. Argyle was facing over twice his own numbers. In terms of infantry, he was facing treble his numbers, though he had a slight numerical advantage in cavalry. These were conventionally heavy odds. According to the laird of Gorthie, the British line was three deep, as was normal. The Jacobite ranks were eight deep, relying on shock rather than firepower, and so the frontage of the two armies was probably roughly equal. He added, 'The Duke had too few troops'.[6]

The district that the two armies had arrived in was sparsely populated. Dunblane had a population of between 1,500 and 2,000, but of these only about 500 actually lived in the town.[7] According to an anonymous account of the battle, it took place on 'a lonely stretch of moor, interspersed with patches of morass, and so uneven as to be almost hilly'.[8] It was a frosty day and there was fog on the muir.[9] In fact there had been frost for several nights prior to the battle, rendering the boggy patches solid and so passable for cavalry.[10]

A contemporary map at the National Library of Scotland suggests that the Jacobite army had its right flank on a road from Perth, just south of the River Allan and its left flank just south of Whithead's Town hamlet, which had hills to its right. It was formed up on a north-west–south-east axis on the muir of Kinbuck and another contemporary map concurs.[11]

The day of the battle was Sunday, 13 November. Before eight in the morning, as day was breaking, the Jacobite army formed itself into two lines, with no reserve, to the left of the road from Dunblane.[12] They then marched two miles to the south, across the Sheriffmuir, positioning themselves to the south of the moor, with the right wing of the second line just in front of the hamlet of Kippendavie.

At sunrise the Jacobites saw a small band of cavalry on the high ground to their south, about a mile away. This could well have included Argyle, who, with Wightman, joined the advance guard because he needed to see where his enemy was. Although the two armies were two miles away, hills and broken ground prevented him from seeing them. He had to consider whether the far larger Jacobite force, some of which was close to the River Allan, might flank him on his right. Argyle was impressed on seeing the Jacobites form up, 'which they did in very good order'. On seeing them the Jacobites sent out their own cavalry to reconnoitre. They returned and reported that Argyle's men were among the enclosures at Kippendavie; this was possibly only a scouting force which withdrew on the Jacobite advance. After that, according to a Jacobite cavalry officer, Sinclair, 'we lost a great dale of time'. According to him, Mar did not expect to see the enemy so close, and did not know what to do, so waited whilst his enemy made the next move.[13]

Argyle had remained on the hill observing the Jacobite army's manoeuvres. Eventually, seeing movement on the left of their line, he became concerned that it might try and outflank him whilst their right attacked his left. Although the marshy ground on his right had hitherto prevented any cavalry action there, it had now frozen over and so could be tenable for troops. He decided that he would have to march his troops to the right in order to avoid being partially surrounded. He rode off his hill and at about 11 o' clock gave his orders.[14] It is possible that the army took the old west/east road eastwards from Dunblane and towards the hamlet of Dykedale a mile to the east, though a contemporary map suggested that they marched eastward through the hamlet of Newtoun and south-east to skirt the north side of Stone Hill, before marching eastward.[15]

It was half past eleven when Mar called all his unit commanders together. According to James Keith, a junior officer, he outlined various possibilities; one being that they could wait, either for the arrival of James, which he daily expected, or for news about the Jacobites in England. He then made a speech, and even Sinclair conceded, 'his Lordship, to doe him justice, which I think I am obliged in conscience to doe, it being the onlie good action of his life, made us a very fine speech'. He spoke of the injustice done to the Stuart family, the misery for Scotland of the Union and the opportunity they now had of righting these wrongs, 'and concluded in very strong and moveing terms'.[16]

Mar put the question of 'Fight or Not' to a vote, when 'all unanimouslie ... with ane unexpressible alacritie, called out, Fight'. They then all went to their posts.[17] Morale was clearly high, for as soon as the officers had got to their posts, and told their men of the council's decision, 'a huzza begun, with tossing up of hats and bonnets and through our whole armie, on the hearing we had resolved to fight'.[18]

Half an hour later, General George Hamilton began to make dispositions for an attack. The infantry, being once in two lines, were now broken up into four columns, presumably to hasten their approach towards the enemy. The four squadrons of cavalry on the right, together with a column of Highland infantry that had been on the right of the front line, were to march and take possession of the high ground (perhaps Stone Hill) from which the British cavalry had been seen. Drummond 'who is always glade to be employed' put himself at the head of the cavalry alongside the Earl Marischal. General Gordon took command of the infantry. They moved quickly forward.[19]

The second infantry column, which had been to the left of the first line, marched by the men who had been to their immediate right, but followed them at some distance. The two other columns advanced and the cavalry squadrons on the right fell into the rear of the last column of infantry. Columns can move faster than lines and clearly the intent was to reduce the distance between the two armies as quickly as possible in order to begin the action without further delay. The cavalry of Southesk, Lord Rupert Rollo (1679–1758) and Sinclair was now on the left. By the time the rear units were beginning to move, the foremost ones 'who had made so great haste to the top, were near the enemie, and beginning to form'. Confusingly, though, Drummond and Marischal's squadrons, which should have formed on the right of the infantry, formed on the left instead and so put themselves in the centre of the Jacobite infantry, 'it seems not knoweing their left hand from their right, thought themselves well there'.[20] According to John Cameron of Lochiel, 'The horse were call'd all to the right of ye Army; none stayed on the left'. A contemporary map shows all the Jacobite cavalry to have found their way to the right wing.[21] This was noted by the enemy; Sir John Anstruther, one of Rothes' volunteer cavalrymen, subsequently wrote, 'the rebels had only Foot upon their left in the first line and some Horse in the second'.[22] The Jacobite army was unable to perform complex drill and so manoeuvres of any type were unlikely to be successful. Such changes in formation were ill-advised as they resulted in confusion and disordered the men. Indeed, Lord Pitsligo later remarked that a Jacobite officer, Colonel Clepham, 'shewed me on paper the first disposition of the battle and how it was broke in the march up the hill, which in all probability deprived us of a complete victory'.[23]

Keith later wrote that Marischal was so eager to attack, having found the enemy, that he wanted Mar to order all of the army forward, to their right. Keith added that the effect was unfortunate, for 'which he did even in too much haste . . . arrived in such confusion that it was impossible to form them according to the line of battle projected, every one posted himself where he found ground'. On the Jacobite left 'a bog hinder'd them from extending themselves and increased the confusion'. Yet nor was the British army formed into a line of battle; 'The Duke of Argyle was no less embarrassed' wrote Keith.[24] This was despite the confusion among the Jacobite army, for the line of battle as planned had now been torn up, with infantry on the left of the front line where the Camerons should have been. First-line troops were in the second line and vice versa and this could not be undone. But morale was high. Cameron claimed, 'never men marched with greater chearfulness towards ane Eneemie'.[25]

The foremost infantry formed up very quickly. The other three columns were 'marching most irregularie at some distance'. They were following each other one by one and then tried to move as fast as possible to the front. These units were running and galloping. An aide of Kilsyth then rode up to Rollo, who was next to the infantry and at the head of the cavalry squadrons. He ordered the cavalry to move to the right of the whole army with all possible haste. Rollo obeyed at once and with speed, and passed the order back to Southesk, who followed Rollo's example. Southesk called back to Sinclair, who followed and then heard a confused Highland cry. He halted his squadron for some minutes and they then 'gallopt as hard as I could after them'. They were soon all posted together on the right. There was a little hill near their flanks and Sinclair thought it an admirable position for they could not be outflanked.[26]

The Government troops then came into view: 'we saw the enemies' colours, and their heads and screwed bayonets, all marching in haste towards our left alonge our front, within two hundred yards of us'. Keith wrote that they were 'marching without beat of drum' and were only twice the distance of extreme musket range from them. Despite the Union flag being visible, apparently many among the Jacobites took these to be Strathmore's Jacobite troops, even though the men they saw were wearing red coats. Meanwhile, Sinclair told his men that they should shoot him down if he turned to run. He told his men to be silent, look straight ahead and keep together in formation 'without which they could be ruined and disgraced'.[27]

Although Argyle had his drummers beat their drums as soon as he returned to his troops at eleven, his force's progress had been slow. This was despite the fact that the army had rested on their arms that night and their officers doing their utmost to bring them together. It was not until noon that the army was ready to march. A letter to John Stirling noted that movement occurred 'after some debate'. There was nothing more that could be done then, and so 'the Duke was forced to pocket up the Matter'.[28]

Since Argyle had returned from his observation of the enemy, he posted himself on the right of his army, which was formed with six battalions of infantry in the front line, flanked each by three squadrons of cavalry. The intention was for the artillery to be placed in three batteries of two guns in the centre of the front line as was customary, to support the infantry. The second line was of two battalions of infantry and four squadrons of dragoons. Also on the right was the squadron of volunteer cavalry, albeit behind the dragoons. Argyle marched the troops on the right wing quickly in order to confront the enemy's left wing, believing that was where the Jacobites would try and outflank him and so it was important that as general he placed himself at the most dangerous point, though this would potentially mean losing control of the overall direction of the battle if he became too much involved in the fight around him. The latter was adjacent to a morass, but the cold weather had frozen it and so it was no longer impassable to troops.[29]

This was a risky manoeuvre, as it exposed the vulnerable left flanks of his marching battalions as they switched from line to columns and marched parallel to their enemy's front line. Argyle was gambling that they would move quickly enough in order to join with his foremost troops and then form into line again to face the foe.

The battle began at about noon, according to Mar.[30] Cornet John Bennett of Portmore's dragoons, in command of the advance guard, reported that the Jacobite army was now in full march, but although this was initially on the low ground, they changed tack and began to march up the hill to the right of the British army. It then became a race to reach the top of the hill on the east of the armies' positions. A letter reported that the advance was 'not in a form of Battle going pretty Quick up the hill were a little breathless', probably in columns although this exposed their flanks to the enemy. Argyle's forces were there first; Portmore's dragoons being at their head, followed by Evans's and then by the volunteer cavalry, and crossed the half mile of the plain at the hill top.[31] It was a shock to see the Jacobites in readiness for them.[32]

Once Argyle could see the Jacobite forces moving to his immediate front, he was delighted, as he later wrote, 'finding them not intirley formed, I judged it was necessary to lose no time and accordingly began the action on the right with the dragoons, charged both their horse and foot without fireing one shot, and tho' they received us with a very good countenance, and gave us their fire pretty close, we broke thro' them'. The infantry battalions 'behaved admirably with Captain [Robert] Walkinshaw [of Shannon's] distinguished himself and a great many more'. The Jacobites had disordered themselves by their climb to the hill and their battalions were quite apart from each other. There were casualties among the British troops, too, as the Jacobites fired. Colonel Henry Hawley (1685–1759) of Evans's dragoons was shot through the shoulder and Lord Forfar was shot in the knee.[33]

A Jacobite account of this part of the battle was as follows, given by Sinclair:

> In what manner our three colums run away, none of those amongst them could tell, nor where the flight begun, everie corps putting it off themselves, on each other, as is usuall. Most agreed that few of them had ever formed, and those who did, begun to fire at a great distance; that the three columns fell in with one another in that running up the hill, and when they came in sight of the Duke of Argyle's right wing, which was alreadie formed, they were in disorder; and the last confusion, when his dragoons made a mine to attack them through the morass, which happned to be bewixt

them; and happie for our foot had they knoun to make the right use of such ane advantage and situation; but instead of that, and falling into forme, they fell into greater confusion, calling for horse against the dragoons, and Generall Hamilton being the onlie officer amongst them, it was impossible for him alone to bring them into order; so they turned their backs that minute we gave the huzza to advance, the Duke of Argyle pursueing them.[34]

A later biographer of Argyle wrote that the Jacobites on the left wing had neither 'courage nor inclination to stand'.[35] In all the fighting on this flank lasted half an hour, according to an anonymous letter written to the Provost.[36] Some of the Jacobite infantry here initially put up a good fight, as Anstruther reported, 'the enemy kept up their fire longer than could have been expected, the fire was very hot upon Evans's regiment for a quarter of an hour they had a deep stripe before them which they could not well pass which made them run about in some disorder'.[37] They were helped in this by having a bog to their front.[38]

Jacobite casualties may have been higher than they appeared. Sinclair saw few corpses on that ground, and he put this down to the fact that 'his [Argyle] being obliged to goe about the morass, which gave our people a great advantage in the flight doun hill, and that the frost was strong enough to bear them on foot, when the dragoons' horses sunk deep in the moor's, our's in the mean time getting over the river of Allen'.[39] There was an alternate suggestion. Lieutenant Campbell believed the body count could have been higher still, 'But had we shown as little mercy as they did they had lost thousands instead of hundreds'.[40]

One Jacobite did fight valiantly there. He was Lord Strathmore, who led a battalion of Atholl infantry. According to Sinclair, 'When he found all turning their backs, he seized the colours, and persuaded fourteen, or some such number, to stand by him for some time, which dreu upon him the enemies' fire, by which he was wounded in the bellie, and, goeing off, was takne'.[41] It was also alleged that an unnamed MacDonald woman died fighting after having refused quarter and having killed or wounded several of her enemies.[42]

A number of infantry battalions under Wightman followed their commander. Wightman later wrote, 'The Moment we got to the Top of the Hill, not above half of our Men were come up, or could form; the Enemy, that were within Pistol-Shot, began the attack with all their Left upon our Right . . . The Enemy were Highlanders, and, as is their custom, gave us a Fire; and a great many came up to our Noses Sword in Hand; but the Horse on our Right, with the constant Fire of the Plattoons of Foot, soon put the Left of their Army to

Rout.'[43] The two-gun battery had been pulled up the hill with the right wing, but they had scarce time to unyoke the horses and turn the guns on the Jacobites, before both sides were intertwined in melee and so artillery fire was out of the question.[44]

An anonymous chronicler gave the following account of the behaviour of various British cavalry units:

> The nobility and gentry of the horse volunteers acted worthy of themselves, and without vanity bore their own share in the victory, and even bore their share of the rebels fire in the attack upon that of Forfar and Wightman's regiments; and tho Evans's dragoons were in some little disorder, it was not throw occasion of the enemy, but through the deepness of the marsh ground, which was near to have bogged their horses.

Evans's dragoons were able to wheel round and found better ground and then 'performed as could be desired'.[45] Initially this unit had reeled back from the weight of a Jacobite volley (and suffered the highest casualties suffered by any of Argyle's cavalry regiments that day – nearly a third) and had disordered the volunteer cavalry to their rear, but both soon rallied and entered the fray.[46] One reason for Evans's men rallying was because 'Rothes' volunteers call out for Shame to them . . . [and] took a terrible vengeance'.[47] Anstruther later gave a graphic account of this part of the battle:

> At the time that Evans's Regiment came amongst us my horse got on and his hind part stuck in the marshy ground where we were formed which made him fall back upon me and I concluded that he had been killed dead but he immediately got off me, I kept the reins and got him mounted again with great difficulty for the balls were flying so thick that the horse did not stand long in one posture and I had the good fortune to escape with some bruises occasion'd chiefly by the fall and was so well as to continue on horseback all the pursuit.[48]

Portmore's dragoons were in the thick of the fighting. Anstruther reported, 'The Greys who are never backward upon these occasions, were the first that cut them to pieces and wherever we got amongst them they fled'.[49] Stair's dragoons also did well, 'no men under Heaven could doe Better and had a full share in Braking through the enemy's line on their left, and who particularly employed in pursuing the enemy into the River'.[50] Those Jacobite cavalry who may have been near their left wing did not take part in the fighting but as Anstruther wrote 'they did not stay till we came up with them and we only saw them flying'.[51] Apparently they were behind the infantry, ironically enough, to prevent the foot soldiers from retreating.[52]

The Jacobites were apparently driven back three miles northwards over the River Allan. Wightman gave it as a mile and a half. Argyle wrote that he 'could not but judge it an entire Rout and thought of nothing but pursuing them as long as we had day light'. This action led to officers being taken prisoner, as well as the capture of a standard and ten colours. The pursuit had taken a long time (possibly three hours) because the Jacobites outnumbered their attackers. The former, being allegedly 5,000 strong, repeatedly made attempts to reform their ranks; after all they outnumbered their pursuers, so as Lieutenant Colonel Harrison wrote, 'this 'obliged us as often to attack and break them'.[53] According to one report, the bodies of eighty Jacobites were later fished out of the Allan.[54] The rout was bloody as is usually the case when exposed infantry are fleeing from the faster-moving cavalry; one eyewitness noting that evening that 'For some tyme our dragoons gave no quarter'. Such was the bloody duty of the cavalry. The eventual rout was utter, Anstruther writing 'they fled in the utmost disorder and there were so very many of them that at first I thought their whole army had been routed and we pursued a good deal too far without knowing what had become of our left'.[55]

Lochiel gave a similar account; his clan, impatient to advance and attack the enemy when they came into view, was behind a Lowland battalion, the latter of whom fired a volley, which was returned. Then the Government troops

> broke in all at once upon my Regiment and carryed them off before the half of them were formed, or of Mckinins men who were drawing up wt them, as well as some of the McPhersons. A little before this Regiment broke in upon mine there was a party of the black dragoons came pretty near us, at whom those who were on my right, and the few of my men who were drawen up in the right of my Regiment, fyred and kill'd severalls, and beat them back. I being advanced some few paces before the right of my Regiment, in order to get sight of the Enemy, me being in a hollow ground, which how soon I had got I look'd about to order my men to advance, but to my great surprise saw them caryed away in this manner, and all those who were nixt to me and drawen up on my right and left gone off. All this time we saw no generall officer, neither received any orders; only by the confusion we observed our right had been broke. So finding myself in this situation, with three or four gentlemen of my friends who chanc'd to be nixt me, made off, and found none of my own men until I cross'd the River of Allan where I found some of them with Apin and some of his men.[56]

Elsewhere on the battlefield, the situation was very different. As Wightman was moving his battalions forward against the collapsing Jacobite left, he felt the need to investigate. He sent his aide and found what had happened there.[57] On the left of the Government line, the battalions (Montague's, Morrison's, Orrery's, Egerton's and Clayton's) and regiments (Kerr's, Carpenter's and a squadron of Stair's) were not formed up for battle, but were marching to follow the lead of those on their right under Argyle. Parker wrote that this manoeuvre was one 'which should have been done before the Enemy advanced so near him'.[58] Argyle, however, had been taken up with what was happening immediately around him.

The troops on Argyle's left had arrived last onto the field and needed to change their formation from column to line and to wheel to face the enemy. Ahead of them, in a hollow way, were concealed part of the Jacobite right wing, which also outflanked them. Robert Henderson wrote, three days later, that the battalions were 'in a marching poster [posture], not expecting the Highland men so near 'em'.[59]

At the head of the clans, Mar, seeing the enemy beginning to form their line on their left, decided to attack them, ordering Clepham and Major Ereskine to pass on his wishes. On their return, he pulled off his hat, waved it with a huzza and the men moved forward; the MacDonalds, the Macleans, the Gordons, Ogilvie's and Huntley's battalions (almost 3,000 men).[60] However, Sinclair and Keith reported it rather differently. Sinclair claimed that an elderly gentleman, who he was told was Captain Livingstone, once of Dumbarton's regiment, went up to Gordon 'calling to him, with great oaths, To attack the eneimie before they were formed', and in the exposed flank. Gordon explained that he could not act without orders from Mar, who could not be seen or found, so Gordon agreed to attack as Livingstone was 'representing to him that he'd loose his time' if he did not immediately attack.[61]

Sinclair gave a graphic description of what happened next:

> The order to attack being given, the two thousand Highlandmen [nearer 3,000], who were then draun up in a very good order, ran towards the ennemie in a disorderlie manner, always fireing some dropeing shots, which drew upon them a general salvo from the eneimie, which begun at their left, opposite us, and turn to their right. No sooner that begun, the Highlandmen threw themselves flat on their bellies; and when it slackened, they started to their feet. Most threw away their fuzies, and, drawing their suords, pierced them everie where with ane incredible vigour and rapidities, in four minutes' time from their receaving the order to attack. Not onlie all in our view and before us turned their backs, but the five squadrons

of dragoons on their left, commanded by Generall Witham, went to the right about, and never lookt back till they had got near Dunblain, almost tuo miles from us; while the Highlandmen pursued the infantrie, who run as hard as their feet could carrie them, a great manie of whome threw away their armes to enable them to run the faster, and were sabred by the Highlandmen, who spared few who fell in their hands.[62]

Keith recorded it more concisely, 'he [Gordon] order'd the troops immediately to charge, which they did with so much vigour that in less than ten minutes they entirely defeated six regiments of Foot and five squadrons of dragoons'.[63] He was exaggerating; Argyle had only eight battalions and no more than five were on his left wing.

One reason why the Jacobites were so successful is that once they reached their opponents' lines, they 'push'd by the bayonets with their targets, and with their broadswords, spread nothing but Death and Terror'. Although their outnumbered enemies 'behaved gallantly, and made all the Resistance they could make; but being unacquainted with this Savage way of Fighting, against which all the Rules of War made no provision, they were forced to give way'.[64] This was very true; regular troops expected to exchange volleys of musketry, possibly aided by adjoining artillery, until one side broke, rather than to engage in melee or even the threat of it. Nor even when in melee, did they expect to fight men with swords, dirks, shields and occasionally even Lochaber axes. In fact melee was rare. As a contemporary chronicler noted, 'It is impossible to express the Horror which some of the Gentlemen of the English Regiments say their men were possess'd with at that unusual and savage way of Fighting'.[65]

When Morrison's and Orrery's battalions were attacked, they gave way to superiority of numbers allied to the force of a charge when insufficiently checked by casualties caused by defensive musketry, but only after an intense and bloody struggle. According to an anonymous eyewitness, the 'Highland rebels, consisting of the clans who were not only their best, but of triple the number to our left, went quite through them and made a considerable slaughter of our men'.[66]

If the Jacobites had about 3,000 men at this part of the battle they can only have been charging at best three battalions otherwise the odds would have been far less in their numerical favour. It was here that most of Argyle's casualties occurred; a total, allegedly, of 516 in all (117 from Montague's foot, 144 from Morrison's, 181 from Orrery's, 22 from Clayton's and 52 from Egerton's; the latter may have fled prior to the others). A few casualties were the result of Jacobite firepower. Lieutenant Colonel Hamars of Morrison's was killed in the first fire. Dennis McMullin, a 28-year-old of Morrison's, a former shoemaker from Colerain, was shot in his left leg.[67] Most of the injuries, though, came from cutting and stabbing weapons, either in melee or in the pursuit. George Studders and Robert Thompson, both of Orrery's, suffered numerous cuts to the head.[68]

Finally, there was no support from the two regiments of dragoons to the left. They were interspaced by fleeing infantrymen, which 'helped the eneimie to put them in confusion'. Whetham's cavalry then allegedly galloped off the field with news of their army's defeat.[69] However, another contemporary stated that Torphichen, lieutenant colonel of Kerr's dragoons, rallied the troops on the left, eventually, and they were able to retire in good order, being covered by the cavalry.[70] The anonymous narrator agrees with this account, admitting that the two dragoon regiments gave way, but later were able to support the fleeing infantry and 'stopt the clans from further slaughter'. The artillery being never unlimbered was thus saved, but some colours and standards were lost by the battalions on the left wing.[71]

Torphichen gave his own account of events. His regiment of dragoons had initially been in the second line of the army and on Argyle marching the army to the right, his men were at the rear, despite galloping uphill behind their comrades. Kerr's dragoons moved between a pass through which they had to travel in order to join the others of the left wing. Yet they did not advance further for the three battalions and the dragoons were running away from the Jacobites. Torphichen had his men make loud cheers and 'threatened them if they did not stand to treat them as enemies which immediately had the desired effect for both dragoons and Foot rallied under my colour and in the mean time cut down what Highlanders had by their eagerness made too great an advance'. Major General Whetham, in command of the left wing, then let Torphichen, because of his gallant behaviour, take charge of the rearguard made up of his regiment, and then they took the guns with them back to Stirling, retreating in good order, facing the enemy and thus deterring another attack.[72]

Yet, according to the account given by Argyle, one of the Government dragoon regiments on the left charged and took a Jacobite standard and the reason for their retreat was because they had heard that the right wing of the army had been surrounded and none had escaped, so they thought the best course was to march to Stirling and defend it as long as possible. Whether this was an excuse is another matter.[73]

A contemporary map disagrees with these accounts, showing the cavalry and infantry divided during the flight. The dragoons rode south-west to avoid a stream and then north-west to ride through Dunblane and then, on the other side of the Allan, southwards to Stirling. The infantry took the more obvious route; southwards to cross the Wharry Burn; Clayton's crossing by

Kippenwright, Egerton's by Kippenwright and the Mill of Penbright, with Orrery's and Morrison's also crossing by the mill.[74]

Once over the Wharry and Allan, finding the pursuit over, there was some discussion as to what to do, based on inadequate information as to what was occurring elsewhere on the battlefield; only seeing their immediate situation. Whetham thought it best to fall back to Stirling in order to secure the place with the fairly unscathed dragoons and what was left of the infantry. Colonel Kerr argued that they should stay on the field of battle until they heard from Argyle. His superior officer, Whetman 'giving all over for lost' had the troops fall back on Stirling Bridge, reaching it at three o'clock.[75] The retreat may have disintegrated into a rout as the men moved further away from the scene of devastation.

As time went on, those in Stirling realized that all was not lost. An hour after the routers arrived, a gentleman who had been riding hard from Sheriffmuir told them that Argyle retained the field and had obliged the Jacobites to retire. Argyle wanted all his troops to march towards him in order to achieve a complete victory. Captain McBride and another officer on guard at the bridge gave three huzzas and their men echoed the cheer. Yet intelligence was conflicting and another report stated that Argyle was dead and all but six of Portmore's dragoons had been taken. Then another rider, arriving at half past four, gave news that Argyle needed all his men and it was only at this second urging that Whetham gathered what troops he could and returned to the moorland.[76] According to Mar the pursuit of the left wing of the Government army lasted as far south as a little hill on the south side of Dunblane. Another account has it lasting the distance of half a mile.[77] In either case, it had not lasted long, suggesting great discipline or that the retreat had been effectively covered by Torphichen's dragoons; the latter seemingly most likely.

It seems that the Jacobite cavalry on the right wing were eager, now that the enemy was broken, to attack them, but Sinclair was against such action, believing that 'there was some more to doe' and so the cavalry needed to be kept together and not loosed against fleeing enemies. One contemporary chronicler suggested that this was a major error as resolute cavalry action could have cut off all of Argyle's left wing. At this point Major Arthur told him that some of the Jacobite left and centre were in full retreat and Sinclair told him to keep that unfortunate news to himself. Although Sinclair tried to maintain all the cavalry near him together, he was not entirely successful as some men had no regard for their officers and 'folloued in the pursuit, in imitation of Drummond and Marichall's four squadrons'.[78]

Mar then arrived and Sinclair 'wisht him joy of the victorie'. As with Argyle and Whitman, he had no idea of what was happening away from his immediate view. Apparently Mar then rode away to reflect, probably sadly, on what had happened on the bloody field without the pretence of giving orders. Sinclair complained about Mar's incompetence to another officer. He then saw a Government squadron on top of a small hill, only 300 yards away. They had taken some of Marischal's squadron prisoner, then surrounded them and 'shot them in our sight', unable or unwilling either to take prisoners or to release them. Sinclair refers to this as 'this small execution' but does not seem to go into the detail of labelling it what would now be termed a 'war crime'. Sinclair's men threatened to advance against the dragoons before they could form up against them, and then 'we made towards them at a trot', but their enemy fled, leaving behind 'some of our's dead or mortallie wounded'. This episode was misreported to Mar as dragoons fighting among themselves.[79]

Sinclair then saw the dragoon squadrons that had been on Argyle's left forming up and returning to the battlefield, but this is probably an error, as Torphichen reported his cavalry only covering the retreat of the left and not returning. There was no sign of either the Government infantry from the left wing or of the Highlanders and Jacobite cavalry who had pursued them. It was a potentially dangerous time for Sinclair's cavalry, with enemy in both directions of them, making it imperative that they form up. Later Sinclair sent a message to Mar to inform him that the cavalry and the Highland pursuers had returned to the scene of strife. There then followed a stand-off between Sinclair's cavalry and Portmore's dragoons.[80]

Afterwards, Mar recovered himself and 'got most of our Horse, and a pretty good Number of our Foot' and re-ordered them. This was a gradual process, as Sinclair related, 'our foot begun to assemble and draw nere, at least some hundred, I believe three or four; and some few of the horse'. He was ignorant as to what had occurred elsewhere on the battlefield, 'We knew not then what became of our Left'. However, on returning northwards, they saw 'a Body of the Enemy on the North of us consisting mostly of the Grey Dragoons [Portmore's], and some of the Black', whilst some Government infantry battalions were further north. He also thought he could see a body of Jacobite infantry to the east. Mar desired to confront the remaining Government troops so as to complete his victory.[81] One contemporary chronicler thought that Gordon was then in tactical command of 5,000 men, but probably less (Hamilton had been on the left wing) and could have attacked the Government troops immediately, rather than halting to form up, with the result that they could have destroyed the enemy, though an unformed mass of men might not have been particularly militarily effective. They did not do so.[82]

Argyle had clearly been taken up solely with what lay before him. During the earlier part of the battle, a large gap had opened up between his right and left wings of his army. Not knowing this, he had advanced with the dragoons rapidly and Wightman, with his slower-moving infantry, took some time to find him. At some point Wightman was able to converse with him. Although no better informed, his subordinate was at least aware that it was worth considering what was happening on the rest of the battlefield and made this point to his leader. They then halted the pursuit – the cavalry were about three miles to the north and the infantry about half that, with the fleeing Jacobites having crossed the Allan – and saw that what had been the right wing of the Jacobite army was now to their rear. Wightman's battalions were no longer in pursuit of the fleeing Jacobite left, but 'not knowing but my Rear might soon be attack'd by the Enemy', he had 'kept what Foot I had in perfect Order'. The Jacobites were now forming up on the top of the hill. No news could be learnt of what had happened to the units on the left of the Government army. At this point Argyle had three, four or five battalions of infantry and five squadrons of dragoons. He marched them towards the Jacobites, extending his left flank towards Dunblane to allow the units that were now on his right to rejoin him and post themselves there. Both sides were half a mile apart.[83]

The remaining Jacobites on the battlefield were now almost all returned from their limited pursuit of the Government left wing. They were formed up 'in tolerable order', with half of the cavalry on each flank of the infantry. The Government troops marched towards them and then halted. The Jacobites did likewise and stood looking at one another about 400 yards distance, for half an hour.[84]

It is not certain exactly how strong each force now was. Argyle wrote that the Jacobites had 4,000 men and Wightman believed they had a three to one numerical superiority. Sinclair believed there were 2,000 Jacobite infantry and the number of cavalry on both sides was equal (perhaps about 400). Those infantry who charged (Huntley's, the Macleans, the MacDonalds and Sir Donald MacDonald's men) had been nearly 3,000 strong, but allowing for casualties and men who had left the battlefield, they may have been rather less. A Jacobite alleged Argyle's force was only made up of four squadrons of dragoons and a 'small Battalion of Foot', which is certainly a considerable under-estimate. Sinclair claims there were about 800 Government infantry. Another contemporary source states that the Government troops 'were scarce a thousand', with the infantry in the centre, in two lines, but it 'did not bring him to ane equall front with us' and a cannon placed to each side. With Argyle at this point were perhaps only three infantry battalions; just under 1,000 infantry in all. Flanking them were the dragoons; Portmore's on the right and Evans's and Stair's on the left (perhaps just over 400). It would seem that the Jacobites outnumbered Argyle; far less than they had done at the onset of the battle. The Jacobites remained on their hill, 'very prudentially' according to

Argyle. This was because he believed that it meant that they could easily withdraw unmolested or if Argyle chose to attack them, it would be the Jacobites who had the advantage of the terrain.[85]

Yet, though Wightman considered that the Jacobites were 'ranged at the Top of a Hill on very advantageous Ground', he thought that his forces were in a better position. He wrote, 'We posted ourselves at the Bottom of the Hill, having the advantage of Ground, where their Horse could not well attack us, for we had the Convenience of some Earth-walls or ditches about Breast high'.[86] These may have been built for agricultural purposes, perhaps as sheep pens.

Mar believed that the Government army might march towards him, but did not do so according to one account, though another states that two squadrons of dragoons marched towards the top of the hill, but on seeing the Jacobites advancing to the attack, retreated downwards faster than they had ascended it. The Jacobites did little further that was aggressive, except to advance two squadrons of cavalry to observe Argyle's movements. According to Sinclair this was, 'I believe without order, by common consent, for I saw no mortall pretend to give orders that day, the one following the others example'. Linlithgow further advanced his squadron, but Sinclair advised him not to do so for his squadron was not advancing and for Linlithgow to do so unilaterally would be to break the line, though 'he was so vaine of that day's behaviour they had [he] would scarce take advice'. They halted in expectation that the infantry would also advance, following the cavalry's example, but Sinclair 'lookt longe in vaine over our shoulders, for they stood like stakes'. Apparently Mar later explained why the Highlanders had not moved forward, 'Mar told the gentlemen, That the Highlanders were so fatigued they had lost spirits, and would not attack; and to the Highlandmen, That he could not find it in his heart to risqué the gentlemen'. Sinclair merely believed this to be an excuse, that 'Mar had no mind to risqué himself' and so 'missed the favourablest [opportunity] that ever offer'd of getting out of the danger he had plunged them in'. He added that it could not be argued that Mar did not know that he outnumbered Argyle.[87]

Keith gave another version of this final confrontation in the afternoon. Mar sent an officer forward to check the enemy's position and then held a council of war:

> to consult whether he should attack them again, but the officer having reported that their numbers were equal to ours, and the Highlanders, who were extreamly fatigued, and, had nothing to eat in two days, being averse to it, it was resolved to keep the field of battle, and to let the enemy retire unmolested, which they had already begun to do under the cover of the earth walls as well as of the night which was now approaching.[88]

Yet according to Keith, the officer who was sent forward – and never named – had blundered and gave Mar faulty information:

> He having taken his remarks more by the number of colours than the space of ground they occupied, made his report that the enemy was betwixt two and three thousand strong, when in reality there was no more than three battalions not making above 1,000 troops, the other colours being what the Duke had just taken on our left, and being almost the same with his own, he now used them to disguise the weakness of his troops by making a show of four more battalions more than he had, the ground and mud walls by which he had cover'd not allowing to see that he had formed only two ranks deep (usually three ranks deep); this mistake hinder'd us from attacking him in the evening; which its probable we might have done with better success than we had in the morning.[89]

Whether the officer had erred is another question: Argyle may well have had such numbers as he suspected; Keith was presumably further away and so his opinion may be less valid. Berwick later commented on Mar's inaction at this stage, 'He ought, however, have tried to induce them to it; for it was of great consequence to him to push on and to hazard everything to Argyle'.[90]

Yet the real reason was somewhat different. By this stage of the battle, Lochiel and Strowan had fled with their men and Sir Donald MacDonald was ill at Perth:

> So that the laird of Glengarry was the only chieftain of consequence remaining with the Earl of Mar, who in a most unaccountable manner took it into his head that he could not attack Argile in his return, & said to Mar that he had done enough for one Day, seeing they beat the Enimy and kept the field of Battle, and although Mar used his utmost endeavours to persuade Glengarry to make the Victory compleat, yet nothing could prevail with him to do so. So that Mar was forced to let the enemy with a very inferior Number of Troops march by him and escape the danger they were in.
>
> Argile in the meantime was very sensible of the disadvantage he lay under, and tho he kept his Troops that were with him in good order, yet he retreated in very good order, yet he retreated in very good heart till he gote into the Town of Dunblane where he reassembled a good many of those who had been routed on his left, and a remained all that night. Mar kept the field of Battle till after sun sett and then marched back to Ardoch, where he encamped that night.

This testimony was from William and Maurice Moray, who formed part of Mar's cavalry escort and were thus better placed than Keith or Sinclair to witness what happened at this crucial juncture of the battle.[91]

Glengarry had about 461 men at the outset of the battle, and so led a sizeable minority of the men who remained with Mar. Without them any attack was even more risky, for the Jacobite's numerical edge was either minimal or non-existent. Furthermore, their holding back may well have discouraged their comrades. Despite all the criticism heaped on Mar ever since 1715, at least he clearly saw that this was the opportunity to defeat Argyle. It was not his fault that inaction resulted. Instead he was let down by a subordinate. In this he was unfortunate that he was not leading a regular army but an army where most of the officers were volunteers, amateurs and not under any formal discipline. As in 1745, Jacobite officers, as gentlemen, valued their independence and did not always agree with their commander-in-chief. Glengarry had been an ardent Jacobite, having fought at Killiecrankie in 1689, but his enthusiasm had evidently waned as he did not support the restoration attempt of 1708; by 1715 he was ageing and though he had vigorously led his clan into battle but clearly thought his men had done all they could.[92]

Unaware of all this, Argyle, finding there was nothing he could do, not having the rest of his men and with darkness now rapidly descending on the moor, marched his troops away from the immediate vicinity of his enemy, whilst still facing the direction of the Jacobites (initially Sinclair thought this was a feint); as did the Jacobites. Wightman later wrote, 'The Enemy behav'd like civil Gentlemen, and let us do what we pleased'.[93] This is not the behaviour expected of enemies in battle. It was about seven o'clock and so was too dark to fight.[94]

Wightman thought that his army had had a lucky escape, writing 'If they had had either Courage or Conduct they might have entirely destroyed my Body of Foot; but it pleased God to the Contrary. I am apt to conjecture their Spirits were not a little damp'd by having been Witness some Hours before of the firm Behaviour of my Foot, and thought it hardly possible to break us'.[95]

In another respect apart from numbers, Mar had held the advantage if he had but known it. Charging downhill gives additional momentum to the attackers and renders it harder for the enemy to fire uphill with any accuracy. The Jacobite charge down the slopes of Killiecrankie had resulted in a decisive victory in 1689 despite being outnumbered.[96] Yet Mar had been let down by Glengarry. Forster and Glengarry were amateurs, not professionals; and when matters become distasteful the amateur often ceases his labours whereas the professional will continue to the grim reckoning.

An hour after the retreat of the Jacobites, some of the units that had been on the left began to rejoin Argyle and explained what had happened there.

Argyle's men passed the bridge of Dunblane and posted themselves 'very securely'. As on the night of the 12th, they were lying with their arms ready for any danger.[97] They camped to the west of the Allan, to the south-west of Dunblane and near the main road to Stirling.[98]

One account claims the Jacobites remained where they were for half an hour before leaving, presumably waiting to see what Argyle would do. Their artillery – never used – had been left where it had initially stood when the rest of the army fled. Some of the carriages were broken, the gunpowder carts were overturned and what little gunpowder there had been was trodden into the wet moor by the horses. Apparently the country people who had charge of the guns and horses fled on being frightened by the sound of the guns. Sinclair suggested burying the artillery which could not be moved, but he was ignored; it is hard to see how this could have been accomplished without a sufficient quantity of the necessary tools even if men could be found who were able and willing to undertake such a menial and physically demanding task at the end of an exhausting day. The Jacobites found that they had lost many of their horses for their baggage carts and artillery, but found a few horses and were thus able to remove some of their material from the field. A total of perhaps six guns were taken away and five abandoned, but as they were pulled away, the horses became exhausted and two of the carriages broke so all the guns were left upon the road. Lacking cover and provisions, they marched away in good order, though Sinclair thought not, with 'everie one shifting for himself . . . there being no one either to command or obey' in the darkness. They camped that night at Ardoch. The rearguard, Sinclair's squadron, did not arrive until midnight, and when they did, could not find either Mar or a quartermaster to give a report nor to be told where their quarters were. Here Mar expected to be joined by the troops that had been on his left and four other battalions; none of the latter having taken part in the battle itself. These forces joined Mar on the following day.[99]

At daybreak on 14 November, Argyle returned to the field of battle of which he was now undoubted master. He found one of his men who had escaped from the enemy after having briefly being captured. This unknown soldier told Argyle that the Jacobites had retreated to Auchterarder and that some had fled over the Allan. Other wounded men were removed from the field.[100] An anonymous contemporary wrote 'all the wounded men came into Towne, some wanting Arms & some Legs, & bloody hands, & that it was the most Dismale sight ever saw. In short I cannot express what crying was in this place, very many officers wounded, soldiers wanting their Arms, wigs & clothes, & officers the same.'[101] He also sent out patrols to take any of the dispersed Jacobites that could be found. Colonel Kerr took a detachment of men with him to bury the dead of both sides.[102] It was probably a melancholy sight; apart from men's bodies there were those of women, 'the damn'd treacherous Rebels had no compassion on the very women was there, but kill'd them downe like dogs'. These were probably female camp followers who accompanied the Government army to succour their menfolk and perhaps seek plunder.[103]

There was little more that Argyle could do. Provisions were running low, his army was numerically reduced and the weather was bad, so encampment on Sheriffmuir was not practical. Nor was it tenable to advance against the Jacobites because of this. As he wrote, 'as for our advancing, our circumstances would by no means admit of it'. He marched his men back to Stirling, leaving Kerr and a few soldiers there in order to put them under cover again, presumably because of the inclement weather. They were, however, billeted in such a way that they would be able to reassemble within a few hours if the need arose.[104]

The Jacobites were in a doleful plight after the battle, too. Sinclair later wrote, 'We found ourselves without provisions, pouder and men'. Having their army reduced by 5,000 men they could not continue fighting. They lacked food so had no alternative but to retreat to Perth. They marched back to Auchterarder on 14 November and cantoned there that night. They arrived at Perth two days later.[105]

The casualties inflicted on the Government army should be easier to ascertain because regular forces keep records and these often survive. Yet in this instance no official record seems to now exist. Rae gives the following figures:[106]

	Killed	*Wounded*	*Prisoners*	*Total*
Infantry	241	120	110	471
Dragoons	25	53	12	80
Officers	14	11	10	35
Sergeants	10	3	1	13
Total Men	290	187	133	610
Horses	42	75	75	157

There are no numbers of casualties among State Papers for Scotland. Figures, broken down by unit, were published in the press a few weeks after the battle. Their accuracy can be doubted, however.

Infantry – killed

Unit	Field officers	Captains	Lieutenants	Ensigns	Sergeants	Others	Total
Forfar			1			11	12
Morrison	1	2	3	4	4	97	111
Montagu	1	3	2			87	93
Clayton			1			6	7
Wightman						7	7
Orrey		1	2		3	85	91
Shannon		1				5	6
Egerton						21	21
Total	2	7	9	4	7	319	348

Infantry – wounded

Unit	Field officers	Captains	Lieutenants	Ensigns	Sergeants	Others	Total
Forfar	1						1
Morrison		1				13	14
Montagu			2			19	21
Clayton						14	14
Wightman						5	5
Orrery		1			1	24	26
Shannon						5	5
Egerton					1	14	15
Total	1	2	2	0	2	94	101

Cavalry – killed

Unit	Officers	Lieutenants	Cornets	Quartermasters	Sergeants	Others	Total
Portmore						2	2
Carpenter						17	17
Evans		1				19	20
Stair						7	7
Kerr						0	0
Total							56

Cavalry – wounded

Unit	Officers	Lieutenants	Cornets	Quarter-masters	Sergeants	Others	Total
Portmore	1			1		2	4
Carpen-ter					1	8	9
Evans	2	2			1	28	33
Stair						6	6
Kerr						1	1
Total	3	2	0	1	2	45	53

Horses

Unit	Killed	Wounded
Portmore	3	8
Carpenter	11	4
Evans	13	44
Stair	11	15
Kerr	1	14
Total	42	75

Troops captured

Unit	
Portmore	2
Carpenter	3
Evans	3
Stair	1
Kerr	0
Forfar	0
Morrison	19
Montagu	3
Clayton	1
Wightman	0
Orrery	64
Shannon	0
Egerton	16
Total	112

To sum up, according these figures, the Government army had lost 404 dead, 154 wounded and 112 prisoners; a total of 670 casualties; roughly a fifth of their total force. A disproportionate loss was suffered by Montague's, Morrison's and Orrery's, who had borne the brunt of the Jacobite onslaught.[107]

Argyle wrote on 15 November, 'My Lord, I have but this moment received the Return of the killed, wounded and missing, which are in so much confusion, that I cannot send them, but I judge that killed, wounded & missing we are 500 men weaker now than the day we marched to the Enemy'.[108] The Return mentioned does not survive, and though commanders often exaggerate the enemy's losses and minimize their own, Argyle's correspondence shows him as a plain speaker in whom duplicity was not a part of his mentality. So his assessment of casualties may be the least inaccurate there is.

Of those 245 men whose wounds are recorded, 122, or 50 per cent, had received injuries from cutting weapons, which would almost all have been inflicted by swords and perhaps occasionally Lochaber axes. Nineteen men (8 per cent) had been injured by stabbing weapons, probably swords and dirks. Nearly a quarter of them, fifty-four men, had been injured by musket balls. Horses trampled on eleven men; five received bruises, two were wounded by bayonets; one by each of the following – a sword pommel, a butt of a gun and a butt of a pistol. For twenty-nine men, or 12 per cent, the cause of injury is unknown.[109] These injuries are very uncharacteristic of those inflicted in conventional warfare at the time; in the Invalides, in 1762, the overwhelming proportion of wounds had been inflicted by muskets balls, some by cannon and only a very small number by hand-to-hand weapons.[110] The majority of these wounds, where their location is known, was to the head; ninety-three (40 per cent), with there being fifty (31 per cent) leg wounds and thirty-nine (24 per cent) were arm wounds.[111]

Lest we become distanced from the human cost of battle through these statistics, recall the words of contemporaries. Captain John Farrar of Evans's Dragoons, who later wrote, 'that unfortunate Day I had the misfortune to Receive a Musquett shott into my left Thigh which broke and shattered all the bone to pieces I lay madam 24 weeks upon my back end'. He was also taken prisoner and lost £200 worth of belongings including his horse, cloak and bag with £70 of cash. On 15 June 1716 he wrote from Stirling 'I could have wished madam that I had escaped that wound that I might have been with ye Regiment when at Brechin'.[112]

Anstruther wrote a week after the battle about four officers who had been wounded, that they were 'much better than could be expected, the surgeons are in no apprehension about the three last but they can't as yet be certain about Forfar who's good heart and strength of constitution will contribute very much to his cure'.[113] Andrew Cockburn, Lord Chief Justice Clerk, also wrote of the wounded a few days later; 'Poor Forfar is dead. James Dormer is in all ill way. I hope my poor brother is out of danger but I am afraid he has lost ye use of his arm; many pieces of bone are already come out and others are coming it will be sometime before he is well'.[114] Campbell thought that Forfar, wounded in seventeen places, was 'a sample of their [the Jacobites'] mercy'. [115]

Then there were the material losses. The Government army had also lost one flag, though another statement gives it as being four.[116] Mar added 'We have taken a great many of the Enemy's Arms'. Three days later his colleague at Burntisland elaborated; 'forty good Horses and one Thousand five Hundred Stand of the Enemy's Arms'. Another Jacobite put captured small arms at 1,400–1,500.[117] Sinclair thought it was 1,200.[118]

No known list of Jacobite casualties survives either, even assuming one was ever compiled. Argyle wrote 'I count their dead my lord to be 500 and believe the number of their wounded to be considerable' (some of whom had drowned in the Allan) as well as having captured 21 Jacobite officers (out of 82 men taken).[119] Harrison put the figure as higher but was uncertain, 'We have as yet no certain Account of the Numbers killed, but its reckoned they may be about 800, amongst whom are several Persons of Distinction'. He counted fifteen officers and numerous subalterns that had been captured.[120] Rae gives two figures for Jacobite dead; 600 and 800, admitting that the Jacobites gave lower figures.[121] Jacobites minimized their losses, Mar writing, 'We have lost, to our Regret, the Earl of Strathmore, and the Captain Clan-Ranald. Some are missing; but their Fate we are not sure of. The Earl of Panmure, Drummond of Logy and Lieutenant Colonel Maclean are wounded.'[122] Another writer gives Jacobite losses as sixty dead and 'very few wounded'.[123] In addition, there were eighty Jacobites taken prisoner, the most exalted being Viscount Strathallan.[124] In contrast to the lenity allowed the Jacobites' prisoners, captured Jacobites were 'close confined'.[125] The injured Panmure was left in a cottage, guarded by a dragoon, but at night the peer was rescued.[126]

It is impossible to ascertain which of these figures is correct, except that the Jacobites' own figures are certainly far too low. Men fleeing the field and being pursued by enemy cavalry as occurred on the Jacobite left are likely to take severe losses, so the figures given by Argyle and Harrison are more probably nearer the truth. In any case, they were present on the battlefield on the following day and so were more likely to be able to give fairly accurate figures. Yet, proportionately speaking, the Jacobite battlefield losses were fewer than those of their enemy. Both sides, therefore, lost approximately the same number of men; proportionately Argyle had lost far more; a fifth compared to the tenth of the Jacobite forces which had been lost. On the face of it, Argyle could simply not afford such losses.

Jacobite losses went beyond manpower. Argyle stated that they had lost four cannon, ammunition carts, baggage carts, thirteen flags and the royal standard, titled the Restoration. Harrison confirmed these numbers.[127]

Furthermore, Argyle's soldiers apparently returned from the field loaded with booty.[128]

So who won the battle? Clearly this was not a clear-cut result, as were Blenheim or Poltava, or Preston, though in the first two cases the wars which these were part of were far from at an end because of their results. Neither army was destroyed and neither was wholly routed. Often it is described as being indecisive for these very reasons. Yet since Argyle prevented Mar's army marching south, the strategic victory must go to Argyle. It was not the decisive battle that Preston had been, for the campaign was to continue for some months. But what it had done is to deny the Jacobite army the prospect of ultimate victory which would have been a possibility had Argyle's army been destroyed.

Following the battle of guns and swords there came a battle of words. Both sides claimed the victory. Argyle, typically modest, informed his political masters in London that 'The Victory we have got is owing to Providence, for my own part, I pretend no further merit than having done my best'. He bestowed praise on the troops, stating that they 'deserve His Majesty's favour' and commended the behaviour of his officers and that of the squadron of volunteers. He was downbeat about the immediate prospects of the campaign, though, writing, 'we cannot hope always to beat three times our number' and looked forward to the arrival of the Dutch auxiliary forces. Colonel Harrison was despatched to London to tell Townshend the news.[129] Yet a contemporary letter stated, 'Our troops . . . are very hearty and desirous of meeting the rebels a second time'.[130] Despite Mar organizing victory celebrations, some of his men knew better. Keith assigned the battle the status of a defeat for the Jacobites, 'thus ended the affair of Dunblane in which neither side gained much, however, but which was the entire ruin of our party'.[131]

On 22 November, Pulteney wrote a similar letter to Argyle:

> I wish I cou'd express my joy to your Grace upon an occasion so happy to your self and Country; in which you have given the Enemys to His Majesty's Crown strong occasion to understand that they are to expect from you when you shall be augmented by the forces designed for you. The Blow you have given them with your small Numbers having already dampen'd their fire, no question but the next will extinguish the last support of the Rebellion.[132]

The medium- and long-term impacts of the battle was even more important to the campaign's outcome than what happened on the field, though these eventualities would not have resulted had the fighting taken a different turn. We shall now examine the battle's later results which only became apparent in subsequent days and weeks.

Chapter 8

The End of the Campaign, 1715–1716

In public both Argyle and Mar proclaimed that their army had been victorious, but in private both were extremely apprehensive. After the battle there was a period of uncertainty for both armies, but both knew that the conflict was far from over.[1] The Jacobite cause was not at an end and nor was their army no longer potentially threatening. Although Argyle acknowledged that he had triumphed at Sheriffmuir, he observed on 15 November 1715 that the Jacobites were 'just in the same situation as they were, before they advanced'. He believed that they were at Perth and Auchterarder, gathering together their forces as a prelude to a second advance against Stirling. He could hardly expect a second 'miracle'. All he could do was to implore the government that the Dutch forces arrive and so an end to the campaign be made, 'I most heartily wish for His Majesty's service that they may arrive in time'.[2]

Ironically, the Jacobites' intelligence was equally poor; they too thought that there might be an offensive against them, Sinclair writing, 'we had several alarmes of the Duke of Argyle's comeing to attack us . . . which frightened us prodigiouslie'.[3] On 22 November, Mar wrote that he had heard that Argyle was about to take the offensive, adding 'He certainly knows our condition and tis not unlikely that the severeness of our numbers may make him attempt it'.[4]

Unbeknown to Argyle, matters in the Jacobite camp made it impossible for them to have mounted an offensive. They just did not have the manpower after Sheriffmuir to have done so. Mar complained, 'Amongst many good Qualities, the Highlanders have one unlucky Custom, not easy to be reform'd; which is, that generally after an action they return Home. Accordingly, a great many went off after the Battle of Sheriffmuir; so that the Earl of Mar not being in a Condition to pursue the Advantage he had by it, was forc'd to return to Perth.' Such had happened in the previous century and it was to do so again. They did not return, in part because the much promised supplies from abroad did not appear, nor had the Duke of Berwick. Many of the leading Jacobites went home because their money was running out and some went without asking leave.[5] Sinclair wrote, 'The greatest part of our two thousand Highlanders, who stay'd with us at the battle went home with the enemies' plunder, and the Chiefs of the neighbouring Clans were sent out to bring back what they could of their men, but with very bad success'.[6]

Breadalbane's 300 men also went home, as did most of Marischal's. Strathmore and Auchterhouse being killed at Sheriffmuir, their men left the army, as did Panmure's, though he was only badly wounded. Some cited their lack of money as a reason for leaving. Sinclair wrote, 'It was easie to see, by no complaints being made of these gentlemen who left us, and as few endeavours to bring them back, and our recruiteing onlie in Perth from one another, that our dissolution was drauing near'.[7]

Keith recalled the demoralizing effects of the result of the news of the surrender at Preston. Several leading Jacobites at Perth, 'seeing that the English, which we always looked on as our principal strength, were quelled . . . began to think of making terms for themselves'.[8] Others did, too 'the melanchollie account was confirmed from all hands' as Sinclair wrote, adding, 'One might imagine that all this storm threatening to break upon us, at a time when we were abandoned by the whole world'.[9] Eventually Mar wrote to James that the surrender at Preston, 'I'm afraid will putt a stop to any more riseings in that country at this time'.[10]

It was not only the news of the surrender of the Jacobite army at Preston that was disconcerting for the Jacobite cause. Sir John Mackenzie, who was in command of the Jacobite garrison at the castle and town of Inverness, had been threatened by the Earl of Sutherland with men of his own clan, and those of Ross, Fraser, Munro, Forbes and Mackay. On 10 November Mackenzie was summoned to surrender the city. Although he initially refused and withdrew his small garrison of 300 men to the castle whilst they occupied the city, he clearly realized the position was untenable and left on the following day.[11]

The loss of manpower in terms of desertions and the Jacobite defeats elsewhere were grim news for those still at Perth. Worse was to come, as some Jacobites clearly saw that defeat and all that implied was staring them in the face and there was no plausible military solution open to them any more. According to Keith, Huntley headed the faction in the Jacobite army which wanted to ask for terms. Some also suspected that Mar, contrary to his pronouncements in public, had also made overtures towards the government, too. Some did not believe that James would ever arrive and so pressed Mar to negotiate.[12]

There followed much discussion, argument and lobbying among the Jacobites. Argyle was aware of this, writing 'I am in hopes tho cannot answer for it that there are some differences among the rebels which may prove fortunate'.[13] Cameron argued, 'it would be the greatest hardship imaginable to enter into any termes with the Government till once we were assured what had become of the King'.[14] Eventually Mar surprised his detractors by proposing that Colonel Lawrence, the most senior Government officer taken by the Jacobites at Sheriffmuir, should be sent from Dundee to Argyle with proposals for negotiation.[15] At the same time, Mar, despite his public utterances, was involved in securing his own safety by employing one Methuen to 'use his credit to get terms from the enemy in favour of Mar' and continued to do so until the end of the year.[16] Yet, unlike the case in 1691, the government decreed that there would be no negotiations with rebels and so the conflict continued.

Mar wrote a despondent letter to James on 24 November, concerned that his master should know the worst before his arrival to a potentially disappointing situation. He tried to present, as ever, an optimistic future, however: 'I have been doing all I can ever since to get the armie together again, and I hope considerable numbers may come in a little time'. Yet, fearing the imminent arrival of the Dutch troops to reinforce Argyle, the immediate military prospects for the Jacobites looked grim, 'I am afraid we shall have much difficultie in making a stand anywhere, save in the Highlands, where we shall not be able to subsist'. He looked forward to James's arrival, which he believed would 'certainly give new life to your friends and make them do all in their power for your service'. But this alone might not be enough, 'but how far they would be able to resist such a form'd body of regular troops as will be against them I must leave your Majesty to judge'. Such a disparity of numerical strength 'unless your Majesty have troops with you, which I am afraid you have not, I see not how we can oppose them'.[17]

Meanwhile, Argyle was optimistic. He was pleased to hear of the success of Scots loyalists at Inverness. According to him, Lovat's retaking of the town was 'of infinite service to His Majesty'. Meanwhile, he learnt that Major General Cadogan would be sent to Scotland, which would be 'very agreeable to me' and was glad to hear that the Dutch troops were on the march towards him.[18] Cornet Kennedy was glad of his arrival, 'I believe he will have this good effect and that his account of things will be more credited at court'.[19] Townshend told him that with the Jacobites in Lancashire defeated, the Dutch could be wholly sent northwards. This would make a considerable force in Scotland and so an additional lieutenant general should be sent – Cadogan – 'as the person who is best acquainted with the Dutch Troops, and who His Majesty judges will be most acceptable to your Grace'. After all, he had played a leading role in the negotiations at The Hague as to their despatch.[20]

Additional troops were only arriving in a trickle. It was on 4 December that the first of the Dutch troops were sighted. Argyle reported that part of the Dutch contingent, Swiss soldiers, had arrived by ship at Leith on that day. Yet another six days passed and there was no sign of any more, nor of Cadogan. Stanhope's dragoons were at Linlithgow on 13 December and Newton's were at Edinburgh on the following day. Another 1,200–1,500 Dutch troops disembarked at Edinburgh. Yet he believed it would be some time before the campaign would be over. After all, it had taken two years to subdue the earlier Jacobite rebellion of 1689–91. Argyle wrote that 'the soonest that the rebellion can be entirely crush'd' was the summer of 1716. In any case, they could not act aggressively against the Jacobites until the weather improved and all the Dutch troops had arrived. Both Cadogan and Argyle wished that they could offer terms to the Jacobites still in arms in order to reduce their numbers, for there were mixed messages about arrivals and departures from the Jacobite base at Perth, but this was not to be.[21]

At least the balance of forces was now in favour of the government. There had certainly been a diminution of Jacobite strength in and around Perth since the brief high-water mark of early November. Cockburn's reports gave the Jacobites 3,000 men at Perth, 200 on the bridge of Earn, with Panmure's battalion at Dunkeld and Strathmore's at Dundee. Their cavalry was housed on the north side of the Tay. Keith estimated their strength was 4,000 infantry and 500 cavalry. Some believed that Huntley might now be raising men in the north. But Mar's attitude was defensive, with a ditch and palisade being built around Perth.[22]

The poor weather certainly put a brake on the progress of Argyle's operations. Artillery from the Tower of London was on board ships in the Nore but could not leave the ice-bound ports. Therefore a train of artillery (ten cannon and four mortars, with ammunition and other accoutrements) was fetched from Berwick by 1,500 draught animals with 500 men.[23] Guns could not be taken from ships because they could not be moved very far on land without carriages. Naval gunners were not of use because they were not 'versant in leading the artillery'.[24]

On 22 December James finally set foot on Scottish soil, for the first and last time, and Mar met him at Peterhead on the following day, but James became ill and so it was not until 9 January 1716 that they made a public entry into Perth. Argyle was not certain how easy it would be to take Perth from the Jacobites, but at least he now had a far stronger army than in the previous year. The troops at their disposal were nine battalions of British infantry, which numbered, on 2 January, 2,895 men plus officers; seven regiments of cavalry, numbering 864 men plus officers, and then Lieutenant General Reiner Vincent van der Beck's Dutch and Swiss troops, theoretically 6,000 strong but numbering 'not over 5,000 men'.[25]

Against these forces, the Jacobites could only offer a vastly depleted force, as calculated in December 1715/January 1716, as being but 4,124 infantry and 269 cavalry.[26] It was on 29 January, despite the snow, that Argyle led the main army northwards from Stirling.[27] A council of war was held by the Jacobites at Perth. The question was whether to fight or to retreat. Most of the officers and soldiers were enthusiastic for a clash of arms, 'so keen for fighting that they could not be restrained'. Mar disagreed with this and with his king, explaining that the great expectations of support from the Duke of Ormonde's projected rising in the South-West had come to nothing and that there had been no aid from abroad.[28] He concluded, 'All this put us into an absolute Necessity of leaving Perth and retiring Northwards, which we did in good order'. The stated aim was to march to Inverness and retake the city, which it was deemed an easy matter to have done, then fight there, 'and so put the affair to the decision of a battle'.[29]

The retreat and the subsequent pursuit began. On 31 January Argyle's men crossed the River Earn without any opposition and advanced to Tullibardine, only eight miles away from Perth. At four that afternoon, Argyle learnt of the Jacobite flight from Perth, so ordered an advance guard of 400 dragoons and 1,000 infantry to proceed towards the Jacobites' former headquarters, and they arrived at ten o'clock on the morning of the first day of February. Cadogan and Argyle arrived the same day.

On 2 February there was no let-up in the pursuit. Argyle advanced with six squadrons of dragoons, three battalions of infantry and a further 800 infantry from various battalions. They reached Errol that day. On the next day this advance guard was at Dundee, which their fellows reached on 4 February. On the 3rd, Argyle had sent a detachment forward to Arbroath, within eight miles of Dundee. Argyle did not think he would be able to overtake the Jacobites. Yet he would pursue the Jacobites until they dispersed.

At Montrose on 4 February, Mar had evidently come to the conclusion that the army's military prospects were minimal. He therefore advised James to depart to France while he still could. Mar initially said he would try and dissuade James from leaving. Yet there was a ship, the *Maria Teresa* of St. Malo, of 90 tons, bound for France in the harbour and on the following day, James, Mar and a few others boarded it and left Scotland forever.

Their departure went unannounced and at a council of war held at Aberdeen the army decided to march to Castle Gordon and there consult with Huntley. If he agreed to join them, they would then march on Inverness. Otherwise they would disperse, which is what they did as Huntley was negotiating with Argyle. It was 14 February that the remainder of the already disintegrating army ceased to exist. Keith added, 'From there every one took the road pleased him best'.[30]

Once Argyle was at Aberdeen, and on hearing reports of the dispersal of the Jacobites either to their homes or in the case of numerous officers, to France, he decided that he did not need to march all the army to Aberdeen. Over the next few days he received in person and by letter, several offers of surrender and requests for mercy. As before, he could only reply that he personally could not give any assurances. Troops and civil magistrates were to search for and arrest any Jacobites found still to be in arms. Four regiments of dragoons were ordered to Inverness and castles (including those of Seaforth and Mackintosh) were garrisoned by troops and militia. Sutherland would disarm the Seaforth men and troops began to march to numerous towns in the Highlands.

Unlike the case of 1691 there was no negotiated surrender. For the hundreds of Jacobite prisoners taken, mostly at Preston, charged with the crime of treason, their fates were variable. Many were put on trial. Those taken in England fared worse. A total of 50, including the Earl of Derwentwater and Kenmure, were executed in the north-west of England and in London in 1715–16, but far more, 638, were transported to the American colonies or the West Indies. Others died in prison. Some such as Forster and Mackintosh, escaped. Yet those taken in Scotland were either released or if they were tried at Carlisle, none suffered death or transportation. In both cases, any still in prison in 1717 were released by an Act of Grace. Landowners often had their lands confiscated; this was more thorough in England than Scotland.

Recently historians have stressed that the government was neither weak nor savage in its treatment of the Highlands in 1716, as was not the norm hitherto. What retribution there was fell mainly on the Catholics in northern England and even this was less than that meted out to the unsuccessful rebels in south-west England in 1685. This policy was dictated by the good sense that civil society needed to be knitted together after the traumatic experience of rebellion. Clemency was thus indicated. Furthermore, Scottish Whig elites were Scottish as well as Whig and were ready to come to terms with their Jacobite neighbours. Whether in retrospect this was sound policy is another question, for some of those reprieved were to rebel again.

Chapter 9

The Battle of Glenshiel, 10 June 1719

After the defeat of the Jacobites in 1715–16 there was little stability either internally or externally for the British state. At home there was a split in the hitherto successful Whig administration under Robert Walpole (1676–1745). He resigned, as did his brother-in-law, Townsend, over the handling of policy in the Baltic. The troops raised in 1715 to deal with the Jacobite threat were disbanded by 1717, Walpole stating that a standing army of only 12,000 men was needed. Although Britain was now enjoying friendly relations with France, there were two foreign challengers allied to the Jacobite cause. The first was relatively easily dealt with. Papers found in the property of the Swedish ambassador, the Count of Gyllenborg, suggested that Sweden had not lost its sympathy for the Jacobite cause and was planning to send troops to invade Britain. He was expelled and in the following year his royal master, Charles XII, was killed during a siege and the beleaguered Swedes, at war with Russia and Denmark, had even less wish for additional foes.

Opportunity for the Jacobites came from Spain, a country sympathetic to the Jacobite cause in 1715, though at that point only interested in delivering financial aid, which arrived too late. In 1717 Spain wanted to reclaim her Italian provinces of Naples and Sardinia, that had been lost to Austria, and Sicily, which had gone to Savoy, at the Peace of Rastadt in 1714. A fleet and army were despatched to Sardinia, in the summer of 1717 in direct breach of international obligations and the lightly-defended island was soon taken.

In November 1716 Britain and France had signed an alliance, with the Dutch Republic joining in January 1717. They promised to assist one another with naval and military aid if one of the other was attacked, and also to provide aid in the case of internal rebellion. They agreed to uphold the provisions of the Peace of Utrecht and Rastadt. It was known as the Triple Alliance and steps were taken to encourage Charles VI of Austria to join but he was reluctant because he refused to acknowledge Philip V as King of Spain, they having been in conflict since 1702 over the Spanish inheritance. Yet with the Spanish invasion of Sardinia he became more interested in their overtures.

Sicily was invaded in the following year and by August 1718 Austria joined what was now known as the Quadruple Alliance. James Stanhope, Secretary of State and leading British minister, travelled to Paris and Madrid to try and resolve the matter diplomatically, at the same time as sending Admiral George Byng with a naval squadron to the Mediterranean. Cardinal Alberoni, Philip V's chief minister, refused to back down, despite Stanhope offering him Gibraltar.

In the meantime, there had been a naval battle at Cape Passarro, which was a major British victory and resulted in most of the Spanish fleet being either sunk or captured. Despite political controversy at home over both the battle and the alliance, when Stanhope returned he obtained Parliamentary approval and so in December 1718 Britain and France went to war with Spain.

Meanwhile, Jacobite representatives, including Ormonde, had arrived at Madrid. As in 1708, British intervention in Europe led to her worsted enemy seeking to play the Jacobite card. Alberoni agreed to send a major fleet to England and a smaller force to Scotland as a diversion. On 15 March 1719, Lord Stair, British Resident in Paris, got wind of the Spanish fleet and implored James Craggs, Secretary of State, 'press ye fitting out of ye ships, raise as many troops as you can and send to the Dutch to have their troops ready. The Spanish could not sail before ye 7 or 8 of the month. I hope our squadron will be ready in time. I think ye Duke of Orlean's heartily in earnest to help us, but it is good not to want French assistance.' Craggs seemed less alarmed than Stair, however, replying that 'I can't say His Majesty is extreaamly alarmed', but agreed that something had to be done: 'However, it will be necessary to take the proper precautions'.[1]

On 10 March an announcement about the suspected Spanish invasion was made. It was not made earlier for fear that it might have an adverse effect on national credit. It was decided to put Cadogan in charge of four battalions of infantry and eighteen squadrons of cavalry and send these to the West Country. Admiral Norris had gone to Portsmouth to take command of seven ships in the harbour there. He was confident enough, 'I do not doubt to be able to give a very good account of a dozen Spanish ships'. Additional ships under the Earl of Berkeley, perhaps eight or ten, would soon be joining him. In the Dutch Republic Lord Stanhope was negotiating for Dutch troops to be sent over as they had been four years previously. He was hoping for only four battalions this time, to be shipped from Ostend.[2]

The Spanish fleet was to have 4,000 infantry and 900 cavalrymen aboard. It would be escorted by seven warships from Cadiz and Ormonde was to accompany them. This was on 7 March NS.[3] Meanwhile, Craggs was informing Stair on 16 March that assistance from both the Dutch and the Austrians had been offered. The best that the French could offer was to attack the Spanish on land and so divert Spanish military effort to Spain.[4] Charles, Baron Whitworth, the

British Minister in the Republic, 'hath had several conferences with the States Deputies and we are assured that if the Pretender or his adherents attempt a Descent . . . their High Mightinesses will send his Britannick Majesty a competent number of Troops to frustrate their Enterprize'.[5]

Colonel John Huske (c.1692–1761) was sent to hire the necessary transport ships and to arrange provisioning. The men were to be embarked at Williamstadt. To ensure that the battalions sent were up to full strength, soldiers from other battalions were to be drafted into them; five were to be sent in all.[6] The actual request came later and Whitworth was in conference with the Dutch deputies at the beginning of April.[7]

By mid-April, 2,500 Dutch auxiliaries had arrived in Britain.[8] Two of these battalions were Swiss, both from Sturler's regiment. They arrived on the Thames and were initially quartered near Tilbury Fort in Essex. The other three battalions were all Dutch; Amerongen's, Huffel's and Sixma's. They were sent to the north of England and then to Edinburgh. In command was Major General Keppel with Major General Welderen as second-in-command.[9] Government troops were also marched to the locations where invasion was anticipated. As in 1715, battalions from Ireland were brought over to the mainland, those of Sabine, Egerton, Chudleigh and Inchingbrooke's foot arriving at Minehead and Bristol.[10]

There was alarm in England more generally, with Joseph Symson, a Kendal merchant, writing on 16 March, 'We are full of fears about the Spanish invasion, which makes all trade of a stand here'.[11] Timothy Cragg, a Lancashire man, wrote in April, 'This spring there was much talk of the Spaniards invading this Land and in the latter end of this month it was said there was some persons landed in the north-west of Scotland who were against this Government'.[12]

The main Spanish invasion fleet left Cadiz on 7 March NS and was joined by other ships at Corunna. There were only provisions for twenty-one days for the men aboard. There were also 30,000 muskets on the ships too. Apparently on 26 March James Stuart arrived at Madrid and was given a sumptuous reception.[13] However, the fleet's voyage was unsuccessful. At the end of March it was dispersed by winds and was scattered 'in a very miserable condition and some were still missing'. There was no need for the Royal Navy vessels off Ireland and Penzance to worry.[14]

Yet there was another threat. On 8 March NS two Spanish frigates sailed from Port Passage to Kintail. On board were 307 Spanish infantry. There were also 2,000 muskets and three Jacobite lords with their servants. They arrived at their destination of 27 April OS. The Spanish lieutenant colonel in charge had been told that they would joined there by 10,000 Highlanders.[15]

On 4 April Keith, veteran of Sheriffmuir, and his companions arrived at the Isle of Lewis. They remained there several days until the two Spanish frigates came. They then went across to Stornoway and Keith was made a colonel in the Spanish army. They had to decide whether to stay on the island, awaiting news of Ormonde and the main expedition, or make for the mainland. Tullibardine was in favour of the first option but the majority were for the latter as to stay risked being trapped there by the Royal Navy.[16]

It was believed that there were only 300 Government soldiers at Inverness, but even so, it was decided to wait until additional support had arrived. It was then that Tullibardine took charge, showing his credentials as lieutenant general. Marischal resigned his command. He had only been in command of the ships due to an order from Alberoni. So they stayed on the island, but there were protests against this and eventually they arrived on the mainland with a view to Marischal and Campbell marching on Inverness with the Spanish and 500 Highlanders as promised by Seaforth.[17]

The troops at Perth were Clayton's battalion, reinforced by dragoons, and the latter had arrived on 30 April. They had marched without a break from Haddington, travelling between 20–24 miles per day. Horses and men were thus exhausted. Montagu's battalion was expected imminently. Clayton and Lord Strathmore met Lord Gordon and were well received. They hoped that he would not be joining the Jacobites. They did not know when or where the Jacobites were to attack, but believed there were only 300–400 Highlanders in revolt and that some had gone to Skye to raise additional support.[18]

Yet, according to Keith, 'the same daemon who inspired them with the design of staying on Lewis hinder'd them from accepting this proposition'. Marischal had already sent a circular letter to the clan chiefs, urging them to do nothing until there was news that the Spanish forces had arrived in England. There was no such news and Tullibardine suggested they should return to Spain.[19] Marischal opposed this and, being in charge of the ships, had them sent back, only three days before a flotilla of Royal Navy vessels arrived. It was believed that the Jacobites had been distributing arms in the form of Spanish muskets; 160 to the Mackintoshes, 700 to the Clanranalds, 400 to the Macleods, 800 to the Camerons and 900 to Seaforth's.[20]

Rumours began to circulate about the Jacobite attempt. Letters from Scotland dated 29 April told of the Spanish landing at Kintail, but that they had soon left due to sickness among the troops. Apparently there had been two ships with 400 soldiers. Another report, two days later, reported that the Jacobites had built huts and houses for themselves within two miles of the landing zone. A total of 500 men had been seen together, these being mainly Spanish, but there was also allegedly 60 Scottish and Irish gentlemen and officers.

Tullibardine was identified as their leader, but his force was revised down to being 400 at most. There were Jacobite outposts 12 miles distant from the main camp, but it was thought that the expedition was to remain stationary until they heard of the Spanish invasion of England.[21]

Additional troops were sent to Scotland. At the beginning of May it was stated that in Scotland and on the borders there were four battalions of infantry and three regiments of dragoons, Dutch troops, totalling 6,000 men in all. Wightman had sent one battalion to Fort William, another to Inverness and had reinforced Dumbarton Castle. The remainder of the forces was being marched to form a camp near Perth. Carpenter was to have overall command, however.[22]

Yet the Jacobite threat was not seen as being particularly dangerous. The king had gone to Hanover, arriving on 18 May, to conduct diplomacy, leaving lords justices to administer the country in his absence (these including Stanhope, Argyle and Marlborough).[23] The Spanish troops were discounted as an effectual force, 'much harassed and fatigued by their voyage': it was deemed that they were merely waiting to surrender. It was not thought that there was any significant number of Scottish Jacobites in being.[24] A later report gave the Jacobites 400 Spanish troops and 140 English and Scottish gentlemen.[25]

At nine in the morning of 10 May three Royal Navy ships arrived at Eilean Donan Castle, garrisoned by forty-two Spanish soldiers. A naval lieutenant was sent under a flag of truce to ask the garrison to surrender. Their reply was to fire cannon at the boat carrying him, so he returned. Later that day, at four in the afternoon, a deserter from the castle told them that the Jacobite force numbered 4,700 at their camp two miles away (a huge exaggeration). At eight in the evening the frigates fired at the castle and sent two boats, each under the command of a lieutenant to land at the foot of the castle. After a short resistance the castle garrison surrendered. After the prisoners of war had been removed, Captain Hardman of HMS *Enterprise* used twenty-seven barrels of gunpowder to blow up the castle. Barns nearby which held corn for the Jacobite army were also destroyed.[26]

On 23 May Captain Hildesley of HMS *Flamborough* arrived in Edinburgh with his Spanish prisoners. One man of the latter supplied information about the Spanish part of the expedition without any reserve. Carpenter told Wightman that if the Jacobites left then 400–500 men should be sent with Colonel Clayton aboard the *Flamborough* to follow them. Clayton had done likewise in 1716.[27]

Wightman arrived on 24 May at Inverness. His task was not thought to be an onerous one as it was thought that the Spanish would surrender when they sighted Government troops and that the number of Jacobites was limited to those who had come from abroad. There was some naval support rendered by HMS *Dartmouth* and HMS *Assistance* observing the Jacobites and destroying what they could.[28]

Apparently the Spanish found the Scottish climate difficult, 'they were surprised with ye temperature . . . of our air . . . and much more of the heat of ye long summer . . . as they marched through Scotland, Colen, one of ye strongest and healthiest of their men suffocated with ye heat, dropt down dead and never recover'd'.[29]

Meanwhile, being unable to retreat, Tullibardine desired to go over to the offensive and 'now he resolved to draw what troops he cou'd together, but it was too late'. The circular letters already sent out gave the chiefs an excuse for inaction, so depriving the Jacobites of support they needed and their enemy was making preparations against them. News that the main Spanish fleet had been dispersed came at this time, but also that another was in preparation. According to Keith, 'They left us still some hopes'.[30]

With the lack of real news, rumours about fighting in Scotland were heard in London. On 6 June there was a report that Wightman had attacked the Jacobites and beaten them. Ten days later a man was arrested in the capital for handing around a forged letter relating how Wightman had been defeated in battle and killed.[31] Yet the danger was seen now as being more severe, with Cobham's and Kerr's dragoons and Chomley's foot being sent to the west coast of Scotland.[32]

Wightman marched his forces from Inverness on 5 June, concerned about his dire supply situation and being unhappy about having to march before it had been resolved. Marching south-west by Loch Ness and then westwards his little army soon found their enemy.

The forces facing each other in battle were the following:

Jacobite Army:
Seaforth's men, 500.
Cameron of Lochiel, 150–300 men.
MacGregors, under Rob Roy's son, and volunteers, 50–100 men.
Lidcoat's, 100.
MacKinnons, 50–80.
Others, 50.
MacKenzies, 200.
MacIntoshes, 170.
Rory Mcleod from Glenelg, 50 men.
Donald MacDonald, 50 men.
MacDougal of Lorn, 10 men.[33]

Keith thought there were 1,000 Highlanders; Wightman wrote of there being 1,640. Another estimate gave 1,660 total and also 900 Highlanders and 270 Spanish.[34] The above numbers suggest an army from 1,380–1,610 men. There were also others on their way, but they never arrived.

>Spanish forces:
>Companies of Don Pedro de Castrois's regiment of infantry.
>Colonel
>Five captains
>Five lieutenants
>Six ensigns
>11 sergeants
>18 corporals
>6 drummers
>221 privates.
>Total 274 men.[35]

The Scots were not in high morale, as Keith noted, 'and even those seemed not very fond of the enterprise'.[36]

Their opponents were as follows:

>Right wing:
>Colonel Clayton
>Major Miliburn's grenadiers (150), Montagu's battalion under Colonel Lawrence (434), Huffell's Dutch battalion, four companies of Amerongen's Dutch battalion, Colonel Harrison's 50 men, Strathaver's 56 Highlanders under Ensign McKay.
>Centre:
>Major General Wightman
>Major Robertson's 120 dragoons.
>4 x Cohorn mortars.
>Left wing:
>Clayton's battalion (406), 90 Monroes under Monroe of Cullcairn.

Total strength: Uncertain. Usually given as 850 excluding Highlanders and dragoons. However, figures for Montagu's and Claytons for July are known and are quoted above. They and the grenadiers alone add up to 900, so estimating 500 for Huffell's and perhaps 200 for Amerongen's, a grand total of all units is perhaps about 2,000. They had, then, a slight numerical edge over their opponents.[37]

Sample of Soldiers who fought at Glenshiel[38]

Name	Unit	Age	Service length	Parish	Occupation
George Thorn	Montagu's	34	12		
William Davis	Clayton's	63	23		
Alexander Gordon		32	2	Galloway	Servant
Thomas Thomson		39	18	Wicklow	Carpenter
John Newby		24	4	Stony Stratford	Weaver
John Young		31	3		
George Mercer		31	7		
Thomas Brende		31	11		
Daniel MacDonald	Montagu's	43	8	Banff-shire	Shoemaker
Thomas Harris	Montagu's	41	9	Near Leeds	Farmer
Bryan Rollins		23	4	Blakesly	Baker
John Bradford		29	2		
Alexander Neil		35	5		
John Baker		40	8		
John Home		48	17		
Hugh Farquharson		41	8		
Martin Rolebanks		30	15		
John McEwan		39	12		
Philip Tingley		45	22		
Robert Nicholson	Montagu's	36	11		
John Childerhouse		40	14		
Patrick Foster		50	17		

Early on 10 June, at six in the morning, the Jacobites marched from their camp at Kintail for the pass of Glenshellbegg, 'which every body thought the properest place for defence.'[39] Reports came to the Jacobites that the British forces were marching from Inverness towards them, with over 1,200 cavalry and infantry.[40] According to Keith, their enemies were made up of four battalions of infantry, a part battalion of the same and 150 dragoons.[41]

Men came in in dribs and drabs to the Jacobite banner. Concerned that insufficient numbers might come in, the Jacobites looked for suitable ground on which to fight, moving three miles from Glenshiel in order to view the passes in the glen, 'hoping to maintain the Rough Ground till the people that were expected should come up on the seventh'. Seaforth met them and told that he had brought 500 of his own men 'who, it was thought, would heartily defend their own Country'. On 8 June Rob Roy's son brought a company of men, who, with volunteers, came to another eighty. Next evening one Lidocat and 100 men arrived, as did Lord George Murray (1694–1760), Tullibardine's younger brother, who had been scouting the enemy's position.[42]

Additional forces arrived, another fifty men at 10 in the morning and at 12 MacKinnon arrived with the same number. There were also men who were on the mountain tops but which did not descend to join the others.[43] These may have been the men who were described elsewhere thus, 'a Corps apart of 500 Highlanders, who were posted on a Hill, to make themselves Masters of our Baggage, it being always one of their Chief Aims'.[44]

It was on 5 June that Wightman's little army left Inverness, halting for one day at the head of Loch Ness.[45] Wightman wrote that he marched from Strachlony to the head of Glenshiel, where he had heard that the Jacobites were planning to defend. The dragoons made the march without the loss of a single horse.[46] Apparently on the evening of 8 June they had marched from Gilly whining to the braes of Glenmoriston. By the end of 9 June they were at Loch Claunie, four or five miles from the Jacobites.[47]

According to him the Jacobites abandoned their first post and retired to defend their camp. This may have been at about four in the afternoon.[48] However, this 'first post' could have been the detachment of men under Murray who Tullibardine noted as having 'retrd, keeping all the way about half a mile from hem till they came in our sight, which was at two o'clock in the afternoon'. The Government force then halted a half mile from the Jacobite lines.[49] Keith wrote that the Jacobite position was a strong one: 'the situation, was strong enough had it been well defended; our right was cover'd by a rivulet which was difficult to pass, and our left by a ravine, and in front the ground was so rugged and steep that it was almost impossible to come at us'.[50]

Wightman agreed, writing that it 'was another very strong Pass called Strachell' and that 'Their Dispositions for Defence were extraordinary, with the Advantages of Rocks, Mountains and Intrenchments'.[51] He later claimed, 'I gave them no Time, but immediately viewed their Situation, and having made my Disposition' attacked. There are various assessments as to when this took place. Wightman claimed it was 'about Five in the Afternoon'.[52]

Wightman's disposition was as follows. To the south of the River Sheil were, on the far left, Munro's Highlanders and then to their right, Clayton's battalion. To the north of the river, in the centre, were the dragoons and in front of them the Cohorn mortars. To their immediate right were the Dutch troops, then Harrison's men and then Montagu's battalion. On the right were the grenadiers, divided into three groups; first 120 men, then an officer and 24 men and lastly a sergeant with a dozen men. Furthest on the right were the Sutherlands.[53]

After a Jacobite council of war, Campbell was left to make the army's dispositions. The Jacobites were disposed as follows; south of the river and upon a little hill were 100–150 of Seaforth's men. They were led by Murray, the laird of MacDougal, Major Mackintosh and John of Avoch. In the centre, over the river, were the Spanish troops, reduced in number through sickness to only 200, another 50 men being left in the rear with the ammunition supplies. In the centre were also Brigadier MacKintosh, the Spanish colonel, Brigadier Campbell of Glenderwell and Tullibardine. Then Lochiel's men, then Lidcoat's, then the MacGregors, then the MacKinnons, then a further grouping of Seaforths led by Sir John Mackenzie of Coul and a final group of Seaforth's to the furthest left of all. These were Seaforth's best men and with them were Marischal and Brigadier Campbell of Ormidale.[54] The baggage was guarded by thirty Spanish infantry in the rear. However, there was disquiet because it was believed that the British knew all that had passed within Jacobite counsels and there were divisions over leadership.[55]

Tullibardine imagined that the enemy would attack in the centre because that was where the land was least uneven and so that was where he positioned himself. There was an attack made on Lord George Murray's position by Clayton's battalion, who fired by platoon. According to Tullibardine, they 'fired several times at other without doeing great damage'. Although outnumbered, the Jacobites 'yet being equall in courage, and superior in their situation', repelled the first attacks, apparently 'with much loss'.[56] Then additional companies of Clayton's were thrown into the attack and by the time the third detachment were sent forward, 'that made most of these with Lord Geo. Run to the other side of a steep Burn'.[57]

One account claimed that they held out for two hours and were only forced to withdraw because of the mortar fire being directed upon them which 'smoaked them out of their stronghold'.[58] However, Murray, MacDougal and Avoch 'drawing their swords as crying to them to stand, but all would not do'.[59] Lacking any assistance, which Keith thought should have provided, the Jacobites had to fall back, though did so without much loss, nor did they inflict many casualties themselves.[60] One observer noted, 'the Rebels always as they had fired their Muskets, skipping off, and never venturing to come to close Engagements, were driven from Rock to Rock, our Men chasing them before them for above three hours'.[61] However, once the Jacobites in this part of the battle had reached the burn, 'they continued till all was over, it being uneasy for the enemy to pass the hollow Banks of that Burn'.[62] Apparently a 'straggling number of Highlanders' fired upon the men from Clayton's and the Munro Highlanders.[63]

There was an assault on the centre, with the dragoons marching towards the plain. They were supported by the mortars which fired shells at the entrenched Spanish infantry. This was followed by an attack by thirty-five dismounted dragoons on the Spanish, whilst other dragoons took part in the main attack on the right.[64] Wightman placed himself in the centre of the ground, 'where everyone had free Access to him for Orders'.[65] The baggage and guards with the field hospital also advanced, though stayed behind the main army, presumably for their own security.[66]

Then the Government troops on the right went over to the offensive. Tullibardine wrote, 'there Right began to move up the Hill from thence, to fall down on our left, but then they saw my Lord Seaforth's people, who were behind the steep Rock, they were oblig'd to attack them least they should been flanked in coming to us'. However, Coul's men, on seeing the attackers, mostly fled. Coul brought up additional forces to relieve the hard pressed Mackenzies. Seaforth also requested assistance. Brigadier Campbell of Ormidale came up to tell him that he feared that the centre was in danger of being attacked imminently. Thus the MacGregors and MacKinnons were dilatory in coming to the aid of the beleaguered left wing and indeed began to give way.[67] Yet another version relates that the fighting on the right lasted for two hours, with only fatigue and casualties causing the retreat. Seaforth tried to rally them, 'upon which he stept out before them brandishing his sword to rally them received a shott in the fleshy part of his arm'.[68]

Seeing this, Campbell then 'made all the despatch he could to join them'. But before he could get his men up the hill 'so as to be fairly in hands with the Enemy', Seaforth's men had mostly left the field. Seaforth himself had been wounded in the arm, presumably by a musket ball, so he had trouble escaping. This led to a more general withdrawal, with the MacGregors 'finding them going off, began to retyre'. Lidcoat, seeing this happen, then followed suit. Tullibardine wrote, 'the enemy, finding all give way on that hand, they turn'd there whole force there, which obliged us to march up the Camerons'.[69]

Yet the Camerons 'likewise drew off as the others had done'. With no other units left to support them, the Spanish had to retreat up the hill to their left. According to Tullibardine, the withdrawal was now universal, 'at last all began to run, tho' half had never once an opportunity to fire on the Enemy, who were heartned on seeing some of ours once give way, and our oun people as much discouraged, so that they could never be again brought to any thing'.[70] One observer wrote, 'Tullibardine, seeing all irreputably lost, called the Spanish and made an orderly retreat without the loss of any of the Spanish or others', keeping up a constant fire.[71]

The fighting had lasted for about three hours. Wightman claimed it concluded 'till past eight'. Although the Jacobites had retreated to the top of the mountain, the height hindered any immediate pursuit. The Government troops 'lay on their Arms all Night, in order to bring off the wounded'.[72] Apparently he withdrew from the field to the extent of leaving some of his wounded behind.[73]

When night came, the Jacobite leaders held a council of war. They lacked provisions and ammunition and morale was poor, 'the few troops they had had behaved in a manner not to give great encouragement to try a second action'. However, the Spanish Colonel Bolano offered to make a second attack, but Tullibardine thought that this would be in vain.[74] Most of the Scots had departed over the mountains.[75]

According to Tullibardine, he proposed next morning that they should continue the campaign, 'I then proposed to my Lord Marshall, Lochiell, Brigadier Campble and all present, that we should keep in a body with the Spaniards and march thro' the Highlands for some time till we could gather again in case of a Landing, or else should the King send instructions, the Highlanders would then rise and soon make up all that was past'. However, his suggestion was unsupported, for he went on to relate, 'But everybody declar'd against doing any thing further, for as things stood they thought it impracticable, and my Lord Marshiall with Brigadier Campble of Ormidale went off without any more adoe or so much as taking leave'.[76]

The Spanish declared 'they could neither live without bread nor make any hard marches thro' the Country'. Tullibardine gave them permission to capitulate and take the best terms they could obtain.[77] There was a lack of meal and flour. What magazines and provisions there were were destroyed on Tullibardine's orders by the MacGregors.[78]

On 11 June the Jacobites broke up: 'everybody else took the road he liked best'. According to a Spanish officer, Seaforth, Marischal and others had embarked that morning. That morning, Wightman's force marched into Glenshiel where he met a Spanish officer, who had a proposition to make to him. The Spanish negotiated a surrender, becoming prisoners on the understanding that their baggage would not be plundered. Wightman granted this and they came to his camp at two in the afternoon. The Spanish arms and ammunition were gathered up and the men marched away under escort. Keith had a fever and hid in the mountains for some months before taking a ship in early September from Peterhead to Holland.[79]

Many of the men on the field had never been engaged in the fighting. Apparently only 400 of the Highlanders fired a shot in anger.[80] Wightman thought that only 850 of his men were involved directly.[81] Tullibardine was not entirely dismayed, though he blamed Marischal, writing of the latter's 'ill concerted expedition'. He wrote 'if a Landing happens soon in England the Highlanders will still act their part'. Yet it was clear that he was not optimistic about the prospects of outside help which he thought was the only possibility of providing success:

> if the Expedition be retarded our being brought away so very unreasonably will I'm afraid ruin the King's Interest and faithfull Subject in these parts; seeing we came with hardly any thing that was realy necessary for such an undertaking of the King's immediate Instructions how to behave on all events that might happen, which was absolutely necessary; seeing nothing otherwise could be one to purpose among the people at Home without a landing in England, I and some others with the Clans concern'd with Endeavour to see private till we know how affairs are like to go . . .
>
>   . . . what a miserable condition we are now reduc'd, and his Majesty's affairs in these parts are infallibly at the brink of ruin unless there be some speedy Succour at hand. It is not to be imagin'd how much people are dispirited at the manner of our Coming and there has not been as yet so much as one word sent us from any that have the manadgement of affairs.[82]

After the battle, Carpenter went to Inverness to meet Wightman on 23 June.[83] Wightman was taking punitive steps against those in rebellion, as he told Carpenter, 'I am taking a tour through all the difficult parts of Seaforth's country, to terrify the Rebels by burning the houses of the Guilty and preserving those of the Honest'.[84]

Carpenter did his best to find who was involved in the campaign among the Highlanders, but given that only a few prisoners had been taken, was unable to do so or to find any evidence or witnesses. Wightman had 'used all possible means to put a Dread upon those who have been more immediately concerned in this late unnatural rebellion'. Carpenter found that it was impossible to capture any of the Highland participants with regular troops and suggested proclaiming that the rebellious clans hand in their weapons and agree to live peaceably in the future.[85] Unlike the case in 1715 or 1745 very few Scots prisoners were taken; a Dr Arnott, a Jacobite surgeon being one.[86]

As to the foreign troops involved, by August the Dutch had departed, with the Swiss leaving England via Newcastle. The Spanish prisoners of war had been marched from Inverness to Edinburgh on 27 June, where they were held for the next four months. Apparently they were treated with 'great humanity', though with money to subsist them running out, Wightman had to lend £50 to keep them fed. On 27 October, they too left Scotland.[87] They were exchanged for British seamen imprisoned by the Spanish.[88] Unlike the case in 1715 or 1745 most of the Jacobites did not suffer any retribution whatever except those who had their property damaged by Wightman's troops.

As for casualties, Wightman wrote on the day after the battle, 'I have not yet an exact Account of our killed and wounded, but judge them not to exceed 150, Officers included. By our next I will send an Exact List of our Loss'.[89] A Jacobite estimate put his losses at 400 killed and wounded, but this is a gross exaggeration.[90]

Killed

Unit	Captain	Lieutenant	Sergeant	Others	Total
Montagu	1	1	1	7	10
Clayton			2	1	3
Harrison				3	3
Huffell		1		3	4
Amerongen			1		1
Sutherlands				1	1
Munroes				3	3
Total	1	2	4	18	25

Wounded

Unit	Captain	Lieutenant	Sergeant	Others	Total
Montagu		2	1	35	38
Clayton	2		1	21	24
Harrison	1	1	1	14	17
Huffell	1		2	26	30
Amerongen				9	10
Sutherlands		1		3	4
Munroes	1	1		13	15
Total	5	5	5	121	137 [91]

Of the wounded, who later received pensions, most had received gunshot wounds (fourteen), but four had been injured in hand-to-hand combat; by sword, musket butt, bayonet and by being stabbed. One man had been hurt by a rock being thrown down during the fighting.[92] The dead captain was Downes, of Montague's.

Jacobite casualties were light. Wightman wrote, 'How much the Rebels have suffered is not yet perfectly known'.[93] Seaforth had been wounded in the arm and Lord George Murray in the leg.[94] One man claimed the Jacobites had lost but ten Highlanders killed or wounded.[95] Another source gives a total of a mere seven.[96]

Perhaps inevitably, Tullibardine was blamed for the defeat, 'for being entirely led by Campbell of Glenderell'.[97] The battle was an unequivocal victory for Wightman, though the Jacobites' initial expedition had been marred by disappointments which had undermined morale and discouraged potential support. It had been an unusual battle for a number of reasons. Firstly the Jacobites had been on the tactical defensive, unlike other battles save Preston and there had been no Highland charge, though the steep terrain barred this eventuality. Secondly it had lasted for about three hours, longer than most of the battles of these campaigns which were over in minutes or at most an hour. This was dictated by geography, the terrain not allowing any speedy movement by anyone. Thirdly it saw the first use of mortars in these campaigns; not seen again until 1745–6. It indicated, too, that the British army could fight and win in difficult terrain, despite taking higher casualties than the defenders, though assaulting troops must expect to incur heavier losses, at least at first. Finally it was the second smallest of the battles in these campaigns, in terms of numbers, but it was also one of the most decisive (ranking alongside Preston and Culloden) in that it ended the campaign, though with the majority of the Jacobites escaping unscathed. The Jacobites had been badly divided over whether to fight or not, lacking the main Spanish invasion as planned and this setback convinced the majority that to continue was hopeless.

With the Jacobite threat extinguished, Britain could spare troops to take the offensive overseas. Later that year a small British force landed in Spain and took the port of Vigo; among those taking part in this were men who would serve in the 1745 Jacobite campaign; Ligonier, Hawley and Wade. The war came to an end in January 1720, with Spain relinquishing the claims to her former Italian possessions and so returning to the status quo of 1714. However, despite the loss of this ally, Jacobite hopes were far from over.

1. Redcoats at the annual Killiecrankie re-enactment, July 2018.

2. Re-enactor Jacobites charge at Killiecrankie, July 2018.

3. Dunkeld Cathedral, scene of fierce fighting in 1689. (Author)

4. James Radcliffe, 3rd Earl of Derwentwater and an English Jacobite leader.
   (Author's collection)

5. Sheriffmuir monument erected in 1915.
   (Author)

6. Statue of Jacobite leader, Rob Roy
   MacGregor, Stirling. (Author)

7. Aberfeldy Bridge, Perthshire, built under General George Wade's supervision. (Author)

8. Charles Edward Stuart (1720–88). (Author's collection)

9. Lord George Murray and Prince Charles, pictured in stained glass windows in the shopping centre, Falkirk. (Author)

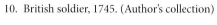

10. British soldier, 1745. (Author's collection)

11. Glenfinnan Monument commemorating the raising of the Jacobite standard in 1745. (Author's collection)

12. The battlefield of Prestonpans, viewed from the south. (Author)

13. Thomas Holles-Pelham, Duke of Newcastle (1693–1768), Secretary of State. (Author's collection)

14. Carlisle Castle, scene of the last two sieges on English soil in 1745. (Author)

15. Pulteney's battalion of infantry; re-enactment unit, outside Carlisle Castle. (Photograph taken by Mr Jepson in 1996)

16. Lord John Drummond, colonel of the French Royal Ecossais, portrayed in a stained glass window in the shopping centre, Falkirk. (Author)

17. Battle of Falkirk monument, erected in 1928. (Author)

William Augt. St : Duke of Cumberland
from a Painting by David Morier.

18. William Augustus, Duke of Cumberland (1721–65). (Author's collection)

19. View of Culloden Moor battlefield. (Author)

20. Monuments on Culloden Moor; clan graves and main monument in background. (Author's collection)

21. Culloden Cottage, scene of an alleged atrocity by Cumberland's men. Postcard in author's collection.

22. Well of the Dead, one of the many nineteenth-century monuments on the battlefield of Culloden. (Author's collection)

23. Main gateway to Fort George, near Inverness. (Author)

24. Main battlefield monument at Culloden to the Jacobites. (Author)

Chapter 10

New Life for the Jacobite Cause, 1720–1745

Internal peace reigned throughout the British Isles for a quarter of a century after the battle of Glenshiel. This is not to say that there was an absence of Jacobite sympathies throughout Britain nor a lack of conspiracies between 1720 and 1745. At the outset, in the wake of the financial crash known as the South Sea Bubble, Francis Atterbury, Bishop of Rochester, and Christopher Layer, a lawyer, had plotted to restore the Stuarts in the light of the said crisis which was also a major political scandal. It came to nothing, but did lay the foundations for the political supremacy of one of the Jacobites' staunchest foes.

This man was the architect of this period of peace, Sir Robert Walpole, once more chief minister to George I and his son and successor, George II, between 1721 and 1742. Walpole was opposed to any foreign entanglements that might lead to war, partly, it is true, for his own political purposes. Despite the wishes of George II, Walpole steered Britain away from military involvement in the War of the Polish Succession (1733–5), the only significant war in western and central Europe in the 1720s and 1730s. This was important because it meant that there would be no potential foreign backer for Jacobite schemes in Britain. Furthermore, the bulk of the peacetime army was on hand for defence if need be. At home Walpole strove to avoid controversy and kept direct taxation low. In Scotland, new fortresses were built, roads and bridges created by the army under Major General George Wade's direction, and a new Highland regiment was formed to police the north.

Yet there were two forces militating against Walpole's pacific desires. The first was that James Stuart had married the Polish Princess Clementina Walkinshaw and produced legitimate male heirs; Charles in 1720 and Henry in 1722. James was now too old and disinclined for further adventures as he had in 1708 and 1715–16, but his eldest son Charles was not and when he reached maturity in the early 1740s, international circumstances were looking favourable for the Stuart cause.

This was because in 1739 Britain and Spain went to war over commercial disputes in the Americas. This had been much against Walpole's wishes, but most of his government and Parliament wanted war. It brought mixed success, but soon became enveloped in a larger pan-European war from 1740, known as the War of the Austrian Succession. Frederick II of Prussia declared war on Austria and France joined in the war against Britain's old ally, with whom she had signed the Pragmatic Sanction to safeguard the succession. In 1743 George II (with most of the soldiers who took prominent commands in the battles in Britain of 1745–6) led an Allied army at Dettingen to victory over the French. As with France in 1708 and Spain in 1718, France now wanted to invade Britain in retaliation and to use the Jacobites in this scheme. By now Walpole had fallen from power and the government was in the hands of former supporters of his, Thomas Holles Pelham (1694–1768), the Duke of Newcastle, and his brother Henry Pelham, who had served as a captain at the battle of Preston.

The French massed ships and troops (twenty battalions of infantry and two regiments of cavalry) under their foremost general, the Marshal de Saxe, at their northern ports. The intention was to sweep across to Essex and seize London. With them would be Charles Stuart, who had left Rome incognito for France the previous year. Yet invasions of Britain are more easily said than done. As in 1708 and 1719, so it was in March 1744. Bad weather played havoc with the French ships before Admiral Norris's squadrons could be brought to bear. A relieved French army remained on the Continent as war was finally officially declared on Britain.

Charles was not easily perturbed. There had been Jacobite agents in both England and France in previous years, canvassing support there for a new restoration attempt. However, much support was contingent on Charles bringing substantial amounts of French aid in the way of arms, money and crucially troops. John Murray of Broughton (1720–77), one such agent, told him, 'if he could prevail upon the French to give him 6000 men and 30,000 lewis d'or and ten thousand Stand of arms, that he was charged to tell him he would be joined upon his landing by a great number of friends, but if he Could not obtain these Succours it was impossible for them to do anything for him.'[1]

French military success in the Austrian Netherlands, which included a costly victory over the Allied army under the King's son, William Augustus, Duke of Cumberland (1721–65), at Fontenoy in May 1745 followed by the capture of a number of towns and fortresses made French intervention less likely. It did mean, though, that much of the British army was engaged on the Continent, leaving a minimum in Britain for home defence. Colonel John William O'Sullivan (c.1700–60) wrote of Charles's determination regardless, 'The Prince being dissatisfied with the treatment he had from the Court of France, & finding yt the Frinch Ministry had no real design to re-establish the King, was resolv'd at any reat, to try what his presence cou'd do among his friends at home, without any other succour'.[2]

Charles was able to find enough money to buy 1,000 guns, ammunition and 1,800 swords, and to pay Anthony Welch for the use of a former privateer, the *Du Teillay*. Along with a handful of companions, the aforesaid arms, a treasury of 4,000 louis d'or and a small number of troops, he set sail from Nantes on 22 June, being joined at Belleisle by the *Elizabeth*, a 64-gun French warship, and sailed for Scotland. They had an eventful voyage for the *Elizabeth* engaged HMS *Lion*, 60 guns, under Captain Brett, in the Channel on 9 July. Both ships were so badly damaged that they had to return to port and the *Du Teillay* soldiered on alone, reaching the Western Isles on 23 July, with Charles arriving at Eriskay and sleeping on shore that night.

Once there, Charles contacted those who he thought would assist him. He met with a varied reception for some would not support him without French troops and others were torn between caution and loyalty. The majority verdict was that he should return home, as O'Sullivan noted: 'yt if he came without troops, yt not a soul wou'd joyn with him, & yt their advise was yt he shou'd go back & wait for a more favourable occasion.'[3]

However, on 25 July Ranald MacDonald of the Clanranalds pledged his support, 'assured him, yt he wou'd do all yt lay in his power to raise his father's men'[4] and began to raise his clan. Eventually there were promises of support from the MacDonalds of Glengarry and the Camerons (despite Lochiel's initial reluctance), all of whom had supported his father in 1715 and his grandfather in 1689. Arrangements were made to raise the standard on 19 August. Meanwhile, the *Du Teillay* deposited the arms and money it had carried and left on 4 August. Charles remained in Borrodale, guarded by the Clanranalds, then on 11 August went to Kinloch-Moidart, whilst messengers were sent out to rally support.

Meanwhile on 1 August the government issued a proclamation of a reward of £30,000 for Charles if he arrived on British soil. Definite news of that arrival only came to Sir John Cope (1690–1760), commander in Scotland, at Edinburgh a week later. He began to assemble the scattered forces in Scotland at Stirling. In the north of Scotland Lord President Duncan Forbes began to assemble the loyalist clans – the Grants, the Mackays, the Sutherlands, the Munros and the Macleods, and to raise units of men to oppose the Jacobites – men who might otherwise join them.

However, first blood was to the Jacobites as two companies of newly-raised infantry of the Royal Scots, marching from Perth on their way to Fort William, had been forced to surrender on 16 August by a small contingent of MacDonalds of Keppoch, after having a few men killed and wounded. Captain Switenham of Guise's battalion was also taken on his way to take command at Fort William.

There was a public gathering at Glenfinnan on 19 August and the Stuart banner was unveiled. Charles was guarded by 50 Clanranalds and was met by another 150 there. In the afternoon there came the Camerons and Keppoch's MacDonalds, though only about 1200 men in all. According to O'Sullivan, proclamations were read out, announcing James VIII and III as rightful King, 'wch was followed by a general Housaw, & a great deal of Allacrety'. Brandy was given to the men to drink his father's health and food was also distributed among those assembled.[5] The campaign was now becoming serious, though many of the men were poorly armed and the force was weak in cavalry and lacking in artillery. They remained in the vicinity another day to take possession of the arms and money that had been brought over.

The next few days saw the little force march to Moy and then to Letterfinlay and on to Invergarry castle, where Charles had assurances that the Frasers would join. The decision now was whether to march north to recruit more clan support or to push southwards towards Edinburgh. The latter course was selected and the chiefs with Charles attested that they would not make a separate peace without universal consent. They were also joined by the Stewarts of Appin; another 260 men.

Newcastle told the Duke of Argyle on 1 August, 'send directions to Sir John Cope to assemble the troops in proper places: and order the dragoon horses to be taken up from grass. Sir John Cope is also to concert with the Lord Chief Justice and the Lord Chief Advocate that may be proper to be done for securing the publick peace and Tranquillity and Disappointing these Designs.'[6] He gathered the bulk of these troops together at Stirling and was ordered by the Marquis of Tweeddale, Secretary of State for Scotland, on 16 August, to march north to stop the Jacobites from gathering support from elsewhere in the country; a strategy similar to that pursued in 1689 and 1719, though not in 1715. The reasoning behind this was, 'the most effectual way of putting a stop to wavering people joining the disaffected, so as to make a formidable body, was immediately to march and to stop their progress'.[7] Cope's two dragoon regiments were unable to march north, due to lack of fodder, and so were stationed at Stirling and Edinburgh. He then took the infantry he had, about 2,000 men, and a small train of artillery with only four aged gunners, marching north from Stirling on 19 August. He also hoped for support from the loyalist clans. None came.

Elsewhere, the lords justices in England contacted the Dutch government to request that they honour their treaty obligations as they had in 1715 and 1719. Given that the Dutch garrison at Tournai had surrendered to the French on parole, they were available for service against a non-French foe and began to be embarked for England. There was discussion between Cumberland and

Lord Harrington about releasing units of the British army for home defence, but Cumberland, facing a stronger enemy, had no wish to increase them and in any case did not see the initial Jacobite threat as being serious. However, he wrote, 'if England wants them, I an intirely of opinion that this country and even the whole alliance ought not to be considered comparatively with our own country', while also being of the opinion that 'I don't see the danger at home as so imminent'.[8]

On 27 August Cope and his men stood near the Correyarrack pass, a difficult ascent to make in the best of times, but almost impossible to force against any serious opposition. As an officer later wrote, 'Formerly several of these officers had marched over that ground and all of them unanimously agreed that to force the rebels in it was utterly impracticable. It must inevitably be attended with the loss of all our provisions, artillery, military stores and indeed of the troops: that giving the rebels any success upon their setting out, was by all means to be prevented, as that might be attended with by bad consequences to the service'.[9] By now the Jacobites had been joined by the MacDonalds of Glengarry and Glencoe, as well as some of the Grants. They were disappointed to learn that Cope was not at the pass. He had decided to march north to Inverness as retreating south would be demoralizing and staying put was untenable due to the lack of provisions. There was discussion among the Jacobites as to whether he should be pursued but this was shunned and the army marched to Dalwhinny on 29 August.

The Jacobites then marched to Blair Atholl and spent the first ten days of September at Perth. Two men came forward to lead the army; Lord George Murray and the Duke of Perth, who were accepted in lieu of any other obvious candidates, both being appointed as lieutenant generals. Murray had limited military experience as a junior officer over two decades previously (having fought at Glenshiel but had been absent at Sheriffmuir); Perth had none. Roberston of Struan brought 200 men to join and Cluny promised to bring his clan in, too. Public money and two ships were taken at Dundee.

The only fly in the ointment at this time was a relatively minor skirmish in which an attempt was made by Gordon of Glenbucket and O'Sullivan to take the lightly-defended Ruthven Barracks on 29 August, as arms and meal was thought to be stored there. This was met with a bloody rebuff from Sergeant Molloy and his dozen men, Molloy declaring 'My answer was that as I was too old a soldier to surrender a garrison of such strength without Bloody Noses . . . I would take my chance'. Attempts to set fire to the main door using barrels failed as the men attempting this were shot. Lacking artillery, the Jacobites had limited options, so left.[10] However, they did surprise and capture the garrison at Inversnaid Barracks.

Charles learnt of Cope's location and a council of war was held to decide whether to confront him in the Highlands or march to the capital. As before, the latter was decided on. On 11 September they were at Dunblane and the Forth was crossed two days later. Stirling, defended by Colonel James Gardiner's regiment of dragoons was their next destination. However, Gardiner retreated to Linlithgow. A plan was made to attack them there on the next day, but once again the cavalry eluded them.

Cope's army had marched north to Inverness, picking up some few additional troops from garrisons en route. He then left on 4 September, marching around the coast to reach Aberdeen a week later. It had been a futile march north, although he had obeyed his political masters. By then matters had altered radically elsewhere in Scotland and England.

In England, George II had returned from the Continent on 31 August. The government and its supporters began to make additional steps to defend the country and England was the priority, as it had been in 1715. This was not because it was thought that the Jacobite threat in Scotland by itself was dangerous but because it was felt that it might be supported by a French invasion. Ten battalions from Cumberland's army were requested and the duke now agreed that they were needed. Less consequentially, perhaps, lords lieutenants and mayors in the counties were recommended to come up with measures for local defence such as keeping tabs on known local Jacobite suspects and raising militia and volunteer forces.

In London Cabinet meetings concluded that Dutch and British troops, under General Wentworth, should be sent to Lancashire, seen as a strong centre of potential Jacobite support, as it had been in 1715. Elsewhere the Dutch troops that were sailing northwards were to be deployed to the north-east under Major General James Oglethorpe, possibly to aid Cope, as it was noted that the Jacobite army might march south and bypass Cope.[11]

With the Jacobite army marching from Perth, and with no army at Stirling to oppose them as in 1715 (the garrison in the castle could safely be bypassed), Edinburgh was looking increasingly at risk. Volunteer forces were raised to supplement the city militia and town guards; the city defences were hastily repaired. The two dragoon regiments (Gardiner's and Hamilton's) which were nearby, could, it was hoped, work with the civilian defenders to protect the Scottish capital. This was not to be. Denied entrance to the city, they withdrew and were unable to prevent the Jacobite army from marching towards the city on 16 September. Their opponents were not without problems; there was only £50 in their treasury, until Lord Elcho (1721–87), a Jacobite officer, supplied 1,500 guineas.[12]

There was also dissension in Edinburgh over what to do next as there were no significant regular troops nearby and the volunteers were increasingly reluctant to risk their lives. The corporation decided to negotiate with the Jacobites, though Charles thought that as prince regent he should not be put to the trouble of negotiating with subjects. Talks began. On 17 September the Jacobites entered the city. A number of Camerons, seeing the coach returning to the city with the negotiators, rushed in when the gates opened and overpowered the guards. Later that day Charles rode in triumph through the streets, watched by adoring crowds. Elcho wrote 'it was mett by vast Multitudes of people, who by their repeated shouts & Huzzas express'd a great deal of joy to see the Prince. When they came to the suburbs the croud was prodigious; and all wishing the Prince prosperity', and expected 10,000 men would join them.[13] This was the first time that a Stuart prince had been in the Scottish capital since his grandfather, as Duke of York, in 1682. Neither Mar nor Dundee had achieved as much. It was a great success, but there was about to be a much sterner test of the Jacobites' military prowess.

Chapter 11

The Battle of Prestonpans,
21 September 1745

There was intense interest in Cope's arrival at Dunbar and so the Jacobites soon learnt that Cope and his forces had embarked at Aberdeen and had arrived on 16 September 1745. The men disembarked on 17 September and the guns and supplies were unloaded on the next day. A volunteer from Edinburgh arrived at the camp to tell Cope that the Jacobites were 2,000 strong, but with more on their way, variously armed and lacking in artillery except for one gun. Cope was joined by Hamilton's and Gardiner's dragoons under Brigadier Thomas Fowke.[1] Many notables from Edinburgh joined them, such as Andrew Fletcher, Lord Justice Clerk, the Earl of Home and Lord Napier. There were also a number of volunteers who came to the camp to offer their services but they were turned down on the grounds that they, being ununiformed, might cause confusion in any battle.[2]

A council of war was held by Cope. The question was whether they should march to attack the Jacobites or wait until reinforcements had arrived (the Dutch battalion of La Rocque was on its way by sea to the Forth, but there was no news of when it would arrive. Cope sent a boat to locate the ship with orders about landing). However, there was much concern about Edinburgh and adjacent parts of the Lowlands being in Jacobite hands. Robert Craigie, the Lord Advocate, feared the Jacobites might bypass Cope and march south into England. The Edinburgh notables encouraged battle sooner rather than later. The officers were of mixed views between taking the offensive and waiting for additional forces. A Mr Wightman, an observer, later wrote that 'I did not approve of it', meaning the former option. Cope was initially of the latter way of mind, too. Having slept on the matter he decided on the morning of the 18th to march forward. Before this could happen, neighbouring gentry and country people supplied carts and horses for the army's baggage, though it is not clear whether they were recompensed for such.[3]

There was a political dimension to this march, Tweeddale writing to Cope on 21 September in response to a letter of his three days previously, 'His Majesty is pleased to find that you intend to proceed without loss of time to rectify this misfortune [loss of Edinburgh]. I heartily wish you good success.'[4] The fall of one of the kingdom's capitals was of clear symbolic importance.

On Thursday, 19 September, Cope's army marched towards Edinburgh. The little army, with its long train of cavalry, infantry, artillery and baggage carts, seemed impressive to onlookers, who were unused to such spectacles.[5] The sequence of the marching column was as follows: a captain and sixty-five dragoons as a scouting party, then the Highlanders, then one of the dragoon regiments, then two guns and the Cohorn mortars, then Lee's companies. Then Lascelles' companies, two more guns, Murray's companies, then the last two guns and the other regiment of dragoons, with the artillery wagons guarded by a sergeant and a dozen men, then the general's baggage, with guards, then the army baggage and then a rearguard of a captain and fifty men.[6]

On the march, Cope did much to encourage his troops, as Lieutenant Colonel Charles Whitefoord noted: 'all along the march, by riding through the ranks and encouraging the men, you rais'd their spirits to such a degree that all express'd the strongest desire for action. Even the dragoons breathed nothing but revenge and threaten'd the rebels with destruction.'[7] George Carne of Berwick noted, 'His men are in good health and in good spirits'.[8]

Given that it was harvest time, the troops requisitioned the produce of John Walker of Beanston's farm; 71 acres' worth of oats, 44 acres' worth of beans and 24 of barley, as well as wines and spirits. These were removed in carts or eaten immediately.[9]

Much hung on the outcome of the battle and news of its result was eagerly awaited. Lord Chancellor Hardwicke in London wrote to his son on the day of the battle, 'We expect every hour to hear of an action, and God grant it may be better conducted and more successful than his march'.[10] Likewise, Newcastle's secretary told the Duke of Richmond, on that same day, 'We are in the utmost impatience for the next letter from that part of the world'.[11]

An anonymous army officer wrote that on the night of the 19th that they camped on fields to the west of Haddington. Edinburgh was only 12 miles away. They stopped here because of the lack of water to be found later on the route. It was there that Captain Brymer of Lee's Foot was sought by his brother-in-law, William Congalton. Finding him in his tent reading, the latter asked him why he was so grave when the other officers seemed to make light of the enemy, was told that he thought they were wrong and that the Jacobites would make an attack on them.[12] Alexander Carlyle, son of a local minister, noted that officers had mixed views about the likelihood of success, with Colonel Gardiner, who 'looked pale and dejected, which I attributed to his Bad Health and the Fatigue he had lately undergone' replying when asked about victory, 'That he hop'd it might be so' and a cornet whe was a kinsman of his 'spake of victory as a thing certain if God were on our side'.[13]

The next day they marched to Tranent, setting out early that morning, planning then to march to Musselburgh links. They had received various intelligence about the Jacobite army which was apparently 'advancing towards us with their whole body, with a quick pace'. This news had been provided by some of the sixteen Edinburgh volunteers whom Cope had ride westwards towards Duddingston, for he was concerned that the Highlanders might attempt a night attack. Whitefoord had also been sent ahead and he reported that the direct route to Edinburgh was too dangerous because there were many places where the army could have been ambushed. Once the army reached Huntingdon they left the main road and took another to Seton. The ground that they had wanted to secure as a battlefield could not be reached, for it was some miles further on and was to be found via a countryside lined with walls. They called a halt at 11 that morning, seven miles from Edinburgh. The Earl of Loudoun, acting as Adjutant-General, who had also ridden ahead, returned with news that the entire Jacobite army was marching towards them. Cope therefore chose the first open ground he could 'and a better spot could not have been chosen for our cavalry to be at liberty to act in'. There were many spectators who accompanied the army and were told by some of the officers that there would be no battle for the Highlanders would not dare attack an army with both cavalry and infantry, though the officers may not have really believed it.[14] The troops initially formed up facing south-west with their right flank to the sea and the village of Tranent to the left.[15]

However, the army only just got into position, though 'in excellent order', before they saw the Jacobites.[16] They were to Cope's south, so he had the army wheel to face them.[17] On that day they arrested a lawyer who had come from Edinburgh. The man's father was a field officer in the Jacobite army and so it was thought that he was a spy. He was facing execution on the following day, but the sentence was never carried out.[18]

Meanwhile, Charles left Holyrood on the Thursday and slept that night at the camp at Duddingston, where Nairn's Athollmen had just arrived the day before and the Grants of Glenmoristons also joined him. A council of war was held with the result that officers were sent out beyond Musselburgh to seek news of Cope and in doing so they took two of Cope's scouts in an inn, who were returning to Cope with news of the Jacobites. On their reports it was decided to fight Cope at Musselburgh. Charles was concerned that Cope might decline battle and retreat to Berwick where he would be joined by the reinforcements from Flanders and 'he assured them that he would not let the first good occasion slip to fight him'. None present dissented, but if Cope could not be found, then he should be sought. It was not certain exactly where he was, but though the Jacobites had a rough idea of the numbers of his infantry and cavalry, they overestimated his artillery as being between twelve and twenty guns. Apparently it was the cavalry and guns that the Highlanders feared most as the infantry had ducked a battle with them in the previous month.[19] According to James Johnstone (1719–c.1800), a Jacobite officer, one reason for fighting was that many Jacobite supporters were awaiting a victory before they declared themselves in Charles's favour.[20] Another question raised at the meeting was how would the Highlanders behave when they met Cope's troops. Keppoch, who had served in the French army, was felt best qualified to answer and he remarked: 'as the country had been so long at peace, few or none of the private men had ever seen a battle, and it was not very easy to say how they would behave; but he would venture to assure His Royal Highness, that the Gentlemen would be in the midst of the enemy, and the private men, as they loved the cause, and loved their chiefs, would certainly follow them'.

Charles then said that he would lead them into battle himself, but this shocked the chiefs, who, perhaps in the knowledge of what had happened to Dundee at Killiecrankie, exclaimed that the cause would be lost if he were killed, for victory or defeat would then be just the same. If he did not back down, they would go home. Unlike Dundee in 1689, Charles acquiesced to this.[21]

At either four or six on the morning of Friday, 20 September, Charles and his army, bagpipers playing, with Murray with the vanguard, marched from Duddingston. Cavalry rode ahead of the infantry as scouts. Charles put himself at the army's head and showed his sword to them, declaring, 'My friends I have flung away the scabbard' which won him many cheers. According to O'Sullivan, 'Yu cant imagine what Courage the Prince's activity, in setting every Regimt in order, the joy yt he had painted in his face, & his talking some wors of Erse to the men inspired to 'um all'.[22]

The army marched across the River Esk at the bridge of Musselburgh, in a column of three men abreast, then to Edge Bucklin Brae. Here they left the road, went by the west side of Walliford and then up part of Fawsise hill, before turning to Tranent.[23]

At Pinkie House the Jacobite cavalry brought news that they had seen several parties of dragoons about Tranent and they believed Cope was nearby. Murray realized that they must seize the high ground before their enemy did, and that there was no time to deliberate nor to await orders, so he marched the men off the road, through the fields and to the top of Carberry Hill, taking half an hour to reach there, where they halted. At last they saw Cope's army drawn up to their north, with cavalry on each flank, infantry in the middle and a small reserve at the rear. It was judged that they were standing on the defensive. Elcho thought that Cope should have attacked them because he had regular troops and they were only militia, 'and his showing an inclination to decline the combat was the Greatest fault he committed, for every motion he made to Shun an Engagement added so much courage to the Princes Army'.[24]

Cope's men prepared for battle, either to defend their position or to take an opportunity of taking the offensive. After exchanging verbal hostilities, the Jacobites ('probably from their liking our disposition' according to the anonymous army officer) carried on the march, about a half-mile from their enemy. The Highlanders shouted at their enemy and would have liked to have attacked, but were restrained by their officers.[25] It was about two in the afternoon. O'Sullivan noted, 'This was not a proper Scituation for highlanders for they must have nothing before them yt can hinder them to run upon the enemy'.[26]

A number of officers were sent forward to examine Cope's position. Murray sent Colonel Henry Kerr of Graden, who, despite being shot at, reported that Cope had chosen a strong position 'where it was impossible to attack him, without risking the loss of the whole army'. To his west were the high walls of the gardens of Preston, where several holes had been made for retreat if need be. To his east was the house of Seton and a small morass. In front of his army was an enclosure surrounded by a ditch three or four feet deep and five or six feet wide. To his rear was the sea. The artillery was placed on the high road to Tranent (to the east) near to the corner of the enclosure and the morass.[27] Johnstone later wrote that the position 'was chosen with a great deal of skill. The more we examined it, the more we were convinced of the impossibility of attacking it'.[28] It was also 'very proper for the dragoons to act in' being a large field.[29]

The Jacobite army faced the dilemma that, though eager to fight, could only apparently do so at a great disadvantage to themselves. Charles moved his forces about, placing some at the several roads which led to Cope's camp. They were fired on by the guns, but these made no impact. Stalemate had been thus reached.[30]

By the early evening the Jacobite army moved off, marching towards Tranent. O'Sullivan put fifty of Lochiel's men in the churchyard there ('for what reason I could not understand' wrote Murray). Richard Jack, a professor of gunnery with no practical experience of artillery, was assisting with Cope's guns and at first noted that it was suggested that the four Cohorn mortars could shell the Jacobites there, but it was decided not to because the mortars were few and faulty and to show the Jacobites this weakness might be accompanied with dire consequences. Thus Cope ordered that two guns be used instead. It was now between five and six o'clock.[31]

The artillery did succeed in injuring a few men, and a Cameron officer reported back that they were exposed to cannon fire and that he could not see for what purpose they were there. The churchyard was at extreme range for the small cannon and the church wall was a strong one, so the casualties were unlucky indeed. Lochiel went to view the situation and told Murray that nothing would more dishearten his men than to be shot at but being unable to advance. O'Sullivan had gone to the rear, so Murray had Lochiel withdraw his men.[32] It appeared to Cope's army that the Jacobite army was in a state of confusion.[33]

Eventually most of the Jacobite army then marched through Tranent to get to Cope's left, and Murray sent word back to tell his master what he had done. When they were rejoined by the men from the graveyard, O'Sullivan reappeared. He asked what Murray was doing. Murray replied: 'It was not possible to attack the enemy on the west side of the village; that the men he had placed at the foot had been exposed to no purpose; and that there were exceeding good fields on the east side for the men to lie well and safe all that night, I would satisfy His Royal Highness how easy it would be to attack the enemy by the east side.'[34]

All this did not go off quietly. At nine that night Colonel Peregrine Lascelles reported hearing dogs barking in the town. He sent a patrol there but, at half past the hour, they found nothing, the Jacobites having already marched on and were to its east.[35] In the meantime, Cope had his baggage guarded by Loudoun's men sent to an enclosure to the north at Cockenzie.[36]

Once the army had passed the village, Charles arrived to be at their head. Lord Nairn went with the 500 Athollmen to guard the road between Edinburgh and Cope to prevent him marching there. Having gone out with several officers to reconnoitre, Cope immediately had his army change their disposition. Presumably he had seen the march of Nairn's command. Therefore the Government troops had their right wing to the sea and their left to the ditches where their front had previously been. Morale seemed high in performing these manoeuvres, for 'our people constantly performed with great alacrity and regular exactness, and in all outward appearance with a cheerful countenance, and eager desire to engage'.[37]

Under the cover of darkness, the Jacobites marched to the south-east of the morass, and though within cannon range, moved so quietly that Cope was unaware of their location.[38] According to O'Sullivan, the dissension between him and Murray continued. Murray was angry that the Atholl men had been sent off and 'threw his gun on the Ground in a great passion & swore God he'd never draw his sword for the cause, if the Bregade was not brought back'. Charles would have complied, but Lochiel interceded and the unit remained where it was. O'Sullivan and Murray also argued about the posting of sentries after the men lay down on the dry stubble field.[39]

Murray then held a council of war. Once all the principal officers were gathered together he told them that he proposed attacking at dawn. He told them it 'was not only practicable, but that it would, in all probability, be attended with success'. He claimed he knew the terrain and there were others there who did. They could march through a defile at the east end of the enclosures, form up and assault the enemy. Charles and all others there applauded the plan.[40] A night attack was ruled out on the grounds that an irregular force would be unable to keep together after the battle.[41]

Once the meeting was over, one Robert Anderson of Whitburgh, who had attended it but who had said nothing, and who knew the country well, spoke to Forbes of Hepburn. He told them that there was a better route through the morass which he could show them. Hepburn advised him to tell Murray, which he did. Grasping the importance of this news, they told Charles who agreed to it.[42]

At either two or three in the morning of Saturday, 21 September, orders were sent to Nairn to have his men there rejoin the main army, which he did. Charles was concerned, however, that their withdrawal would allow Cope to march unhindered to Edinburgh.[43]

The army was then drawn up as follows:

Front line, right to left, MacDonalds of Clanranald (250–300), Glengarry (350–500), Keppoch and Glencoe (420–450), (commander on right, Perth), Camerons (500), Stewarts of Appin (200–250), (commander on left Murray). Second line, Atholl men (350), Menzies (300), MacLauchlans (200) and Duke of Perth's men (200).
Reserve of Viscount Strathallan's cavalry, 25–100.[44]
Total according to Andrew Lumisden, Charles's secretary, 2,200.[45]

James Maxwell (1708–62), a junior officer, put the total as 3,000 infantry and 40 cavalry and Elcho concurs with thus almost to a man, though he lists 36 cavalry.[46] According to Andrew Henderson, an Edinburgh schoolmaster, these latter were about 100 'and these very unfit for Action'.[47] There was a single cannon which had been taken to Edinburgh but there is no reference to its being employed.[48] In light of what was to happen at Culloden, it is interesting to note that when Lochiel announced that his clan wanted to be positioned on the right of the line of battle, Clanranald asserted the right of the MacDonalds to be there, which was claimed as being an ancient right. This was granted to the latter on this occasion.[49]

They were fairly well armed, though prior to arrival in Edinburgh only half had been 'Completely armed, the others with pitchforks, scythes, a sword or a pistol, or some only a staf or stick'. However, on entry to the city they seized 1,000 muskets 'which gave him and his Army a great deal of joy as they stood in need of them'.[50]

An Edinburgh volunteer recorded that their guns were of various kinds, from muskets to fowling pieces, and that their swords were a mix of Highland broadswords and French-made swords.[51] According to Johnstone, some men only had bludgeons and MacGregor's company of Perth's regiment had scythe blades attached to poles. An Edinburgh volunteer thought that about 100 men were so armed, and that these weapons resembled Lochaber axes.[52] An anonymous Edinburgh man observed the quality of their arms: 'they were guns of difernet syses, and some of innormowows length, some with bolts turned uplick a leven, sometyd with puck threed to the stock, some withowt locks and some matchlocks, some had swords over ther showlders instead of guns, one or two had pitchforks and some bits of scythes upon poles with a cleck, some old Lochaber axes'.[53]

Their appearance may have been disconcerting too, as an Edinburgh volunteer reported to Cope: 'most of them seemed to be strong, active and hardy men; that many of them were of a very ordinary size . . . the Highland garb favoured them much, as it shewed their naked limbs, which were strong and muscular; that their stern countenance and bushy uncombed hair, gave them a fierce, barbarous and imposing aspect'.[54]

An anonymous Edinburgh observer was less complimentary, noting that there were 'a greate many old men and boys' in the army, yet also stating that 1,000 of them were 'as good men as any in Europe', with the same number 'indifferent good' and the 1,400 others 'good for nothing old men, shepherds and boys'.[55] Carlyle was also disparaging about the Jacobites, 'In General they were of low stature, and Dirty, and of a contemptible appearance'.[56]

Their opponents comprised the following:

Commander-in-chief: Sir John Cope.
Second in command: Brigadier Fowke.

Infantry
Lascelles' (eight companies) and Guise's (two companies only), 570 men, Lee's (five companies only, 291 men), Murray's (580 men), and Loudoun's (183 men).
Total infantry: 1,624 men, plus officers and NCOs (c.88, based on Culloden figures of 5.5 per cent of rank and file).

Cavalry
Gardiner's and Hamilton's dragoons (567 men in total).
Total strength: 2,279 men.

Artillery
Six 2½-pounders.
Two Cohorn mortars.
Four small Cohorn mortars.
Manned by Colonel Whitefoord and Major Griffiths, Richard Jack, four elderly gunners and between six and nine sailors from HMS *Fox*.[57]

The Government army was thus outnumbered by almost 2:1 in the case of the infantry. Yet in cavalry and artillery it would appear to have had a crushing advantage. These assets, were more apparent than real, however.

It is often noted that Cope's men were inexperienced in warfare and this is one reason why they were routed with ease. Of the rank and file (and these almost all infantrymen) who later were awarded pensions, and whose nationality is known (152), 92 were English, 45 Scottish and 15 Irish. They had come from a variety of occupations, but the most common were labourers (37), followed by weavers (33) and shoemakers (24). There were nine men who had been husbandmen, six were former tailors and five who had been shepherds and five former servants. At the battle, most of the men were aged between 20 and 40, though twenty were over 40 and two were over 50, the eldest being 54. There were also three teenagers. Their numbers of years in the army was variable, but mostly was low; 97 having had four years of life in the army; 24 having had three years, 17 two and a dozen had but a year. Ten men had served for over 10 years and nine had between 20–26 years of experience. Almost all had joined between the ages of 16 and 38.[58] Yet these battalions had not fought in the recent Continental battles; the dragoon regiments, though raised in 1715 and had fought at Preston in 1715, had been stationed in Ireland for over two decades, and most of the dragoons were Irishmen.

Fowke later stated of the dragoons, 'I found many of the horses' backs not fit to receive the riders, many of the men's and some of the officers' legs so swell'd that they could not wear boots, and those who really were to be depended upon, in a manner overcome for want of sleep'.[59] Gardiner was also concerned about the troops under his command, confiding on the eve of battle, that he believed the men had not recovered from their panic after having fled the enemy only several days ago, and 'I have not above 10 men in my regiment whom I am certain will follow me. But we must give battle now and God's will be done.'[60] The anonymous Edinburgh critic noted, of the cavalry, 'two dastardly Irish regiments of dragoons. These poltrown squadrons.'[61]

There were problems with the artillery, too. Cope lacked any men from the Royal Artillery. He only had one elderly gunner and three other men from the Invalids company that was Edinburgh Castle's garrison and a number of sailors from the ships they had travelled on from Aberdeen. The latter were 'generally drunk upon the march . . . and he [Cope] could never have any dependence on them the two days they were with him'.[62] Cope had tried to remedy this; on 20 September he sent a Lieutenant Craig to Edinburgh castle to ask the garrison commander, General Guest, for the castle's chief engineer. Craig did not arrive there until 11 at night and then Guest told him that he could not spare the man in question, but offered a bombardier and four gunners. The men disguised themselves as tradesmen to avoid any Jacobite patrols, but were too late for the battle.[63] As well as the men, there were questions raised over the effectiveness of the mortars, which had been stored in Edinburgh Castle for years, and many of the shells' fuses were faulty.[64] The guns themselves were described as follows after their capture. The six guns had barrels six feet long; two had been made in 1719, two in 1721 and two in 1741. All were 2½in bore. The two Cohorn mortars had 5¾in bore and the small ones 4in bore. They had plentiful ammunition; the cannon had 162 roundshot and 61 bags of grape shot; there were 28 Cohorn grenades and 40 for small Cohorns, along with 11 barrels of gunpowder.[65]

Meanwhile, Charles addressed his men, echoing his previous words on the day before, 'Follow me, gentlemen, by the assistance of God, I will this day make you a free and happy people.' In good spirits, the Jacobite army advanced. It was now four o'clock. Perth and his men were in the vanguard, being guided through the morass by Anderson, along with the major of Clanranald's and forty of his men. Behind them were the army in a column three abreast. They were very quiet and their march was cloaked by darkness and mist. It was narrow and 100 men could have held up the entire force had they been posted there. As it was 'it was so difficult that every step the men made they sunk to the knee in mud. This made them pass in some disorder.' Yet since they were undetected, this mattered not.[66] Murray was in the rear of this advance guard.

Once out of the morass, the army could draw itself up into a line of battle. Perth marched his men towards the sea in order to avoid the risk of detection. This led to the wings of the front line being out of alignment with one another and Murray's left wing was thus rather nearer to Cope's men than was Perth's. This went uncorrected, it being dark and the men and their leaders inexperienced in warfare.[67]

Charles had spent the night encouraging his men, assuring them that the enemy would not stand against them (after all, he was the son of the man he deemed was their rightful king). It seems that Charles once again raised the question of his leading his men into battle. Murray and the officers urged Charles not to risk himself in the ensuing battle. If he was killed, all would be lost as his presence united them and inspired them. He replied, 'Tis for yt reason yt they must see me, you all expose yourselfs, for the King & contry's cause, & I am as much obliged to it, as any of yu'. He agreed to dismount and remain with the Atholl brigade.[68]

The night was dark and cold. According to John Home, an Edinburgh volunteer, some among Cope's army were feeling apprehensive, boxed in as they were. They felt that the enemy had the advantage, as they were secure from attack and so could rest, and rise fresh and vigorous with the initiative, whilst Cope's men had to stand at arms all night. Cope sent out patrols of infantry and dragoons and had fires lit in front of his army.[69]

Major Talbot of Murray's posted sentries and they made constant reports to the commander. He also sent out patrols and Lieutenant Colonel Peter Halket and Lascelles went on their rounds, asking Cope for instructions at half past two. Cope had reports every half an hour. They were especially concentrated on the east, towards the marsh. It was suggested that the mortars be fired at the Jacobites in the night though Whitefoord wrote, 'but by the experiments you made, you found that few of them bursted, which you apprehend if they perceived, would take off their fear of them'. The sentries 'could not perceive any motion they [the Jacobites] made, every thing seemed so quiet'. This could have been because 'The first line crawled upon their knees, like Hunters in quest of their prey'. It was about three that they detected any movement among the Jacobite army. And they reported them being in full march eastwards. An hour later they found that they were marching north-east and it was thought that an attack was to be launched on their left flank. Cope had his army change face yet again 'in less time than one would think possible', with the left flank on the sea.[70]

The ground between the two armies 'was an extensive cornfield, plain and level, though sloping towards the sea, without a bush or tree. Harvest was just got in, and the ground was covered with thick stubble, which rustled under the fee of the Highlanders as they ran'. There was mist, which lifted as the distance between the armies was being closed by the Jacobites.[71] It was thus ideal for charging infantry and cavalry. Carlyle wrote that 'The Field was entirely clear of the crops, the last sheaves having been carried in the Night before, and neither Cottage, tree or Bush were in the whole extent, except one solitary Thorn bush, which grew on the march between Seaton and Preston Fields'.[72]

The battle proper was about to begin. Initially the Jacobites were stood 100 men abreast and 20 men deep.[73] Perth and Murray were both on foot and at the head of their troops.[74] The Highlanders pulled off their bonnets, looked up to Heaven and made a short prayer. They then moved forward. Murray noticed that his troops risked being outflanked because there was a large space between his left flank and the ditch of the enclosure that had been to the fore of Cope's army. He had the Camerons move towards the left.

This meant that the gap between the two wings of the Jacobite army, already not inconsiderable, widened further. As a remedy, the men in the second line was ordered to advance into this interval and form a centre force.[75] Despite their speed, they had to stop twice to dress ranks which due to their haste.[76]

According to the anonymous army officer, the Jacobites appeared thus, 'three large bodies in columns, of their packed-out highlanders, came in space though in a collected body, with great swiftness'. He added, 'it was so dark when they came to attack us, that I could only perceive them like a black hedge moving towards us'.[77] Henderson wrote that they were 'in a declining posture, covering their Heads and Breasts with their Targets'.[78] The Jacobite columns of attack were irregular, with men in some places ten deep, in others, only two. At the front were their officers, all on foot, presumably to encourage the men but also to present less obvious targets.[79] This also reduced their mobility, visibility and their capacity to control their men after the initial impact.

Cope's men were arrayed thus, from left to right:

Line 1
2 squadron of Hamilton's dragoons, c.125.
Murray's.
Lascelles.
Lee's.
Guise's.
Total infantry in Line 1, 1,158.
Trained (Artillery) Guard, 100 men of Lee's Foot, led by Captain Cochrane.
Artillery under command of Lieutenant Colonel Whitefoord.
2 squadrons of Gardiner's dragoons, c.125.
Line 2
1 squadron of Hamilton's dragoons, c.100.
1 squadron of Gardiner's dragoons, c.100.
Baggage guard made up of Loudoun's and two of Murray's companies, 230.
Other troops
Infantry at Gardiner's house, 70.
Infantry patrols, 66.
Dragoon patrols, 118.[80]

By now they had been seen by their enemies. Cope's men had already realigned themselves and so were facing eastwards rather than to the south. The infantry were in lines three deep, the cavalry two deep.[81] Unlike Charles, Cope does not seem to have ever made a formal speech to encourage the troops.

However, as an officer noted, of Cope, 'the diligence and activity which the general behaved himself. He first order'd the right to form, and then gallop'd to the left, and brought the dragoons up to their ground: from thence I saw him hasten back along the front of our line, to the right, upon his observing that the rebels were advancing to attack it.'[82] Cope himself later wrote, 'I returned again the same way to the right, encouraging the men as I went along the line, to do their duty'.[83] According to Forbes, 'the general rode from the right to the left in the front, encouraging the men, begging them to keep up their fire, and keep their ranks and they would easily beat the rebels'. When he reached the left he noticed that Hamilton's dragoons had not drawn their swords. He became 'very angry' and ordered them to do so.[84]

Lascelles dismounted and put Lee's men in order so that they could attack or defend.[85] There were some difficulties. The infantry outposts were unable to join their own units so formed up to the right of Lee's men. This meant that Gardiner's two dragoon squadrons did not have enough room to form up, so Gardiner's own command had to form up behind that of his subordinate, Lieutenant Colonel Shugborough Whitney's squadron. Furthermore, the artillery guard was now before Whitney's dragoons, thus blocking their movement forwards.[86] Cope also wanted to redeploy two of his guns to the left flank, 'I sent Major Masson to the right, to Colonel Whitefoord, for cannon immediately to annoy them'. Yet by this time the civilian artillery drivers had decamped with the horses and there was insufficient time for the guns to be manhandled to the other end of the line.[87]

Naturally the guns went into action first. Whitefoord and Griffiths fired the guns and mortars at 100 yards, the sailors and elderly gunners having run away.[88] Lumisden reported that 'they played their artillery furiously upon our left: yet only one private man was killed, and one officer wounded'. Jack wrote of the potential of the artillery, 'the great advantage that would have been of breaking of their ranks and putting them into confusion with the shells had these been in good order, was lost'.[89] However, guns cannot win a battle unaided, as Jack wrote, 'though the artillery broke the ranks of the rebels, and obliged them to divide into small partys as they advanced, yet being unsupported by the dragoons . . . Those who commanded and managed the train were so much pushed that they were obliged to retire'.[90] Recent archaeological evidence has shown that the guns fired canister rather than roundshot, which would have been more effective at short range, though clearly insufficiently so here.

The guns never fired again on that day as 'the Highlanders ran on with such eagerness that they immediately seized the cannon'.[91] It was the Camerons on the Jacobites' left who hit the enemy first. Apart from the guns having been taken, the body of 100 infantry guarding the artillery were thrown into disorder.[92] Jack wrote that 'Captain Cocheran behaved somewhat better', his men firing two volleys on the Jacobites once the latter had the guns, but being intimidated by the charge, fled.[93] John Marchant, a contemporary historian, claimed that they may have been fearful that the guns might have been turned against them.[94]

The Jacobites had fired, which they could not have been prevented from doing, but at too long a distance and so did little damage.[95] However, seven men later claiming wound pensions attested to having been shot at this battle, so their fire was not wholly ineffective.[96] Then there were the dragoons to deal with; their avoiding battle a week previously did not bode well. Apparently they 'made a very regular fire'. The Jacobites were undeterred, cheered and fired back, 'which was very brisk' and 'the dragoons were immediately thrown into disorder'.[97]

The fact that of all the cavalry only one dragoon, a former farmer of Inniskillen, 41-year-old Henry Smith (and with 21 years of soldiering behind him one of the most experienced soldiers in the battle) from Hamilton's later claimed a wound pension from injuries inflicted in the battle suggests that the cavalry played only a very minor role in it.[98] Apparently Hamilton's fled after firing only a few shots and escaped by the sea shore, one commentator writing 'Hamilton's dragoons never engaged, but galloped off without stricking a stroke'.[99]

Wightman agreed, noting that they routed 'without firing, or being fired upon, and without drawing a sword'. In fact their manoeuvre disordered Loudoun's Highlanders, too.[100] Sir John MacDonald, a Jacobite officer, referred to 'the cavalry flying before the Highlanders on the plain like a flock of sheep which after having run away, gathers together and then begins to run again when seized by a fresh fear'.[101]

Whitney saw a column of Jacobites moving to attack Gardiner's regiment when Loudoun approached him and suggesting it would be advantageous if he wheeled his squadron to the right and took the enemy in the flank. Whitney concurred and the manoeuvre 'was done with all the calmness, silence & Resolution that I could wish from brave men'. The squadron was a mere 20 yards from the Jacobite flank and as Whitney recalled, 'I gave the word of command to my squadron to charge into the middle of them'. It was at this crucial moment that a musket ball shattered Whitney's left arm, 'otherwise I thought I had the fairest opportunity of doing a notable piece of service'.[102]

Whitney retired to the rear of his squadron but not before he ordered his lieutenant to lead the charge. This officer 'came with great Alacrity to the head of the standard, but having a wild, unruly horse he fell a plunging & never ceased till she threw the lieutenant on his back on the ground, by which means a second occasion of doing good service was lost'.[103] Gardiner's regiment fled by Preston.[104] Jacobite firing had been 'very irregular', though one man thought that they had 'receiv'd a terrible fire' which had struck panic into Gardiner's dragoons, presumably unused to gunfire, and the colonel's squadron fled, leaving Gardiner to vainly call them to stand. Fowke also 'endeavoured for Gardiner to rally ye dragoons'.[105]

According to Henderson the cavalry horses were young and became 'affrighted at such a noise in the morning, fell a capering, fled off at once'. Some riders were dismounted in the process. Apparently these riderless horses ran through the Jacobites towards Dunbar.[106] The Jacobite infantry had been encouraged to attack the cavalry by aiming for the horse' noses, which would then wheel about with their wounded faces and a few so afflicted will throw a whole squadron into disorder. Scythe-armed men could cut a horse in two with their lethal weapons.[107]

Nathaniel Cox later wrote that when 'the rebels came running up with a confused noise and hallowing a good number of the soldiers behind you [Lascelles] took off their hats, crying to give a huzza'. Lascelles at first wanted to stop this, but joined in and took off his hat, waved it in the air and cried 'in the name of God, huzza'. Although apparently looking exhausted, Cox thought that Lascelles was 'exerting himself very much at the head of the army'.[108] With the rout of the dragoons on the right, Lascelles hoped that the platoons nearest him could wheel to their right and so cover the right flank, now exposed. Yet the men were 'crouching, and creeping gently backwards with their arms recovered'. He reproached them for their retreat and initially stopped it. The dragoons' flight also had the effect of throwing the infantry into 'ye utmost disorder'. When attacked by Highlanders coming out of column and charging sword in hand, they fled. It was then that Lascelles fell to the ground and was forced to surrender his pistol and sword, but he was then left and later escaped.[109]

Major Talbot later wrote, 'I recommended it to the men to keep up their fire, and be attentive to their officers'.[110] Yet another report stated, 'Our men had orders not to fire till they had the word from their officers, but that no orders were ever given by the general . . . the men fired at random, some one shot, some more, not any above two'.[111] The British infantry fired, as trained, by platoons. As with the fire of the dragoons, it had little effect, though Maxwell wrote 'The foot gave one good fire from right to left' but were unable to deliver a second.[112] One Jacobite casualty was Captain Malcolm MacGregor of Perth's, who was struck by five musket balls, and cried out to his men, 'My lads, I am not dead, and by God, I shall see if any of you does not do his duty'.[113] Others hit by musketry were Malcolm and John Cameron, respectively shot through the ankle and sustaining a fractured thigh due to gunshot wounds; Gilbert Campbell was also wounded in the leg.[114]

The confusion into which their mounted comrades had been thrown into also affected the infantry. The Jacobites then attacked, 'threw down their muskets, drew their swords, and carried all before them like a torrent'.[115] Apparently the men fired too soon, and had not fixed their bayonets. Some fled even before that.[116] There seems to have been little or no melee, the infantry fleeing before they were attacked.[117] On the right was O'Sullivan, realizing that they had outflanked the enemy, 'Cryed out "let the MccDonels come to this hedge, we have out wing'd them"'.[118]

Jacobite aggression was noted: 'never were such strokes seen by sword as on the above occasion; not only were hands and feet were cut off, but even the legs of horses; and what I saw may be affirm'd for truth; that a Highland gentleman (who led up a division after breaking through Murray's regiment) such a blow at a grenadier, the poor fellow naturally put his hand over head and not only had his hand lop'd off, but also his scull, cut above an inch deep that he expired'.[119] Similarly, O'Sullivan wrote, 'broadsword played their part, for wth one stroke, armes, & legs were cout of, & heads split to the shoulders, never such wounds were seen'.[120] A Jacobite account read, 'they could not withstand the impetuoisity, or rather fury of the highlanders, and were forced to run when they could no longer resist'.[121] Carlyle noted that Elcho 'had an air of savage ferocity, that Disgusted and alarmed'.[122]

Morale was collapsing, 'And from this example, the whole body became possessed with the same fatal dread; so that it became utterly impossible. . . to put an end to their fears or stop their flight'.[123] Jack wrote of the flight thus, 'in a manner that no language can give a just idea of'.[124] According to Whitney it was only two minutes from the first rattle of musketry that 'the field in their rear covered with Runaways without Arms who ingloriously left their Brave officers a sacrifice to the merciless fury of these tartars of the worst kind'. Furthermore, 'an universall panick seized the whole body of foot & Dragoons & every thing ran into Irreparable Confusion'.[125] James Johnstone, an aide to Murray, wrote, 'The panic terror of the English surpassed all imagination. They threw down their arms that they might run with more speed, thus depriving themselves by their fears of the only means of arresting the vengeance of the Highlanders. Of so many men in a condition, from their numbers, to preserve order in their retreat, not one thought of defending himself'.[126] The anonymous Edinburgh observer wrote 'never deer ran faster before hownds than these poor betrayed men'.[127]

Apart from the one volley of fire (according to a military observer, only twelve platoons actually fired), very little resistance was put up by the majority of the infantry. George Carne noted that only two platoons of Lee's 'gave a tolerable fire', for 'the rest was no better than the fire of a bad militia from the end of the line to the other . . . our men acted as if they had wanted arms'. He added that Jacobite musketry was poor, 'the enemy fired likewise but without doing any execution'.[128]

According to Henderson, 'The infantry in the first line were miserably massacred by the rebels. Such as threw down their Arms, and begged for Quarters upon their knees, were inhumanely mangled; and such as fled into the Enclosures were pursu'd and killed.'[129] Another writer put it thus, 'The followed a prodigious slaughter, for the Highlanders quickly fell upon them wt their broadswords and almost hewed them to pieces'.[130] According to Johnstone, a youth of 14 knocked down or killed fourteen soldiers with his sword. Another Highlander captured ten men, 'driving them before him like a flock of sheep'. He had ordered them to surrender armed with only a sword and pistol and the men had been so 'terror-struck' that they obeyed.[131]

Seeing the Jacobites were attacking his right first, Cope rode over but by now the cavalry and artillery guard were in flight, 'We endeavoured to get them to order but it would not do'. The infantry could not be rallied either.[132] Attempts were made to rally the men. Cope wrote, 'Seeing the dragoons go off in this manner, I went to the Foot, to try by their means to retrieve the affair . . . I endeavoured all I could to rally them, but to no avail'.[133]

Talbot added, 'He and the rest of the officers did everything in their power to stop the men running away, but to no purpose'.[134] The unknown officer wrote, 'All remedies, in every shape, were tried by the General, Brigadier Fowke, the Earls of Loudoun and Home, and the officers about them, to remedy this disorder'. Yet these officers 'did all that was in the power if men to do, and in doing so it exposed themselves in such a manner to the fire of the rebels'.[135]

At this point, the Jacobite army was in a confused state, too. Elcho wrote that the battalions in the front line were in 'the Greatest Confusion', mainly occupied in pursuing the enemy or pillaging the dead. Lochiel was able to re-form his men by having his piper play the pipes for he was concerned that the dragoons might rally. The second-line battalions, were, however, still formed in their ranks.[136]

Fowke, hearing firing to his rear, thinking it was from a body of troops still resisting, galloped towards the noise. He hoped to retrieve the situation, but found it was Jacobite musketry and the men being concealed by gunsmoke. He almost was made a prisoner, but one Captain Wedderburn saw him and called out to him to let him know of the danger he was in. Likewise, Lascelles had a fortunate escape. Abandoned by his men, he was taken prisoner, but in the confusion and hurry of battle he managed to escape and eventually got to Berwick.[137]

Some dragoons, who were being fired upon, fled through the town of Preston. Gardiner's dragoons fled through the defiles in the park walls on the right and Hamilton's taking those on the left. At the west end of Preston, Cope, Loudoun and Home stopped the dragoons' flight and tried to have them return to the field. Cope hoped that they could now charge the disordered enemy who were in pursuit of fleeing infantrymen.[138] When the cavalry were alongside Lord Grange's Park, some Jacobite musketry came their way and so they retired again.[139] According to Carlyle, two men were shot dead here.[140] Whitney 'and some officers of distinction made to yt narrow lane near Gardiner's house and appos ymselves sword in hand threatened to kill those dragoons who would not return, but these officers were carry'd off by ye violent press of men and horses'.[141]

Finding he could not rally his men, Cope at the head of his dragoons (some 450 strong), now in an orderly body, and some volunteers, took the road to Carberry Hill. About fifteen infantrymen joined them. The Jacobites lacked the cavalry and the time to pursue. The defeated men rode to Lauder and then to Berwick on the following day.[142]

MacDonald wanted to stop the escape of some of the dragoons and found an officer with fifty Athollmen. They initially agreed to his suggestion, but then desisted because they thought that they had too few men. Once the bulk of the dragoons had passed, MacDonald then suggested that now they might seize a few men and their horses. MacDonald's servant captured one horse but that was all.[143] Some of those in flight were fired upon. Captain John Maclean of the Jacobite army wrote 'We met some of them that was making their escape and fired our pieces at them'.[144]

There were a few acts of resistance. Most famously there were the actions of Colonel Gardiner, who, having tried and failed to rally his dragoons and seeing the officers of a nearby infantry unit fall:

> the colonel immediately quitted his horse, snatch'd up a half pike and took it upon him the command of the Foot, at whose head he fought, until he was brought down by three wounds, one in his shoulder with a ball, another in his forehead by a broad sword, and the third, which was the mortal stroke, in the hinder part of his head by a Lochaber axe: this would was given him by a Highlander, who came behind him, when he was fetching a stroke at an officer. With whom he was engaged.[145]

Some from both sides saw his death as being heroic for he could have taken the opportunity to escape.[146] Murray of Broughton was unsympathetic, claiming that Gardiner's fate was caused 'by his obstinacy occasion'd his own fall'.[147]

Other officers fought on. Major Bowles of Hamilton's, having fallen with his horse, 'was desperately hacked by the Boys who followed the rebels'. Others were Captain Stuart of Phisgil of Lascelles' ('mangled in a most miserable manner'), Captains Brymer and Rogers of Lee's, Howell of Guise's and Bishop and ensign Forbes of Murray's.[148] Brymer had fought at Sheriffmuir and so was the only officer who had seen Highlanders attack regular troops. Apparently he disdained to run and so was killed with his face towards the enemy.[149] As to Phisgill, according to Murray of Broughton, 'nothing but a mistaken notion of honour occasion[ed]' his death'. Apparently, Ensign Donald Stuart of Ardshiel's offered him his life, but was insulted and eventually Stuart was obliged to kill him, albeit reluctantly, in self defence.[150]

Another eyewitness reported of Captain Rogers:

> after his men had surrendered themselves prisoners of war that asked him to surrender Likewise and his answer was that he was fighting for his King & Country and that he would sooner Loose his life than surrender himself to any such Rebelous rascals as thay were and he killed 4 of the highlanders with his own hand when one of them came behind him with an ax and cut off his lower jaw and he fell to the ground and thay knockt him in the head with the same weppon.[151]

Elsewhere a lieutenant colonel, five other officers and fourteen privates got into a ditch and fired at the Jacobites. Murray assembled 100 men who presented their muskets at them. He persuaded his men to hold their fire and 'nothing gave me more pleasure that day than having it so immediately in my power to save these men'.[152]

But not all officers may have behaved bravely. According to Whitney, he heard that Lascelles left his command to Major Severen, who stood 'at the head of the colours' where the colonel should have been. Whitney heard that Lascelles 'were out of the field before the Action was over' and was seen at Haddington, eight miles away at half past six on the morning of the battle.[153] Lascelles hotly denied this allegation, however. The last senior officer from the field was Fowke, who was fired upon three times.[154] According to MacDonald, fifty dragoons took refuge in an enclosure. He suggested that the Glengarrys and Kappochs attack them. They refused to do so. He mused that 'Highlanders will never do anything more after their first charge had been stopped'.[155]

The companies of Loudoun's and Murray's infantry, about 350 men, who were guarding the baggage, seeing that all was lost on the flanks, retired to take up a position in Prestonpans churchyard, 'being resolved to sell their Lives at the greatest price had made preparation for their defence'. Halkett, now a prisoner, approached them at Lord George Murray's suggestion (Murray of Broughton stated that Captain Cochrane, not Halkett, was the go-between), and proposed a treaty by which they laid down their arms so no more blood be shed. They accepted.[156] Murray suggested that the men surrendered because they learnt that the Jacobites had possession of the artillery and because they could now expect no assistance.[157]

The fighting, such as it was, was over in seven or eight minutes. Dead and dying were lying all around. Carlyle wrote 'their Groans and Agonies were nothing compar'd with the howlings and cries of the women'.[158] The walls of Pinkie were an obstacle to flight, despite the few breaches that had been made hitherto. According to O'Sullivan, 'it was there really where the great slautter was, for the poor souldiers yt cou'd not pass in those breaches, because of the Dragons yt fill'd 'um up, were cut to pieces'. Dragoons dismounted in order to escape. They were chased by the MacDonalds.[159] Henderson adds, 'But the great Carnage was at the Grange Park Dyke, which when the poor men were climbing, they were massacred in the most barbarous manner; twenty were killed by the sword, for one who fell by a bullet. At last the slaughter was stopt by Perth and Lochiel'.[160] Yet not all in these heaps were dead; Murray of Broughton stating, 'At first one would have imagined that few or none of the troops had escaped the slaughter, they lying in heaps down by the park wall, then in less than quarter of an hour 9 of 10 found their feet, for to evite death numbers thrown themselves on the ground, the greatest part not so much wounded'.[161] Elsewhere, the 'field of battle presented a spectacle of horror, being covered with heads, legs, arms and mutilated bodies, for the killed all fell by the sword'.[162] Corpses were stripped of their clothes.[163]

Charles had spent the battle on foot in the second line. Once the battle was over, he mounted his horse, rode forward and ordered the killing to cease, 'make prisoners; spare them, spare them, they are my father's subjects'.[164] Murray of Broughton added 'nor was there ever more mercy shown as upon any occasion'.[165]

According to Lumisden, 'All care imaginable was taken of the wounded, plenty of able surgeons having been provided for that purpose'.[166] According to Henderson, Perth advised Charles to send to Edinburgh for surgeons. He alleged that Charles, after the battle, was clad as an ordinary captain, 'in a coarse plaid and blue Bonnet, his Boots and knees much dirtied' having fallen into a ditch. According to Henderson he was laughing heartily and unconcerned about the wounded, even eating beef and drinking when in the earshot of the sounds of the dead and dying.[167] Murray of Broughton denied such allegations, 'falsely inserted by a little ignorant school Master'.[168] Cunningham and Trotter, surgeons to the dragoon regiments, surrendered themselves in order to tend to the wounded.[169]

Jacobite losses were slight. Lumisden notes that four junior officers and thirty rank and file died and six officers and seventy privates were wounded.[170] However, a study of the Jacobite army of 1745 reveals that six officers were killed; one each from Keppoch's, Glencoe's, Perth's, Stewart of Appins and two from the Camerons.[171] Most of the dead were among the Camerons and MacGregors, according to O'Sullivan.[172] The dead officers ('these people of no distinction', wrote Murray of Broughton) were Captain Robert Stewart, Angas MacDonald, Archibald MacDonald of Keppoch, Lieutenant Allan Cameron, James Cameron and Ensign Drummond/MacGregor, of Perth's battalion. A further seven Jacobites died of their wounds in hospital.[173] James Ray, a contemporary historian, claimed that the Jacobites concealed the true number of their dead by hiding the burials from prying eyes.[174]

As to the losses suffered by the British army, Jacobite estimates of killed, captured and taken prisoners were sizeable, but exaggerated.

Officers Killed

Unit	Field Officer	Major	Captain	Lieutenant	Cornet/ Ensign	Other	Total
Gardner	1						1
Hamilton							
Lord jorn Murray					2		2
Lascelles			1				1
Guise			1				1
Lee			2				2
Loudoun							
Total	1		4		2		7

Officers Wounded/Captured

Unit	Field Officer	Major	Captain	Lieutenant	Cornet/ Ensign	Other	Total
Gardner	1			1/1		1/3	2/5
Hamilton	1/1	1/1			½	0/1	3/5
Lord John Murray			0/1	0/1	0/1		0/3
Lascelles		0/1	0/6	2/4	0/5		2/16
Guise			1/1	0/2	0/2		1/5
Lee	0/1		0/4	3/6	0/3	0/1	3/14
Murray	0/1	0/1	2/5	3/5	1/5	0/1	6/19
Loudon			0/3	0/2	0/3		0/8
Others	1/1	0/1		0/1		0/4	1/7
Total	2/4	¼	3/20	9/21	2/21	1/10	18/82

Rank and file

Killed/missing: 357 (no breakdown by unit is available).

Escaped: 175 infantry (to Carlisle, Edinburgh castle and Berwick), 450 cavalry

Captured: 958

These were as follows:

Unit	
Gardner	52
Hamilton	62
Lord John Murray	155*
Lascelles	266
Guise	40
Lee	157
Murray	226
Loudoun	155*
Total	958

*denotes total prisoners taken from Highland regiments

Many of these prisoners were also wounded.[175]

Gardiner was buried three days later in the churchyard at Tranent, where eight of his children were already interred (his widow and a surviving daughter were currently at Stirling Castle). The nearby Bankton House was his home.[176]

Of those wounded who later claimed pensions and whose wound location is known (100), 26 had head wounds, 19 had been injured in their legs, 21 arm wounds and 30 to the hand. Only four were abdomen wounds. Seventeen men had been injured in more than one place. Occasionally the cause of this damage is known; eleven being due to cuts and seven by musket ball.[177] Henderson gave a graphic account of the suffering he saw, 'The private men's heads were almost cut through, the greater Number in the back part; some had 7 or 8 Wounds. Noses, Hands, Arms, Legs &c. were promiscuously to be seen scatter'd o'er the Field.'[178] Horses were also slain, even after their riders had fled or being killed. According to Elcho, horses as well as men fought.[179]

Apart from men, Cope lost all his artillery, small arms, flags (seven in all), drums, tents, baggage and the money, estimated at between £2,500–£4,000, in his military chest. Cope's carriage was also taken.[180] Charles sent O'Sullivan to make an inventory of the material gains which were fit for military service, but Murray obstructed him so that he was unable to make such a list.[181] Murray makes no mention of this but stated that he took care of the guns.[182] There was also some thefts. Some of the officers had their money and watches taken from them. Officers' servants and country gentlemen were treated likewise.[183] One of Mr Walker's sons attempted to retrieve the carts and horses used by the army, but was pursued by the Jacobites. Wounding one pursuer and losing one horse, he was successful.[184]

Of the prisoners, a number of NCOs and privates joined the Jacobite army (including Alan Stewart, hero of the Robert Louis Stephenson novels *Kidnapped* and *Catriona*). A report of 4 October referred to 160 former prisoners seen in Edinburgh with white cockades in their hats and an English sergeant was seen with such a decoration, recruiting men in Edinburgh streets with the aid of a drummer. Only thirty, however, were later found in the Jacobite army and several were subsequently hanged for desertion.[185] Apparently none of the Mackays and Munros taken prisoner enlisted.[186] Many deserted afterwards and found their way to Berwick, where by the end of October there were about 200; another 37 escaped to Carlisle. Charles wrote, 'I am in great difficulties how I shall dispose of my wounded prisoners'. They were conveyed to Edinburgh in sixteen carts, organized by Lochiel.[187] According to one eyewitness, 'betwixt 2 & 3 Hundred of our men prisoners of war at Edinburgh and they youse them very unmercifull'.[188] Alexander Walker, a surgeon of Haddington, sent his apprentices out with carts to bring wounded men to his house to care for them, spending money on medicines and oatmeal to the total of £350.[189]

Rank and file prisoners were confined in 'the church' and in Cannongate prison in Edinburgh. The officers were better treated, with one declaring 'We are very well used, and have the liberty of the town on our parole'. They also had to promise not to write to the government.[190] Charles asked one wounded officer why he fought against him, his true prince come to rescue the country form a foreign yoke, and 'He said he was a man of honour, and would be true to the Prince, whose bread he ate and whose commission he bore'.[191]

Murray saw to it that the officers who were wounded were placed in Gardiner's house and seen to by surgeons; others were sent to Musselburgh. Next day he arranged for the rank and file prisoners to be given food.[192] Seventeen of those wounded died in hospital in the following week.[193] About 70–80 of Loudoun's men were freed on condition they promised not to fight the Jacobites and were given money to return home. In early October about fifty of these were in Inverness, in Loudoun's service but the remainder had gone home saying that they could not break their oaths not to serve against the Jacobites. By the end of the month other prisoners were sent to Logie Rate, Atholl and officers were sent to Perth.[194] Many were later rescued in January 1746.

The reason for this defeat was a breakdown in morale, as the anonymous officer explained:

> Neither officers nor General can divest men of dread and panick when it seizes them, he only can do that who makes the heart of man. To their being struck with a most unreasonable panick, and to no one thing else, the disgraceful event was owing. The ground was to our wish, the disposition was unexceptionable, and we were fully formed.[195]

Michael Hughes, a volunteer in Bligh's battalion, put the defeat down to the inexperience of the troops, 'A few Flanders Regiments of ours, with a good Commander, would have disputed the Cause much better with them'.[196] Certainly very few of the men had seen service abroad. On the other hand, many (though crucially not all) of the veteran battalions were to flee in the subsequent battle against the Jacobite army. In both cases the unorthodox fighting tactics of their enemies in their rush forward and the threat of a mêlée may have been crucial, and this was something most regular troops were unused to.

Cope wrote to Newcastle on the evening of the battle and on the day thereafter at Berwick to explain his defeat, 'I cannot reproach myself, the manner in which the army came on, which was quicker than can be described (of which the men have been long warned) possibly was the cause of our men behaving amiss'. He added on the next day, 'to the ill behaviour of some of the dragoons, in consequence of which the whole line took a pannick'.[197]

Other explanations were that the Jacobites had an overwhelming superiority of numbers; Whig historians giving the Jacobites as being 5,000 men as opposed to less than half that.[198] Henderson pointed to 'the Bravery of the clans, (a virtue which they carry to such extremes, that it degenerates into Madness)' and that some had served overseas, and the fact that the British troops were inexperienced.[199]

Craigie was fearful over the battle's consequences, writing on the day afterwards, 'One thing is certain that this defeat will make it a dangerous experiment for His Majesty's troops to engage the rebels a second time without a visible superiority'.[200] Yet some of the old contempt remained. Jack was contemptuous of the enemy, '1500 raw undisciplined and desperate Highlanders, no better than a mob . . . in no sense can it be called a battle'.[201] Wightman agreed, writing 'I say scuffle for battle it was not' as he thought it lasted a mere four minutes.[202]

Condemnation by the officers of the rank and file (who had few advocates) was universal. Craigie wrote, 'The officers in general condemn the soldiers and in a particular manner the dragoons who they say did not strike one blow before they fled . . . We think this accounts for the defeat', not the bravery of their enemies nor their numbers.[203] Yet according to Philip Doddridge, the officers of Gardiner's were blamed, for in a letter to the colonel's widow, 'it is said that the King has resolved to try all ye officers of it for their late conduct', though this never happened.[204]

Charles had a different reason why the Government soldiery did not fight well, 'yet they did not behave so well as I expected. I thought I could plainly see that the common men did not like the cause they were engaged in . . . their officers, who by their own ambition and false notions of honour, fought more desperately'.[205]

Charles stayed at Pinkie on the night of the battle, returning to Holyroodhouse on 22 September. His army went back to Duddingston on that day, too.[206] According to Maxwell, 'Nothing could be more complete, or more important than this victory; nevertheless, the Prince did not seem to be much elated with it'. When he returned to Edinburgh with 800 of his men he was greeted 'with all the demonstrations of joy and affection imaginable'.[207]

There was much regret by loyalists on hearing the news of Cope's defeat, which arrived in London on 24 September. Edinburgh loyalists wrote that it had been 'a melancholy day for those that love peace and quiet'.[208] Andrew Stone, Newcastle's secretary, wrote of 'the melancholy news which we received this morning, of the rebels having attack'd the King's troops . . . & entirely defeated them'.[209] Horace Walpole (1717–97), son of the late Sir Robert, wrote, 'The defeat has frightened everybody but those it rejoices'. London spinster

Miss Gertrude Saville wrote in her diary 'This defeat shook the whole Nation (except Papists and Jacobites) . . . into terror and confusion'.[210] She put the blame on 'Scoundrelly' Cope, who she alleged was asleep at the time of the battle and was the first to run away. This comment was as accurate as hers about Gardiner's having been shot dead.[211] Of Cope, Walpole was less harsh in his characteristically waspish and backhanded comment, 'I pity him, who with no shining abilities, and no experience [!] and no force, was sent to fight for a crown'.[212] Carlyle wrote that 'Nothing but the weakest, and most unaccountable Bad Conduct, on our part, could have possibly Given them the Victory. God forbid that Brittain should ever again be in Danger of being overrun by such a Despicable Enimy. For at best the Highlanders were at that time but a Raw Militia.'[213]

There was a great deal of contemporary criticism of Cope's behaviour in battle from both friends and enemies. Marchant remarked that he had exposed the artillery by having them a distance from the main body. He thought that they should have been centrally positioned.[214] Henderson blamed Cope, 'his counsels were infatuated, and by his conduct he ruined himself'. He also suggested that he should have attacked the Jacobites at Musselburgh or at the Esk.[215]

According to Henderson, when he asked some of the wounded on the field, 'what was become of Cope? And they all, but especially the English soldiers, spoke most disrespectfully and bitterly of him.'[216] Murray of Broughton stated that Cope should not have rushed into battle but should have awaited reinforcements, that he left a better battlefield than the one he had, that he should have not intimidated his own men, that he should have marched earlier on the 20th to seize the bridge at Musselburgh, have had better reconnaissance of the morass, and could have marched to Edinburgh when the Athollmen were withdrawn.[217] In the following year there was a Board of Enquiry into Cope's conduct on the campaign and on the battlefield carried out by a number of brother officers. Cope was cleared but never again held a battlefield command and the popular Jacobite song 'Hey Johnnie Cope' has damned his memory as a fool and coward.

There is no doubt that this was a spectacular Jacobite victory, surpassing even Killiecrankie. Elcho wrote that it was 'undoubtedly, one of the most complete victorys ever was gained' yet claimed it went to Charles' head, 'The Prince from this battle entertained a mighty notion of the Highlanders and ever after imagin'd they would beat four times their number of regular troops' and also believed that 'regular troops would not fight against him, because of his being their natural Prince'.[218] According to Carlyle, 'the Almighty had blessed them with this almost Bloodless Victory (on their part)'.[219]

Charles wrote a letter to his father on the evening of the battle, telling him that 'it hath pleased God to prosper your Majesty's army under my command with a success that has even surprised my wishes'. It had not quite been complete, he admitted, for 'if I had a squadron or two of horse to pursue the flying enemy there would not one man of them have escaped'. Yet he was not wholly content, writing 'if I had obtained this victory over foreigners, my joy would have been compleat. But as it is over Englishmen, it has thrown a damp upon it that I little imagined. The men I have defeated were your Majesty's enemies, it is true, but they might have become your friends and dutiful subjects.' In the meantime he sent one Stewart, 'a faithful honest fellow' to tell his father the news.[220]

This was the Jacobites' greatest victory. They had won the battle and killed or captured the bulk of the enemy army and with only minimal casualties to themselves. Although the former had occurred at Killiecrankie too, that had been at the cost of not only about a quarter of their army but also their leader. Furthermore, now the Jacobites had cleared Scotland of all field armies opposed to them, unlike in 1689. They had succeeded in part because the calibre of the troops opposed to them was low, their artillery ineffective and their cavalry incapable of offensive action; they had the added advantage of charging at daybreak, which is never a time when courage is highest. Yet this was only one battle won over a small part of the Government forces. More successes would be needed to achieve another Stuart restoration. The victory was thus the first step to potential future triumphs. For their enemies, this had been the chance to snuff out what might only have been a little local difficulty, as at Glenshiel. Now the British state faced a much more difficult challenge which would require a substantial amount of troops and resources.

Chapter 12

The Jacobite High Tide, 1745–1746

With Cope's army effectively destroyed, there were only the isolated garrisons in Scotland's castles and fortresses who resisted the Jacobite cause in the northern kingdom. They could do little immediately against them. One of the British kingdoms now had an undisputed Stuart in the royal palace in Edinburgh. The Jacobites were in their strongest position ever. However, this was not enough. The Stuarts wanted all of their ancestral lands possessed from 1603–88, not just the one inherited by James VI in the sixteenth century.

Almost as soon as the battle of Prestonpans was over, there was talk of an immediate thrust into England, via the north-east. This was soon dismissed for Berwick was strongly defended, being held by over 1,000 troops with artillery. The Jacobite army was not numerically strong enough to try such a move. However, over the next few weeks, additional recruits came in, especially from the Lowlands. These included Lord Ogilvy and Farquharson, Gordon of Glenbucket, Lord Pitsligo and additional Camerons and MacDonalds. Cavalry units were formed under Elcho and Balmerino and there was now a proper train of artillery. There was even a form of international recognition from the French as an envoy, one Du Boyer, Marquis d'Aigulles arrived with golden promises, explaining that a treaty had been made between Louis XV and the Jacobite representative and that the former would send troops to assist the Jacobites. Later that month ships arrived at Montrose and Stonehaven with artillery and crews under James Grant, an engineer.

Perhaps the only snag was that an emissary sent into England was arrested at Newcastle and so no further attempts were apparently made to contact the English Jacobites. Even in Scotland, Jacobite authority was being challenged, both in towns such as Perth and Dundee and in the Highlands amongst the loyalist chiefs. Edinburgh Castle held out and the Jacobites were unable to blockade it following an artillery barrage from the Castle when they briefly attempted to do so.

In England the government's position was much stronger, too. The arrival of ten battalions of infantry on 23 September prevented any panic that might otherwise have occurred following the news of the defeat at Prestonpans. These troops were sent northwards to join an army under Wade which was forming in Doncaster, eventually marching to Newcastle, along with the Dutch/Swiss troops. Field Marshal George Wade had five regiments of cavalry and two troops of auxiliary cavalry, twelve battalions of British infantry and eight of Dutch/Swiss troops. More troops were sent from Cumberland's command. An additional army was being formed under Lieutenant General Jean Ligonier's charge in the Midlands. Many of these men were from Flanders, too, for on 30 September, Cumberland was told to despatch another 6,000 men to England and on 25 October, two regiments of cavalry, four battalions of infantry and the remainder of the guards battalions came over. Cumberland arrived himself on 18 October, but was initially not given a field command. In November additional cavalry regiments came.[1] New battalions and regiments were controversially raised by loyalist noblemen and in the counties militia and volunteer troops were raised.

Wade's command was made up of the following:

Commander-in-Chief
Field Marshal George Wade
Subordinates: Lord Tyrawley, Lieutenant Generals Wentworth and Handasyde, Major Generals Huske, Howard and Oglethorpe.

Infantry
1st Brigade
    Brigadier Mordaunt
    Battalions of Wolfe's, Munro's, Blakeney's and Royal Scots.
2nd Brigade
    Brigadier Cholmondeley
    Battalions of Howard's, Cholmondeley's, Ligonier's* and Pulteney's.
3rd Brigade
    Brigadier Fleming
    Battalions of Price's *, Battereau's, Fleming's and Barrell's.

Cavalry
Horse: Wade's and Montagu's.
Dragoons: St. George's, Gardiner's* and Hamilton's*.

Artillery
Major Belford, with 65 men.
16 x 3-pounders
8 x 1½-pounders
10 Cohorn mortars

Volunteers
Royal Hunters (cavalry).
William Thornton's infantry.
Oglethorpe's Georgians.

Dutch/Swiss

Commander: General Nassau

Subordinates: Lieutenant General Schwarztenburg, Major General Villattes.

1st Brigade

Hirzell's three battalions (1,700 men) and Holstein Gottrop (500 men).

2nd Brigade

Brackell's, Patot's, Villatte's and La Rocque's (500 men in each).

Dutch artillerymen: 9

Strength in October 1745: 11,300 infantry and 1,380 cavalry.

Units marked * detached on 12 November with Handasyde to Edinburgh.

By 5 December, 805 cavalry, 5,425 British infantry and 3,502 Dutch were fit for service at Wetherby.[2]

The Jacobites in Scotland had to decide what to do. They were running out of money so could no longer stay where they were for much longer. Movement was crucial. Should they invade England, which a Jacobite army had last done in 1715, with unhappy results? Or should they remain in Scotland? Charles was adamant for the first course of action – throughout the campaign he always advocated boldness – and his wish was backed at the council of war held in Edinburgh, after he had made promises of significant English support. The next question was where should this march take place. There was the route through the north-east of England, taken successfully by the Scots in 1640, or the north-western route, taken with disastrous results in 1648, 1651 and in 1715. Charles proposed the first in order that they could defeat Wade's army and achieve another resounding victory to encourage supporters in England to declare for him. Murray was the voice of caution – as he was to be throughout the campaign – and proposed marching through the county of Cumberland, avoiding immediate battle and allowing supporters to join before such fighting. His opinion was taken.

On 4 November the Jacobite army of 5,000 infantry (divided into 13 battalions), 500 cavalry and 13 guns left Edinburgh and its environs. In detail the army's composition was as follows:

Infantry

Unit	Commander	Strength
Camerons	Cameron of Lochiel	500
Stewarts of Appin	Ardshiel	150
MacPhersons	Cluny of MacPherson	300

Unit	Commander	Strength
MacDonalds of Clanranald	Clanranald	200
MacDonalds of Keppoch	Keppoch	150
MacDonalds of Glengarry	Lochgarry	500
Ogilvies		200
Edinburgh Regiment	Roy Stuart	200
Glenbuckets		200
Perth's		300
Atholl Brigade battalion 1	Lord Nairn	350
Atholl Brigade battalion 2	Shian Menzies	300
Atholl Brigade battalion 3	Lord George Murray	350

Cavalry

Unit	Commander	Strength
Pitsligo's Horse	Lord Pitsligo	150
Hussars		70
Guards	Lord Elcho	150
Perthshire Horse	Lord Kilmarnock	130[3]

It divided into two columns. One under Murray feinted to the east. Wade's advance guard had marched north to Morpeth on 3 November but he was uncertain as to the Jacobites' intended destination, so fell back on Newcastle. He did, however, send two battalions of infantry and two of dragoons under Lieutenant General Roger Handasyde to Edinburgh which they reoccupied without a fight. Meanwhile Murray's men rejoined the rest of the army and on 9 November they were arranged outside the border town and castle of Carlisle, which had been bypassed by the Jacobites in 1715. However, en route southwards into England the army suffered from desertions to the tune of about 500 men, as it had in 1715, some of the Scots being unwilling to travel so far from home.

Following an abortive summons for Carlisle to surrender on 9 November, the Jacobite army began to make preparations for a siege. Trenches were dug and cannon mounted under Perth's directions. The city's and castle's walls were far from robust, neglected after decades of domestic peace. The garrison of the castle was but eighty elderly soldiers under Lieutenant Colonel James Durand. The city had the county militia and the city volunteers. It was not an impressive defence, but then the Jacobites lacked the heavy artillery necessary to make breaches in the walls.

However, when a messenger was sent to Wade in Newcastle to request relief, Wade refused, believing that Carlisle must hold out as the Jacobites lacked heavy guns. The receipt of this news caused morale among the militia and volunteers to plummet. The Jacobite army had moved some troops to Brampton to the east of the city lest a relief force arrive. They were now pulled back to Carlisle and negotiations began following the refusal of the militia to continue to defend the city. Durand was forced to surrender and on 15 November, the first English city and castle had been taken by the Jacobites, despite the latter's internal dissension when Murray resigned his post before being reinstated.

The next question was whether they should continue marching southwards or return to Scotland. There had been, disappointingly, no rush of English supporters to the Jacobite cause. Meanwhile Wade, on 16 November, marched his army from Newcastle to Hexham, intending to attack the Jacobite army at Carlisle. Bad weather, appalling roads and scanty provisions all combined to seriously weaken his men after a mere two days. On hearing on 18 November that the city had fallen the decision was taken to retire to Newcastle for shelter. The Jacobite army left a small garrison in Carlisle and then pressed on, in search of additional support.

Marching through Penrith, Kendal and Lancaster was, as it had been in 1715, a disheartening experience, for only a handful of men volunteered to join them. However at Preston and especially Manchester, matters were looking up, but only just. Elcho later wrote that at the latter:

> The mob Huzza'd him to his Lodgings, the town was mostly illuminated, and the Bells rung, their were several substantial People came and kiss'd his hand, and a vast number of people of all sorts came to see him supp. After all these proceedings it was natural enough to imagine that their would be a great joining, but everybody was astonish'd to find that all that was to join was about 200 common Fellows.[4]

At the latter, on 30 November, there were finally enough men to form a predominantly English Jacobite battalion of infantry, led by Francis Towneley, whose uncle had fought for the Jacobites in 1715. Yet even here, much more had been expected and the relatively low social status of the recruits was depressing. Yet there was, as in Edinburgh, cheering for Charles in the streets. This was enough to impress him and encourage the army to continue its march, after some discussion about its viability, but some were less sanguine about their hopes for success.

Although there had been no resistance to the Jacobite march through Lancashire with the outnumbered and isolated county militia disbanding and the Liverpool Blues retreating to Chester after having broken bridges, there was now a greater threat. Ligonier had been replaced by Cumberland in charge of a substantial army in the Midlands. Philip Stanhope, fourth Earl of Chesterfield, was looking forward to a battle, writing on 25 November, 'our regular troops, I am convinc'd are fully equal to three times their own number of undisciplined rabble . . . I see an end, and a speedy one of the rebellion'.[5]

Cumberland's army was composed of the following:

Commander: The Duke of Cumberland
Subordinates: Lieutenant General Ligonier and St. Clair, the Duke of Richmond, Major Generals Bland and Skelton, Brigadiers Sempill, Douglas and Bligh.

Infantry
Guards: three battalions.
Regular battalions: Sowle's, Sempill's, Royal Scots Fusiliers, Johnston's, Skelton's, Douglas', Handasyde's, Howard's and Bligh's˙ (7,500 men).

Cavalry
Horse: Ligonier's.
Dragoons: Bland's, Kerr's, Cobham's (1,400 men).
Newly raised
Dragoons: Kingston's Light Horse, Montagu's (800 men).
Infantry: Halifax's, Bedford's, Montagu's, Granby's, Gower's˙ and Cholmondeley's ˙ (3,000 men).

Artillery
2 x 6-pounders
14 x 3-pounders
2 howitzers
Units marked ˙ detached on 29 November for the defence of Chester under Brigadier Douglas.[6]

Murray marched the army into Macclesfield, then into Derbyshire. By a feint he had made, Cumberland marched his army to Stone in Staffordshire. On 4 December the Jacobite army was in Derby. On the face of it, this was a remarkable achievement. No Jacobite army had ever penetrated this far south into England with the potential for reaching the capital and thus success. Wade's forces were only as far south as Yorkshire and Cumberland's had been side stepped.

Charles was elated. So it must have come as a shock, despite discussions at Carlisle and Manchester for a retreat, that the majority of his council was opposed to any further advance. Murray led the discontent and came up with seemingly plausible reasons for a return to Scotland. He remarked, 'if there was any party for in England, it was odd that they never had so much as sent him money or intelligence or the least advice what to do'.[7] There had been no French support, no significant English support and with an army smaller than it had been when it left Edinburgh it was folly to think they could fight and beat three stronger armies (there was another force defending London led by George II). With reinforcements in Scotland, including a few French troops, it was surely for the best to join their compatriots north of the border. Charles was furious, 'The Prince heard all these arguments with the greatest impatience, fell into a passion and gave most of the Gentlemen that spoke against him very Abusive Language and said that they had a mind to betray him'.[8] Following a second meeting that day he had to concede to his council's demands and so preparations for retreat were made, despite the men's evident high morale. In retrospect this was the nearest the Jacobite army came to victory – or an immediate and bloody defeat. The strategic initiative now passed to the British army. As John Daniel, an English Jacobite, later recorded, 'How far they acted amiss or well, I know not'.[9]

London was not wholly undefended. Units for the defence of the city, December 1745 (numerical strength if known in brackets), were as follows:

Horse
Two troops of Ligonier's (110).
Dragoons
Hawley's (360).
Rich's (431).

Infantry
Three battalions of Foot Guards.
St. Clair's (660).
Huske's (611).
Mordaunt's (623).
Bragg's (641).
Murray's (616).
Beauclerk's (490).
Richbell's.
No numbers given for Guards or Richbell's.
En route, Frampton's. Bragg's unable to march until relieved at Tower of London by Harrison's.[10]

Both Cumberland and Wade might have been able to have defeated the Jacobite army in England. Yet Wade's forces marched too slowly. By the time the advance guard was in Halifax the Jacobites were in Manchester and so were too late. Cumberland made haste with his cavalry and mounted infantry northwards; Wade despatched Oglethorpe and the cavalry from his army westwards. However, Cumberland was delayed in his pursuit by letters from London telling him of a French invasion on the south coast. Once it was confirmed that this was illusory, the Jacobite army was even further away. Oglethorpe failed to stop the escaping army which once considered stopping for battle but never did. There was discussion among the Jacobites about fighting near Lancaster and Murray looked for a suitable field, but this came to naught. Despite resistance from the country people in Cumberland and Westmorland, the bulk of the Jacobite army reached Carlisle by 18 December.

It was on this day that Cumberland's pursuit force finally caught up with the Jacobite rearguard under Murray. Requesting more men, Murray had his men (the MacPhersons, the Appin Stewarts, Roy Stuart's battalion and the MacDonalds of Glengarry) line the hedges of the village of Clifton. After a brief firefight the Jacobites charged and pushed back some of the dragoons, who were fighting on foot. Casualties were minor on both sides. The Jacobite army was able to retreat unscathed as Cumberland had retained the ground. This was the last skirmish between formed armies on English soil.

At Carlisle, Charles decided to leave a garrison of mainly non-clan troops and the remainder of the Manchester regiment, about 400 men, with artillery. It was a controversial decision, though O'Sullivan believed that they would delay Cumberland's pursuit of the main army, which they did. On 21 December, as the Jacobite army reached Scotland, Cumberland and his advance guard began to lay siege to Carlisle. Lacking heavy guns, he sent for them from Whitehaven and a week later they began their bombardment. After a small breach had been made, surrender negotiations were entered into but the garrison had to surrender at the king's pleasure: as in Preston in 1715 the Jacobites were seen as rebels and traitors, not legitimate prisoners of war. By 31 December, England was clear of the Jacobite army once again.

Meanwhile, Wade had been superseded in command by Lieutenant General Henry Hawley, a veteran of Sheriffmuir. With news of another French invasion scare, Cumberland travelled south and so the main army opposed to the Jacobites was that led by Hawley. Because of the French fighting alongside the Jacobites, the Dutch/Swiss troops could no longer participate in the campaign so were withdrawn from his force as the government negotiated for Hessian troops to be sent. Hawley therefore marched his men to Edinburgh.

The main Jacobite army marched to Dumfries, reaching it by 21 December and then to Glasgow, five days later, taking contributions from both of these towns. They stayed in Glasgow for a week and then marched to Stirling in order to take the town and castle. The former fell after a few days' siege on 8 January 1746, being only held by militia. Major General William Blakeney, the lieutenant governor, was unwilling to surrender the castle without a siege, 'he was always look'd upon as a man of honour, and the Rebels should find that he would die so', and the Jacobites began to assemble their heavy artillery that had arrived from France.[11]

The difficulty was that these guns were at Alloa and the only way to transport them to Stirling was by water. There were Royal Navy sloops there to prevent them but these were eventually evaded and by 12 January the Jacobite siege artillery was in position. The siege began, mainly conducted by the Lowlanders and the newly-arrived French and Irish troops.

Hawley began to push parts of his army towards Stirling and supplies were gathered for his army at Linlithgow. On 13 January, hearing of this, Murray marched with five clan regiments and two of cavalry to seize it to retard Hawley's march. They reached the town but by noon heard word that a strong force of British troops under Major General John Huske had left Edinburgh and were attempting to cut them off from the rest of the army. Murray managed to extricate his forces, but heard on the following day that this had been the advance guard of Hawley's force with the remainder on their way. Another battle could not now be long delayed.

Chapter 13

The Battle of Falkirk, 17 January 1746

This was the biggest battle of the Jacobite campaigns in terms of men involved. Once in Scotland the Jacobite army was reinforced by Scottish forces raised in their absence, as well as contingents of French infantry. Yet this battle is one of the least studied, perhaps because it was strategically indecisive. In some ways the reason why it was fought was a very common one in eighteenth-century warfare; the relief of a fortress, but more was expected. On the day of the battle, Horace Walpole wrote to Sir Horace Mann with anticipation, 'what a despicable affair is a rebellion upon the defensive! General Hawley is marched from Edinburgh, to put it quite out . . . [he] will give a mortal blow to the pride of the Scotch nobility . . . He is very brave and able; with no small bias to be brutal'.[1] Others of the elite shared Walpole's views, too, with Newcastle writing to Chesterfield on 6 January, 'I hope General Hawley will not only be able to prevent their return [into England], but entirely to reduce and beat them'. His correspondent's letter of five days later included the wish, 'if Hawley acts with spirit, as I verily believe he will do, you will see the trouble in Scotland ended in two months time at the furtherest'.[2]

On 15 January 1746 the Jacobite army was drawn up on a plain or moor which was a mile to the east of Bannockburn. Cavalry were sent off to Falkirk to reconnoitre and found a large body of Government dragoons near the town, but no infantry were seen there. The Jacobite army returned to its quarters, 'in the scattered huts around Bannockburn' but leaving some of the cavalry to patrol that night as near to Falkirk as possible. According to MacDonald, the cavalry was 'composed chiefly of gentlemen without discipline or experience, whose horses, worn out and ill cared for, were in a very bad state', so that he thought the army's protection in case of attack was minimal.[3]

Next day the patrols reported that Government infantry had arrived at Falkirk from Linlithgow, consisting of eight battalions, Hamilton's and Ligonier's (formerly Gardiner's) dragoons and the Glasgow militia under Huske. They were in a camp just to the north of the town. The cavalry had advanced as far as the bridge of Carron. Meanwhile the Jacobite army drew up again on the same plain as they had on the previous day. By three o'clock they had seen no sight of the enemy and so returned to their scattered – and thus vulnerable – camps. Had Hawley's army attacked them in that condition, although he could not as not all the army was together, Elcho estimated that only 3,000 men could be brought together to resist them. Additional troops joined the Jacobite army in the shape of Lord Lewis Gordon's 800 men, Sir James Kinloch's 600 and Lord John Drummond's 350-strong regiment of Royal Eccossais, part of the French army. Morale was high.[4]

That evening a council of war was held and a unanimous decision was taken to attack on the next day.[5] Later that day the remainder of the Government army arrived at Falkirk, with Hawley (he stayed at Callendar House from eight that night, turfing some Glasgow militia officers out of their rooms to do so). The artillery arrived at seven in the evening. The Argyllshire militia and Cobham's dragoons arrived from Edinburgh at eight in the morning on 17 January. The Earl of Hopton gave the infantry battalions 12 guineas each and the same to the first two of the dragoon regiments in order that they might buy beef for themselves. The plan was to attack on 18 January.[6]

The Government camp was in a strong position, 100 paces to the west of the town. In front of the camp was a deep hollow, with a morass to the right flank and to the left was an enclosure with large wet ditches. Brigadier James Cholmondeley wrote that it was 'very strong'. The tents were lined up in two ranks. The evening of the 16th was frosty.[7] Hawley was looking forward to battle and victory. He had a poor opinion of his enemy, writing on 11 January, 'I do and always shall despise these rascals' and that the 'rascally scum ... will go off or they are mad'. Cumberland agreed with him, believing 'that despicable enemy' would flee before them. So Hawley was eager to fight; on 15 January he had written, 'I am resolved to strike while the iron is hot'. Another reason for his eagerness was that he was concerned that Stirling Castle might fall to the Jacobite siege, 'The rebels are busy at Stirling, but I hope they'll find it a tough nut, tho' I fear we can't be time to save it'.[8]

Meanwhile, on 17 January the siege of Stirling Castle began, the Jacobite besiegers being under the command of Perth with 1,400 men.[9] These were made up of the Duke of Perth's regiment, 700 strong, John Roy Stuart's regiment, 400 strong and Glenbucket's 300 men. There were also two 18-pounder guns and some 12- and 16-pounders.[10] They remained on guard there on the day of the battle.

According to MacDonald, it was three in the morning when one Brown 'came to rouse the Prince telling him that the enemy were beating to quarters. It was then feared that we might be surprised and we sent all around to collect the troops, which were not assembled until about 10 o' clock', though there is no evidence that they were under any threat whatsoever.[11]

Early that morning, Murray gave a scroll detailing the line of battle to Charles. It showed that the French and Irish regulars should be split between each flank of the second line in case the army was attacked in the flank by the dragoons. Murray asked Charles that he appoint officers to command and suggested their location. However, no such appointments were made.[12]

For the third time in as many days, the Jacobite army formed up. Johnstone thought that everyone believed that the review was merely to choose a battlefield and find out what the ground was like there as they believed that they would be attacked there imminently.[13] Again the cavalry was despatched to ascertain Hawley's movements. Once more there was nothing to report. A council of war was held, where Murray explained that whereas the Jacobite army was divided and so vulnerable, their enemies were united. He added, 'by holding above the Torwood, we would gain the hill of Falkirk as soon as them, as it was a thing they did not expect. I knew the ground well, and thought there was no difficulty of taking it before they could.' O'Sullivan added that additional reasons were that because the enemy was not stirring from their camp, it would be 'fatiguing his men to keep them under armes every day'. Charles approved the plan and so the decision was taken to take the offensive.[14] O'Sullivan wrote that 'every one was of yt opinion, & it is very happy they were, for the enemy was to march yt night and attack us in our quarters'.[15]

Lord John Drummond, commander of the French troops, would take the main road to Falkirk as far as Torwood with his own regiment, the Irish troops and the cavalry. Murray would lead the two columns of infantry on the south side of Dunipace and began to ascend the hill there.[16] This was so that the main force would be hidden from the enemy's sight by the trees of Torwood. Following behind the main column were the train of artillery (except for the heavy siege guns), with Farquharson's men escorting them. It was noon when the army began to move.[17] This was because, as Murray noted, 'how difficult it was to bring our men together from so many cantonments for several miles round'.[18]

Morale seemed high among the Jacobite army as they marched to possible battle. Daniel wrote, 'the soldiers shewed the greatest alacrity; the foot marching with such celerity as kept the horse on a full trot'.[19] Maxwell wrote that 'they were all in fine spirits, and confident of victory'.[20] Charles did his best to keep up the men's morale, 'was occupied of encourgaeing the men, & forming them, as they us'd to come out of those bad steps, to get them to march in order & presse them on, yt there should be no interval nor time lost'.[21] In fact, according to one soldier, the men had been so disappointed in not being allowed to march on the previous two days that they would have advanced towards the enemy with or without orders on the 17th anyway.[22]

Half an hour after the march began, O'Sullivan rode up to Murray and told him he had been talking to Charles. The two had decided that it was in-advisable to cross the river until nightfall, when it could be done without being seen, for to do so before then would be dangerous in the face of the enemy. Murray was surprised and pointed out that it was only a quarter of an hour before they would have to make the crossing and that was two miles distant from the Government army's camp. Murray did not halt and O'Sullivan returned to see Charles. He added that if they stopped, the enemy would gain the high ground they desired and if the Jacobites did not move forward before night fall they would have to take shelter in the houses and villages nearby and so not be brought together until noon of the next day.[23]

Charles was riding between the two Jacobite columns. He, O'Sullivan, Brigadier Walter Stapleton, commander of the Irish Picquets, and others soon rode up to Murray. The latter expanded on his reasoning why halting the march would be folly. It would mean that the men would have to 'lie in the open fields all night' and in the cold January weather this would lead to men leaving to find food and shelter elsewhere. They must either march forwards or return to their quarters. Stapleton agreed, 'To be sure if the enemy were not near enough to dispute our passing, there could be no other objection'. Murray surmised that their enemy were still at dinner and that the Jacobites should march forward with all haste so as to secure the high ground and that would give them the initiative. Charles and Stapleton agreed with him and, as they had been riding forward all this time, the crossing was near at hand. It was then that they first saw their enemy.[24]

The Government army had been unaware of their peril, as Daniel noted, 'thinking it not worth their while to take the necessary precaution of having spies out, as other prudent generals would have done, notwithstanding the contempt they might have for us. We now roused them out of their lethargy.'[25] They were not completely caught napping for there were sentries placed a mile distant from the camp.[26] So far the day's weather had been fine. But then it turned for the worse. According to Daniel, 'all the elements in confusion, so that the heavens seemed to fulminate their anger down upon us, by the impetuous storm of hail, wind and rain, that fell just at the time of the engagement'.[27] It beat down on the faces of Hawley's men.[28]

Hawley had gone to the camp at five in the morning and at ten went to the hilly ground nearby to the left of the camp but neither he nor one Corse, a Glasgow militia officer, could see the enemy.[29] Cholmondeley later wrote, 'I saw them very plain with a glass' at eleven that morning. Yet, there were several hills between them and the Jacobite army, so he was uncertain where they were marching to. The men were turned out.[30] Hawley recalled that this was 'when the men were all boyling their kettles' and were stood to arms within minutes of the call. However, he then claimed that the next news was that the Jacobites had halted their march and were merely changing their grounds by the evidence of camp fires being lit. So he ordered the troops 'to lodge their arms and go on with their kettles'.[31]

It was only when Drummond's force was on the hill at Torwood that there was movement seen on the part of the Government army. They seemed to believe that all the Jacobite army was with Drummond and it was only later that the majority were seen.[32] It was one o'clock that repeated reports came of the Jacobite march towards them and these then had to be confirmed. The Jacobite army was three miles away.[33] In the interim, the troops were permitted to eat their dinners, which they just finished before the crisis developed.[34]

Just before one, two officers from Howard's battalion, one being Teesdale, climbed a tree near the camp and fixed a telescope. With it they saw the main bodies of the Jacobite army, not just the cavalry. They immediately told Lieutenant Colonel Howard and he went to Callendar House, to tell Hawley of the news. Hawley gave orders for the men to put on their equipment but not at this point to stand to under arms. During the next hour, horsemen rode about to gain more intelligence and they came back quickly with the news that the Jacobite army was on the march to the south of Torwood, about to cross the river at Dunipace, three miles from Falkirk. It was clear that the Jacobite army was marching to Falkirk moor, which was to the left of the army's camp.[35]

This news became widely known throughout the army and because Hawley was still at Callendar House, alarm began to rise among the officers who wondered where he was, what should be done and that they lacked orders. Senior officers had the infantry battalions formed up in front of the camp.[36] Apparently Hawley later stated that he believed that the Jacobite plan was to bypass him altogether and march to Edinburgh, but to think that the Jacobite command were deliberately leaving a hostile army in their rear seems incredible.[37]

According to Corse, 'I was surpriz'd to see in how little time ye regular troops were form'd (I think in less than half an hour)'.[38] Once the men were stood to, they were marched in two columns for a half mile from the camp, Cholmondeley wrote, 'but as we had hollow roads, and very uneven Ground, to pass, we were in great confusion'. They formed up for battle again, 'in my opinion a very good situation'. They then had to form up for a second time, to the left of the first position. When Hawley arrived, he had the cavalry march to seize the high ground and for the infantry to follow. The former soon outpaced the latter and a noticeable gap grew between them.[39] Corse noted that the infantry were 'running & quite out of breath with the Fatigue'.[40] It was now about two in the afternoon. The armies met on Falkirk Moor, about a mile to the south-west of the town.

Murray later wrote that the Jacobites had all the advantages that they could wish for. These were that they were close to their opponents before the assault, they were descending a hill to do so, that the wind was at their backs and at their enemies' faces, that they had boggy ground on their right to prevent the cavalry outflanking them, and that due to poor roads and steep hills the artillery could not be brought to bear against them. To summarize, 'in a word the Highland army had all the advantages that nature and art could give them'.[41]

O'Sullivan claimed that Charles told him to arrange the front line according to the order of battle as planned. He arrived at the right and saw the ground that Murray had occupied was 'full of old stone walls, & had one of them just at the heels of his last rank'. O'Sullivan said that such a position was dangerous and that he should advance the men to a better position, which Murray consented to. O'Sullivan was also concerned about the vulnerability of the right flank and suggested that the Atholl brigade be placed there, advancing in column, so they could face any way which was necessary. Murray refused this suggestion. O'Sullivan then went down the front line, telling all the colonels and majors that 'the second & third rank shou'd fire only, & yt as near the enemy as possible'.[42]

Before the battle, Charles made a speech, which was recorded by an unknown French officer, 'My friends, there are your enemies and mine, I rely on your bravery for the justice of my cause, for your lost country and your rightful King. I will be with you'. The same officer emphasised Charles's popularity with his men because 'He exposes himself despite all representations of the army, as the bravest Highlander, he has seen many officers killed close to him without making any wrong orders which as much calm as if he was in his tent'.[43]

The Jacobite army was forming up as follows (right to left), with the clan units in the front line, the Lowland ones in the second and Drummond's in the third.

Line 1 (left, commander Lord Drummond, to right, commander Murray).
    Lochiel, including McKinnons and MacGregors, 800–900.
    Stewarts of Appin, 300, led by the clan chief.
    Frasers, 300–400 led by Master Lovat.
    Mackintoshes, 200.
    Farquharson, 200.
    Cromarties, 200.
    MacPhersons, 300–400 led by Cluny of MacPherson.
    Clanranalds, 400, led by Clanranald.
    Glengarrys, 800–900, divided into two battalions, led by Lochgarry, the chief's son.
    Keppoch, 400–500, led by Keppoch.

Line 2
    Lewis Gordons, 400–900, led by Lord Lewis.
    Lord Ogilby, 700–1,000, divided into two battalions.
    Atholl Brigade, 600–1,000 led by Murray and Nairn.
Line 3 (commander Charles Stuart)
    Pitsligo's Horse, 100–120.
    Perthshire Horse, 40.
    Kilmarnock's Horse, 40–150.
    Irish and French, 300–450 led by Drummond and Brigadier Stapleton.
    Hussars, 40.
    Balmerino's, 40–60.
    Elcho's, 100–120.
    Unregimented gentlemen with Charles, 100.

Artillery
Two Swedish guns, 4–6-pounders, two French guns, 18-pounders.

According to Elcho there were 6,000 infantry and 360 cavalry.[44] Maxwell claimed the army was 7,000 strong.[45] The figures cited above suggest 5,900–7,350 infantry and 360–630 cavalry, so a minimum of 6,260 and a maximum of nearly 8,000. The bulk of the infantry were in the front line. This meant that there were large gaps between the units in the second line, especially between the centre and the wings.[46]

Their opponents were as follows:

In front of line 1
Ligonier's two squadrons of dragoons (253).
Hamilton's two squadrons of dragoons (266).
Cobham's three squadrons of dragoons (253).
Line 1 (left (commanded by Hawley) to right (commanded by Huske).
    Glasgow Militia (572 men, divided into 10 companies).
    Cholmondeley's (540).
    Pulteney's (504).
    Royal Scots (532).
    Price's (255).
    Ligonier's (318).
    Howard's (554).
Line 2
    Wolfe's (522).
    Blakeney's (460).
    Munro's (525).

Fleming's (426).
Barrel's (378).
Battereau's (474).
Line 3
Campbell Militia, led by Lieutenant Colonel Campbell and three companies of Loudoun's, (950 men).
Add 5.5 per cent based on figures for Culloden for non-rank and file; 301, so total of 5,789 regular infantry.
Reserve
Paisley Militia (174 men, divided into three companies), Captain Thornton's Yorkshire company of volunteers (150 men).
Total infantry strength: 7,635 (including 1,846 militia).
Total cavalry strength: 772 (assuming strength of Cobham's that as recorded later that year)
Total strength: 8,407

Artillery
Ten guns, including 4-pounders and 1½-pounders (Hawley claimed there were ten 3-pounders from Edinburgh Castle).
Captain Cunningham and 28 men, including 12 civilian drivers.[47]

Hawley had more men, especially in cavalry and more guns, although nearly 2,000 of his men were militia and volunteers.

As with Cope, Hawley had difficulties with the artillery. On 13 January he told Newcastle, 'no diligence shall be wanting in me, but my lord, no body can worke without tooles, and as to that point, my situation is as bad as ever any body was'.[48] He wrote 'We are in the greatest want of Guns . . . We want nothing but Gunns to go to Stirling and drive them from there'. But he was also disappointed in the senior artillery officer that he was provided with, 'Major Belford dos not come at all & this Cunningham is so ignorant & such a beast, he is no use'.[49] Belford was allegedly unwell, 'the sickness I suspect to be only a young wife he wants to be with, I know him'.[50] Cunningham was despised by Hawley, 'ane old trooper of the Duke of Argilles . . . who is such a sot and so ignorant that as I live he and I shant agree long'.[51] Finding the crews to man his guns was another headache. Walter Grossett, Collector of Customer at Alloa, was ordered by Andrew Fletcher and Hawley to go to Borristownness to find some men. He went there and recruited 'nine or ten sailors for that purpose who had been Gunners on Board Men of war' at the cost of £16 8s to be advanced to their families.[52] Hawley later wrote, 'the train is more for show than for use'.[53] Nor was he impressed with the cavalry, writing 'the debris of two Irishe regiments of dragoons, very weak and all the rest intimidates and cowed since the battle of Prestonpans', yet at least 'All the Foot except two regiments were good old battalions from Flanders'.[54]

The relatively few men (sixteen) who were later in receipt of pensions for wounds inflicted at the battle give less scope for analysis than is the case for those at Prestonpans. They were from thirteen different occupations prior to enlistment, with a preponderance of weavers, labourers and farmers. The overwhelming majority were English, though one was Scottish and two from Ireland. The years served varied between one and twenty-one with an average of between six and eight and they were aged in their late twenties on average, with a few being in their thirties.[55]

Hawley had given some thought to defeating the Jacobites, (whom he had fought at Sheriffmuir) for on 12 January he had drawn up a memorandum, expressing his contempt for their fighting abilities and outlining how they could be beaten:

> The Manner of the Highlanders way of fighting which there is nothing so easy to resist. If officers and men are not prepossess'd with the Lyes and Accounts which are told of them . . . The sure way to demolish them is at 3 deep to fire by ranks diagonally to the Centre where they come, the rear rank first, and even that rank not to fire till they are within 10 or 12 paces but if the Fire is given at a distance you probably will be broke for you never get time to a load a second Cartridge, and if you give way you may give your foot for dead, for they being without a firelock or any load, no Man with his Arms, accoutrements &c. can escape them, and they give no quarters, but if you observe the above directions, they are the most despicable Enimy that are.[56]

Both armies began to march up the hill, though neither side could see the other. The Jacobites hoped to gain the summit and then march directly on the enemy if there was enough daylight remaining. Otherwise they would remain here at night and then attack next morning. Whilst they were doing so, they could see some dragoons at the top of the hill, which they first assumed was just a small party of scouts, but then numbers were rising. However, 'The sight of an enemy gave fresh spirits to the Highlanders and it was impossible to restrain their ardour, but they still kept their ranks and marched up in the finest order imaginable, though at a prodigious rate'.[57]

The three regiments of dragoons made feints towards the Jacobite right, trying to entice them into firing at long range so that they could charge safely home against troops who could not fire a second time. In this they were unsuccessful. Meanwhile the armies continued their march and when they saw one another it was clear that each flank outlapped the other; the Jacobites outflanking the Government on the right and vice versa, so the Jacobite left was opposite the Government centre.[58]

Murray later wrote that this misalignment might have been remedied if two or three of the battalions in the second line had been brought up to extend the front line. But battalion commanders and clan chiefs only commanded their own men and the latter would take orders from no one else. Furthermore, the left wing was leaderless, though Drummond was allegedly in charge there, the reality was that 'he had no directions to do it, and was not there when the battle began'.[59]

Drummond had ridden at the head of the cavalry on the march, making a feint. When the infantry were crossing the Carron, he turned the cavalry towards the crossing and followed the infantry there. By the time the army had formed, he was in the rear and the he joined the troops on the third line.[60]

The three regiments of dragoons formed up in front of the camp 'in a moment'. Hawley told Captain John Masterton, a staff officer, to have them 'march immediately to him which was on a hill and ordered General Huske to follow with the Foot in two lines'. This having been accomplished, Hawley's next instructions for Masterton was 'to go to Lieutenant Colonel Whitney (who was on the left of the whole as all our dragoons were in two lines) to desire him to file more to the left than the rebels might not outflank us and make room for the Foot to march up the hill, upon wch ye sd colonel told me he could march no further for they were a morass on his left'.[61]

The men on the Jacobite right had seen the dragoon regiments after the former had crossed the Carron. They marched quickly ahead to secure the advantage of terrain that their enemy sought. Yet they kept their ranks and gave time for the rest of the army to come up on their left.[62] Murray sent Colonel Roy Stuart and Anderson, who were both on horseback, ahead to ascertain whether there were any infantry in support of the dragoons, which meant them riding close to their enemies. This they did and in answering Murray in the negative he continued his men's advance.[63]

The dragoons were formed up as seven squadrons, and once Hawley had seen to his infantry, he returned to find Colonel Ligonier at the head of the cavalry. Hawley ordered him to go to the left of the dragoons to head Cobham's there, with Whitney at the front of the adjacent squadron.[64] The dragoon regiments attempted to attack the Jacobite right wing in the flank. Murray realized what their plan was and then he and Colonel Roy Stuart 'made a very quick motion till he gained a morass, by which he saved being flanked'.[65] Once again the dragoon regiments attempted to unnerve the regiments opposite them. Elcho recorded their next move that they, 'at last came down in a line at full trot & attacked them sword in hand'.[66]

Daniel was initially overawed by the sight, later writing: 'Here I must acknowledge, that when I saw this moving cloud of horse, regularly disciplined, in full trot upon us down the summit, I doubted not but that they would have ridden over us without opposition (I mean the front line) and bear us down without difficulty in their impetuous progress.'[67] However, as Hawley noted, the cavalry charge was uneven. Cobham's three squadrons and Ligonier's two 'went on very handsomely', but 'Hamilton's who were in the centre, never stirred'.[68]

Elcho recorded the Jacobite response: 'The Highlanders march'd up to them very slowly, with their pieces presented, every man taking his aim, and when the dragoons came within half pistol shot of them, gave them a full discharge, which kill'd a great many of them.' Elcho claimed 400 were killed but this is a huge exaggeration, as shall later be noted.[69] Johnstone wrote that there was then hand to hand fighting:

> The cavalry . . . rushed upon the Highlanders at a hard trot, breaking their ranks, throwing down everything before them and trampling the Highlanders under the feet of their horses, the most singular and extraordinary combat immediately occurred. The Highlanders, stretched on the ground, thrust their dirks into the bellied of their horses. Some seized the riders by their clothes, dragged them down and stabbed them with their dirks, several again used their pistols, but few had sufficient space to use their swords.

MacDonald of Clanranald found himself trapped under a dead horse and was unable to extricate himself. He saw a Highlander struggling with a dismounted dragoon. The former was triumphant and then aided Clanrald. Johnstone concluded, 'The resistance of the Highlanders was so incredibly obstinate that the English, after having been for some time engaged pell-mell with them in their ranks, were at length repulsed and forced to retire'.[70]

Among the dead was Whitney, who had escaped Prestonpans, albeit wounded, of whom Hawley later wrote, 'poor Whitney had devoted his life to redeem the character of his men and I saw him lose it, just by me, a gallant good man, and he the only one I would have recommended [for promotion?]'.[71] Corse, who as a member of the Glasgow militia was stationed behind the cavalry, had a good view point, wrote that he could see daylight between the cavalry.[72]

The dragoons who remained alive fled, 'who in their flight run down all along the Princes first line and got the fire of the whole line'. This was because their own infantry had by now advanced close to them and so they could not go straight back without breaking their own lines. Masterton was shocked, 'for such pannick God keep me from ever seeing again that our forces was in'. Hawley tried to rally them. He drew his pistol, 'but threats and fair words would not do for they never stopped till they got to camp wch was a good mile distant'. He was almost ridden down by the fleeing horsemen.[73]

Hawley himself later wrote: 'The Lieutenant General in trying to stop the dragoons was beat downe, him and his horse, by them twice and bothe times was very near being killed or taken by the Highlanders . . . He was at last forced along with the crowde to the bottom of the hill'.[74] Apparently some fled to Linlithgow where they reported that they were all that remained of Hawley's forces.[75] Some even rode as far as Edinburgh, bearing similar news and causing panic there.[76] The cavalry's flight also disordered the infantry battalions on the left and the Glasgow militia who were to their rear, some of whom were in some farmhouses.[77] However, for the Jacobites, 'This beginning greatly inspired our men, as it had a contrary effect on the enemy'.[78]

The only mishap from the Jacobite point of view was that Major MacDonald of Keppoch took a dragoon horse, mounted it and was then carried away by the horse with the rest of the dragoons.[79] MacDonald, however, later found himself looking at the artillery which was stuck in the mud and asked about it, 'I am diverting myself looking at these pieces of cannon'. He was then warned that the Campbell militia might arrive and so he decided to return to the nearest Jacobite unit. Looking for one, he saw red-coated infantry and assumed that these were the Irish Picquets. Walking amongst them, his white cockade in his hat denoted he was a Jacobite and the men of Barrell's battalion cried out, 'Here is a rebel'. Huske had him take his sword from the scabbard for examination and there was blood and hair on it, which sealed his fate. He then ordered his men to shoot him, but his life was saved by Captain Rich of that battalion who stopped his men from firing on him. MacDonald then drew his sword and pistol to give to Rich as part of his surrender, but Huske feared that this was a prelude to an attack, so once again wanted the man killed but again Rich prevented this and led him away to captivity.[80]

After the melee, the MacDonalds then charged with Murray, who was on foot, at their head. They pursued the dragoons in disorder and failed to keep their ranks. Murray wrote, 'it was not in my power to get them rallied so as to carry them down in the enemy's foot regularly'.[81] It was not only the infantry that pursued the fleeing dragoons, but a detachment of Jacobite cavalry also did so and were rebuked by John Roy Stuart, 'Gentlemen, keep your ground, these are only Cope's dragoons: You have the battle yet to fight'.[82] Yet the success on the Jacobite right wing resulted in 'there was no possibility of making the MacDonalds keep their ranks; many of the first line of the right, pursued the horse and fell in with some of the enemy's militia'.[83] O'Sullivan noted that 'our highlanders according to their usual custom, pursued them sword in hand, & destroyed as many as they cou'd overtake'.[84]

Apparently Lord Hume, commander of the Glasgow militia, ordered some of his men to fire and they did so, 'and brought down some of their horses'. Presumably this is a reference to the fleeing dragoons. Thornton's company of Yorkshire volunteers was clearly nearby for he later wrote, of the said militia, 'they stood and maintained their ground most heroically, so as to secure in a great measure, the retreat of the army at the hazard of their lives and liberties, many of them being cut in pieces'[85]

The next stage of battle was confusing because the irregular terrain made it impossible for anyone to have a grandstand view as to what was happening. Lumisden wrote of 'the inequality of the ground, being interspaced with risings and hollows, whereby there was no seeing from right to left what was doing'.[86] The other issue was that many of the men were less than rigorous in the pursuit at John MacLeod noted, 'When they came to the brow of the hill, they then stop'd their pursuit, and walk'd about, talking with each other and telling what marvels they had perform'd, with the same unconcern as if no enemy had been near'.[87]

It was now past four o'clock and the skies were darkening, not just with impending nightfall but with foul weather which was to play a decisive part in the battle. Daniel wrote, 'there blew such a storm of wind and hail; which was before on our side, and now turned miraculously, as we turned on our backs; and notwithstanding that almost disabled us to bear up against them, it so harassed the enemy'.[88] The elements had been favourable towards the Jacobites but not for their opponents. Corse wrote 'Had it been fair weather, I believe the Troops would have beat them at last . . . The great storm of Rain & Wind wch began about 10 minutes before the action had rendered their arms useless, & wet all the soldiers' cartridges'.[89] The Government infantry were disordered by the weather.[90] Cholmondeley also noted, 'as we march'd, all the way uphill, and over very uneven ground, our men were greatly blown'.[91] Hawley wrote 'It was difficult to see or hear'.[92]

The Government infantry were 100 yards apart from one another.[93] According to Maxwell, 'the left of the Prince's army having spent their fire upon the dragoons, found the enemy's whole foot before them, and by this time, the rain, which had begun with the battle, was become so violent, that it was impossible for the Highlanders, who do not use cartridges, to load again; nevertheless they drew their broadswords and went on with abundance of resolution'.[94]

Meanwhile, the clans on the Jacobite right 'as usual Threw down their Guns and advanced very quick sword in hand'. Some fell on the Glasgow militia who were to their front. But, because the Jacobite right outflanked that of their opponents, most found no enemy before them, 'made a Stop and went into the greatest confusion'.[95] Others met some opposition, 'Our left in pursuing the horse, met with the four or five battalions yt I spoke of before, recd their fire, for the highlanders had non to oppose 'um, & rished in upon them sword in hand, immediately after the enemy's discharge, & cut them to pieces. This was perhaps one of the boldest and finest actions, yt any troops in the world cou'd be capable of'.[96] Captain George Fitzgerald of Munro's battalion was grenadier captain of his company and he wrote how part of the front line collapsed, 'Blakeney's regiment being put into some disorder on the left of ours by being attacked on their flank by the rebels, occasion'd ours likewise to give way'.[97]

Infantry fire was limited, Cholmondeley writing, that they gave but a 'faint fire'.[98] Many of the Government infantry merely fled without firing, Hawley writing 'the whole second line of Foot ran away without firing a shot'.[99] A private from Barrell's battalion in the second line stated, 'at the running of –'s regiment, like a catching infection, the whole front follow'd, and likewise the rear, not one regiment being left in the field but ours'. It is worth noting that these battalions had a great deal of battle experience, as Sir John Penicuik wrote, 'whole regiments ran off without firing or receiving fire from the enemy . . . who had behaved well in Flanders'. Cumberland later noted, 'they did not use to run away formerly'.[100]

As with Prestonpans, sometimes officers found themselves abandoned by their men, hence the large proportion of casualties among them. Captain Fitzgerald was knocked down by a musket ball, which went through his hat and wig and grazed his forehead, stunning him and knocking him to the ground. He was soon attacked by a 'party of the rebels who cut me in the head and knock'd me down a second time, when they began to rob me'. Fortunately a French officer, on hearing his cries, intervened and saved his life.[101]

Worse was to come for the battalion's commander, Sir Robert Munro of Foulis. In a letter by a relation, it was claimed that he was deserted by his men and 'was attacked by Cameron of Lochiel's regiment & for some time defended himself with his half pike. Two of the six, I'm informed, he kill'd, a seventh coming up, fired a pistol into my father's Groin, upon him falling, the Highlander with his sword gave him two strokes on the face, one over the eyes & another on the mouth, with instantly ended a brave man. The same Highlander fired another pistol into my uncle's breast & with his sword terribly slashed him; whom he killed, he then despatch'd a servant of my father'.[102]

Apparently Munro, 'who was heard much to blaspheme during the engagement and as a punishment, for which, his tongue was miraculously cut asunder by a sword and that struck him directly across the mouth'.[103] Some British soldiers were killed in the pursuit, Daniel writing, 'We pursued them sharply for about sixty paces, and fetched down a good many of them'. Munro was joined by his brother-in-law, a Dr Duncan, who rode unarmed to his assistance. Both were killed. Contemporary historians elevated these two deaths to the status of atrocities, 'they were both miserably slaughtered' and then mutilated.[104]

A number of other infantry officers stood more or less alone, abandoned by their men, and were killed or wounded. These included, among Munro's battalion, his lieutenant colonel, Biggar, and three captains, Hall, Fitzgerald and Witherall. Blakeney's also resisted the Jacobites, with Captains Tod, Kellet, Dalrymple and Edmondson falling, along with six lieutenants, Fairfield, Garing, Hamilton, Launders, Hele and Kirkson. Howards' battalion lost two captains and Cholmondelys' and Wolfe's one officer each; in the former case it was lieutenant colonel Powell.[105]

The left wing of the Jacobite army fell against Hawley's centre and leftwards battalions, attacking sword in hand, without recourse to musketry which would only have slowed them down and exposed them to greater firepower. In any case, many of the men had already fired their guns. The Government battalions broke, probably after minimal resistance ('irregular fire') at best.[106] Hawley went with these retreating infantry.[107]

However, on the Government right the advantage lay with them in having no Jacobites to their front to directly threaten them. Furthermore, there was a 'ravine or gulley' separating them from their nearest enemies and there was a small farm house securing their left. Barrel's and Ligonier's, in the first rank, under Brigadier Cholmondeley, stood firm. The latter wrote, that the battalions' officers 'deserve the greatest praise, for the spirit they shew'd'. Cholmondeley wrote 'I got the men to be quite cool, as cool as ever I saw men at exercise; and when the rebels came down upon us, we not only repulsed them, but advanced, and put them to flight'.[108]

Other infantry under Huske, the Royal Scots and Howard's, joined them. They began by firing in platoons against small bodies of Jacobites. Cholmondeley told them 'if they will keep their ground and will go back and rally the dragoons'. They did so, and 100 men of Cobham's dragoons were added to the force. Cholmondeley addressed them all, 'I told them that I had repuls'd the Enemy, with two weak battalions and that if they would march up, I would beat them, and that I would order the two battalions, to march up Briskly at the same time, & give them their Fire, and that they should fall in, sword in hand, they were greatly pleased with this, and with many oaths and Irish Exclamations, swore they would follow me'.[109]

The dragoons marched 100 yards behind the infantry battalions as they advanced. They found some Jacobites formed behind houses and barns.

Cholomondeley fired his pistol to have the men form for action. Cholmondeley remarked that if he and Huske could gather more troops, they could drive the Jacobites off the field. Nightfall, however, brought their venture to an end.[110] The weather led to only one musket in five being able to fire, nor was there any artillery support. When Huske's forces retreated they found the guns abandoned and stuck in the mud. Grenadiers from Barrell's battalion drew one away and horses were taken from the camp to drag another two away.[111] A private from Barrell's later wrote, 'Brigadier- [Cholmondeley?] was pleased to express his satisfaction at our Behaviour, by kissing our men and making us a present of 10 guineas'.[112]

The artillery had played no part in the battle, as was the case with the Jacobites' guns. Yet there had been an expectation that it would have done so. Hawley had not given Cunningham any orders, presumably due to the haste that he gave orders to the rest of the army. Cunningham rode up and down the line to find him but was unable to do so. He asked Huske, but he only told him that he had to see Hawley. Eventually a staff officer eventually told Cunningham to 'march the artillery up to an adjacent hill in the rear of the front line of the army'. It seems that the mortars were never moved from the camp. Yet the road that the train had to take was 'very bad and intricate'. Progress was slow and they fell behind the second line of the infantry as it moved forward. Two of the heavy guns became stuck in the mud and so were abandoned. With only three guns left (two 4-pounders and a 1½-pounder) they carried on, but on seeing retreating infantry, the civilian drivers deserted with the horses and the majority of the men left, too. A soldier noted that 'the carelessness and cowardice of the people belonging to the horses, who cut the traces and made the best way to save themselves'. Cunningham later observed, 'In such a situation, deserted by his men and the rebels within 20 paces of him, it was impossible for him to do any service with three guns, he thought it most prudent to order them down the hill'.[113]

Huske's force was faced by a body of 400 Jacobites returning from the pursuit, but lacking muskets, having thrown these away, the latter were unable to stand up to them in a firefight. Roy Stuart thought that this might be an ambush, so called out to the men to stop their pursuit and the call 'flew immediately from rank to rank and there the while army into disorder'. He later wrote, 'The Highlanders were in complete disorder, dispersed here and there with the different clans mingled pell-mell together'.[114] Macleod wrote, 'if they [the enemy] return'd to the charge, he was afraid that they wou'd still take the victory out of our hands, considering the great confusion we were in'.[115]

The trio of Government officers won plaudits from contemporary historians. Cholmondeley's activity was particularly praiseworthy because he was 'dangerously wounded, and contracted a palsy from the cold he caught in the field'. Huske had shown 'great vigilance and Presence of Mind [and] acquired the Highest Reputation'. Brigadier John Mordaunt 'was allowed to have done all that could be expected from the most knowing and experience Officer'.[116] Meanwhile, the Argyllshire militia, stationed to the right of the army to the east end of Callendar Park, in order to secure the camp, saw no action. As night fell they marched back to Linlithgow and arrived at Edinburgh on 18 January, in an orderly manner.[117]

As with Prestonpans, this had been a short battle. Officers who had taken part in it discussed its length thereafter. They concluded that the time between the first firing and the retreat of the Government army's right wing, was about 20 minutes.[118]

The counter-attack also had an effect on the second line of the Jacobite army. They did not move further to the left to face these battalions head on, nor did they stand still and wait for new orders, but rather crowded in with the first line. Those that did, 'went down upon the enemy with them; the rest of the second line fell into confusion with their ranks, being thinned by those who had run in with the first line'. They fell back to their initial positions on the battlefield.[119] Some went back to Bannockburn or even Stirling, 'where they gave out yt we lost the day'.[120] When Farquharson's men heard firing they left their artillery and rushed forward, but were met by 200 or 300 men flying westwards, though he forced them to turn back.[121] MacDonald claimed that the Lowland battalions in the second line 'smitten apparently with terror took to flight' and he and O'Sullivan managed to rally them.[122]

According to Murray, O'Sullivan was the man to blame. He should have brought up troops from the second line or the reserve to have extended the first line. Murray wrote, 'nothing was more easy; but that gentleman had certainly no knowledge in these affairs, nor was he ever seen to do any thing in the time of action'.[123] Eventually Murray tried to take charge. He had his Atholl battalions, 'who kept their line in perfect good order'. Seeing the enemy's confusion, he resolved to exploit it to the full. Marching down the hill, he attempted to rally the MacDonalds. This was difficult because there were none to play the bagpipes, the pipers having already thrown away their pipes and taken part in the charge. He sent Kerr to plead that the reserves might advance to their left. Kerr thus brought up the Irish Picquets and the Royal Eccossais. Drummond and other officers accompanied them. Marching forward to the foot of the hill they passed the abandoned cannon. It was then realized that there were four Government infantry battalions and a regiment of dragoons intact and now to the Jacobites' rear. The remainder of their opponents, though, was long gone. 'The other part of their army were in the utmost confusion, running off by forties and fifties to the right and left to get into Falkirk, so that their line was in the greatest disorder.'[124]

According to some Jacobites the battle represented a lost opportunity. Daniel wrote, 'we let an opportunity slip out of our hands, which never afterwards presented itself again'. He blamed this on Murray, 'who would not permit the army to pursue any further'.[125] John Macleod wrote, 'Had our army been disciplined or have been commanded by experienced generals, I am fully convinced that we would have cut the King's army to pieces'.[126] At least one of their opponents thought so, too, Corse writing: 'Why they did not use their advantage, & enter when the troops were broke, sword in hand, as is their way; & in the next place, why they did not pursue when the army marched to Linlithgow, when all firearms were useless is not to be comprehended. They cant, in all human probability, ever have such another opportunity.'[127]

According to Elcho, 'all the generals & their aid de camps were on foot, whereas they ought to have been on horseback, for Generals' business in a battle is more to command than to fight as common soldiers'.[128] He stated elsewhere, 'if it had been dry and our right wing had been able to see the confusion which our enemies found themselves . . . the whole army of Hawley would have been destroyed'.[129] Murray stated that at this point he only had 600–700 men 'the rest being all scattered on the face of the hill, he judged it would be risking all the advantages they had gained'.[130] Drummond suspected an ambush. On seeing the Royal Scots file away he remarked, 'these men behaved admirably well at Fontenoy, and yet they are flying; I fear there is an ambuscade.'[131]

The victory was far from complete, 'The honour of remaining masters of the field was of little avail to us. We had no reason for believing that we had lost the battle as the English army had retreated, but as we supposed them still in their camp, we considered it at most as undecided'.[132] However, Lumisden put the delay down to the need to re-order the army in order to defeat the Government forces at their camp. Yet only half the army could be got together. They then saw the camp being burnt and the men retreating to Falkirk. Three officers went forward, disguised as peasants to reconnoitre. On their return, they told how the enemy was in full retreat to Linlithgow. Lumisden deemed that this was an error: 'a few men properly posted could have hindered the highlanders from entering that night, and obliged us either to have abandoned the field of battle, or to have stood all night under arms, wet and fatigued as we were, and exposed to the inclemency of the weather, a thing impossible'.[133]

In fact there was even the suggestion that at this point the Jacobite army should retreat towards Dunnipace and places nearby. This was because of the weather, 'it being a prodigious rain', and the men needed to be under cover.

There was a great deal of confusion among the Jacobite army. Many did not know what had happened on either wing of the army. Bad weather and poor light did nothing to help.[134]

Hawley had been carried away with the rout of the troops he was trying to rally and was at the camp before any other of the senior officers. He spent his time there forming up what troops there were, when Mordaunt joined him with additional forces. They had these men formed up, but knew nothing of the whereabouts of Cholmondeley, Huske and their four battalions as all firing had ceased. Hawley feared that the Jacobites might march to Linlithgow to cut him off from Edinburgh so had Mordaunt take some of the men and march to Edinburgh to secure the city.[135]

Once Huske and the remainder of the battalions arrived, Huske suggested they should stand and fight. Hawley sent for his two other horses, had two of the abandoned cannon taken off and then disagreed with Huske. It was now a full hour since the last shot had been fired. It was not possible for them to return to the fray because the rain had spoiled their arms and ammunition, and so lacking provisions and ammunition, and finding that their horses had been taken from the camp by the drivers, orders were sent to burn the tents. The army then retreated to Linlithgow, where Hawley believed was a wagon with ammunition and gunpowder (it turned out to be a bread wagon so Hawley had the food distributed to the troops) then to Edinburgh on 18 January. On their way back they found some officers and men concealed in houses so these were arrested for deserting their posts.[136]

Some fleeing troops had already arrived at the Scottish capital with tales of being defeated, but shortly afterwards Grossett was sent there to give Fletcher an alternative version of events. He told him that 'the Kings Troops had at last beat the Rebels from and kept the Field of Battle 'till obliged to leave it for want of Provisions, and leave seven of their Cannon on the Field for want of Horses to carry them off'. This dissipated the alarm that was becoming widespread among Edinburgh loyalists.[137]

In the evening the Jacobite army were permitted to take hold of the town of Falkirk. According to Murray, 'he would either lye in the town or in paradise' and strongly advocated marching towards it. Charles, who rode up to him, agreed. Murray advised him to stay in a house at the foot of the hill until word could reach him that Falkirk had been secured.[138] As they marched towards it they found the guns which had been abandoned by Cunningham's men earlier that day. Drummond, Murray and Lochiel led the column entering the town by three different routes. They had but the Atholl men and the Irish Picquets with them and a handful of MacDonalds, Ogilvie, Appin Stewarts, Camerons and Roy Stuarts, headed by their colonels. There was little opposition.

The army was merely 1,500 strong in Falkirk, the remainder being scattered throughout the district, with some back at Bannockburn.[139] Daniel and seventeen men were told to take a house three miles away which housed some of the enemy. The door was shut against them. They surrounded it and made a summons to surrender. On the first refusal, the Jacobites opened fire and then the inhabitants gave in. There were fifty-four in all.[140] A few other prisoners were taken and by the day's end, Charles arrived, too. It was eight o'clock.[141]

In the town were found many of the supplies belonging to Hawley's army, especially those of his officers, including 'hampers of good wines, & liquors & other provisions'. O'Sullivan, wrote, 'The Prince profited of General Hally's supper wch he wanted very much, for he had not a bit of his own, nor either did he eat a morsel yt day'. He also had 'a great quantity of bread found, wch was distributed' among the men. He stayed at Falkirk that night and the next two days.[142]

Inclement weather persisted until the night. Daniel wrote 'we went thoroughly wet and cold, to repose ourselves a little while on straw, and some in the open fields or air, so that it was impossible to find any resource or ease for our excessive hunger, wet and cold'.[143] Yet some men did take shelter, 'every one putting himself under cover to dry his cloaths and refresh himself after the fatigue of the day'. This meant that the intended 1,000 men who were to pursue had been whittled down to a mere 50 and so these were insufficient to do much apart from mounting sentries that night, though some cavalry did pursue and rounded up a few stragglers. Hawley's army, elements of which had been departing Falkirk from the east as Drummond's column arrived at the other end, were clean away. The Jacobite army's behaviour was allegedly due to their being irregular troops.[144] Elcho wrote, 'Had the Prince's army been able to have followed them, the same night to Linlithgow there is no doubt he would have destroy'd them'.[145]

Murray wrote about why the army's behaviour went awry;

> Had the MacDonalds on the right either not broke their ranks, or rallied soon after, they, with the Atholl men, would have cut the whole enemy's foot to pieces, for they were close at them, and must have drove them down the hill before them; and by speed of foot, not a man of them would have got off from them.
>
> Had there been any officer on the left, to have ordered two or three battalions from the second line, or reserve, to have faced those of the enemy that outflanked them, they would have had a complete victory. Most of the officers were with his Royal Highness in the reserve; had they come up, and with the left of the second line followed the first, extending a little farther to the left, the enemy's

whole army, or at least the foot, must have been taken or killed, and, in that case, even but few of the horse would have escaped.[146]

He also listed the enemy's failings. They were unready and so failed to reach the summit first. Later, they could have lined the camp or the town and repulsed the Jacobite attack, assuming the Jacobites would have ever attacked.[147] Johnstone wrote that if this had happened the Jacobite army would have had to have retreated because they 'could not pass the night in the open air, during such a terrible tempest' and so this would have 'been a sort of victory for General Hawley'.[148]

On the following day the field of battle was surveyed by the victors. Numbers were counted; apparently, according to Jacobites, there were 600–700 Government and 50 Jacobite dead. The corpses of both armies were buried. Social distinctions were maintained in death as those men identifiable as officers were brought down to the town and were buried there, and these included Munro and Whitney.[149] Johnstone recounts the awful reality of seeing corpses on a large scale, 'the horrid spectacle I had witnessed was for a long time, fresh in my mind . . . when we coolly proceed over a field of battle, we are seized with horror at the sight of dead bodies, a spectacle repugnant to human nature, though when living, they may have been perfectly unknown to us'.[150] The belongings of the dead were stolen. O'Sullivan wrote of 'Gold watcheses were at a cheap reat'.[151] Officer prisoners were housed in Stirling town house and the men in the church; later they were rehoused in Down Castle. They included a number of Presbyterian priests and hangmen.[152]

Daniel wrote, 'But this cheap bought victory, you will say, merited a better exit!' There were about 100–700 prisoners and one remarked, 'By my soul, Dick, if Prince Charles goes on in this way, Prince Frederick will never be King George'.[153] Johnstone was certain it was a Jacobite victory, writing, 'Mr MacDonald of Lochgarry . . . revived our spirits by announcing for certain that we had gained a most complete victory'.[154] There were too few Jacobites to exploit the victory, however. According to Daniel, only 3,000 remained to hand, 'many of them having loaded themselves with booty, returned up to the hills'.[155]

Jacobite loses were light. Lumisden counted them as three captains, four lieutenants and forty privates dead, with double that wounded. This was a little more than at Prestonpans, but far fewer proportionately.[156] Elcho counted fifty dead and sixty wounded including Cameron of Lochiel and his brother being slightly injured.[157] Of the senior officers, Drummond had been shot in the fleshy part of his arm and three officers from the Royal Eccossais were also injured.[158]

Jacobite estimates of the number of the enemy who had become casualties varied; Johnstone wrote that 600 had been killed and 700 made prisoner; Elcho that there were 500–600 dead and 600 taken and Maxwell gave lower figures; 400–500 killed and hundreds taken captive.[159] The reality is that all these figures were wild exaggerations. A muster roll taken 11 days after the battle gave 6,755 infantrymen, more than had fought at the battle.[160]

The casualty returns of the army were thus: 14 officers, 71 other ranks, total of killed 85, 83 wounded and missing 283, totalling 451, though contemporary accounts list 25 officers as killed, wounded or missing.[161]

Officers Killed

Unit	Field Officer	Captain	Lieu-tenant	Ensign/ Cornet	Staff/Quart-master	Total
Barrel						
Cholmon-deley	1					1
Munro	1	2			1	4
Wolfe		2				2
Blakeney		4	1			5
Battereau						
Pulteney						
Price						
Royals						
Howard						
Fleming						
Blakeney						
Cobham					1	1
Ligonier	1					1
Hamilton						
Total	3	8	1		2	14

Officers Wounded

Unit	Field Officer	Captain	Lieu-tenant	Ensign/ Cornet	Staff	Total
Barrel						
Cholmon-deley						
Munro						
Wolfe						
Blakeney						
Battereau						
Pulteney						
Price						
Royals		1				1
Howard			1			1
Fleming						
Ligonier					1	1
Cobham	1					1
Ligonier						
Hamilton	1		1			2
	2	1	2		1	6

Officers Missing

Unit	Field Officer	Captain	Lieutenant	Ensign/ Cornet	Staff	Total
Barrel						
Cholmondeley	1					1
Munro	1					1
Wolfe		3				3
Blakeney						
Battereau						
Pulteney						
Price						
Royals						
Howard						
Fleming						
Ligonier						
Cobham						
Ligonier			2	2		4
Hamilton				1	2	1
Total	2	3	2	3	2	12

Soldiers' Casualties

Unit	Sergeants killed	Sergeants wounded	Sergeants missing	Others killed	Others wounded	Others missing	Total
Royals			2	6	1		9
Howard				1		12	13
Barrell					1	11	12
Wolfe			1	5	9	20	35
Pulteney				1	3	10	14
Blakeney	1			39			40
Price				1	2	31	34
Cholmon-deley		1			9	7	19
Fleming					4	7	11
Munro					11	28	39
Ligonier	1			1	5	11	18
Battereau				2		35	37
Cobham				9	11	18	38
Ligonier	1	1	1	1	15	28	47
Hamilton					4	59	63
Total	3	2	4	66	75	267	419

All told there were 452 casualties among the regular forces.[162]

Ligonier died ten days after the battle, not by wounds, but because he had been unwell prior to the battle, but could not be persuaded not to lead his men. Despite being bled and blistered beforehand, he was drenched to the skin by the rain on the day of the action, contracted a cold and quinsy and died.[163]

There is no record of how many of the militia and volunteers were killed, wounded or captured. Many fell into the latter category, however. Yet, at least nineteen Glasgow militia privates lost their lives and their widows later received £5 each.[164] Apart from these men, some of the volunteers present were also taken prisoner. Prisoners included William Thornton and eighteen of his Yorkshire volunteers, though he escaped fairly quickly afterwards, as did his men and another twenty-five detainees.[165] A number of the Glasgow militia, perhaps twenty-five, were also taken, as were some of the spectators.[166] The lot of the prisoners was dismal, with most of the provisions intended for them eaten by their guards. When those remaining marched north in early February they were described as being 'in a miserable condition, some wanting shoes and stockings'.[167] Material losses include seven brass cannons, three iron ones, several mortars, ammunition for these, wagons, tents, three standards and two colours, a kettledrum, some muskets and baggage.[168]

Despite Hawley writing, 'I flatter myself that nobody will lay many faults to my charge', they did so, as they had with Cope.[169] After the battle the recriminations began. On 28 January Walpole told Mann, 'you will find there [in the newspapers] an account of another battle lost in Scotland – our arms cannot succeed there. Hawley, of whom I said so much to you in my last, has been as unsuccessful as Cope, and by almost every circumstance the same, except that Hawley had less want of skill and much more presumption. The very same dragoons ran away at Falkirk, that ran away at Prestonpans'.[170] Trooper Enoch Bradshaw of Cobham's dragoons had no love for his commander, writing 'General Hawley who does not love us because our regiment spoke truth about Falkirk job' and he was sorrowful over 'the brave Englishmen that are now in their graves had not been lost'.[171]

An officer wrote to Lady Elizabeth Hastings thus:

> I am alive and well at present though, it is only by God's blessed will than our general's conduct. For he drew only 400 dragoons, sword in hand, up against 1,000 of our enemy and we had orders not to draw a pistol or fire and as soon as he had given these orders to the rest of the officers he moved away from us and we never saw him move until the next morning. We lost the day for we were all sold to our enemies by treacherous general Hawley, for we could have got the day if he had done us justice or let us fight like Englishmen as we are. I wish the Duke [of Cumberland] had been with us.[172]

One Wightman saw Hawley shortly afterwards and wrote, 'Hawley seems to be sensible of his misconduct . . . he looked most wretchedly; even worse than Cope did a few hours after his scuffle'. Like others he was critical of the general's conduct, 'Hawley is in much the same situation as General Cope; he was never seen in the field during the battle'. Wightman thought it could all have been much worse 'if General Huske had not acted with judgement and courage, and appeared everywhere'.[173]

Not all blamed Hawley. Private Michael Hughes believed it was outside the general's control, writing later that year: 'The Miscarriage in this Battle must, in Truth, be laid to the badness of the Weather, and Night coming on so soon; for had the Royal Army but advanced out of their tents a small time sooner, and made proper Dispositions for an Ingagaement, what could have hindered such a regular Body of Forces with so many good officers from getting a sure Victory.'[174]

News of the battle reached the Jacobite court in Rome and the French court as one Brown, an Irish officer, was sent from Scotland to Louis XV, where it was presented as a great victory (Brown was awarded the Cross of St. Louis). The Jacobite account included the line, 'After a compleat Victory, gained by 8000 over above 12,000, we remained masters of the field'. Charles wrote an effusive letter to Louis XV on the triumph.[175] Sir Horace Mann despairingly reported to Walpole, 'Hawley's affair for example frightened us out of our Senses. The French accounts magnified it an hundred fold.' He could not believe that an outnumbered army of '6000 Vagabonds' could defeat 18,000 troops.[176]

Hawley realized that, like Cope, he needed to defend himself and wrote to Cumberland on the evening of the battle thus:

> My heart is broke. I can't say we are quite beat today, but our left is beat, and their left is beat. We had enough to beat them, for we had 2000 men more than they. But such a scandalous cowardice I never saw before . . . I must say one thing, that every officer did his duty, and what was in the power of man, in trying to stop and rally the men, and they led them on with as good a countenance, till a Halloo began.[177]

Yet Newcastle, as well as Cumberland, was very solicitous towards Hawley, writing on 24 January:

> His Majesty was extremely concerned for the unfortunate event of the Engagement on Friday last near Falkirk: But I have the satisfaction to answer you, that the King is persuaded you did everything in your power to prevent the misfortune that happened; and will not fail to do your utmost to retrieve it in the best and most expeditious manner possible.[178]

Other reasons were ascribed for the defeat, with Miss Saville recording in her diary, 'The reasons given are, the same cowardly dragoons who ran away when Cope was beat, did so again; also a storm of hail, rain and wind not only blinded our men . . . but wet their powder, so that most of their guns would not go off'.[179]

Yet in recent years, a revisionist account of the battle suggests that this battle was not a defeat for the Government army.[180] This is, in part, because of comments made by Major James Wolfe (1727–59), who wrote, ''twas not a battle as neither side would fight . . . possibly it will be told you in a much worse light than it really is. Though we can't be said to have totally routed the enemy, yet we remained a long time masters of the field of battle and of our cannon.'[181] A private from Barrell's battalion was not at all downcast, writing after the battle that 'We expect in a few days time to give them another meeting which I pray God it may be attended with a better opportunity'.[182]

Hawley held court martials on those deemed to have misbehaved during the battle. In this he had been sanctioned by Newcastle. Two captains, one lieutenant and six privates of Hamilton's regiment were found guilty and sentenced to death by shooting, to take place on 27 January. However, they were reprieved. Two men, though, were 'punished by severe whipping'. Cunningham, who had also earned Hawley's annoyance, tried to commit suicide by slitting his arteries to escape trial but survived, was found guilty and cashiered before the whole army on 24 February at Montrose. His sword was broken over his head and he was forced out of the army for cowardice.[183] Hawley was probably influenced by Fletcher, who suggested that 'I therefore submit to your consideration that it may not be for the general good, that the execution of these private men be delayed at least for some little time'.[184] However, four army deserters, all Irishmen, and including one who had gone over to the Jacobites after Prestonpans, were hanged at Grassmarket, Edinburgh, on 24 January.[185]

One contemporary newspaper likened the battle to that of Sheriffmuir, in that both armies saw their left wing rout from the field of battle. Yet, as with most comparisons, the differences are also evident on closer examination. At Sheriffmuir, Argyle's army held the field and their enemy retreated back to Perth. Their enemy's march south has been thwarted. In this instance the Jacobite army held the field and had prevented their enemies' march to Stirling to relieve the castle. Neither battle ended the campaign. Falkirk, though, must be counted as a Jacobite victory, as Hawley's aim had been defeated and he had been forced to retreat.

A better comparison was made by our anonymous officer in the Royal Eccossais:

> *je regarde comme une bataille de Fontenoy, en petit, par rapport a 'effet qu'elle produit. Les Ennemis ont ete arretes dans leurs projects comme a Fontenoy, & et le siege de Sterling est continue, comme celui de Tournay* ('I compare it to the battle of Fontenoy, in small scale, by the effect it produced. The enemies were stopped in their aim just as at Fontenoy and the siege of Stirling continued, just as that of Tournai did').[186]

The battle was not a decisive Jacobite victory as Prestonpans had been. They had caused only minimal casualties; a roll call of the twelve battalions engaged taken ten days after the battle showed a greater number of men in the ranks than before the battle (presumably caused by men returning from hospitals).

Bad weather, nightfall and a lack of formed troops under orders had prevented a rigorous Jacobite pursuit on 17/18 January. Yet they had retained command of the field of battle and had prevented Hawley from relieving the siege of Stirling Castle or destroying the Jacobite army or forcing it to retreat. The British army had been checked, temporarily, but that was all. The campaign was not at an end and so the fighting would continue as both sides' armies were largely intact.

Chapter 14

Endgame in the Highlands

As in the case of the aftermath of Sheriffmuir, both sides ended up where they had begun prior to the battle, though this time the advantage was with the Jacobites because Hawley had not broken the siege of Stirling castle. The Jacobites carried on, carefully watched by Blakeney. The siege was overseen by Mirabelle de Gordon, a French engineer. However, there were losses through the defenders' fire and the accidental shooting of a Clanranald by a Glengarry soured tempers within the Jacobite army.

In London it was now realized that there would not be a French invasion. This meant that Cumberland could be spared and he rode northwards to take over command of the army in Scotland. There were additional troops, too; three infantry battalions, two cavalry regiments, forty-eight gunners and matrosses from Newcastle and, by sea, Prince Fredrick of Hesse and a strong force of his countrymen to replace the Dutch/Swiss. Cumberland arrived at Edinburgh the end of January 1746. To raise morale he pardoned all the troops under threat of execution following the court martials.

Hessian Corps, 1746
Prince Frederick
Hussars (98).
Grenadiers (830).
Prince Maximillian's battalion (829).
Mansburgh's battalion (836).
Guards' battalion (833).
Dunop's battalion (833).
Prince Frederick's battalion (907).
Total: 5,068 men and 655 horses.[1]

Conversely, Jacobite fortunes were on the decline. Once their siege guns were in position, on 29 January, they began to fire, but Blakeney had his cannon return it. He was successful and so the Jacobite guns fell silent even before they had the chance to bombard the castle. Cumberland was impressed. Well aware that the Government army in Edinburgh had been reinforced and had a new leader, there was a need to decide how to react to what would surely be a renewed assault. As ever, Charles, who was at Bannockburn, was in favour of a battle and asked Murray, who was at Falkirk, to prepare a plan to do so. Murray and the chiefs argued for a retreat northwards, citing desertion and sickness as having reduced the size of the army so that it was in no fit state to take on and beat the army that would be led by Cumberland. Charles was disappointed, but as at Derby had little option but to reluctantly agree.

A retreat to the Highlands, however, would enable the Jacobites to 'destroy Lord Loudoun's army and all his Enemies in that Country, to take and demolish all the forts in the north, by which means he would be intire master of that Country'. Finally, once spring came, they would be in a position to counter attack with an army 8,000 strong. In the meantime all the heavy guns and ammunition which could not be carried were destroyed. The retreat caused surprise in an army which was ready to fight; whether a battle here would have been favourable is a question which in hindsight the answer was probably positive. However, as was the case throughout these campaigns, caution was often preferred to the risk of an immediate decision.[2]

The retreat, which was initially shambolic, began on 1 February and on the next day the army had arrived at Perth. They then decided to split; with one column of the Highlanders marching straight to Inverness and the others marching by the north-east coastal route. Detachments from the former under Gordon of Glenbucket, with artillery, forced the little garrison at Ruthven under lieutenant Molloy to surrender, albeit conditionally, on 10 February.

Cumberland was disappointed that there was to be no battle, writing

> I hop'd that the Rebels flush'd with their late Success would have given us an opportunity of finishing this affair at once, & which I am morally sure would have been in our Favour as the Troops in general shew'd all the Spirit that I could wish, & would have retrieved whatever slips are past.[3]

Cumberland marched his army to Linlithgow on 1 February, then to Stirling and via Dunblane and Crieff to Perth by 6 February. In order to prevent another Jacobite thrust south he had Blair Castle garrisoned by Sir Andrew Agnew, with troops in support in Coupar and Dundee. Forces were sent ahead by sea to seize Montrose. Fort William was also strengthened. The main army then went along the coast, halting at Aberdeen on 27 February. He had difficulties of his own to contend with, principally concerning the question of supplying such a comparatively large force. He was also unsure whether the Jacobites would stand and fight or would dissolve into the hills, as in 1716. For both these reasons, the Hessian troops, who arrived at Leith on 8 February, were initially seen as more of a hindrance than a help, being extra mouths that needed feeding.

He also ordered his troops to attack Jacobite property wherever it could be found. This was in order to sap their morale and even encourage some to desert and to reward his own troops. So, on 5 February, when at Crieff, having marched through territory once in Jacobite hands, 'I thought fit to let the soldiers a little loose with proper precautions that they might have some sweets with all their fatigues'.[4] Just over two weeks later he instructed the garrison at Fort William, to 'Send out Parties to Burn & Destroy all the Country belonging to the Rebells in your Neighbourhood, as far as you dare go with safety to your Garrison'.[5]

Yet this was not indiscriminate plundering in the Scottish Highlands, as Major General John Campbell, who had ordered troops to attack Jacobite property, wrote, 'I can take the liberty to assure you that it is by no means His Royal Highness' intention that His Majesty's innocent subjects should suffer with the Guilty and that I have the confidence in His Majesty's officers by land and sea that they will take care to distinguish the one from the other'.[6] He also had a proclamation published to grant pardons to 'command all ordinary common people who have bore arms, or otherwise have been concerned in this rebellion, bring in their arms to the magistrate or minister . . . and are to submit themselves entirely to the King's mercy'.[7]

Cumberland was convinced that there had to be a final military reckoning with the Jacobite army, as he explained to Newcastle:

> For, should this rebellion end any way but by the sword, I apprehend that the lenity of our government and from all the ill places compassion which be had, when our Frights are over, the authors and actors of, and in this rebellion, will not be sufficiently punished to prevent another.

However, he added:

> As His Majesty has been graciously pleased to entrust me with the power of promising his pardon to those who shall entitle themselves to it, I will endeavour to make the properest use of that power.[8]

Once the Jacobites were ensconced in Inverness on 18 February, after Charles had avoided being taken by Loudoun's militia in a surprise night raid at Moy on 16 February, there were a number of enemies to deal with. There was Loudoun's militia, who had taken boats to the Black Isle, a number of Argyll militia outposts to deal with, three forts and a castle to take. Operations against all of these were feasible because Cumberland's main army was in and around Aberdeen and the Hessian forces were at Perth, and all were not planning to move against the Jacobites in force just yet. Three ships brought additional troops from France, but two were captured en route by the Royal Navy. The third arrived at Aberdeen with 160 men from Fitzjames' Horse, though they lacked horses and so some of the Jacobite cavalry were obliged to dismount to give their horses to these regulars.

Fort George stood near Inverness. As with the other forts, it was garrisoned by Government troops. It could not be taken by artillery fire, so the Jacobites began mining operations. The garrison could not depress their guns low enough to fire at this method of attack and so on 20 February the governor, Major Grant, surrendered. This was much criticised, with Henderson alleging the capitulation was 'solely owing to Grant, whose cowardice and bad conduct cannot but reflect dishonour on himself'.[9]

Other Jacobite forces, the French troops, the Camerons and the MacDonalds of Keppoch under Brigadier Stapleton, marched to the end of Loch Ness to try and take Fort Augustus. This was newly built but poorly designed for defence against artillery. Its powder magazines were dangerously exposed. Maxwell wrote,

> He attacked the old barrack without waiting for the artillery and carried it; the soldiers behaving with surprising intrepidity on this occasion. The 3d March, a trench was opened before Fort Augustus, which held out but two days. What hastened the reduction of the place was, that some shells had been thrown into it had set fire to the powder magazine and blown it up.[10]

The governor surrendered the fort on 5 March.

With two down there were two to go. Firstly there was Blair Castle, central to the Jacobite campaign of the summer of 1689. The garrison under Sir Andrew Agnew was menaced by a force led by Murray. Unlike the two other sieges, there were no French gunners nor heavy artillery; only two 4-pounders which were quite ineffective against thick castle walls. The defenders were aided by lukewarm efforts on their behalf by nearby battalions of Hessian infantry. Eventually Murray had to withdraw his troops.

Toughest nut of all was Fort William, which Cumberland deemed the only fort in Scotland that had to be held, so he sent Captain Caroline Scott, an engineer, to take command. Jacobite troops appeared outside the fort on 5 March and the French artillery began their bombardment there on 7 March under Grant's supervision. However, he was wounded and Mirabelle took over, proving no more of a success than he had been at Stirling. The Jacobite bombardment had been serious enough, but had been disrupted by an effective sally by the garrison on 31 March. Eventually the siege was lifted and the Jacobites marched away on 4 April as Stapleton realized his guns were insufficient to take it.

Elsewhere, though, there had been other Jacobite successes. Two posts held by the Argyll militia had fallen; Cumberland discounted them anyway. Loudoun's militia had been dispersed as the Jacobites under Perth commandeered vessels in order to approach Sutherland and on seeing them they gave up the fight on 20 March. Yet all these encounters were relative side shows to the impending struggle that could not be long delayed.

There were other clashes between relatively small parties of troops. Major General Humphrey Bland marched on Strathbogie on 17 March and nearly took Roy Stuart, who heard of this, drew up his men and retreated to Fochabers in good order, the Government cavalry not risking an attack. Stuart only lost one man and was at Keith on 18 February and then marched westwards. After that all troops were retired to the west side of the Spey.

However, Major Glascoe marched on the night of 20 March with a mix of 200 infantry and cavalry to attack a Government army scouting party of 100 men who had arrived at Keith. This was made up of Argyllshire militia and some of Kingston's Horse. Arriving there at one in the morning, Glascoe attacked. After a firefight in which both sides had several men killed, the Jacobites captured the remainder of their surrounded enemies.

According to Maxwell, these skirmishes were highly effective and successful, 'This is without dispute the finest part of the Prince's expedition, and what best deserves the attention of judicious readers'.[11] Yet, although this kept the army occupied and maintained morale, where it was successful, it did not strike at the root cause of the campaign. The main body of the Government army was still in and around Aberdeen, well fed and paid and ready to march when the weather permitted.

Not that Cumberland's troops had been idle at Aberdeen. He spent some of the time there in training the infantry to resist the attacks of the Jacobites, which had resulted in setbacks in the previous year. Convinced that the infantry were the most important part of the army, he needed to restore their confidence and implant the idea in them that the Jacobites were not invincible when it came to hand-to-hand fighting, or even its threat, so that they would stand their ground rather than run away as previously.[12]

On 26 March General Albermarle and Bland with six battalions were established at Strathbogie, with Mordaunt and another three battalions being at Old Meldrum. Cumberland was determined to raise the morale of his own men and lower that of the Jacobites. According to him, the property of anyone in the Jacobite army was fair game. So he allowed his troops to plunder Jacobite property on their march from Falkirk. He sent out raiding parties, such as the one led by Major La Fausille, to burn the houses of known Jacobites. At the same time, troops found overstepping the mark were punished, whether officers or men.

Heavy rain had raised the level of the River Spey thus making it an impenetrable barrier for longer than usual. However, news from Jacobite deserters, relaying the difficulties that the Jacobite army was experiencing with supplies and money were welcoming. It was only in early April when two officers returned from the Spey with intelligence that the river was now shallow enough to be forded that the army could advance.

It was on 8 April that Cumberland had his army march towards Inverness, gathering together at Cullen three days later. The only physical barrier was the Spey and this had been left unguarded. Once over that, the Jacobite army was in reach. Cumberland later wrote:

> They were continuing to retire towards the Water of Nairn, & the Town. Upon which, I ordered fifty of the Campbells, who were the most advanced, with fifty of Kingston's under Lord Robert Sutton, to push their Rearguard, which was still at the further end of the Town. This they immediately did & drove their Rearguard in upon their Main Body & formed at the other End of the Town. In the mean time, all the Remainder of the Campbells and cavalry forded over the Water of Nairn, & pursued them five miles without any loss on our side, and on theirs, of eight or ten men killed, & three or four taken.[13]

The Jacobite forces just to the west of the river were led by Perth and Drummond and included the bulk of the French troops and the cavalry. However, there were several places where the river could be forded. They were too weak to successfully contest the crossing. They pulled back in an orderly manner towards Inverness and their main body of troops. A counter-attack with the Clanranalds, the Stewarts of Appin and part of Fitzjames's Horse was advocated but on finding that the advanced guard of Cumberland's army was made up of three regiments of cavalry, they withdrew. They were pursued, but apart from a harmless exchange of shots at long range, neither side gained any advantage.

Next day they were at Elgin and then at Alves. After six days' marching the Government army stopped at Nairn on 14 April. They would rest on the following day, which coincidentally was their young commander's 25th birthday.

Matters were not going well for the Jacobites, despite the string of successes enjoyed in the past two months. Little money remained with the Jacobites and now their headquarters was stationery, there was no prospect of taking tax collectors' money and their only hope was cash from abroad. With the loss of the eastern seaboard and the supremacy of the Royal Navy, prospects were slim.

The one hope was the ship *Hazard* from France carrying much-needed gold to the tune of £12,000 to pay the troops and to keep them supplied. This fell into the hands of the loyalists on 25 March and subsequent attempts by Lord Cromarty to recover it ended in failure. There were supplies at Inverness but baking them and getting them from there to the army was problematic. Elcho wrote, 'As money was very scarce with him, he paid his troops mostly in meal, which they did not like and very often mutiny'd, refused to obey orders, and sometimes threw down their Arms and went home'.[14] Other depressing news was that 'the French had laid aside all thoughts of Sending any men over either to England or Scotland'.[15] The increasingly desperate state of the Jacobite army in April was to lead to the final act of the drama.

Chapter 15

The Battle of Culloden, 16 April 1746

After Cumberland's army had successfully crossed the Spey the endgame had begun in earnest. Charles had been unable to concentrate enough men to march them eastwards towards the enemy and thus needed to fight near Inverness, his base for the past two months. In London, Walpole wrote to Mann, on 15 April, 'The Rebellion seem once more at its last gasp; the Duke is marched, and the Rebels fly before him, in the utmost want of money'.[1]

Another difficulty for the Jacobites was that only part of their army was present. There should have been about 8,000 men.[2] Despite messages that had been sent out imploring their return to Inverness, many were still absent. On Monday, 14 April, only some of the Camerons had arrived, for many would not leave their homes as Fort William was still a threat to their homesteads. On the next day, when Keppoch's MacDonalds came, 'as much reduced in proportion as the former', Clanranald 'had but a mere handful of his people'. The MacPhersons were still in Badenoch, the MacKenzies were in Sutherland, as were the MacGregors and MacKinnons. Some of the MacDonalds were in Barrisdale and only part of the Frasers were on the march to rejoin, the latter 'with a considerable Recruit of his men'. Overall, over 2,000 'of his very best Highlanders' were absent. This was because some men had returned to their wives and families and others were out collecting money.[3] Yet Charles was adamant for fighting, being 'resolved to attack the enemy without waiting for those who were to join us'; and claimed he would fight even if he had only 1,000 men.[4]

That evening, what there was of the army was formed up in and around Culloden Park, whilst the artillery and ammunition was brought up from Inverness. The whole force was then drawn up on Culloden Moor on the next day, with two lines and a small reserve. 'All the men seemed to be in great spirits, expecting the enemy any moment.' Charles and his officers rode along them, smiling and saluting the men from each unit and they cheered in return. False alarms of the enemy's march were given to animate them further. They expected that the Government troop would march towards them and fight them on that day, as it was Cumberland's birthday. It was known that the enemy was at Nairn.[5]

Yet not all was well. It was an 'open muir' and Murray declared, 'I did not like the ground: it was certainly not proper for Highlanders'. Others agreed, 'Many were for retiring to stronger ground till all our army was gathered: but most of the baggage being at Inverness, this was not agreed to'. In the early afternoon, Murray sent Kerr and Stapleton to view ground to the south of the River Nairn. They reported back at two o'clock that it was hilly and boggy and Murray thought that this would hinder the enemy cavalry and artillery if they had to fight there. O'Sullivan disagreed, noting the presence of a ravine there, that any obstacles to a Jacobite charge would give the advantage to the Government infantry and artillery with their unbeatable volley fire (as it had on the Jacobite left wing at Falkirk). In addition, the same objections to this new site were made; that it would mean abandoning all the army's supplies and baggage at Inverness.[6] He also noted that 'he was sure Horse could be of no use, as there were several Boggs and Marshes'.[7]

O'Sullivan wrote at length why avoiding battle was not a serious option:

> how cou'd yu keep nine or ten thousand men together with out meal or mony, there was none to be had in the mountains. Yu cou'd not get them even Cows without mony, yu cou'd not keep them out in the feelds, in the season we were in, they must be quarter'd in villedges, yu cou'd never assemble them time enough in case the enemy come upon yu, & where are those villedges unlesse yu occupied nine or ten mils, besides peoples, yt are starving, finding themselves in their neighbourhood, the most of them wou'd go to their homes, & you'd have no Army. There was no replique to this. It was better to risque a battle, where it was morally sure yu wou'd abeat them if his royal Highness orders were follow'd, than give up all for lost, as yu wou'd if yu retired.[8]

Or as Lumisden put it more succinctly, 'He was obliged either to fight or starve'.[9]

By noon it was clear that Cumberland was not marching towards them on that day. It was his birthday and they were having a day's rest after a week of marching, and 'every man had a sufficient Quantity of Biscuit, Cheese and Brandy allowed him at the sole Expense of the Duke'.[10] In the Jacobite camp, a council of war was called. Elcho recalled, 'Lord George Murray made a speech, wherein he enlarged upon the advantages Highlanders have by surprising the Enemy, and rather attacking in the night time than in day light'. His plan was for the army to march at dusk to surprise the enemy and attack them whilst they were in their tents. The army would march in one column and on reaching Nairn the vanguard under Murray would attack the enemy's rear whilst the rearguard under Charles would attack at the front. According to Elcho, 'Every body Agreed to Lord George's opinion'.[11] In detail, the army would march at dusk to avoid being seen, and on reaching Kilvarock, the front third would cross the Nairn whilst the remainder would go to the north side, until both could see the enemy camp. The van would then recross the river and attack from the south. They would have to be ready to attack no later than two in the morning.[12]

Yet there were difficulties: many men had not arrived on the field, that in the case of being repelled it would be hard to rally and a retreat would be difficult. In any case they had little intelligence about Cumberland's dispositions and that he might have his spies in the Jacobite camp and so would be ready and waiting for them. Yet Charles was convinced 'he had men enough to beat the enemy whom he believed were utterly dispirited and would never stand a bold and brisk attack'. Perth and Lord John Drummond were positive for the attack but Cameron of Lochiel and Murray were aware that there were dangers therein.[13] Morale may have been high, with Kilmarnock later noting 'on the Day before the Ingagement, the Rebels were drinking together very chearfully'.[14]

The march was scheduled to begin at 7–8pm 'which [was] obeyed with the greatest pleasure and alacrity by the whole army'.[15] It was intended to be within striking distance by 2am on the next day at the outside. A number of Mackintoshes who claimed to know the lay of the land would act as guides. According to Kerr, 'The Prince . . . was very well pleased to see them in so good spirits'.[16] Apparently it was 'the Prince's conviction that the English would on that day be intoxicated'.[17] However, once the vanguard, headed by Murray, had marched the first half mile, he was told that there were gaps developing in the column as the men in the rear were finding it hard to keep up. The going was modest as the van was requested to slow the rate of their march. Some men were deserting to look for food and shelter.[18] This was because they had only been issued with a biscuit apiece that day.[19] O'Sullivan later wrote, 'The inevitable fate of night marches. It was extremely fatiguing and accompanied with confusion and disorder'.[20]

The van arrived at Kilvarock at about 2am as planned. Their destination was still three or four miles away and it would soon be daybreak. Perth arrived from the rear to consult Murray. O'Sullivan told Murray that Charles was adamant for an assault to be made. No one agreed with him, but Hepburn advocated that Cumberland's men would be still drunk after celebrating his birthday of the day before. The decision was then taken to retire. Murray later wrote: 'We had not half our men, and it was found impossible to make the attack in the time proposed. What else could be done? Was there any anything left but to retire as quiet as possible, so as the men might have a little rest and refreshment, in case they had to fight that day?'[21]

A suggestion made by a soldier in the Government army was that the Jacobites could hear their drums three miles away and realized that a surprise attack was no longer possible.[22] However, it is uncertain how close the vanguard was to Cumberland's camp and so it has been argued that the march should have been continued and a night attack attempted. Such had succeeded at Cromdale in 1690.

Charles was very angry, as Maxwell wrote, 'The Prince was incensed beyond expression at a retreat began in direct contradiction to his inclinations and express orders'.[23] On returning to Culloden, via Croy church, Elcho wrote, 'Everybody seemed to think of nothing but sleep. The men were prodigiously tired with hunger and fatigue' and many departed from their units to look for food or find sleep. The officers were lodging at Culloden House, where 'Everyone lay'd himself down where he could, some on beds, others on tables, chairs & con the floors, for the fatigue and hunger had been felt as much amongst the officers as soldiers'. They only had a couple of hours to rest before news came of their enemies being on the march.[24] The army had gambled and they had lost; subsequently were in an even worse condition in which to fight a battle. As Sir Robert Strange later wrote, 'Judge, then, what was to be expected from such an army, worn out with fatigue, and at this moment short of the necessaries of life. What, then can justify the deliberate folly and madness of fighting under such circumstances?'[25]

Whilst all this was going on among the Jacobites, Cumberland had treated his men to brandy to celebrate his birthday, though this was no immoderate amount as imagined by the Jacobites (O'Sullivan had thought that 'They'l all be drunk as beggars').[26] Ever since taking charge of the army in the previous year, Cumberland had been looking forward to a battle, but he later admitted, 'I never expected they would have had the imprudence to risqué a general engagement but their having burnt Fort Augustus the day before convinced me that they intended to stand'.[27] The regimental officers were all gathered together by Cumberland. He gave them their marching orders for the next day and told them that there was the possibility of a battle on that day, how the leading battalions would act and that he expected victory if his orders were obeyed.[28]

For Cumberland's men, Wednesday, 16 April began between four and five in the morning when they were roused from their tents to dress, arm and march from the camp near Nairn westwards towards Inverness. Battalion commanders 'received their full Instructions in writing in what manner to act, and how the Men were to be formed'. General orders of the day were read to each company, reminding them that if any soldier failed to do his duty he risked being court-martialled and executed. Hughes wrote 'It was quite necessary and prudent to have a regular and strict Order preserved, that a finishing Period might be put to the scandalous Progress of these rebellious Vermin'.[29]

It was not a prepossesing day, as Private Alexander Taylor of the Royal Scots later wrote: 'It was a very cold, rainy Morning, and nothing to buy to comfort us. But we had the Ammunition loaf, thank God; but not a dram of Brandy or Spirits, had you given a Crown for a gill, nor, nothing but the Loaf and the water. We had also great Difficulty in keeping the Locks of our firelocks dry; which was absolutely necessary'.[30] A fellow Scot, the 51-year-old Private Edward Linn of Campbell's, also wrote of the dispiriting march to Culloden, 'We waded to our knees in mud & dirt through the Moor Severall times that day with a good will to be att them, & no Wonder, considering the fatigues we have undergone this Winter by hunger & Cold & Marching, Night & Day, after them'.[31]

The army marched in four columns. The first three were all composed of five battalions of infantry. The fourth column, to the right of the others, consisted of the three regiments of cavalry. Behind the first column of infantry, on the left, were the artillery and baggage. To the army's fore were the Argyll Highlanders and forty men of Kingston's Horse. This was a cautious army that was feeling its way forward. Whitefoord explained that the formation had been organized thus in order that were they attacked on the march, they could form up to repel any attack.[32] Ashe Lee wrote of the formation, 'he [Cumberland] settled the disposition of our march and the order of battle, in a manner most justly admired, and worthy the experience of the oldest and ablest general'.[33]

The effects of the abortive night march were proving to be dismal among the Jacobites. Apparently, 'the fatigue of this night's march, joined to the want of sleep for several nights before, and the want of food, occasioned a prodigious murmuring among the private men, many of them exclaiming bitterly'. Many left in search of food, to Inverness and elsewhere.[34]

Meanwhile, to the west, there was further discussion among the Jacobites as to what they should do. Some advocated a retreat to Inverness, where the stores were located. Such a move would allow stragglers and others to join them, as well as enabling the men to be adequately fed.[35] However, no council of war was held, as Elcho noted, 'everyone knew that he wished to fight, and yet there was only one proper course to follow, viz to retreat, but there were no provisions'.[36]

Yet there seems to have been some further discussion. O'Sullivan stated that 'he was sure horse could be of no use, because there were several bogues and morasses'. Yet Murray replied that 'he was afraid the enemy would have great advantage in that plain muir both in their horse and cannon'.[37] However, Murray had made no such complaint about the fairly featureless terrain that had been fought over at Prestonpans several months previously.

Jacobite cavalry observed the approach of the Government army. The Jacobites had only two hours of repose after the night march before they had to face their foes again, only this time it would be in actuality. Drums were beat and pipes played 'which Alarm Caused great hurry & Confusion amongst people half dead with fatigue'. They were also reduced in number, too, with perhaps 2,000 men being absent, either asleep or looking for food. Some were too far away or otherwise unable to hear the reveille.[38] The weather was also discouraging; it being rainy and both this and the wind blew westwards into their faces, which had been the reverse at Falkirk. Johnstone wrote, about the vulnerability of the Jacobite army: 'Indeed, he [Cumberland] must have been blind in the extreme to have delayed attacking us instantly in the deplorable situation in which we were, worn out with hunger and fatigue, especially when he perceived from our manoeuvre that we were impatient to give battle under every possible disadvantage, and well disposed to facilitate our own destruction.'[39]

When news of Cumberland's advance came, there were only 1,000 men gathered together at Culloden, so they drew up on a site further to the west of the grounds selected on the previous day in order to allow more men to join. Others left as the army gathered together. It was only by noon that 'the lines were brought to some confused form'.[40] Strange reported a similar scene, 'No line was as yet formed; the men were standing in clusters; and stragglers in small numbers were coming up from all quarters'.[41]

The Marquis d'Eguilles made one final attempt to persuade Charles not to fight and later wrote:

> The Prince who believed himself invincible because he had not yet been beaten, defied by enemies whom he thoroughly despised, seeing at their head the son of the rival of his father, proud and haughty as he was, badly advised, perhaps betrayed, forgetting at this moment every other object, could not bring himself to decline battle even for a single day.

The French envoy stated that the army was under strength, it was tired and hungry. A retreat to Inverness or into mountains would put them in a better condition to fight. It was a fruitless exercise, and so, 'finding him immovable in the resolve he had taken to fight at any cost', D'Eguilles rode to Inverness and burnt all his papers.[42] Similar entreaties were brushed aside by Charles's advisers, who apparently 'having lost all patience and hoping no doubt for a miracle . . . insisted upon a battle'.[43] Apparently 'Sir Thomas Sheridan, and others from France . . . insisted upon a battle, and prevailed'.[44]

Stapleton added fuel to the fire when he goaded those clan chiefs who were ambivalent about the prospect of fighting on that day. He remarked that 'the Scots were always good troops until things came to a crisis'. Lochiel answered 'he did not believe there was a Highlander in the army who would not have run up to the mouth of a cannon, in order to confuse the odious and undeserved aspersion'.[45]

Charles and Murray were at odds again, as Johnstone recalled, 'The Prince, on his return to Culloden, enraged against Lord George Murray, publicly declared that no one in future should command his army but himself'. Pleas to avoid a battle when the men were scattered, exhausted and hungry went unheeded. Falling back to either hilly ground or to Inverness in order to allow the men rest and food, to let stragglers come in, and to fight on better terrain were ignored. Johnstone was clear 'The Prince, however, would listen to no advice, and resolved on giving battle, let the consequences be what they might'.[46] Perhaps the observer who summed up Charles's reasoning best was in the following 'he felt it due to his reputation rather to be defeated, arms in hand, than to flewe before the English whom he had already vanquished at Prestonpans, Aberdeen and Falkirk, with forces much inferior to their own'.[47] For Charles fighting the battle was a matter of honour and among the princes of Europe in the eighteenth century this was no small matter.

Meanwhile, Cumberland's army, having marched on the main road, now left it to march to Culloden, to the south-west of the highway. Hearing that the Jacobites were advancing towards them, he had the men form up in line for battle. However, finding that the Jacobites were not so forward, he ordered the men back into columns to march again. These changes of formation were carried out quickly and efficiently. There was another, equally unnecessary switch of formation and back again. Colonel Joseph Yorke, a staff officer, noted, 'the Duke made the army form immediately in line of battle, which they did with the ease and alacrity as surprised every spectator, and gave the greatest hope for eventual victory'.[48]

It was an unsettling march for the men, however. Taylor wrote: 'We marched but four miles till we were alarmed by their Out-parties and drew up in order of battle, and marched that way for two miles with our arms secured and Bayonets fixed (a very uneasy way of marching.'[49]

Taylor's alarm may refer to the sighting of Jacobite scouting parties, presumably cavalry, who apparently sighting their Government counterparts a mile to the south-east of Culloden House, with the latter retreating. In fact, Charles ordered Murray to attack with the handful of men they had before the enemy could form up. Murray refused to do so, preferring to wait until more men had been assembled on the moor. Charles then spent time 'expressing his displeasure of Lord George's conduct', not for the first nor the last time. John Stuart who heard this remarked that had any man but the Prince criticised Lord George he would have had words with him.[50] Further evidence that the Jacobite army was at hand was provided by five deserters from Drummond's regiment.[51]

The weather continued to be dull, with Linn writing 'it was a very bad day both for Wind & Rain, But thank God it was straight upon our backs'.[52] Lumisden gave the Jacobite perspective on the weather, 'the great storm of hail and rain that blew in our faces'.[53] On the advance, the cavalry were able to take a few prisoners, presumably stragglers or sleeping Jacobites.[54]

The Government army was initially arrayed on the battlefield thus:

Infantry
Front line
Commander: Earl of Albermarle
Barrell's, Munro's, Royal Scots, Price's, Cholmondeley's, Royal Scots Fusiliers (from left to right)
Second line
Commander: Major General Huske
Wolfe's, Howard's, Fleming's, Bligh's, Sempill's, Ligonier's (from left to right)
Reserve
Commander: Brigadier Mordaunt
Battereau's, Blakeney's, Pulteney's
Lord Loudoun's and Argyll Militia companies (total of four)

Cavalry
Kerr's Dragoons and two squadrons of Cobham's on the left
Kingston' Light Horse and one squadron of Cobham's in reserve

Artillery
10 x 3-pounders (in batteries of two between each battalion in front line).
6 x Cohorn mortar (in front of second line)
Major William Belford and Captain John Godwin
2 lieutenants, 2 sergeants, 2 corporals, 1 fireworker, 21 gunners, 47 matrosses and 7 bombardiers.

Strength of the Army

Infantry

Unit	Field Officers	Captains	Lieutenants	Sergeants	Drummers	Others	Total
Royals	2	5	19	29	25	401	481
Howard	2	4	10	21	14	413	462
Barrell	2	5	13	18	10	325	373
Wolfe	1	7	14	17	11	324	374
Pulteney	2	6	14	23	19	310	374
Price	2	7	14	21	11	304	359
Bligh	2	5	13	22	13	412	467
Campbell	1	5	13	21	14	358	412
Sempill	3	5	15	20	14	358	415
Blakeney	2	4	14	24	12	300	356
Cholmon-deley	2	7	15	21	15	399	359
Fleming	2	6	18	25	14	350	415
Munro	2	6	15	23	19	426	491
Ligonier	3	5	16	21	16	325	386
Battereau	1	7	19	24	18	354	423
Total	27	84	222	330	225	5521	6409

Argyllshire Militia: 140 men in four companies on the field; another eight companies (about 361 and officers) in reserve/baggage guard.
Murray's company: strength unknown

Cavalry
Officers

Unit	Field Officers	Majors	Captains	Lieutenants	Cornets	Others*	Total
Kingston	0	1	2	5	6	8	22
Cobham	0	1	3	2	2	5	13
Kerr	1	1	2	6	6	5	21
Total	1	3	7	13	14	18	56

*indicates adjutants, surgeons and quartermasters: none had a chaplain

Men

Unit	Sergeants	Drummers	Troopers	Total
Kingston	11	7	166	184
Cobham	12	8	219	239
Kerr	13	12	249	274
Total	36	27	632	697

Also 225 men on sick list
Total cavalry strength: 56 officers and 697 men (753 men)
Total strength: 7,246, plus John Murray's company.

A word about the men in the ranks of the regular army is probably worth making. Based on an analysis of the pension records of over 3,000 of the rank and file, the following comments can be made. 1,745 (52 per cent) were English, 1,145 (34 per cent) were Scottish, 246 (7 per cent) were Irish and 77 (2 per cent) were Welsh. Given that the Scots formed only about 10 per cent of Great Britain's population, they were represented in Cumberland's army far beyond the expected proportion. More Scots fought for the Jacobites at Culloden, but many fought against them; and the number cited above excludes the militia companies. Of their former occupations, 1,296 (39 per cent) were labourers, 320 were weavers (10 per cent). At the time of the battle, the average mean age was 33 and the average mean length of service in the army was eight years. A forthcoming paper will deal with the men in the ranks of the army in more detail.[55]

When the army reached Culloden, they drew up about a mile to the east of the Jacobites. They were arrayed with six battalions in the first two lines and three in the third, with 50 yards between each line. Albermarle and Sempill were in command of the first line, Huske the second and Mordaunt the reserve. Two cannons were placed between each of the battalions on the front line and the six mortars were before the battalions on the right of the second line. Two squadrons of Kingston's Horse and one of Cobham's dragoons were in the reserve at least initially. Kerr's squadrons and the remainder of Cobham's were stationed on the left of the infantry, with Hawley and Bland in command. Most of the Argyll Highlanders were placed in the rear to guard the baggage but 140 accompanied Hawley. There was considerable manoeuvring by both sides before the battle.[56]

As usual, the Jacobites' strength was in the battalions in their front line. There were fourteen battalions, mainly clan units here. There were also twelve guns divided into three batteries. Numbers of men are unclear because many men were absent from their units and the numbers of absentees are indeterminable. One source suggests a total of 6,626 men, with 4,150 of these in the front rank and 1,600 in the second, with a reserve of 700 and only 176 cavalry. It is possible that these numbers are based on those of 15 April. On the day of the battle Elcho estimated that Jacobite strength was about 5,000 in all. Their formation was such that the left wing battalions were considerably farther away from their enemies than was the case on the right. It is also worth noting that the battlefield was not the one selected on the previous day, but was to its south-west.[57] There was allegedly half a mile between the front and second lines.[58]

The Jacobite army was, according to one estimate, on 15 April as follows, from right to left:

Unit	Possible strengths	Line
Atholl Brigade	500	1
Camerons	600	1
Stewarts of Appin	200	1
Roy Stuarts	100	1
Frasers	500	1
MacIntoshes	700	1
Farquharsons	200	1
Macleods	100	1
MacLeans	100	1
Clanranalds	250	1
Keppochs	300	1
Glengarrys	600	1
Glenbuckets	200	1
Perth's	300	1
Lord John Drummond	400	2
Ogilby's	500	3
Irish Picquets	300	2
Kilmarmnock's	50	2
Fitzjames's Horse	70	2
Balmerino's and Strathallan's	70	2
Hussars	36	2[59]

Cumberland had his men make additional movements to improve their position. Although a morass protected the battalions on his right flank, as they advanced it no longer did so. Thus he ordered the cavalry from the reserve to form the right wing of the front line. Pulteney's and Battereau's battalions were moved from the reserve to the right of the first and second lines respectively, thus lengthening his first two lines at the expense of reducing the reserve to a single battalion.[60] Maxwell was impressed by them, 'They made a very good appearance' whilst Daniel was less so, 'they continued proceeding, like a deep sullen river'.[61]

Hawley had apparently been reconnoitring the Jacobite position, 'having been some time before to see the ground, had been up near the right of the enemy'. Cumberland expressed to him the concerns he had over his left flank. Hawley said, 'Sir, if youle give me the conducting of the dragoons, I'll answer for your left flank'. Cumberland answered, 'Do so: I depend on you'. Hawley then had Bland divide the dragoons on the left (Cobham's and Kerr's) into 'as many little squadrons as there were troops' and put them in two lines of two men deep, which made twelve small squadrons. He did this 'knowing they had no cavalry to deale with worthe thinking of'.[62]

To the right of the Jacobite front line were the 6ft-high walls of Culwhinniac, which would appear to have protected their flank here. O'Sullivan suggested to Murray that these walls could be defended by putting troops inside them and piercing the walls to enable musketry. This would deter any potential threat to the flank, but Murray disagreed with him and reminded him that he was the superior officer of the two.[63] Protecting the left flank were the walls of Culloden Park. It was a 'high boggy moor' according to Wolfe.[64]

There was a degree of discord within the Jacobite army, not just between Murray and O'Sullivan. Charles was 'enraged against Lord George Murray', presumably because of his having halted the night march without consulting him.[65] The MacDonalds were unhappy that they were sited on the left of the front line, not the right, as this should have been their place as they had been on the left on the previous day, but there had been no time to change formation that morning so the previous day's order of battle was adhered to.[66] Daniel wrote that they 'were now displaced, and made to give way, at the pleasure of Lord George Murray, to the Athol men, whom he commanded'.[67] Charles was unable to decide who had the right of the matter, but he found it easier to ask the MacDonalds to be posted on the left than he could prevail upon the headstrong Murray to drop his case, but it left the MacDonalds dissatisfied with their leaders.[68] French officers were impressed with their enemy's advance, one later saying, 'he was sure the day was lost' and on being asked why, replied, 'he had observ'd the Duke's men come on, but never in his Life saw an army move in a more cool and regular Manner; for they would often break and move again with great Dexterity and Fine Order.'[69]

The armies were now only 500 yards apart, which was cannon range, and so hostilities could not be long delayed. Morale seemed to be high on both sides and last minutes efforts were made to maintain that. In order to encourage his men, Cumberland rode down the lines and made a short speech:

> My brave boys, your toil will soon be at an end; stand your ground against the broadsword and target, parry the enemy in the manner you have been directed, be assured of immediate assistance, and I promise you that I shall not fail to make a report of your behaviour to the King, and in the meantime, if any are unwilling to engage, pray let them speak freely, and with pleasure they shall have a discharge.[70]

Michael Hughes, a volunteer in the ranks, later wrote that the speech was 'followed by a full acclamation of all the soldiers, testifying their intire satisfaction and loyalty.'[71] The last sentence of the speech is reminiscent of Shakespeare's *Henry V* Agincourt speech, which presumably Cumberland was aware of. Apparently, he spoke to each battalion and platoon, 'Had you seen him as I did, you could never forget him. His presence and intrepid Behaviour was enough to inspire the most pusillanimous with courage' and he told them to 'Depend my lads on your Bayonets: let them mingle with you; let them know the Men they have to deal with.'[72] He then rode over to the battalions on the right wing, posting himself in front of Howard's in the second line, 'imagining the greatest push would be there' as he later wrote.[73]

Cumberland seems to have played an active role in the battle. John McCoull wrote of 'the Duke was imploying in riding through the Ranks during the heat of the Action spiriting up the men.'[74] Donald Campbell of Airds wrote, 'His Royal Highness acted not only the part of a Generall, but an ADC, was all the time in the line, giving orders, with the same coolness as a Judge sitting on his bench.'[75]

Meanwhile, despite their privations ('the men were nodding with sleep in the ranks'), the Jacobite army was also in good spirits as battle became imminent. Daniel wrote, 'Those, however, who staid, put the best face on the affair they could, and all of us presently appeared surprisingly courageous, who only seemed to survive animated by the spirit of loyalty and love for our dear Prince'. When they saw their enemies approaching, 'we began to huzza and bravado them in their march upon us'. Part of this enthusiasm may have been engendered by Charles and other Jacobite leaders who 'rode from rank to rank, animating and encouraging the soldiers by well adapted harangues'.[76]

Maxwell added 'The Highlanders, though faint with hunger, and ready to drop with fatigue and want of sleep, seemed to forget all their hardships at the approach of the enemy'.[77] After all, this was an army which to date had not been beaten in battle.

Charles had ridden to the battlefield with the Camerons. According to O'Sullivan he did much to try and improve the men's morale, 'Not the least concern appear'd on his face, he has yt talent superiorly, in the greatest concern or denger, its then he appears most cheerful & harty, wch is very essential for a Prince or a general, yt incourages much the army'. He also went among the officers and men, talking to them and telling them "'here they are comeing, my lades, we'l soon be wth them. They don't forget, Glads-mur [Prestonpans], nor Falkirk, & yu have the same Armes & swords, let me see yours", takeing one of the men's swords. "I'l answer this will cut of some heads & arms today. Go on, my Lads, the day will be ours & we'll want for nothing after". This & the like discource heartened very much our men, tho' the Prince in the bottom had no great hopes'.[78] Apparently he made a speech which was greatly applauded, 'Whereupon they all threw up their Bonnets in the Air with great Clamour, saying God bless the King and Prince Charles; and immediately were ordered a double portion of Oatmeal and Whisky for Incouragement'.[79]

As with Falkirk, the weather played a part in the battle and we have already noted that it was poor. One effect of this was that the ground in places was wet underfoot. Horses pulling the guns of the Royal Artillery began to sink and had to be unharnessed, obliging soldiers to manhandle the guns into position, but being only three pounders this was manageable. Elsewhere, Wolfe's battalion were sinking up to their ankles until they moved position.[80] The weather was variable at this point, there being a rainstorm, followed by wind and by one o'clock there was fair weather.[81] Soldiers on neither side found this bad weather beneficial, as the wind blew into the Jacobites' faces, but the rain made some of the regulars' cartridges wet. Most men, though, kept their muskets dry with their coats and so only a few failed to fire.[82]

Apparently, Cumberland was not entirely sure what to do next and sent an aide to Hawley, as a more experienced general, for his opinion, and Hawley sent a message back, ''twas his opinion to attacque immediately and that he would very soon be in upon their flanque with the dragoons, that he saw nothing but what he liked for they seemed to be all in confusion'.[83] Possibly bearing in mind the repulse of the attack made at Falkirk, Cumberland sent quite possibly the same aide forward to verify this. This was Lord Bury (1724–72), in order to take a closer look at the Jacobite army, and in particular to note where their artillery was situated.

Meanwhile, on the left of the Government infantry, the dragoons were moving away from them, Hawley planning to move towards the river and out of sight of both armies, in order to attack the Jacobite right flank. Learning of the walls ahead, it was thought that they could be 'tumbled down in a minute' and the Argyll militia did so.[84]

It was about one o'clock when the first shots of the battle were fired, and these were by the Jacobite artillery. This was the first time in the campaign of 1745 that the Jacobite artillery had fired a shot on the battlefield and was the most numerous array of artillery ever fielded by a Jacobite army in the entire period of 1689 to 1746. The general consensus was that they were, in Cumberland's words, 'extremely ill served and ill manned'. Ray added that they, 'did us little or no damage'.[85] Apparently 'the Balls flew mostly over the heads of the Royalists'.[86] An anonymous contemporary from Edinburgh blamed this on the ineptitude of the crews manning the guns. Maxwell stated that there were no trained crews for the guns on the left, the men could not be found and so some 'common soldiers were sent to do the best they could'.[87]

Yet it was not wholly ineffectual. One soldier wrote that 'the shot when [*sic*] entirely over the army (except a few) and killed some person guarding the baggage, a great distance behind the army'. Furthermore, there were a number of battalions who were not directly engaged otherwise in the battle and these took some minor casualties which were probably the effect of this artillery fire.[88] According to John McCoull, it was 'mostly over our lines and only a little hurt in the corps de reserve'.[89] Some of this fire was directed against Cumberland himself, as an observer noted, 'tho' by exposing his own valuable Person too much, it had often like to cost us too dear . . . a particular Providence guards him, and he trusts to it', though 'severall balls having fallen within a yard of him' and the artillery fire killed two men in the battalion nearby.[90] Other than those men killed or wounded in the two battalions that took the weight of the Jacobite charge, there were nine killed and sixty-nine wounded, and some of these may have been caused by Jacobite cannon fire. Apparently, the guns fired from right to left twice before any reply was made.[91] According to Hughes the guns fired on the battalions on the left of the Government army, 'but did not do the Execution as was first expected' and considered the guns well placed.[92]

It was then the turn of the Royal Artillery to open fire with roundshot and mortar fire, the delay being caused by 'the boggy Ground hindered the immediate bringing up of our Cannon', wrote Hughes.[93] This was the first time in the campaign, indeed, in the whole of the Jacobite campaigns from 1689, that there had been effective artillery fire directed against the Jacobite army on the battlefield. It is impossible to state exactly how long this fire was and how many casualties it caused. However, it was not insignificant, as attested by contemporary observers. Wolfe later wrote, 'they were greatly surpris'd and disordered by it'.[94] 'Ours immediately answered them, which began their confusion', wrote Cumberland.[95] Hughes wrote of 'the great Execution performed with our Cannon'.[96] Ker wrote that they were 'playing with great execution'.[97] Elcho stated, 'they suffer'd the Cannonade very impatiently, a great many of them threw themselves down flatt upon the Ground, and some of them, but few, gave way and run off'.[98] Some fire focussed on one of the three Jacobite batteries and 'made a strange slaughter-house' of it.[99] Not all the artillery fire was directed at the troops in the front line, with Daniel writing 'the whole fury of the enemy's Artillery seemed to be directed against us in the rear, as if they had noticed where the Prince was' for some balls went towards those behind them, killing one of Charles' servants and endangering him and another eyewitness wrote 'Some of the cannon balls went over their targets'.[100] It is not known how long the cannonade lasted. According to Yorke, the cannonade lasted only two or three minutes, but Wolfe thought it was fifteen, though this may refer to the entire time guns of both sides were firing; in another letter he put it as eight or nine. Another contemporary gave it as nine minutes.[101]

Meanwhile, on the Jacobite right, 500 yards beyond the first wall was another, 8ft high, which was taken down and the British squadrons marched through 'as soon as possible and upon a trot in two lines'. Yet the last wall was held by the two Jacobite battalions 'drawne up with their noses close to this eight foot high wall' posted on the right to defend the flank against any such attack.[102] Charles, on horseback on an eminence next to Fitzjames Horse, saw the destruction of the walls and sent repeated orders to Murray to attack them, but apparently 'Lord George paid no attention to this order'.[103] The units posted to prevent any further attack were Avuchies's, Elcho's and Fitzjames's Horse.[104] Apparently 'They seemed quite astounded and never faced nor fired one shott'.[105]

The main Jacobite army needed to advance into contact with its enemies. Murray, on the right, asked Kerr if the attack should begin. To do so they needed orders. Charles did send an order for them to attack, but the messenger was killed by a cannon ball. Another man was subsequently sent and then another. Other sources suggest that several messengers had to be despatched before the men began to move. It was envisaged that the battalions on the left would move first and then movement would continue all along the line with those on the right moving last in order that they hit their enemy at the same time to rectify the misalignment of the line and Kerr was sent to ride along to ensure these orders were followed.[106]

Maxwell wrote 'It was indeed high time to come to a close engagement, for the enemy had infinite advantage in cannonading'. He believed that it was Murray who was responsible for the delay in launching an attack. According to him, 'they were as yet at too great a distance, and what vigour the men had left would be spent before they could reach the enemy'. The risk of being out-flanked was another possible cause of delay. Yet there was no advance against them and the cannonade was constant. 'At length the Highlanders, who grew very impatient, called aloud to be led on, which Lord George Murray did without further delay'.[107]

When the infantry finally advanced the clans on the left of the line were remarkably reluctant to charge. This was probably because they had further to charge, the ground in their front was boggy and there were squadrons of dragoon on the right of the British line who could counter-charge once they left the protection of the walls to their left. It seems that they made several feints as Cumberland later wrote: 'they came down three separate times within a hundred yards of our men, fireing their Pistols & brandishing their Swords, but the Royals & Pulteneys hardly took their firelocks from their shoulders, so that after those faint attempts, they made off'.[108] Some firing did take place, as Captain Ronald MacDonald recalled seeing 'Keppoch fall twice to the ground . . . upon that second fall, looking at Donald Roy MacDonald, he spoke these words "O God, have mercy upon me. Donald, do the best for yourself, for I am gone"'.[109]

Instead it was the right wing, the Atholl men, the Camerons and the Stewarts of Appin, who were nearest the British line, who were the first to charge. The enclosures to their right funnelled them in a large mass towards the two battalions on the left of the British line, Barrell's and Munro's, which they cumulatively outnumbered.

Cumberland, as with Hawley at Falkirk, was convinced that the infantry's musketry was the key to success. He had written, 'I put all the cavalry in the third line, because by all accounts the rebels don't fear that, as they do our fire, and on that alone I must depend'.[110] Both the men in his ranks and those in the Jacobite ranks attested to the impressive, deadly fire of the Government infantry at Culloden. Linn wrote, 'we gave them so warm a reception that we kept a continuall close firing upon them with our small arms' and Taylor wrote of 'the thunder of our fire'.[111]

Those on the receiving end concurred. Daniel noted, 'our hopes were very slender from the continual fire of musketry that was kept up upon them from right to left'.[112] O'Sullivan agreed, 'the enemy's musquetary begins, & continues as regular & is nurrished a fire as any troops cou'd. Our men advances, but slolly, & really it is not possible yt any troops yt cant answer such a fire as the enemy kept can do otherwise'.[113]

Artillery could now switch from roundshot to canister to inflict even greater casualties. Linn recalled its effectiveness, '2 or 4 of our cannon gave them such a closs with grape shott which galled them very much'.[114] Maxwell concurred: 'their cannon, which were now charged with grape shot, did a great deal [of damage], particularly an advanced battery on their left, which outflanked the Atholl men'.[115] Fire was from three sources, as Forbes later noted, 'Field pieces and cohorns, and by a perpetuall Regular . . . platoon firing which brought them down in hoops'.[116] Hughes wrote of 'our Cannon began to play so very briskly upon them, and their Lines were formed so thick and deep, that the Grapeshot made open Lanes quite through them, the Men dropping down by Wholesale'.[117]

The Jacobite attack, led by Murray at the front, was a chaotic one. Wolfe wrote that they moved forward 'with more fury than prudence'.[118] They were unable to see their foes 'which they could not see till they were upon them, for smoke'.[119] Elcho wrote that 'the Centre join'd the right, and in a sort of a mob, without any order or distinction of Corps, mixt together, rush'd in and attack'd'.[120] Archaeological evidence in the form of musket and cannon shot found there suggests that some men broke over the Leanch enclosures on their right, which would have further disrupted any ordered formation.[121]

In part the reason for this confusion was the wind and smoke which blew against them as Maxwell noted, 'the wind which had been so favourable to the Highlanders at Falkirk, was now directly in their faces, and more detrimental, as there was much more firing. They were buried in a cloud of smoke, and felt their enemies without seeing them.'[122] The Jacobite charge was described by several witnesses. Yorke wrote of 'they broke from the centre in three large bodies like wedges and moved forward'.[123]

According to Henderson, they came 'in a stooping posture, with their Targets in their left Hand, covering their Head and Breast, and their glittering swords in their Right, they ran swiftly upon the Cannon, making a frightful huzza'.[124] According to Ray, they were 'running forward in their furious wild way' and 'in a noisy, confus'd, tumultuous manner'.[125] There was also a degree of respect for the enemy among some. Taylor referred to their charge at Culloden thus, 'they betook them to their small Arms, Sword and Pistol, and came running on our Front-Line like Troops of Hungry Wolves, and fought with intrepidity'.[126] Likewise, Linn wrote 'they came up very boldly & very fast all in a Cloud together, Sword in hand'.[127] Hughes wrote that 'like Wildcats their Men came down in swarms'.[128] The sight might also have unnerved some men, however, as a contemporary historian noted, 'Everybody allowed, who saw them dead in the field of battle, that men of a larger size, larger limbs and better proportioned, could not be found'.[129]

The Jacobites were fired upon at almost point-blank range – at pistol shot, one Jacobite claimed. The Government battalions immediately before them were three ranks deep. The second and third ranks fired within 30 yards but the first rank fired just as the Jacobites were at the muzzles of their muskets. The cannon fired 'within two yards of them they received a full Discharge of Cartridge shot which made a dreadful Havock'.[130] Apparently 'they received a most terrible fire, not only in front, but also on the flank' from the Argyllshire militia behind the Culwhinniac enclosures.[131]

According to Wolfe the attackers were 'throwing down their arms without exploding them', but not all did so.[132] There was some Jacobite fire on these two battalions, for an officer of Munro's referred to later finding six musket balls in his coat and hat, though none of these harmed him.[133] Yorke referred to the Jacobites 'firing very irregularly at a considerable distance', so the balls were probably spent by the time they hit the aforesaid officer.[134] But not all incoming fire was harmless. Three of Munro's and two of Barrell's men later claimed wound pensions for having been shot in the legs at Culloden.[135] Archaeological evidence also suggests that there was some musketry on the Jacobites' part.[136]

Firepower alone was insufficient to check the charging Jacobite infantry, however, who outnumbered the men in the two battalions in front of them. Huske rode over to Barrell's and Munro's battalions 'bidding the men push home with their bayonets, was so well observed by these brave fellows, that hundreds perished on their points'. Lord Robert Kerr, a captain in Barrell's, was thrusting his weapon ahead and had 'his spontoon in the heart of a rebel'.[137]

There were several comments on this mêlée. It was reported, 'There was scarce a soldier or officer in Barrell's or Munro's which engaged, who did not kill one or two men each with their bayonets or spontoons'. Of Barrell's it was alleged, 'After the battle there was not a bayonet in this regiment but was either bloody or bent'.[138] An officer of Munro's attested, 'Our lads fought more like Devils then Men'.[139] Captain Clifton, of the same battalion, wrote that a Cameron offered him quarter, 'which I replied and bid the rebel scoundrel advance. He did, and fired at me, but providentially missed his mark. I then shot him dead and took his pistol and dirk, which was certainly neat'. He added, 'we gave no quarter nor asked for any'.[140] A soldier from Barrell's later wrote, 'the old Tangerines bravely repulse those Boarders with a dreadful slaughter, and convinced them that their Broadswords and Target is unequal to the Musket and Bayonet, when in the hands of Veterans who are determined to use them'.[141] According to Elcho, Jacobite losses were all the greater because 'it was the more easy as they had no targets, for they would not be at the pains upon a march to carry them'.[142] This fearsome hand-to-hand combat is in stark contrast to the behaviour of the men in Cope's army at Prestonpans who fled before contact and where it was said that not a bayonet was used throughout the battle. These two veteran battalions stood and held their ground instead.

Contemporary historians laid much stress on the effectiveness of the new bayonet drill which had been taught to the troops at Aberdeen. Douglas wrote:

> The alteration was mighty little, but of the last consequence. Before this, the bayonet man, attacked the sword man right fronting him, now the left hand bayonet attacked the sword fronting his next right hand man. He was then covered by the enemy's shield where open on his left, and the enemy's right open to him. The manner made an effectual difference, staggered the enemy, who were not prepared to alter their way of fighting, and destroyed them in a manner rather to be conceived than told.[143]

Lord Robert Kerr was the most prominent fatality in the Government army. Apparently, 'not noticing his men's going back, [he] remained a few yards alone. He had struck his pike into the body of a Highland officer, but before he could disengage himself, was surrounded and cut to pieces.'[144] He 'was covered with wounds [over thirty according to Walpole]; his head was cut by a lieutenant of Keppoch's regiment, from the crown to the collar Bone, yet he was in a manner hacked in pieces . . . There were other officers were likewise cut to the pieces . . . their mangled Corpses.'[145] Wolfe recorded another act of heroism, when Ensign John Brown was 'obstinately defending one of the colours but was knocked to the ground, but not carried off'.[146] It could then have been that David Robertson, a private from Sempill's battalion, came forward to guard the standard for the wounded ensign.[147]

Yet even this heroism was not enough, for the Jacobites had the advantage of numbers, overlapping Barrell's battalion on the latter's left flank, and with a third of Barrell's men killed or wounded on the spot, they were able to break through and reached the ground behind the first line of battalions. Hughes wrote 'they begun to cut and hack in their own natural way without Ceremony'. They were urged on by their officers, 'their Commanders kept continually riding through their Lines, forcing the Highlanders down upon us'.[148] Apparently they 'would have been cut to pieces had they not been immediately supported'.[149] Wolfe wrote that Barrell's were surrounded and risked destruction.[150]

But there were troops there ready for the Jacobites. This had been foreseen by Huske. As Hughes noted, he 'gave us this Charge, That if we had Time to Load, so to do, and if not, to make no Delay, but to drive our Bayonets into their Bodies and make sure Work'.[151] Wolfe's and Fleming's battalions wheeled to the left and Bligh's and Sempills' to the right, firing on the Jacobite front and flanks. They 'received a full fire from the centre of Bligh's'.[152] Murray recalled, 'my horse plunged and reared so much, that I thought he was wounded: so I quitted my stirrups and was thrown'.[153] Disciplined fire into the mass of charging men 'made great havoc of 'em and the greater for them being (unusually) fifty deep'.[154] William Oman, who was in the ranks of one of these battalions, wrote, 'The perpetual fire of our troops made for five minutes . . . which beat them off, and obliged them to turn their backs and run away'.[155] Of the 500 men who broke through towards the second line, Ray was of the opinion that 'I believe there was a not a single man who escaped'.[156] However, it was later alleged that ''tis thought by their fire killed several of Barrell's men mixed with the enemy' in a case of what would late be termed 'friendly fire'.[157]

Several of the rank and file captured Jacobite standards at this point. These men were Edward Patridge from Bligh's, Sergeant Dunn, Charles Robinson and John Brown (a 42-year-old former weaver from Glasgow), the latter three from Sempill's. Later Patridge was rewarded with £16 and the other three shared £50 18s with Robertson, who had saved one of Barrell's colours.[158]

During the encounter, 'Lord George behaved himself with great gallantry, lost his horse, his periwig and bonnet, was amongst the last that left the field, had severall cuts with broadswords in his coat, and was covered with blood and dirt'. He had behaved like an admirable battalion commander but not as a general. Meanwhile, as some of the Camerons fled, Lochiel tried in vain to rally them. When he returned to the remaining Camerons he was shot by the Argyllshire militia and four of his men took him to a barn. They narrowly missed being captured or killed by dragoons, and later were able to escape.[159] Duncan Forbes later reported that several of the chiefs begged the men to 'return to the charge, but to no purpose'.[160]

It was about at this point that the frustration among some of the Jacobites was noted by Cumberland, writing, 'in their rage that they could not make any impression upon the battalions, they threw stones at them, for at least a minute or two'.[161] Johnstone wrote, 'the flight began to become general, which spreads from the right to the left of our army with the rapidity of lightning. What a spectacle of horror! The same Highlanders, who had advanced to the charge like lions, with bold, determined countenances, were in an instant seen flying like trembling cowards in the greatest disorder'.[162] Henderson referred to the Jacobites 'now flying like flocks of sheep before them'.[163] According to Wolfe, 'they ran off with the greatest precipitation'.[164]

There had been less action on the left of the Jacobite army, though some of the men advanced to within twenty paces of the British line. Johnstone was there with his friend Scothouse, and when the latter was shot dead:

> I perceived all the Highlanders around me turning their backs to
> fly. I remained for a time motionless, and lost in astonishment; then

in a rage, I discharged my blunderbuss and pistols at the enemy and immediately endeavoured to save myself like the rest. But having charged on foot and in boots I was so overcome by the marshy ground, the water on which reached the middle of the leg, that instead of running I could scarcely walk.

Johnstone eventually found a horse and with the aid of a Cameron, took it from the servant holding it and rode off.[165] Burdell MacDonald later recalled how he jettisoned his horse, his greatcoat, his case of pistols, his boots and his shoulder belts in order to escape, merely keeping his sword and gun 'which I thought heavy enough'.[166]

Once the infantry began to falter and turn tail, they were fired on by the artillery again, as Linn wrote, 'our cannon & a few royalls sent them a few small bomb shells & cannon balls to their farewell'.[167] This is the only contemporary reference to the mortars being fired during the battle. Recent archaeological digging has shown that mortar fire had been used earlier in the battle, fragments of such bombs being located in the inappropriately-named 'Field of the English'.[168]

There was also an advance of the Government infantry 'with shouts of victory', firing by platoons and using the guns, as the first line of the Jacobite line had been broken and the second was under attack. The French troops there were initially holding firm by the Culwhinniac walls, but were being surrounded. The wounded Daniel was urged by Drummond to 'come off with him, telling me all was over'.[169] Much of the troops in the second line were in flight, covered by the French and Irish regular troops, who had 'march'd up in front to sustain it, & gave & received Several fires, and then retreated towards Inverness'.[170] Apparently the Irish fired upon the dragoons and forced them to veer off, before the former took up position in the park and continued to fire, though Stapleton was mortally wounded.[171] Three battalions in the second line 'were brought up and gave their fire very well, yet the ground and everything else was so favourable to the enemy that nothing could be done'. The French Royal Ecossais exchanged fire with the Government infantry.[172] Hawley put himself at the head of the Government battalions on the left 'who were moving on and nothing left in any body before them'. The infantry advanced in line for two miles.[173]

Most commentators noted that Charles tried to rally his troops, though Elcho remarked that he left the battlefield without making any attempt to do so, though claimed it would have been futile for him to have attempted 'for none of the Highlanders who Escaped ever Stop'd until they gott home to their own houses'.[174] According to Johnstone he should have acted decisively, 'This was a critical moment when he ought to have displayed the courage of a grenadier, by immediately advancing to put himself at the head of his army, and commanding himself these manoeuvres which he wished to been executed. He would never have experienced disobedience on the part of his subjects.'[175]

According to O'Sullivan, after trying to rally some of the men, Charles had to change horses. 'The Prince wont retir notwithstanding all yt can be told him.' O'Sullivan could see Government troops marching to cut off their line of retreat, and so redoubled his urging that Charles should leave immediately.[176] Charles, with a bodyguard of sixteen men from Fitzjames's Horse, retired across the River Nairn, unmolested.[177]

The four companies of Argyllshire militia, led by Captains Campbell of Ballimore, Glenuchay, Ackinbas and Dougald Campbell, having broken down the walls of the Culwhinniac enclosure to let the cavalry pass through, had advanced against the Jacobite right flank. They used a dyke as a breastwork and fired 'closs in a strong party of the rebels than formed the right', including Drummond's men. The latter were thrown into disorder, but on advancing as the cavalry did, they crossed the dyke and cut some of their enemy down. Ballimore was shot dead, however, and a fellow captain was also shot, later to die of wounds.[178]

Wolfe wrote, 'as soon as the rebels began to give way to the fire of our own foot ceased, he [Hawley] ordered General Bland to charge the thickest of them with three squadrons and Lord Ancrum to support him with two. It was done with wonderful success and completed the victory with great slaughter'.[179] The cavalry 'went all along theyr rear and tooke all the runaways in the flanque and made great havock'. Meanwhile, Hawley had the remaining four squadrons wheeled against the flank of the two battalions posted by the walls, whilst the Argyll militia engaged these two battalions in musketry from the rising ground on the other side of the wall. The Jacobites broke and were pursued, though not before causing some fatalities and other casualties among the militia. According to Hawley, the cavalry were 'killing them, to a pass by the river where they made a short stand, the dragoons being all dispersed in the pursuit and not there together'.[180]

Elsewhere, the other Government cavalry could be used to their full effect, as Argyle had at Sheriffmuir. O'Sullivan recorded, 'The cruelty of the enemy cant be imagined. The Dragoons & Horse yt follow'd the MccDonells, MccIntoshes & another clans of about a hundred & twenty that joined some time before the battle, as they were the last yt staid upon the field, what slattor they made of them, & if it was not for the Parks & inclosiers of Castle Hill, where the horse cou'd not follow them, not a man would wou'd escape.'[181] According to Marchant, 'the cavalry cut down great numbers, without the least opposition'.[182] Wolfe wrote, 'It was done with a wonderful spirit and completed the victory with much slaughter. We had an opportunity of avenging ourselves, for that and many other things, and indeed we did not neglect it. As few Highlanders were taken prisoner as possible'.[183] In another letter he explained why this happened: 'The Rebels, been their natural inclinations had orders not to give quarter to our troops'.[184]

The cavalry which had charged from the 'right, & left met in the centre, except two Squadrons of Dragoons which we miss'd, & they were gone in pursuit of the Runaways; Lord Ancrum was ordered to pursue with the horse as far as they could & which he did with so good effect, that a very considerable number were killed in the pursuit'. Major General Bland 'had also made great slaughter, & gave quarter to none but about fifty French officers, & soldiers he pick'd up in his pursuit'.[185] Kingston's Horse 'galloped up briskly, and falling in with the fugitives, did excellent execution'.[186] Ray referred to 'there was much knapping of Noddles' and claimed 500 were killed in the pursuit.[187] Three former Nottinghamshire butchers in Kingston's Horse later bragged of having killed fourteen Jacobites each.[188] According to Yorke, 'Had not fear added wings to their feet, none would have escaped the edge of the sword'.[189]

The Jacobites streamed away. Those who fled downhill towards Inverness were unfortunate, as Johnstone wrote: 'Having been pursued by the English cavalry, the road from Culloden to that town was everywhere strewed with dead bodies'.[190] According to Hawley, 'The dragoons had cleared all the country for three miles before them and had made great slaughter every way, even downe to Inverness'. They took no prisoners.[191] Some arrived in Inverness, 'There were vast numbers ran thro' the Town, some crying, others mourning, some stood astonished and did not know whither to turn themselves'.[192] Meanwhile, the Government infantry switched from line to two columns and marched to the Highland town.[193]

Slaughter by pursuing troops who are faster-moving than their victims is commonplace after battles. It had happened after Killiecrankie and Prestonpans where the Jacobites slew their routing enemies; it had happened after Sheriffmuir when Argyle's dragoons struck down Jacobites from the defeated left wing. The cavalry's actions after Culloden was not a unique 'war crime' therefore, but the bloody reality of the cavalry's business.

As to Jacobite casualties, Cumberland wrote

> By the best calculation we can make, I think we may reckon the rebels lost <u>2000</u> men upon the field of battle, & in the pursuit, as few of their wounded could get off, & we have here <u>222</u> French &, <u>326</u> Rebel Prisoners, as by the inclosed list. Colonel Howard certainly killed Lord Strathallan, as his seal &, his different commissions from the Pretender were found in the pocket of the Person

killed by him. It is said I believe with some foundation, that Lord Perth, Lord Nairne, Lochiel, Keppoch, & Appin Stuart are also killed.[194]

According to Hawley, many 'were found dead of their wounds for 20 miles around on all the rounds and hills'.[195]

Cumberland added, 'All their Artillery, & Ammunition, of which I shall inclose a list, is taken, as was the Pretender's, & all their baggage, which was in general plundered, there are also twelve Colours taken'.[196] Cumberland gave the men a shilling for each sword they brought in from the Jacobites, two shillings and sixpence per musket, and 16 guineas per standard or flag.[197] The haul of military equipment taken 'at and since the battle of Culloden' consisted of the following: three 1½-pounders, eleven 3-pounders and four 4-pounders, all brass cannon, and four 4-pounder iron cannons. Six brass swivels and two iron swivels were captured. A total of 2,320 muskets and pistols, together with 190 'swords and blades', 1,500 musket cartridges, 1,019 cannon shot, 37 powder barrels and 22 ammunition carts. There were also a quantity of stores, tents, canteens, pouches, cartouche boxes, pistols and saddles.[198]

Soldiers also took what they would from the dead, with a contemporary historian writing that some were seen 'strutting about in rich laced waistcoats, hats, &c.' However, he added, 'Our men got the plunder of the field, but it was not very considerable'.[199] A Jacobite cook was waylaid in his flight and his valuables stolen. One sergeant paid him half a crown for his 34-guinea horse.[200] Some of the looting was the work of civilians, Bishop Pococke later being told, 'They were all instantly stripped by the women who went loaded with spoils to Inverness, and the bodies were soon naked all over the field. It is said the few that fell of our soldiers were not stripped'.[201] Ronald MacDonald later recalled lying wounded and having his breeches and shirt stripped from his body.[202]

The battle had lasted little over half an hour from the first artillery fire to the final flight of the Jacobite army.[203] Cumberland was very pleased with his men, writing two days later, 'I have the satisfaction to say, that all the General Officers, & the Corps did their utmost in his Majesty's service, & all strove to shew their zeal & bravery on this occasion'.[204] On the day of the battle, he told them so himself. Linn wrote, 'after it was over, he Rode along the same line & Returned us a great many thanks for our good behaviour & said he never seed better ordered or well done'.[205] An anonymous observer concurred with the commander in chief, 'Not a man in the whole army behaved ill. On the contrary an uncommon spirit appeared through the whole of them'.[206] Campbell of Airds wrote, 'The Troops all behaved remarkably well, and what I believe is very singular, not a single man turned his back or came off from the line. Even the few wounded men came off in spirits.' The Scots Fusiliers 'had the Duke's

Particular thanks, saying it was owing to them the victory was so cheap', but he also singled out the men from Barrell's and Munro's, too.[207] The soldiers cheered him, 'Flanders! Flanders! We'll follow your Highness against any enemy.'[208] At four that afternoon Cumberland issued each man with a glass of spirits.[209]

Cumberland himself won plaudits, too. Oman referred to him privately as 'Our gallant Hero' and 'His Royal Highness' behaviour was like his noble predecessors, viz., with great calmness and Bravery'.[210] Another observer noted 'The Duke behaved as usuall, led on his men on foot in a plain soldier's coat with a common gun and bayonet'.[211] John Clark later wrote, 'The Duke shew'd himself a brave as well as a Cautious and prudent commander on this occasion, and discovered with what attention he discerned the behaviour of several regiments . . . by the suitable compliments he payed them . . . He was pleas'd to distinguish the Fusiliers and our regiment in a particular manner'.[212]

Sir Edward Fawkener gave credit to him for the victory, writing:

> His Royal H. gave Life & Spirit to the Army. He settled all the Marches, & by His activity got together the necessary Fund of provisions for putting the Army onto Motion towards this barren Country, & He provided so well, that we have not wanted any thing. The Disposition of the Army for the Action as well as the Directions for the Execution were also entirely owing to his R.Hs.[213]

Another soldier agreed:

> Under God, wholly to the conduct and valour of His Royal Highness the Duke of Cumberland . . . Behaved as if he had been inspired, constantly riding up and down giving his own orders. And what do we not owe to Almighty God for giving us so great a deliverance, and preserving that young glorious hero, whom he made the instrument of delivering us.[214]

There was much congratulation among the government's supporters about the battle's outcome. Walpole wrote, 'The defeat is reckoned total, and the dispersion general . . . it is a brave young Duke. The town is all blazing round me, as I write, with fireworks and illuminations.'[215] Stone told Richmond, of 'this great and glorious news'.[216]

En route to Inverness, the French troops surrendered to Bland, sending him a note 'to hope for every thing which is to be expected from the English Generosity'.[217] On the way to Inverness the Duke was cheered and on his entry to the city, church bells were rung in his honour. However, he asked that no cheers be given. Once outside the city gaol he was given the keys to it and had the soldiers held there freed: 'Brother soldiers, you are free'. They were given food and drink as well as arrears of pay.[218]

Casualties on the Jacobite side are hard to ascertain. That there were many there is no doubt, with estimates ranging from 1,000 to 4,000, with the latter being far too high. An officer later wrote, 'The moor was covered with blood, and our men, what with killing the enemy, dabbling their feet in the blood, and splashing it about one another, looked like so many butchers'.[219]

Jacobite officers who were killed and captured were reported by name. The former included Colonel MacLuchlan, Major MacLauchlan of Inchonell, Colonel MacGillvra and Major Macbean of the Mackintoshes, and MacDonald of Keppoch who died of gunshot wounds. Cameron of Lochiel was shot in the ankles but was hauled away by his men. Those captured were Kilmarnock (who mistook Government cavalry for Fitzjames's Horse, both being red-coated soldiers on horseback), Sir John Wedderburn, Colonel Farquharson and Major Stewart of Perth's regiment.[220]

British Army casualties are easier to ascertain, but many of those wounded subsequently died of those wounds.

Infantry

Battalion	Killed	Wounded
Royal Scots	0	4
Howard	1	2
Barrel	17*	108*****
Wolfe	0	1*
Pulteney	0	0
Price	1*	9*
Bligh	4	17*
Campbell	0	13
Sempill	1	7
Blakeney	0	13
Cholmondeley	1	2
Fleming	0	6
Dejean	14	68*****
Conway	1	5*
Battereau	0	3*
Total	40	245

*denotes number of officer casualties

Artillerymen, Cavalry, Highland units

Unit	Killed	Wounded
Gunners	0	1
Men	0	5
Loudon	6	3*
Argyllshire Militia	0	1*
Kingston	0	1
Cobham	1	0
Kerr	3	3
Total	10	14

*denotes one man wounded who subsequently died thereof.

Horse

Unit	Killed	Wounded
Kingston	2	1
Cobham	4	5
Kerr	4	15
Total	10	21[221]

For the victors, the Guildhall Fund paid out sums to all the rank-and-file survivors; for sergeants this was 19s 1½d, corporals, 12s 9½d and privates and drummers, 9s 6½d. For the artillerymen, sergeants received £1 18s 3s, bombardiers, £1 11s 11d, gunners £1 5s 7d each and the others, 19s 1½d. The subalterns were given £1,000 between them, so about £4 apiece. Widows and orphans of soldiers having been killed were also given sums varying from £10–£30. Widows of officers killed received higher sums.[222]

For the British army it was a remarkably cheap victory in terms of lives lost. Some battalions had emerged wholly unscathed, though the brunt of the casualties were borne by the two battalions who took on the cutting edge of the Jacobite charge: Barrell's and Munro's. Linn wrote, 'We lost very few men of our Army, only a few wounded; our loss is about 200 men Wounded & Killed. Thank God we lost not one man of our Regiment, only a few wounded, we never had such good Luck befor.'[223] However, Lord Rich of Barrell's, who had had his hand cut off, a cut through other fingers and a deep wound near his elbow, later died of his wounds in June.[224] Grievous though the human losses had been – 'the bloodiest engagement that was ever known in the memory of man', as a Government officer noted, even excluding the far higher butcher's bills in Continental warfare – the casualties had been proportionately far higher at Killiecrankie, and probably more in absolute terms, too. Yet very few in 1746 had any personal memories of the events of 1689.

Soldiers were affected by the battle in different ways. Cumberland was in a contemplative mood, walking over the battlefield, apparently in deep meditation, laying his hand to his breast and lifting his eyes up to Heaven before declaring, 'Lord! What am I! That I should be spared, when so many brave men lie dead upon the spot?'[225] One of his admirers was Trooper Bradshaw, who wrote after the battle, 'No history of battles can brag of so singular a victory and so few of our own men lost'.[226] Linn was more modest, 'I give you the trouble of these to acquaint you what great things God almighty hath done for us'.[227]

Lord Bury was sent southwards by ship to north Berwick and then on horse to London to relay the news to the court. On doing so he was given £1,000 and the offer of being made an aide to the King himself.[228] George II asked 'What's become of my son?' to which Bury replied, 'He is very well'. The King then remarked, 'Then all is well to me' and was unable to speak further for joy.[229]

The controversy over this battle is not the actual fighting but its aftermath. Jacobite accounts talk of great severity on the behalf of the victors, Elcho noting 'Every body that fell into their hands gott no quarters, except a few who they resrv'd for publick punishment'.[230] Henderson noted in the aftermath of the battle: 'The Field was clear, and the Victory being compleat, the soldiers, warm in their Resentment, did Things hardly to be accounted for; several of their wounded Men were stabb'd, yea some who were lurking in houses, were taken out and shot upon the Field, tho' others were sav'd, by those whose Compassion was raised at the sight of so many victim.'[231] Apparently the Earl of Kilmarnock begged for mercy, 'which was granted him with difficulty'.[232] This may have been because when a Jacobite officer had earlier in the battle being taken prisoner by Captain Alexander Grossett of Price's battalion, the man had, when Grossett fell off his horse, snatched one of his pistols and shot Grossett dead before being killed by the dead man's colleagues.[233]

Henderson then went on to explain why such behaviour happened:

> The rebels had enraged the Troops, their Habit was strange, their Language still stranger, and their way of fighting was shocking to the Utmost degree: The Rebellion was unprovoked and the King's Troops had greatly suffered by it: the fields of Preston[pans] and Falkirk, were fresh in their Memory, they had lost a Gardner, a Whitney, a Munro besides other officers . . . their mangled corpses could not but stir up the soldiers to revenge. Therefore, if they found

Vengeance in their Power, they violated the stricter rules of Humanity, some allowance ought to be made for the Passions they were
inspired with at that time.[234]

As with other battles, spectators came along to view this one, some with the
desire to take what spoils they could from it, and were caught up in the killing,
as at Sheriffmuir, for example, as Hughes explained, 'many of the inhabitants,
not doubting of success, who came out of curiosity to see the Action, or perhaps to get plunder, never went home again to tell the story: for their being
mixt up with their own people, we could not know one from another'.[235]

One story that has received much credence is that related by Johnstone,
who was not an eyewitness: 'He [Cumberland] ordered a barn, which contained many of the wounded Highlanders, to be set on fire and the soldiers
stationed round it drove back with fixed bayonets the unfortunate men who
attempted to save themselves into the flames, burning them alive in this horri-
ble manner'.[236] Others who were there contradict the story. Captain Kinnier of
Munro's 'avers that to his certain knowledge none of the wounded rebels were
carried to that house, that only a few of the common soldiers of the Rebels
were there and two sergeants, but not one ensign, nor any of the superior
rank. He adds that not one of these had received any hurt and that they did
not remain in the house above two hours'.[237] In any case, the house where this
massacre was alleged to have occurred was not built until after the battle and
there is no archaeological evidence to support the atrocity story.[238]

After the battle a note was found on the corpse of a dead Jacobite which
included the following ominous phrase:

> It is His Majesty's orders, that every person attach himself to some
> Corps of the Army and remain with the Corps Night and Day, until
> the Battle and Pursuit be finally over, and to give no Quarter to any
> of the Elector's Troops on any account whatsoever. This regards
> the Foot as well as the Horse. Sign'd George Murray, Lieutenant
> General.[239]

One soldier later wrote, of this, that it was not known about until after the battle, 'so that many were saved by our Army', implying that if it had been known
about then the body count would have been higher.[240] Some Jacobites have
claimed that this order was a forgery. Balmerino attested, 'I do declare that it
is without all manner of foundation . . . I believe rather that this report was
spread to palliate and excuse the murders they themselves committed in cold
blood after the battle of Culloden'.[241] Yet fellow Jacobite Kilmarnock thought
otherwise, 'I have had all reason in the world to believe that there was such
an order'.[242] In fact, it is possible that the order refers to the previous night's

planned attack, where no quarter could be granted when sleeping troops were to be killed.

On the day after the battle, Cumberland issued the following order: 'A Capt. & 50 men to march immediately to the field of Battle& search all cottages in the neighbourhood for Rebels. The officer & men will take notice that the publick orders of the Rebels yesterday were to give us no quarter'.[243] This is often taken to mean that Cumberland was sanctioning mass murder. That some of the Jacobites were killed is undeniable. John Murray, writing in 1748, claimed 'Gentlemen and officers, not only refused to give quarters, but damn'd the more compassionate soldier for loading themselves with prisoners'.[244] Ronald MacDonald, wounded in the legs and after lying on the battlefield, stripped of his clothes, recalled that some men were shot but that Lieutenant Hamilton of Cholmondeley's battalion saved his life and took him to a nearby country house, though when on the next day he was conveyed to Inverness with a group of wounded Government soldiers, they were 'cursing and abusing him all the way for a damned rebellious rascal'.[245] Hughes related a similar story, though with Lieutenant Colonel Cockayne being sent out with 500 men 'to go on Quest of them that should be found lurking after the Battel'. He stated that 12 miles from Culloden 'they found several wounded, and others endeavouring to hide themselves, all which were shot directly'.[246] That some of the troops were angry cannot be doubted: 'they were really mad; they were furious and no check was given them' and 'the fury and madness of the sogers'.[247]

Yet many Jacobites were taken into captivity, rather than being bayonetted or clubbed on the spot. Linn wrote, 'we send out every day strong parties of Foot and Horse and they bring in great heaps of prisoners every day'. Hawley made a similar remark.[248] David Calder wrote of 'continual processions of prisoners and wounded', the latter word giving the lie to the oft-told accounts of a universal massacre in cold blood.[249] Similarly, Campbell of Airds wrote of 'There are many prisoners, but as more are still brought in, the exact number cannot be ascertained'.[250]

There is no doubt that Culloden was a decisive battle. On 18 April Cumberland wrote:

> I had the honour to acquaint his Majesty the 16 by Lord Bury of the compleat Victory we gained that day over the Rebels; I must own I never expected They would have the impudence to risk a general Engagement, but they having burnt down Fort Augustus the day before convinced me They intended to stand.[251]

Others among the army agreed with him. Yorke wrote, 'I flatter myself that this is the last time blood will be shed on the field by fellow subject of this island'[252] Others lower down in the army had similar views, with Richard Webb opining, 'they have not had such a threshing since the Days of Old Noll [Oliver Cromwell]'.[253] Bradshaw told his brother, 'In short, tis mine and every bodies' opinion no history can brag of so singular a victory'.[254] Finally Private Taylor wrote that it was:

> so compleat a victory . . . We are now here encampd and I hope soon to be south again, most of our work now been over, except among the Highlands and taking them that have escaped . . . And it is my opinion his Royal Highness will use Lenity to all, but Non-jurant Episcopal ministers, who all thinking parts of Scotland must own to be the Nursers and Former of this and all Rebellions since the Revolution.[255]

Henderson agreed: 'The Rebellion was dashed to pieces: The flame of it was not only extinguished, but the very Embers of it quenched'.[256]

Jacobites believed that they had lost the battle by default. According to Johnstone, it 'was lost on the 16th of April rather from a series of mistakes on our part than any skilful manoeuvre of the Duke of Cumberland'.[257] Similarly, Maxwell wrote that 'Their strength and spirits were quite exhausted through want of food, and rest for several days; they were allowed too much leisure to contemplate an enemy, more than double their number, and they were cannonaded for a considerable time at very small distance'.[258]

Henderson replied to these criticisms. He admitted that many of the Jacobite troops were not present at the battle, but then went on to state that many of the Government troops were in garrison or otherwise absent, too. He agreed that the Jacobites were fatigued after the fruitless night march, but 'What General will not take advantage if he can?' and added that the Government army had had a tiring march from Nairn immediately as a prelude to the battle and were further incommoded by having to shelter their muskets from the hail. As to the breakdown of Jacobite supplies, 'this was their misfortune; and is it not a finesse, in the Art of war, for a commander to improve upon the Straits of his Enemies?'[259]

There are a number of positive reasons why the Government army was successful, quite apart from the weaknesses of its enemy. It was the best equipped army to fight the Jacobites in 1745–6, enjoyed the best morale and was the best led. Unlike the case at Prestonpans this was an army of experienced men who had seen the Jacobites in action before and, unlike at Falkirk, knew what to expect. The artillery was, for the first time, properly manned. Cumberland had done his best to prepare the men for the battle to come, by seeing to their welfare and instilling in them that victory was possible if they stood their ground and fought well. On the day of the battle the troops played to their strengths and the Jacobites' weaknesses. There was no headlong rush to fight as at Falkirk, and the brief Jacobite triumph on the right was soon dealt with by an immediate and successful counter-attack which sealed the fate of the battle.

Civilian reactions were positive. Miss Saville wrote that on 24 April, in London, 'The Guns at the Tower and Park were fired twice. At night such rejoicing, so many Bonfires, such illuminations were never seen. Scarce the meanest house that had not some candles . . . Great honour and thanks are due to him who thou was pleas'd to make thy Instrument, the Young Duke, whose Courage and Conduct were extraordinary.'[260] At Edinburgh, 'publick rejoicings were ordered and such as either from a natural reluctancy to joy in the day of the fall of their friends and Relations did not put out candles or whose houses were only inhabited by Stuarts had their windows broke or were mobb'd'.[261] Clerk of Penicuik noted, 'The success of this Battle gave universal joy, especially to the friends of the government, but there were even Jacobites who were at least content at what had happened, for peace and quietness began now to break in, whereas Anxiety and Distress of various kinds had possessed the breath of most people since the rebellion broke out. All Trade and Business in this Country were quite at a stand.'[262]

Yet for all that, the Jacobite army was not destroyed nor were all their leaders captured or killed. It was not the losses in men, arms and equipment that made the battle so important, but rather its effect on the army's leader, as we shall soon see.

Chapter 16

The End of the Jacobite Campaigns

Although the battle of Culloden was a decisive setback for the Jacobites, it did not necessarily mean the end of the campaign. Not all the Jacobite army had fought at Culloden nor was that which did was utterly destroyed. Many men rallied at Ruthven along with Murray and Perth. John Daniel recorded, 'At first we had great hopes of rallying again'.[1] There were possibly between 2,000 and 3,000 Jacobites there. Yet a message came from Charles, 'to tell them that they might disperse and every body shift for himself the best way he could'.[2] Johnstone believed that 'partisan warfare' would have been success-ful. He argued, 'Our numbers increased every moment, and I am thoroughly convinced that, in the course of eight days, we should have had a more pow-erful army than ever.'[3]

Yet as Maxwell noted about the dispersal:

> There was indeed hardly anything else to be done. There were no magazines in the Highlands. The meal that had been carried to Fort Augustus, had been brought back to Inverness, or embezzled by the people of the country. There was at that time a greater scarcity than usual in the Highlands, which if themselves afford nothing in that season. It would have been impossible for a considerable body of men to subsist together. The Lowlanders at least must have starved in a country that had not subsistence for its own inhabitants and where they neither knew the roads nor the language. These consid-erations had determined the Prince to lay aside all thoughts of mak-ing a stand at present, and to make the best of his way to France.[4]

This was the real impact of Culloden. The Jacobites had lost not only men, but also their logistical support. Their leader had no wish to immediately continue the struggle. The campaign was, then, at an effective end and the Jacobites had lost again.

Despite this, some Jacobite clans desired to fight on and made resolutions to stand by one another. Charles wrote to his followers, urging them to remain defiant in the cause whilst he went to France to summon help. French ships brought, too late, substantial amounts of gold in May 1746, but most of this was lost or stolen. All this did no good; when the Camerons were confronted later that month by loyalist militia they fled and it was only then that all formal resistance was over.

There were no clear instructions as to what the Government army was to do, nor how, in the aftermath of the campaign. Cumberland shared the view common among the senior members of the political, legal and military establishment that the Jacobites who had participated in the rebellion must either surrender or, being classified as being rebels, be dealt with as being such, and be acted against militarily. Initially Cumberland was based at Inverness.

Two days after Culloden, Cumberland wrote:

> Brigadier Mordaunt is detach'd with <u>900</u> Volunteers this morning into Frazers' country, to destroy all the Rebels he finds there. Lord Sutherland & Lord Reays people continue to exert themselves & have taken <u>100</u> Rebels whom I have sent for, & I have great reason to believe Lord Cromarty, & his son are also taken. As I don't know where the greatest bodys of them are, or which way they have taken to shift for themselves, I can't as yet determine which way we shall march.[5]

Cumberland stated, 'you will constantly have in mind to distress whatever Country of Rebels you may pass through, & seize or destroy all Persons you can find who have been in the Rebellion or their abettors and to be particularly diligent in the search & pursuance of their Chiefs'.[6] His officers were clear as to what he wanted them to do. Wolfe wrote to a subordinate that 'You know the manner of treating the houses and possessions of rebels in this part of the country. The same freedom is to be used where you are as has been hitherto practised, that is seeking for them and their arms, cattle and other things', though he was clear that those who had submitted were to be left alone.[7] Four hundred cattle were taken from the estate of leading Jacobite Lady Mackintosh. Lord Lovat's house was destroyed, but not before anything of value – 1,000 bottles of wine, a library worth £1,400 and his stores of malt – were removed.[8]

This did not mean that Jacobites would be indiscriminately massacred wherever they were found. Many were taken prisoner. Private Linn wrote, 'we send out every day strong Parties of Foot & Horse . . . & they bring in great heaps of Prisoners every day'.[9] General orders given two days after Culloden were that wounded Jacobites were to be brought to Inverness. To have left the enemy wounded lying on the field of battle for two days may well have been callous, but it is indicative that there was no general massacre of the wounded in its aftermath as often alleged.[10] Cumberland told the Earl of Crauford,

'Wherever you hear there are any of the Rebells returned, you are in the like manner to take them Prisoners & to send them to the said Castle or to some other Secure Prison as shall be most convenient all those who are not sent to Edinburgh Castle you will keep under a Military Guard'.[11]

Wolfe certainly believed that prisoners were to be taken and told a subordinate on 19 May, 'be carefull to collect all proofs and accusations against them'. This clearly shows that these men were envisaged as being eventually put on trial, and thus evidence against them would be crucial.[12] The result of all this was, as Ray noted, 'all the Gaols were soon full of prisoners, notwithstanding the great Number that was shipped off to Newcastle'.[13] Cumberland was told that he prepare lists of prisoners with their whereabouts and the proofs against them, placing more emphasis on 'officers and persons of note' than 'the private men'.[14]

Possessions belonging to unrepentant Jacobites was to be forfeit. Cumberland told Crauford, 'The Forrage taken from Kunachie, as it belongs to Mr Auchinleck, actually in the Rebellion, is not to be paid for, neither is any other Forrage belonging to Persons, that are or have been in the Rebellion or its abettors, to be paid for'.[15]

Likewise, chapels used for non-juroring, Episcopalian or Catholic worship were destroyed. Since these were illegal as their ministers supported the Jacobite cause, this was merely enforcing the existing laws. Cumberland wrote 'I have demolished all mass houses & meeting houses as we marched allong'.[16] Lord Ancrum reported that in the month after Culloden he had burnt two Catholic chapels and five Episopalian ones, as well as a priest's library. He had also had Catholic books burnt in Cullen marketplace.[17]

The insignia of the Jacobite army was to be destroyed. Cumberland wrote, 'I shall immediately put into Execution the king's orders in sending to Edenburg the colours taken from the Rebels to be burnt by the hands of the common Hangman'.[18] The flags arrived at 31 May and were burnt four days later. Another was burnt in Glasgow on 25 June. These were burnt with great ceremony.[19]

Cumberland had been allowed to grant an amnesty to Jacobites who delivered their weapons. Many took the opportunity to do so. The MacDonalds of Glencoe gave up their arms to Major General Campbell on 13 May. The Stewarts of Appin did so, too.[20] A newspaper reported 'Rebels coming in daily and laying down their arms and submitting to the King's mercy . . . It is to be hoped that this precedent will be imitated by others in the same situation, that themselves and families may be saved.'[21] Apparently 8,000 guns, 7,000 swords, 57 cannon and many shields were eventually handed in.[22]

There was doubt cast over whether this was an effective policy in preventing another rebellion. Cumberland wrote to Newcastle that 'I hope His majesty will not imagine that by these peoples laying down their Arms, the country is a jot safer from any fresh rising. For at this time almost very Highlander is possessed of 2 or 3 sets, which are hid.'[23] However, Newcastle was more optimistic, suggesting that disarming would be enough to secure the future peace of the Highlands.[24]

There were also attempts made to capture Charles. He was determined to escape from Scotland after being defeated at Culloden and did not desire to lead a guerrilla campaign as some of his followers advocated. Cavalry were despatched to the towns on the north-east of Scotland to prevent his leaving from there. Trooper Bradshaw of Cobham's dragoons looked forward to the task with relish, 'I pray God I had him in this room, and he the last of the Stuart race; it would be my glory to stab the villain to the heart'.[25]

Cumberland marched with numerous battalions to Fort Augustus on 19 May after being at Inverness for a month. He was doubtless aware that some of the clans there were still in arms against his father's government. He wrote:

> I am still of opinion that the Pretender's Son went off with those French ships, but yet the Highlanders have still a notion of his being concealed some where amongst them. For which reason my Lord George Sackville is marched with 800 Foot, divided into two partys; the one of 500: the other of 300: He & Major Wilson are marched to the Barrack of Bernea with 500: from whence he is to march southward along the coast, till he comes over against the head of Loch Arkek, where Lieutenant Colonel Cornwallis is, with the other 300 men. From thence the corps are to march southward to drive through the countrys of the MacDonalds of Moidart, & Knoidart, and the Camerons, north of Lockly; which Captain Scott with the old garrison of Fort William which was relieved two days ago by Houghton's Regiment, will advance from the south to meet them: & Major General Campbell or the officer commanding the Argyleshire Militia in his absence, is to scour the country about Megarny Castle.
>
> The Reasons why I have sent such a force into that country, are to convince them that it as much in his Majesty's power to march his Forces into that country which they have hitherto boasted is inaccessible as into any other part of his Dominions, to disperse the small Remains of the Rebels which may be got together, & to be certain whether the young man is still amongst them. I shall wait here the Return of this Detachment & that will prevent my marching from hence so soon as I expected, the obstinacy of the Highlanders is inconceivable. The MacPhersons have indeed acted honestly enough in bringing in their arms, but the rest are no way to be prevailed upon but by Force.[26]

Troops also searched for military equipment belonging to the Jacobites. Captain Duncan Campbell took a detachment of Highlanders by Loch Sheil in Lochaber. They found eight pieces of cannon sunk in the loch. Captain Noble of the Scots Fusiliers found nineteen barrels of gunpowder and thirty-two chests of arms and ammunition, buried beneath the ground. Other similar discoveries were also made.[27]

A number of leading Jacobites were captured in the months following Culloden. A patrol of soldiers were sent, following information, to seize John Murray, Charles' secretary. Lord Lovat was also taken up by parties of soldiers sent from sloops making descents on the coasts of Knoidart and Arisaig.[28] The property of leading Jacobites was often destroyed. The houses of Cameron of Lochiel's at Achnacary was burnt on 28 May. Those of his colleagues such as the MacDonald's of Keppoch, Glenrarry's, Cluny MacPherson's and Glengyles's were dealt with similarly. Their followers also suffered, as a contemporary Scot wrote, 'vast numbers of the common people's houses or huts are likewise laid in ashes'. Cattle were carried off; sometimes 2,000 in a drove towards Fort Augustus in June. Apparently 'several poor people, especially women and children have been found dead in the hills, supposed to have starved'.[29] Soldiers were allowed to sell these animals to the dealers who came from England to buy these goods.[30]

Indiscriminate plunder in the Highlands was not countenanced by the Duke. When complaints were brought to his attention, he was conciliatory and determined to deal with them. He wrote to Lord Fortrose on 11 June,

> I received this Morning your Letter of the 9th from Braan Castle, & am extreamly sorry you should have any sort of reason to complain on Injury or violence from those who were sent out with no other design than to annoy, & distress such as are stil in Arms, & acting in maintenance & support of this wicked Rebellion.
>
> In this disagreeable circumstance, it is a satisfaction to me it so falls out that by the return of Lord George Sackville this instant with his Party I have the means of enquiring into the affair, & that I can tell you it did not happen from any mischievous purpose in the Soldiers of the Party to plunder all People indiscriminately, but from the indiscretion of some of your Tenants, who in their first alarm upon the appearance of the Troops amongst them, fired upon them, & from thence the disorder took its rise.
>
> I am, I assure you, very much concerned it should have happened. Lord George Sackville tells me the Cattle, & other things taken have been return'd, & if anything yet remains, I will give the necessary orders about it, & if I can do anything more towards repairing the

injurys, & losses your Tenants have sustained, I shall be pleased with an opportunity of giving such proofs as may be most satisfactory of the just sense I have of the firm attachment & zeal you have shewn on all occasions, & especially in the course of this wicked Rebellion, to his Majestys Person & Government, & if the particular regard, & friendship you have expressed for me; I must likewise acknowledge the great regards to the publick what have all along accompanied your services in avoiding to raise the Militia when you did not see they could not be of so great use as to answer the expence, & it no doubt raises the value of these services, that you have been careful to perform them in such a manner as must be most agreeable to his Majesty in this light. I have all along considered & represented them. I hope therefore you will not admit the least suspicion that in the orders given the Troops there were in any such distinctions made as could be injurious to you, or that the utmost regard would not have been had to your concerns, if any accident of this kind could have been foreseen.[31]

The Jacobite version of events in the Highlands paints a picture of terror, murder and rape. Some officers in particular were deemed notorious. These were Colonel Cornwallis, Majors Lockhart and Ferguson, and Captains Scott and Grant. Apparently, 'In several parts of the Highlands in Scotland the soldiery spared neither man, woman, nor child . . . They marched through scenes of woe, and marked their steps with blood'.[32]

However, Ferguson's correspondence with Cumberland presents a rather different story. He refers to burning property, capturing livestock and men, but does not even hint at further activity. If he was lying, his account suggests that he was acting beyond his orders and without the blessing of his commander.[33] Not all soldiers acted likewise, for General Campbell prevented a prisoner being flogged for information and later treated Flora MacDonald, the woman who more than any other helped Charles escape, with great respect.[34]

Indiscriminate plunder by the troops was against Cumberland's rules. A general order of 24 May read that there was to be 'No plundering nor Moroding on pain of hanging'. Soldiers found outside their encampments were to be searched by patrols. There were also curfews in the evening, too. Courts martial were held on men found indulging in theft and on 4 June four men were flogged for 'plundering under pretended orders from His Royal Highness'.[35]

Cumberland believed, 'It will be absolutely necessary, that new Forts be erected here, & where Fort Augustus stood, & whoever his Majesty may think proper to order to inspect their construction, should be sent down immediately, as the season is now come for works of that kind'. Fort Augustus, which had fallen after a short siege earlier that year, was not rebuilt, but a larger structure, Fort George, was constructed near Inverness in the decade after Culloden.[36]

Cumberland was well aware that he and his troops could only do so much. He wrote, 'It will be absolutely necessary that the new laws take place before His Majesty's forces quit this country, and I flatter myself that within a month or six weeks we shall have done all what can be done by the military'.[37]

Cumberland returned to London on 25 July, after having spent three months in Scotland after Culloden. He was not certain whether his work had been successful, writing to his successor that 'this country is in so unsteady a station' and he feared that there might be another campaign and so warned him 'keep the whole in a Readiness to take to the field at a moment's notice'.[38] Yet these fears proved groundless. The Jacobites never rose again and the campaign of 1745–6 was to be the last on British soil.

Almost 3,500 Jacobite prisoners had been taken during the course of the campaign, though mainly after Culloden. The most detailed study reveals that the most common fate of these was to be released; 1,287 in all (37 per cent), though of these 387 were French and Spanish troops. Only a very small number were executed, and leaving aside army deserters and spies, this was a mere 80 (2 per cent). However, in most cases the alternative to execution was transportation to the Americas, and this was the fate of 936 people (26.87 per cent). Another 358 were banished (11 per cent), whilst 92 enlisted in the British army (3 per cent). Although only 88 are recorded as dying in gaol, there are 684 whose fates are unrecorded and whilst some of these may have escaped, probably the majority died in prison.[39]

After many adventures, and with a price of £30,000 on his head, Charles left Scotland on 19 September, never to return. Although initially feted in France, by 1748 he was ordered to leave the country as a condition of the Treaty of Aix la Chappelle, ending the War of the Austrian Succession. There was another attempt to attempt to restore the Stuarts, the Elibank Plot of 1750–2, which aimed at a coup d'etat in London and a rising in Scotland, but this was exposed and a principal conspirator for the second element, Dr Archibald Cameron, was executed, the last man to suffer death (in 1753) for the Jacobite cause. In 1759, there was a plan for a French invasion of Britain with Charles to accompany them, but naval defeats scuppered this scheme. Charles became less attractive and declined into alcoholism; his later marriage failed to provide a legitimate heir and his brother became a cardinal. Following the accession of George III in 1760 and the rehabilitation of the both the Tories in England and the clan chiefs in Scotland, support for the

Stuarts sank even lower and finally was banished from the realm of practical politics, though some still held Stuart sympathies. James Stuart died in 1766 and Charles was not recognized by the Papacy or any other court as Charles III as his father had been recognized as James III. Charles died in 1788 and his brother 19 years later, the last direct descendants of James II. The Jacobite cause was over and could now safely become a topic for romantic novelists and poets.

Conclusion

The Jacobite campaigns consisted of nine battles. Of these, the Jacobite army was victorious in only three (Killiecrankie, Prestonpans and Falkirk) and there was some equivocation over the first and last. The British state was successful in the other six (Dunblane, Cromdale, Preston, Sheriffmuir, Glenshiel and Culloden). It is arguable that what was noteworthy is not that the Jacobite armies ultimately failed, but that they were able to succeed at all, having been built up from nothing, with minimal financial backing and little overseas support and with only a few professional soldiers in their ranks. After all, rebellions against the English and Scottish states in the decades after 1660 were all dismal failures, when faced with a regular standing army, as in 1666, 1678 and 1685.

That they were able to win battles was perhaps due to the circumstances surrounding the creation of their armies. They fought in an unorthodox manner; lacking time and expertise to train the men in formal drill and musketry, they were forced to rely on the rush to the offensive, which was unconventional at that time, and only became commonplace in western Europe during the French Revolutionary Wars of 1793–1801. Unconventionally disciplined troops were able to defeat their more formal and conventional opponents who expected to exchange volley fire until one side gave way. They were unused to a foe which fought in such an aggressive fashion. When faced with the Jacobite columns morale often collapsed and a rout resulted.

The way to overcome such assaults was to surprise the Jacobite army or defend a built up area as at Cromdale or at Dunkeld. Or, if fighting in open terrain, to use two or three arms against the predominantly infantry force of the Jacobite army. Argyle, at Sheriffmuir, used cavalry and infantry on his right to rout a superior Jacobite force, or at Culloden, when artillery and infantry worked together to repel the Jacobite onslaught, with dragoons giving the *coup de grâce* to the remnant of the Jacobite army.

These battles were small by Continental standards. Yet by British or American standards they were not. After all, though often featuring troops from more than one state on each side, such as at Killiecrankie, Glenshiel, Falkirk and Culloden, these contingents were relatively small.

The question is, whether the Jacobite armies could have ultimately triumphed. Nothing is inevitable nor obvious until it has happened. The odds were certainly stacked against them. The Jacobite campaigns were improvised with scant resources. Support from abroad, whether the Spanish or the French, was always minimal, enough to support them but not enough to decisively tip the scales in the Jacobites' favour. Jacobite leadership was also variable. Most of its leaders were men inexperienced in warfare; the one man who was not was Dundee and he was killed at the moment of his one and only victory in 1689. Often the Jacobite leaders were rift in conflict as in 1715 and 1719 as well as in 1745. They were faced with the resources of a great European power, often with active European allies. Once a capable leader was able to lead a significant force against the Jacobites, the balance of probability was very much against a Jacobite victory. As John Home remarked, the wonder is not that they were defeated, but that they, and here he refers to 1745–6, secured so many triumphs. He wrote:

> The conclusion of this enterprise was such as most people at home and abroad expected: but the progress of the rebels was what nobody expected; for they defeated more than once the king's troops; they overran one of the united kingdoms and marched so far into the other that the capital trembled at their approach, and during the tide of fortune, which had its ebbs and flows, there were moments when nothing seemed impossible: and to say the truth, it was not easy to forecast, or imagine, anything more unlikely, than what had already happened.[1]

Yet it had been no cakewalk for the Government army. They had to adapt to fight enemies whose tactics were far different to those they were used to. They had to fight in difficult terrain and often outside the conventional campaigning season. Often their initial encounters, such as at Prestonpans and at Killiecrankie were failures. It took time and men's lives before they could fight back effectually and successfully.

The campaigns' outcomes were settled by the men who fought, willingly or not, on these nine fields of battle, and on those who led them. There was bravery and there was wisdom, there was cruelty and there was cowardice. When we put down this volume, we should remember them and their deeds and perhaps ponder what we would have done in those heroic yet terrifying days long gone. Most of those who fought are unknown to history and it is only the officers, especially the leaders, and a very small number of the rank and file, whose names are recorded.

The importance of these battles was not just what happened on the bloodstained fields. It was what happened afterwards, because of what had occurred and how it affected men's minds. After all the Jacobites had been victorious after the first day's fighting at Preston, at Glenshiel they lost far fewer men than their enemies and at Culloden there were still thousands of men to fight for the Stuarts. Yet in all these instances, the Jacobite leaders deemed, rightly or wrongly, that the campaign was at an end.

These battles and the campaigns of which they were important episodes, resulted in James II and later his son, not returning as de facto King of Britain. They ensured that William and Mary, and later, the first two Georges, would continue as monarchs, with all that implied as regards domestic and foreign policy. The course of history as set in motion after the end of 1688 therefore continued without major interruption. There was no second Stuart restoration.

Appendix: The Battlefields Today

The Campaign of 1689–1690

Much of the geography of the battlefield of Killiecrankie remains today; the pass, the hills and the river. However, Urrards House no longer exists as it was burnt down in the nineteenth century; a Victorian house now stand there, once the home of Sir William Gull, a royal surgeon. The A9 road run right through the battlefield, parallel to the river, however, and there is currently a risk that it might be expanded into a dual carriageway, being built over some of the most archaeologically sensitive parts of the battlefield. There are also far more trees now there was at the time of the fighting (this is also the case at Dunkeld, Sheriffmuir and Falkirk).

However, at the pass of Killiecrankie can be seen the famous Soldier's Leap, allegedly made by Private McBane, and this is marked by a plaque. Further along the trackway is the Balfour Stone, allegedly, although certainly incorrectly, where Brigadier Balfour was killed. There is also the National Trust for Scotland Visitor Centre, open from April to October; only two other Scottish battlefields have such. There is a little about the battle there, though there are three swords of the time, one allegedly being that of Dundee.

In the middle of the battlesite, there is the Tomb Clavers or the Grave of the Officers, marking Ian Steward Fitzgerald Campbell the Younger, killed in the Malayan Emergency in 1950 as well as the battle of 1689. This is the focus of an annual commemoration, The Soldiers of Killiecrankie, established in 2012. There is also the Claverhouse Stone, allegedly where Dundee was killed, but in fact dating back to Prehistoric times. Finally, there is Dundee's grave and a plaque marking his remains in the former church of St. Bride's, near to Blair Castle. At the castle is Dundee's helmet and breastplate with bullet hole (made many years after the battle), as is at least one of the three 'leather guns' used at the battle.

At Dunkeld, two of the houses existing at the time of the battle still stand; though much modified; they are at the west end of Cathedral Road, to the north side and plaques denote their survival. Atholl's house and grounds no longer exist. Then there is the church and the adjoining ruined cathedral. The church boasts a small museum, in an annexe, with a little information about the battle. There is also a plaque in the nave, erected in 1903 to Cleland, who is buried there. Inside the ruined cathedral is a stone with the alleged initials of one of Cleland's men carved onto it. Another plaque, outside the cathedral, relates a concise account of the battle. To the north of the church there is an information board about the battle.

Cromdale's surviving buildings are the old kirk by the river and Lethendry Castle/Tower, which is currently in a ruinous situation. There is also a plaque to the battle, on the outer wall of the kirk near to the ford where Livingstone's troops crossed.

The 1715 Campaign

There is very little in Preston to mark that a battle was fought there in 1715, but the Harris Museum in the town centre has a small display of relevant material. Sheriffmuir is a little better served; the Dunblane Museum has a display of artefacts and some explanation boards. On the ground is a large memorial to the Macraes killed in the battle, erected in 1915, and there is, not far away, a more recent memorial erected by the 1745 Association.

The 1719 Campaign

There is a small roadside wall with a plaque briefly describing the battle. The embankment used by the Spanish troops can also be seen.

1745 Campaign

The Forty-Five is well served with memorials, as one would expect, given the number of books on the topic and the interest shown in it more generally. At Prestonpans there is a stone cairn marked simply '1745'. Bankton House, once home to Colonel Gardiner, still stands as does a nineteenth-century obelisk to the fallen colonel. The churchyard where some of the Camerons were bombarded is still there, and its thick walls indicate how well protected they were. Recently there has been erected a series of illustrative explanatory boards about the battle on an incline overlooking the battlefield.

In 1927 an obelisk was erected at the battlefield of Falkirk, and more recently there is an explanation board about the battle nearby. This is close to the ravine which hindered part of the Jacobite advance. Callendar House, where Hawley briefly stayed, is now Falkirk's museum and there is a little about the battle in the section on the town's history in the basement.

However, it is Culloden which has the lion's share of memorials and a great visitors' centre, akin to those seen in the USA for the American Civil War. The battlefield itself is full of memorials of all sizes to numerous clans, of nineteenth-century provenance. The Visitors' Centre has been much improved of late, reopened and revamped in 2007, and sells numerous books and other items about the last Jacobite campaign. It is the focus of commemoration each year on 16 April and on the nearest weekend.

There are other visible monuments to the period such as a column at Glenfinnan to mark the unfurling of the Stuart banner there in 1745, a statue of Charles Edward Stuart at Derby and a statue of Rob Roy MacGregor in Stirling. Although there was once a statue of the Duke of Cumberland in Cavendish Square, London, only the plinth with its inscription now remains. In this case, history has tended not to have been written by the victors, but by the losers.

Notes

Abbreviations

BC	=	Blair Castle
BL	=	British Library
CTB/CTP	=	Calendar of Treasury Books/Papers
EUL	=	Edinburgh University Library
HMC	=	Historic Manuscripts Commission
LRO	=	Lancashire Record Office
NLS	=	National Library of Scotland
NRS	=	National Records of Scotland
RA	=	Royal Archives
RPCS	=	*Registers of the Privy Council of Scotland*
TNA	=	The National Archives
TWAS	=	Tyne and Wear Archive Service
WAYS	=	West Yorkshire Archive Service

Preface

1. Christopher Duffy, *Fight for a Throne: The Untold Story of the Last Jacobite Rising*, Solihull, 2015; Stuart Reid, *1745: A Military History of the Last Jacobite Rising*, Staplehurst, 1996.
2. John Baynes, *The Jacobite Rising of 1715*, London, 1970; Daniel Szechi, *1715: The Great Jacobite Rising*, New Haven, 2006; Stuart Reid, *Sheriffmuir: 1715*, London, 2014 (covers whole campaign).
3. Paul Hopkins, *Glencoe and the End of the Highland War*, Edinburgh, 1989; Jonathan Oates, *Battle of Killiecrankie and the First Jacobite Campaign*, Solihull, 2018; Stuart Reid, *Killiecrankie: The Last Act of the Killing Times*, Barnsley, 2018; Charles Stanford Terry, *John Graham of Claverhouse, Viscount Dundee*, London, 1905; Alastair and Henrietta Tayler, *John Claverhouse*, London, 1938; Magnus Linkwater and Christian Hesketh, *John Graham of Claverhouse, Bonnie Dundee: For King and Conscience*, Edinburgh, 1989; Andrew Scott, *Bonnie Dundee*, Edinburgh, 2000.
4. Daniel Szechi, *Britain's Lost Revolution? Jacobite Scotland and French Grand Strategy, 1701-1708*, Manchester, 2015; Jonathan Worton, *The Battle of Glenshiel: The Jacobite Rising of 1719*, Solihull, 2018.
5. Charles Petrie, *The Jacobite Movement*, London, 1932; Bruce Lenman, *The Jacobite Risings in Britain, 1689-1746*, London, 1980; Michael Barthorp, *The Jacobite Rebellions, 1689-1745*, London, 1982; Daniel Szechi, *The Jacobites: Britain and Europe, 1688-1788*, Manchester, 1994; John Roberts, *The Jacobite Wars: Scotland and the Military Campaigns of 1715 and 1745*, Edinburgh, 2002.

6. Stuart Reid, *Killiecrankie*, Leigh on Sea, 1989; Jonathan Oates, *The Last Battle on English Soil: Preston, 1715*, London, 2015, and *The Crucible of the Fifteen: Sheriff-muir*, Solihull, 2017; Kathleen Tomasson and Frances Buist, *Battles of the Forty-Five*, London, 1962; M. Marguiles, *The Battle of Prestonpans*, Stroud, 2007; Arran Johnston, *On Gladsmuir Shall the Battle Be!: The Battle of Prestonpans 1745*, Solihull, 2017; G. Bailey, *Falkirk or Paradise: The Battle of Falkirk Muir, January 1746*, Edinburgh, 1996; John Prebble, *Culloden*, London, 1963; P. Harrington, *Culloden 1746: The Highlanders' Last Charge*, Oxford, 1991; Stuart Reid, *Like Hungry Wolves: Culloden Moor, 16 April 1746*, London, 1994, and *Culloden*, Barnsley, 2005; Stuart Reid and G. Embleton, *Culloden Moor, 1746* Oxford, 2002; P. Sked and S. Horrocks, *Culloden*, Edinburgh, 1997; Tony Pollard, *The History and Archaeology of the Last Clan Battle*, Barnsley, 2009; Murray Pittock, *Culloden*, Oxford, 2016.

Chapter 1: The Origins of the Jacobite Campaigns, 1688–1689

1. Andrew Murray Scott (ed.), 'Letters of John Graham of Claverhouse', *Scottish History Society Miscellany 11*, 5th series, Vol. 3 (1990), p. 249.
2. Ibid., pp. 256, 260, 263.
3. Historic Manuscripts Commission (HMC), *The Manuscripts of the Duke of Athole and the Earl of Home*, London: HMSO, 1891, pp. 38–9.
4. William Fraser, *Melvilles Earls of Melville and the Leslies Earls of Leven*, Edinburgh, 1890, III, p. 127.
5. National Records of Scotland (NRS), GD406/1/3065.
6. Hugh Mackay, *Memoirs of the War carried on in Scotland and Ireland, 1689-1691*, Edinburgh, 1833, p. 226.
7. Ibid.
8. Ibid., pp. 41, 237.
9. Ibid., pp. 44–5.
10. Ibid., p. 245.
11. Ibid., pp. 46–7.
12. Ibid., pp. 47–8.
13. Ibid., p. 48.
14. NRS, GD406/1/3608, 3609.
15. Mackay, *Memoirs*, pp. 48–9.
16. Ibid., p. 49.
17. J. MacKnight (ed.), *Memoirs of Sir Ewen Cameron*, Glasgow, 1842, p. 256.
18. Ibid., p. 257.
19. HMC Report VI, London, 1877, p. 700.
20. NRS, GD406/1/3068.
21. Mackay, *Memoirs*, p. 49.

Chapter 2: The Battle of Killiecrankie, 27 July 1689

1. NRS, CH12/12/1717; J. McKnight (ed.), *Memoirs of Sir Ewen Cameron*, p. 258.
2. NRS, CH12/12/1717.
3. Mackay, *Memoirs*, pp. 56, 263–4; Edinburgh University Library (EUL), Laing MSS II 89/338.
4. Mackay, *Memoirs*, pp. 49–50.

5. EUL, Laing MSS II, 89/338.
6. McKnight (ed.), *Memoirs of Sir Ewen Cameron*, p. 258–65.
7. Ibid., p. 265.
8. Mackay, *Memoirs*, p. 50.
9. Ibid., p. 51.
10. Ibid.
11. Ibid., pp. 52, 53, 56.
12. James MacPherson (ed.), *Original Papers, containing the Secret history of Great Britain*, London, 1775, p. 369.
13. Anon, *Memoir of Lord Dundee, by an Officer in the Army*, London, 1711, p. 31.
14. NRS, CH12/12/1717.
15. John Creighton, *Memoirs*, London, 1731, p. 268.
16. McKnight (ed.), *Memoirs of Sir Ewen Cameron*, p. 268.
17. Ibid., p. 266; James Graham (ed.), 'The Grameid', *Scottish History Society*, Series 1, Vol. 2, 1886, pp. 128, 122–3; NRS, GD26/8/71.
18. McKnight (ed.), *Memoirs of Sir Ewen Cameron*, p. 265.
19. MacPherson, *Original Papers*, p. 369.
20. Creighton, *Memoirs*, p. 268.
21. Mackay, *Memoirs*, p. 248.
22. Ibid., p. 46.
23. National Library of Scotland (NLS), MS 3740, 96.
24. EUL, Laing MSS II, 89/338.
25. *Registers of the Privy Council of Scotland* (RPCS), 14, 1689, pp. 351, 421.
26. Mackay, *Memoirs*, p. 3; Evan Whyte Melville Balfour-Maitland (ed.), 'Estate Proceedings, An Account of the Proceedings of the Estates of Scotland, 1689-1690', *Scottish History Society*, series 4, vol. I, 1954, pp. 95, 114.
27. EUL, Laing MSS II, 89/338.
28. Charles Grant, *From Pike to Shot: Armies and Battles in Western Europe 1685-1720*,Wargames Research Group, 1986, p. 32.
29. EUL, Laing MSS II, 89/338.
30. Mackay, *Memoirs*, p. 263.
31. Ibid., p. 61.
32. RPCS, 13, p. 542.
33. Ibid., 14, p. 20.
34. McKnight (ed.), *Memoirs of Sir Ewen Cameron*, p. 265; NLS MS 3738, f28r.
35. NRS, GD112/39/145/11.
36. Mackay, *Memoirs*, p. 54.
37. Ibid., p. 53.
38. Ibid., pp. 53–4.
39. Ibid., p. 267.
40. Ibid.
41. Mark Napier, *Memorials and Letters of Dundee*, Edinburgh and London, 1862, Vol. 3, p. 724.
42. Donald McBane, *The Expert Sword-Man's Companion*, Glasgow, 2015, p. 78.
43. Mackay, *Memoirs*, p. 55.
44. Ibid.; NRS, CH12/12/1717.

45. MacPherson, *Original Papers*, p. 369.
46. EUL, Laing MSS II, 89/338.
47. Mackay, *Memoirs*, p. 55.
48. McBane, *The Expert Swordsman's Companion*, p. 78.
49. McKnight (ed.), *Memoirs of Sir Ewen Cameron*, p. 266.
50. Ibid., p. 267.
51. Ibid.
52. NRS, GD112/39/145/11; Mackay, *Memoirs*, p. 55.
53. McBane, *The Expert Swordsman's Companion*, p. 78.
54. Anon, *Memoir of Lord Dundee* pp. 31–2.
55. McKnight (ed.), *Memoirs of Sir Ewen Cameron*, p. 267.
56. Anon, *Memoir of Lord Dundee*, p. 32; Napier, *Memorials*, 3, p. 724.
57. McBane, *The Expert Swordsman's Companion*, p. 78.
58. David Blackmore, *Destructive and Formidable: British infantry firepower, 1642-1765*, London, 2014, pp. 37, 49–53.
59. John Dalrymple, *Memoirs*, Dublin, 1773, II, p. 82.
60. Tony Pollard and Neil Oliver, *Two Men in a Trench II*, London, 2003 , pp. 233–4.
61. Mackay, *Memoirs*, pp. 263–4.
62. Ibid., p. 56.
63. *A9 Dualling Programme: Killiecrankie to Pitagowan – Archaeological Metal detecting Survey at the battlefield*, 2015, p. 17.
64. Pollard and Oliver, *Two Men in a Trench II*, p. 234.
65. Lord Elcho, *Short Account of the Affairs of Scotland, 1744-1746*, Edinburgh, 1907, p. 460.
66. McKnight (ed.), *Memoirs of Sir Ewen Cameron*, p. 271.
67. Royal Archives (RA), Stuart Papers Main Series, 9, ff.47-48n.
68. McKnight (ed.), *Memoirs of Sir Ewen Cameron*, p. 267.
69. Mackay, *Memoirs*, p. 281.
70. NRS, CH12/12/1717.
71. Mackay, *Memoirs*, p. 264.
72. NRS, CH12/12/1717.
73. A.H. Miller (ed.), 'Eyewitness Account of Killiecrankie', *Scottish History Review*, III, 1905, p. 67.
74. McBane, *The Expert Swordsman's Companion*, p. 78.
75. McKnight (ed.), *Memoirs of Sir Ewen Cameron*, pp. 267–8.
76. MacPherson, *Original Papers*, p. 370.
77. Mackay, *Memoirs*, pp. 281–2.
78. EUL, Laing, MSS II, 89/338.
79. RPCS, 15, pp. 307, 181.
80. Mackay, *Memoirs*, pp. 59–60.
81. EUL, Laing MSS II, 89/338.
82. Mackay, *Memoirs*, pp. 266, 282.
83. Pollard and Oliver, *Two Men in a Trench II*, pp. 232, 234.
84. Mackay, *Memoirs*, pp. 56, 265.
85. McKnight (ed.), *Memoirs of Sir Ewen Cameron*, p. 268.
86. EUL, Laing MSS II, 89/338.

87. *A9 Dualling Programme: Killiecrankie to Pitagowan – Archaeological Metal detecting Survey at the battlefield*, p. 16.
88. NRS, CH12/12/1717.
89. EUL, Laing MSS II, 89/338.
90. NLS, MS 3738, f28v.
91. RPCS, 13, p. 351.
92. Mackay, *Memoirs*, p. 56.
93. Ibid., p. 57.
94. Ibid., p. 255.
95. McKnight (ed.), *Memoirs of Sir Ewen Cameron*, p. 271.
96. NLS, MS 3738, f28v.
97. Anon, *Memoir of Lord Dundee*, p. 32.
98. NRS, CH12/12/1717.
99. McBane, *The Expert Swordsman's Companion*, p. 79.
100. McKnight (ed.), *Memoirs of Sir Ewen Cameron*, p. 268.
101. MacPherson, *Original Papers*, p. 370.
102. EUL, Laing MSS, II, 89/338.
103. R. Kane, *The Campaigns of King William and Queen Anne*, London, 1745, pp. 120, 122.
104. McBane, *The Expert Swordsman's Companion*, p. 79.
105. Ibid.
106. *London Gazette*, 2476, 1–5 Aug. 1689.
107. McKnight (ed.), *Memoirs of Sir Ewen Cameron*, p. 299.
108. Ibid.
109. Ibid., p. 271; Mackay, *Memoirs*, p. 265.
110. Mackay, *Memoirs*, p. 59.
111. NLS, MS 3740, 96.
112. Thomas Morer, A *Short Account of Scotland*, London, 1702, p. 93.
113. McKnight (ed.), *Memoirs of Sir Ewen Cameron*, p. 273.
114. EUL, Laing MSS II, 89/338.
115. NRS, GD26/13/98.
116. EUL, Laing Mss, II, 89/338.
117. NRS, GD26/13/98.
118. Fraser, *Melvilles and Leslies*, I, p. 253.
119. Anon, *Memoir of Lord Dundee*, p. 33.
120. Mackay, *Memoirs*, pp. 57–8.
121. McKnight (ed.), *Memoirs of Sir Ewen Cameron*, p. 269.
122. Ibid.
123. T. Thomson, *Acts of the Parliament of Scotland*, 1814–1875, IX, p. 56.
124. McKnight (ed.), *Memoirs of Sir Ewen Cameron*, p. 270.
125. NLS, MS 3738, f28v.
126. Mackay, *Memoirs*, p. 58.
127. Ibid., p. 266; NLS, MS 3740, 96.
128. Mackay, *Memoirs*, p. 266.
129. Ibid., p. 61.; *London Gazette*, 2476, 1–5 Aug. 1689.
130. McKnight (ed.), *Memoirs of Sir Ewen Cameron*, p. 268.
131. Ibid., p. 280.

132. Mackay, *Memoirs*, p. 59.
133. *Dundee Letters: Letters of John Graham of Claverhouse, Viscount Dundee*, Edinburgh, 1826, p. 84.
134. John Atholl, *Chronicles of the Atholl and Tullibardine Families*, Edinburgh, 1908, Vol. 1, p. 303.
135. McKnight (ed.), *Memoirs of Sir Ewen Cameron*, p. 270.
136. MacPherson, *Original Papers*, p. 370.
137. NRS, CH12/12/1717; NLS MS 3738, f29r.
138. NRS, GD112/39/145/11.
139. E. Berwick, *The Rawdon Papers*, London, 1819, p. 310.
140. Mackay, *Memoirs*, p. 262.
141. NRS, GD77/189.
142. RPCS, 14, pp. 180, 256, 38, 523.
143. Trevor Royle, *The British Civil Wars*, London, 2004, pp. 340–1, 345, 349; David Chandler, *The Art of Warfare in the Age of Marlborough*, London, 1976, pp. 334–5; John Barratt, *Battles for the Three Kingdoms*, Stroud, 2006, p. 118.
144. RPCS, Vol. 15, pp. 123, 151, 181.
145. Ibid., Vol. 16, p. 76.
146. NRS, GD124/15/808.
147. Thomson, *Acts*, XI, pp. 56–7.
148. Ibid.
149. J.S. Clarke, *The Life Of James II*, II, London, 1816, p. 353.
150. EUL, Laing MSS, II/89/338.
151. NLS, MS 3740, 96.
152. NRS, GD77/189.
153. MacPherson, *Original Papers*, p. 370.
154. EUL, Laing MSS, II/89/338.
155. NRS, GD112/39/145/11.
156. Thomson, *Acts*, IX, p. 57.
157. McKnight (ed.), *Memoirs of Sir Ewen Cameron*, pp. 270–1.
158. NRS, GD406/1/3647.
159. Ibid., 3595.
160. Ibid.
161. Mackay, *Memoirs*, pp. 255, 257.
162. Ibid., p. 309.
163. Ibid.
164. A.W.C Lindsay (ed.) *Memoirs of the Earl of Balcarres*, Edinburgh, 1841, p. 48; McKnight (ed.), *Memoirs of Sir Ewen Cameron*, p. 282.
165. Fraser, *Melvilles and Leslies*, II, pp. 140–1.
166. Mackay, *Memoirs*, p. 248.
167. Ibid., p. 249.
168. NRS, GD406/1/3595.
169. Calendar of State Papers Domestic, 1689–1690, p. 205.
170. Mackay, *Memoirs*, pp. 251–2; NRS, GD406/1/3595; NLS, MS3740, 96.
171. NRS, GD406/1/3595.
172. McKnight (ed.), *Memoirs of Sir Ewen Cameron*, p. 299.

173. Fraser, *Melvilles and Leslies*, III, p. 142.

174. NRS, GD26/13/23.

175. Creighton, *Memoirs*, p. 269.

176. McKnight (ed.), *Memoirs of Sir Ewen Cameron*, p. 282.

177. Atholl, *Chronicles of Atholl*, p. 303.

178. NRS, GD112/39/145/11.

Chapter 3: The Battles of Dunkeld and Cromdale, 1689–1690

1. John Slezar, *Theatrum Scotiae*, 1693, p. 8.

2. Mackay, *Memoirs*, pp. 68–9; RPCS, 14, pp. 62, 84.

3. Kane, *Campaigns*, p. 6.

4. Mackay, *Memoirs*, pp. 68–9.

5. Balfour-Maitland, 'Estates', I, p. 220.

6. RPCS, 13, pp. 34, 20.

7. G. Neil (ed.), 'Journal of a Soldier in the Earl of Eglington's Troop of Horse', *Transactions of the Glasgow Archaeological Society*, I (1868), p. 44.

8. McKnight (ed.), *Memoirs of Sir Ewen Cameron*, p. 286.

9. Mackay, *Memoirs*, p. 69.

10. Ibid., p. 68.

11. Anon, *Exact Narrative of the conflict at Dunkeld*, Edinburgh, 1689, p. 1; Balfour-Maitland, 'Estates', I, p. 223.

12. Anon, *Exact Narrative*, p. 1, Balfour-Maitland, 'Estates', I, p. 223.

13. McKnight (ed.), *Memoirs of Sir Ewen Cameron*, p. 286.

14. Balfour-Maitland, 'Estates', I, p. 223; Anon, *Exact Narrative*, p. 1.

15. Anon, *Exact Narrative*, pp. 1–2.

16. Balfour-Maitland, 'Estates', I, p. 223; NRS, GD26/9/229.

17. Balfour-Maitland, 'Estates', I p. 223; Anon, *Exact Narrative*, p. 2; RPCS, 13, lviii p. 82; Neil (ed.), 'Journal of a Soldier', p. 44; NRS, GD26/9/229.

18. Balfour-Maitland, 'Estates', I, p. 223; Anon, *Exact Narrative*, p. 2; RPCS, 13, p. 82; Neil, 'Journal of a Soldier', p. 44.

19. Fraser, *Melvilles and Leslies*, II, p. 119.

20. Mackay, *Memoirs*, p. 69.

21. Ibid., p. 68.

22. Ibid.

23. Anon, *Exact Narrative*, p. 3; Balfour-Maitland, 'Estates', I, p. 223; RPCS, 13, p. 82; Neil, 'Journal of a Soldier', p. 45.

24. NRS, GD26/9/229.

25. Fraser, *Melvilles and Leslies*, II, p. 120.

26. Mackay, *Memoirs*, p. 71.

27. NRS 26/9/251; Balfour-Maitland, 'Estates', I, pp. 221–3.

28. Balfour-Maitland, 'Estates', I, pp. 223–4; Anon, *Exact Narrative*, pp. 3–4; RPCS, 13, p. 82; Mackay, *Memoirs*, p. 71.

29. Anon, *Exact Narrative*, pp. 2–3; Neil, 'Journal of a Soldier', p. 45.

30. Charles Dalton, *English Army Lists, 1660-1714*, London, 1892–1904, III, p. 87; NRS, E100/13.

31. NRS, E100/13.

32. McKnight (ed.), *Memoirs of Sir Ewen Cameron*, p. 286.
33. Anon, *Exact Narrative*, p. 1.
34. RPCS, 13, p. lviii.
35. NLS, MS 542, f10-12.
36. Balfour-Maitland, 'Estates', I, p. 223.
37. RPCS, 13, p. 82.
38. Anon, *Exact Narrative*, p. 4.
39. McKnight (ed.), *Memoirs of Sir Ewen Cameron*, p. 286.
40. Ibid., pp. 266, 283; RPCS, 13, p. 82.
41. McKnight (ed.), *Memoirs of Sir Ewen Cameron*, p. 286.
42. Anon, *Exact Narrative*, p. 4; Balfour-Maitland, 'Estates', I, p. 224.
43. Anon, *Memoir of Lord Dundee*, p. 35.
44. Mackay, *Memoirs*, p. 69.
45. McKnight (ed.), *Memoirs of Sir Ewen Cameron*, p. 286.
46. Anon, *Exact Narrative*, p. 4.
47. Balfour-Maitland, 'Estates', I, p. 224.
48. Ibid., p. 221.
49. Ibid., p. 224; McKnight (ed.), *Memoirs of Sir Ewen Cameron*, p. 286.
50. www.lochiel.net/archgives/arch173.html.
51. Anon, *Exact Narrative*, p. 4.
52. MacPherson, *Original Papers*, p. 371.
53. Anon, *Exact Narrative*, pp. 4–5; Balfour-Maitland, 'Estates', I, p. 224.
54. McKnight (ed.), *Memoirs of Sir Ewen Cameron*, p. 286.
55. Anon, *Exact Narrative*, p. 5; McKnight (ed.), *Memoirs of Sir Ewen Cameron*, p. 286.
56. McKnight (ed.), *Memoirs of Sir Ewen Cameron*, p. 286.
57. Balfour-Maitland, 'Estates', I, p. 224.
58. Anon, *Exact Narrative*, p. 5.
59. Balfour-Maitland, 'Estates', I, p. 224.
60. Anon, *Exact Narrative*, p. 5.
61. Balfour-Maitland, 'Estates, I', p. 224.
62. McKnight (ed.), *Memoirs of Sir Ewen Cameron*, p. 287.
63. Anon, *Exact Narrative*, p. 5.
64. Ibid., p. 6.
65. McKnight (ed.), *Memoirs of Sir Ewen Cameron*, pp. 287.
66. Anon, *Exact Narrative*, p. 7.
67. Ibid., p. 6.
68. *Dunkeld its Straths and Glens*, Dunkeld, 1879.
69. MacPherson, *Original Papers*, p. 371.
70. Anon, *Exact Narrative*, p. 6.
71. Balfour-Maitland, 'Estates', I, p. 224.
72. Anon, *Exact Narrative*, p. 6; Balfour-Maitland, 'Estates', I, p. 224.
73. Anon, *Exact Narrative*, p. 7; Balfour-Maitland, 'Estates', I, p. 224.
74. Anon, *Exact Narrative*, p. 6–7; Balfour-Maitland, 'Estates', I, p. 224.
75. RPCS, 14, p. 82.
76. *London Gazette*, 2484, 29 Aug.– 2 Sep. 1689.
77. McKnight (ed.), *Memoirs of Sir Ewen Cameron*, p. 287.

78. MacPherson, *Original Papers*, p. 371.
79. NRS, E100/13.
80. *London Gazette*, 2482, 29 Aug. – 2 Sep. 1689.
81. Anon, *Exact Narrative*, p. 7.
82. McKnight (ed.), *Memoirs of Sir Ewen Cameron*, p. 287.
83. MacPherson, *Original Papers*, p. 371.
84. Balfour-Maitland, 'Estates', I, p. 226.
85. NRS, GD26/9/251.
86. Fraser, *Melvilles and Leslies*, II, p. 120.
87. Ibid.
88. Ibid., p. 121.
89. Mackay, *Memoirs*, pp. 70–1.
90. McKnight (ed.), *Memoirs of Sir Ewen Cameron*, p. 287.
91. Balfour-Maitland, 'Estates', I, p. 220.
92. Atholl, *Chronicles of the Atholl*, II, p. 322.
93. The National Archives (TNA), WO5/5, pp. 231, 233.
94. D. and J. Stewart, *The Stewarts of Appin*, Edinburgh, 1880, p. 120; Anon, *Memoir of Lord Dundee*, p. 35.
95. NLS, MS 3740, 135; Mackay, *Memoirs*, pp. 142, 145, 146.
96. NLS, MS 3738, 32r.
97. Ibid.; McKnight (ed.), *Memoirs of Sir Ewen Cameron*, p. 294; Mackay, *Memoirs*, p. 104; Anon, *Memoir of Lord Dundee*, pp. 35–6.
98. Mackay, *Memoirs*, p. 93.
99. Anon, *A True and Real Account of the Defeat of General Buchan and Brigadier Cannon*, London, 1690; HMC, *Manuscripts of S.H. Le Fleming Esq. of Rydal Hall*, London, 1896, p. 270.
100. Mackay, *Memoirs*, p. 94.
101. Anon, *A True and Real Account*.
102. Mackay, *Memoirs*, p. 93.
103. Dalton, *Army Lists*, III, p. 92. NRS, GD26/9/302.
104. Mackay, *Memoirs*, p. 93; Anon, *A True and Real Account*.
105. Mackay, *Memoirs*, pp. 97, 104.
106. RPCS, 15, p. 304.
107. www.lochiel.net/archgives/arch173.html.
108. Anon, *A True and Real Account*; Mackay, *Memoirs*, pp. 93–4.
109. Mackay, *Memoirs*, p. 94.
110. Anon, *A True and Real Account*; Mackay, *Memoirs*, p. 94.
111. Mackay, *Memoirs*, p. 95.
112. Anon, *A True and Real Account*; Mackay, *Memoirs*, p. 95.
113. Ibid.
114. Ibid.
115. McKnight (ed.), *Memoirs of Sir Ewen Cameron*, p. 294.
116. Ibid.
117. Anon, *A True and Real Account*.
118. Ibid.

119. George Carleton, *The Military Memoirs of an English Officer*, London, 1728, p. 56.
120. Ibid., pp. 56–7.
121. Ibid., pp. 57–8.
122. McKnight (ed.), *Memoirs of Sir Ewen Cameron*, p. 295.
123. Anon, *A True and Real Account*; Mackay, *Memoirs*, p. 97.
124. Balfour-Maitland, 'Estates', II, p. 157.
125. HMC, *Le Fleming*, p. 270.
126. www.lochiel.net/archgives/arch173.html.
127. Balfour-Maitland, 'Estates', II, pp. 171, 174, 181–2.
128. NLS, MS975, f63.
129. Anon, *A True and Real Account*.
130. Balfour-Maitland, 'Estates', II, p. 153.
131. Mackay, *Memoirs*, p. 96.
132. Ibid., pp. 96–7.
133. Anon, *Memoir of Lord Dundee*, p. 36.
134. Anon, *Great News from Scotland and Ireland*, 1690.
135. McKnight (ed.), *Memoirs of Sir Ewen Cameron*, p. 295.

Chapter 4: Peace and Storm, 1692–1715
1. James Fitzjames (ed.), *Memoirs of the Duke of Berwick*, II, London, 1798, p. 56.

Chapter 6: The Battle of Preston, 12–14 November 1715
1. Robert Patten, *History of the Late Rebellion*, London, 1745, p. 80.
2. Anon, *A Letter about the Occurrences from and at Preston*, Edinburgh, 1718, p. 5.
3. Peter Rae, *History of the Late Rebellion*, Dumfries, 1746, p. 318; William Matthews (ed.), *The Diary of Dudley Ryder, 1715-1716*, London, 1939, p. 231.
4. Clerk, *Memoirs*, p. 92.
5. *Political State of Great Britain*, XI, 1716, p. 167.
6. TNA, SP54/9/92.
7. J.O. Robinson (ed.), 'Military Memoirs of Lieutenant General the Hon. Charles Colville', *Journal of the Society of Army Historical Research*, XXV, 1947, p. 60.
8. TNA, WO5/20, pp. 116, 182.
9. *Daily Courant*, 4388, 16 Nov. 1715.
10. Ibid.; KB8/66.
11. *Political State of Great Britain*, XI, 1716, p. 167.
12. *Weekly Journal*, 255, 19 Nov. 1715.
13. Rae, *History*, p. 324.
14. *St. James' Evening Post*, 73, 15–17 Nov. 1715.
15. West Yorkshire Archive Service (WYAS): Wakefield Archives, QS10/13, 112a.
16. Robinson (ed.), 'Military Memoirs of Colville', p. 61.
17. Patten, *History*, pp. 80–1.
18. Rae, *History*, p. 318; Lancashire Record Office (LRO), QSP 1091/8.
19. William Page (ed.), *VCH Lancashire, VII*, London, 1911, p. 74.
20. Patten, *History*, p. 81.
21. Henry Paton (ed.), 'Journal of the Several Occurrences', *Scottish History Society Miscellany* I (1893), p. 521.

22. Tyne and Wear Archive Service (TWAS), CP3/22.
23. Patten, *History*, p. 81.
24. Ibid., p. 104.
25. Blair Castle (BC), Atholl Papers, 45/12/77.
26. TNA, SP54/9/107.
27. Patten, *History*, p. 83.
28. Paton (ed.), 'Journal', p. 521.
29. *Weekly Journal*, 10 Mar. 1716.
30. BC, Atholl Papers, 45/12/77.
31. *Weekly Journal*, 10 Mar. 1716.
32. Robinson (ed.), 'Military Memoirs of Colville', p. 60.
33. Paton 'Journal', p. 521; LRO, DDX2244/1.
34. Anon, *A Letter*, p. 6.
35. TNA, SP54/9/107
36. LRO, DDX2244/1.
37. Robinson (ed.), 'Military Memoirs of Colville', p. 60.
38. Patten, *History*, p. 82.
39. Rae, *History*, p. 319.
40. Charles Hardwick, *History of the Borough of Preston and its Environs in the County of Lancashire*, I, Preston, 1857, p. 229n.
41. Paton (ed.), 'Journal', p. 521.
42. Patten, *History*, p. 49.
43. Paton (ed.), 'Journal', p. 521.
44. BC, Atholl Papers, 45/12/77.
45. Robinson (ed.), 'Military Memoirs of Colville', p. 60.
46. TNA, WO116/1
47. Patten, *History*, p. 85.
48. Ibid., p. 50.
49. Ibid., p. 102.
50. Charles Radcliffe, *A Genuine and Impartial Account*, London, 1747, p. 38.
51. Patten, *History*, p. 39.
52. Ibid., pp. 98, 105.
53. Anon, *A Letter*, p. 6.
54. TNA, SP54/9/107.
55. Robinson (ed.), 'Military Memoirs of Colville', p. 60.
56. Patten, *History*, p. 84.
57. BC, Atholl Papers, 45/12/77.
58. Patten, *History*, p. 90.
59. Ibid., pp. 90–1.
60. Ibid., pp. 44–5.
61. TNA, SP54/9/107.
62. Patten, *History*, p. 86.
63. Anon, *A Letter*, p. 7.
64. BC, Atholl Papers, 45/12/77.
65. Paton (ed.), 'Journal', p. 521.
66. Patten, *History*, p. 88.

67. Rae, *History*, p. 320.
68. Phillip Doddridge, *Some Remarkable Passages in the Life of the Hon. Colonel James Gardiner*, Hedley, 1812, pp. 95–6.
69. Robinson (ed.), 'Military Memoirs of Colville', p. 60.
70. Patten, *History*, p. 68.
71. Rae, *History*, p. 320.
72. Anon, *A Letter*, p. 7.
73. Paton (ed.), 'Journal', p. 521.
74. TNA, FEC1/246-250.
75. *Political State of Great Britain*, XI, 1716, p. 165.
76. Samuel Hibbert-Ware (ed.), 'Lancashire Memorials of 1715', *Chetham Society*, V (1845), p. 169; Patten, *History*, p. 61.
77. TWAS, CP3/22.
78. Patten, *History*, dedication.
79. *Political State of Great Britain*, XI, 1716, p. 165.
80. Hibbert-Ware, 'Lancashire Memorials', p. 136.
81. Rae, *History*, p. 324.
82. *The Daily Courant*, 4391, 19 Nov. 1715.
83. WYAS: Wakefield, QS10/13, 112A; Northumberland Record Office, QS44/51.
84. TNA, KB8/66.
85. Patten, *History*, pp. 85, 88–9.
86. BC, Atholl Papers, 45/12/77.
87. TNA, SP54/9/107.
88. HMC, *Manuscripts of the Marquess of Townshend*, HMSO, 1887, p. 170.
89. Patten, *History*, p. 87.
90. TNA, SP54/9/107; Anon, *A Letter*, p. 7.
91. *Weekly Journal*, 10 March 1716.
92. HMC, *Various Collections*, II, p. 409.
93. *Evening Post*, 980, 15–17 Nov. 1715.
94. Patten, *History*, p. 89.
95. CTB, XXXII, 1716, p. 18.
96. Patten, *History*, pp. 89–90; *St. James' Post*, 131, 5–7 Dec. 1715.
97. LRO, DDX1788/1.
98. Paton (ed.), 'Journal', p. 522.
99. HMC, *Townshend*, pp. 170–1.
100. Patten, *History*, p. 90.
101. Ibid.; Radcliffe, *Genuine and Impartial*, p. 39.
102. BC, Atholl Papers, 45/12/77.
103. Rae, *History*, p. 321.
104. HMC, *Townshend*, pp. 170–1.
105. Robinson (ed.), 'Military Memoirs of Colville', p. 121.
106. *Political State of Great Britain*, XI, 1716, pp. 113, 115.
107. Patten, *History*, p. 92.
108. Ibid., pp. 92–3.
109. Rae, *History*, pp. 321–2.
110. *Political State of Great Britain*, XI, 1716, pp. 344, 355.

111. HMC, *Various Collections*, II, p. 409.
112. *Evening Post*, 980, 15–17 Nov. 1715.
113. Anon, *The Life of the Late Right Honourable George, Lord Carpenter*, London, 1736, p. 25.
114. W. E. Matthews (ed.), *Diary of Dudley Rider, 1715–1716*, London, 1939, pp. 173–4.
115. HMC, *Various Collections*, II, p. 409.
116. Patten, *History*, pp. 94–5.
117. Anon, *Life of Carpenter*, p. 23.
118. BC, Atholl Papers, 45/12/77.
119. Patten, *History*, p. 93.
120. Ibid., pp. 96–7.
121. *Weekly Journal*, 10 Mar. 1716.
122. BC, Atholl Papers, 45/12/77.
123. TNA, SP54/9/107.
124. BC, Atholl Papers, 45/12/77.
125. Anon, *A Letter*, p. 7.
126. *Weekly Journal*, 10 Mar. 1716.
127. BC, Atholl Papers, 45/12/77.
128. TNA, SP54/9/107; TS23/34.
129. Patten, *History*, p. 96.
130. Ibid., pp. 96–7.
131. Peter Addy and Peter McNiven (eds), 'Diary of Henry Prescott', II, *Record Society of Lancashire and Cheshire*, 1992, p. 475.
132. Thomas Hearne, *The Remains of Thomas Hearne*, ed. John Buchanan-Brown, London, 1966, p. 240.
133. *Oxford Dictionary of National Biography*, 20, pp. 426–7.
134. Patten, *History*, pp. 98–9.
135. HMC, *Stuart Papers*, III, pp. 456–7.
136. HMC, *Townshend*, p. 171.
137. Patten, *History*, p. 103.
138. NRS, 220/5/60.
139. TNA, FEC1/213; Patten, *History*, p. 103.
140. Lady Newton (ed.), *Lyme Letters 1660-1760*, London, 1936, p. 307.
141. HMC, *Stuart Papers*, II, p. 138.
142. Addy and McNiven (eds), 'Diary of Henry Prescott', II, p. 475.
143. *Flying Post*, 3758, 24 Feb. 1716.
144. Robinson (ed.), 'Military Memoirs of Colville', p. 60.
145. HMC, *Townshend*, p. 169.
146. Rae, *History*, p. 32; HMC, *Townshend*, pp. 170–1.
147. Rae, *History*, pp. 323–4.
148. *Flying Post*, 3734, 8–10 Dec. 1715.
149. Patten, *History*, p. 102.
150. Paton (ed.), 'Journal', p. 522.
151. Anon, *A Letter*, p. 7.
152. NRS, 220/5/601.
153. *St. James' Evening Post,* 73, 15–17 Nov. 1715.
154. HMC, *Townshend*, p. 170.

155. Patten, *History*, dedication.
156. Ibid., p. 102; Rae, *History*, p. 324.
157. Paton (ed.), 'Journal', p. 522.
158. Anon, *A Letter*, p. 7.
159. Patten, History, p. 85.
160. CTBP, 1716, p. 18.
161. Joyce Ellis (ed.), 'The Letters of Henry Liddell to William Cotesworth', *Surtees Society*, 197 (1987), p. 200.
162. Spencer Cowper (ed.), *Diary of Lady Mary Cowper*, London, 1865, p. 57.
163. TNA, WO4/17, p. 276.
164. *Daily Courant*, 4376, 2 Nov. 1715, 4391, 19 Nov. 1716.
165. TNA, SP54/10, 64.
166. Ibid., 60.

Chapter 7: The Battle of Sheriffmuir, 13 November 1715

1.   TNA, SP54/11/2b, 9/92.
2.   Rae, *History*, pp. 308n, 300n.
3.   NRS, GD220/5/817/5.
4.   NLS, MS 1498, folio 1r and v.
5.   Scott, *Memoirs*, p. 200.
6.   NRS, GD220/5/817/9b.
7.   William Inglis, *The Battle of Sheriffmuir*, Stirling, 2005, p. 7.
8.   Anon, *The Battle of Sheriffmuir*, Stirling, 1898, p. 15.
9.   NRS, GD220/5/817/5.
10. Anon, *Annals of the Reign of George I*, London, 1716, p. 147.
11. Stuart Reid, *Sheriffmuir: 1715*, London, 2014, pp. 124–6; www.data.historic-scotland.gov.uk/data/docs/battlefields/sheriffmuir-full.pdf; RA, HT, 7411-24-138.
12. James Keith, *A Fragment of a Memoir of Field Marshal Joseph Keith*, London, 1845, p. 17.
13. Scott, *Memoirs*, p. 209; TNA, SP54/10/48; Patten, *History*, p. 161; Rae, *History*, p. 303.
14. Rae, *History*, p. 303.
15. www.data.historic-scotland.gov.uk/data/docs/battlefields/sheriffmuir-full.pdf; RA, HT, 7411-24-138
16. Scott, *Memoirs*, pp. 212–13; Keith, *Fragment*, p. 17.
17. Scott, *Memoirs*, pp. 213–14; Keith, *Fragment*, p. 17; www.lochiel.net/archgives/arch173.html.
18. Scott, *Memoirs*, pp. 213–14.
19. Ibid., p. 214.
20. Ibid., pp. 214–15.
21. www.lochiel.net/archgives/arch173.html.
22. NRS, GD220/5/498/4.
23. H. Tayler (ed.), 'The Jacobite Court in Rome, 1719', *Scottish History Society*, 3rd series, vol. 31, 1938, p. 68.
24. Keith, *Fragment*, p. 18.
25. www.lochiel.net/archgives/arch173.html.
26. Scott, *Memoirs*, pp. 215–16.

27. Ibid., pp. 216–17; Keith, *Fragment*, p. 17.
28. Rae, *History*, p. 304; NRS, GD220/5/787/A.
29. TNA, SP54/10, 48, 51; Rae, *History*, p. 308n.
30. Rae, *History*, p. 304; NRS, GD220/5/489/4; 220/5/787/A.
31. NRS, GD220/5/787a.
32. Patten, *History*, p. 161; *The Spottiswoode Miscellany* 2, Edinburgh, 1845, p. 427; NRS, GD220/5/489/4.
33. TNA, SP54/10/48; WO116/3; Patten, *History*, p. 155; Rae, *History*, p. 304; NRS, GD220/5/787A.
34. Scott, *Memoirs*, p. 225.
35. Robert Campbell, *The Life of the Most Illustrious Prince, John Duke of Argyle and Greenwich*, Edinburgh, 1745, p. 191.
36. TNA, SP54/10/47.
37. NRS, GD220/5/489/4.
38. Ibid., 787/a.
39. Scott, *Memoirs*, p. 225.
40. NRS, RH15/14/149.
41. Scott, *Memoirs*, p. 227.
42. *St. James' Evening Post*, 77, 24–26 Nov. 1715.
43. Patten, *History*, p. 159.
44. Rae, *History*, p. 308.
45. HMC, *14th Report Appendix* III, p. 168.
46. Ibid.
47. NRS, GD220/5/787a.
48. NRS, GD220/5/489/4.
49. Ibid.
50. Ibid.
51. Ibid.
52. NRS, GD220/5/787A.
53. TNA, SP54/10/48; Patten, *History*, p. 153.
54. *St. James' Evening Post*, 77, 24–26 Nov. 1715.
55. NRS, GD220/5/489/4.
56. www.lochiel.net/archives/arch173.html.
57. TNA, SP54/10/48.
58. Parker, *Memoirs*, p. 264.
59. HMC, *Report on the Laing Manuscripts preserved in the University of Edinburgh*, London, 1925, p. 180.
60. Patten, *History*, pp. 166–7.
61. Scott, *Memoirs*, p. 217; Keith *Fragment*, p. 18.
62. Scott, *Memoirs*, pp. 217–18.
63. Keith, *Fragment*, p. 18.
64. Anon, *Annals of the Reign of George I*, p. 151.
65. Campbell, *Life of Argyle*, pp. 190–1.
66. HMC, *14th Report Appendix*, III, p. 168.
67. TNA, WO116/1-3.
68. Ibid.

69. Campbell, *Life of Argyle*, pp. 190–1.
70. Anon., *Steuart News Letters of 1715-16*, London, 1910, p. 71.
71. HMC, *14th Report Appendix* III, p. 168.
72. TNA, SP54/11/95.
73. TNA, SP54/ 10/48.
74. RA, HT 7411-24-138.
75. NRS, GD220/5/787/A.
76. TNA, SP54/11/97.
77. Patten, *History*, pp. 161, 167.
78. Scott, *Memoirs*, p. 226.
79. Ibid., pp. 219–20.
80. Ibid., p. 220.
81. Patten, *History*, pp. 161, 167; Scott, *Memoirs*, p. 221.
82. Anon, *Annals of the Reign of George I*, p. 152.
83. Patten, *History*, pp. 159–60.
84. Scott, *Memoirs*, p. 222.
85. TNA, SP54/10/48; Patten, *History*, p. 160, 167–8; Rae, *History*, p. 308; Scott, *Memoirs*, p. 223.
86. Patten, *History*, p. 160.
87. Scott, *Memoirs*, pp. 222–3.
88. Keith, *Fragment*, p. 19.
89. Ibid., p. 21.
90. Berwick, *Memoirs*, p. 235.
91. NRS, GD24/1/872/1/3:279.
92. Elcho, *Short Account*, pp. 415–18.
93. TNA, SP54/10/48; Patten, *History*, p. 160; Rae, *History*, p. 308; Scott, *Memoirs*, p. 222.
94. NRS, GD220/5/787/A.
95. Patten, *History*, p. 160.
96. Pollard and Oliver, *Two Men in a Trench II*, p. 214.
97. Patten, *History*, p. 160.
98. RA, HT 7411-24-138.
99. Patten, *History*, pp. 162, 168; Scott, *Memoirs*, pp. 224–5; Anon, *Annals of the Reign of George I*, p. 153.
100. TNA, SP54/10/48; Patten, *History*, p. 160.
101. T.K. Kington-Oliphant (ed.), *Jacobite Lairds of Gask*, London, 1870, p. 44.
102. HMC, *14th Report, Appendix III*, pp. 168–9.
103. Kington-Oliphant (ed.), *Jacobite Lairds of Gask*, p. 44.
104. TNA, SP54/10/48.
105. Scott, *Memoirs*, p. 241.
106. Rae, *History*, p. 310.
107. *Flying Post*, 3732, 3–6 Dec. 1715.
108. TNA, SP54/10/51.
109. TNA, WO116/1-3.
110. Christopher Duffy, *The Military Experience in the Age of Reason*, London, 1987, p. 245.

111. TNA, WO116/1-3.
112. NRS, GD45/14/263.
113. NRS, GD220/5/489/5.
114. NRS, GD27/3/37/6
115. NRS, RH15/14/149.
116. TNA, SP54/10/48; Patten, *History*, p. 168.
117. Patten, *History*, p. 168.
118. Scott, *Memoirs*, p. 228.
119. TNA, SP54/10/48, 54.
120. Patten, *History*, p. 154.
121. Rae, *History*, p. 310.
122. Patten, *History*, p. 162.
123. Ibid., p. 169.
124. Rae, *History*, pp. 309–10.
125. NRS, GD220/5/787A.
126. Anon, *An Account of the Battel of Dunblain in a Letter from a Gentleman at Stirling to his friend at Edinburgh*, Edinburgh, 1715.
127. TNA, SP54/10/48; Patten, *History*, p. 154.
128. Anon, *An Account of the Battel of Dunblain*.
129. TNA, SP54/10/48, 51.
130. *Spottiswoode Miscellany*, p. 430.
131. Keith, *Fragment*, p. 20.
132. TNA, WO4/17, p. 285.

Chapter 8: The End of the Campaign, 1715–1716

1. Patten, *History*, p. 171.
2. TNA, SP54/10/51.
3. Scott, *Memoirs*, p. 256.
4. NLS, ADV MS 13.1.8/44.
5. Patten, *History*, p. 212.
6. Scott, *Memoirs*, p. 244.
7. Ibid., pp. 260–4.
8. Keith, *Fragment*, p. 23.
9. Scott, *Memoirs*, pp. 251–2, 256.
10. HMC, *Report on the Manuscripts of the Earl of Mar and Kellie preserved at Alloa House*, London, 1904, p. 514.
11. Patten, *History*, p. 171.
12. Keith, *Fragment*, p. 23; NLS, ADV MS 13.1.8.44.
13. TNA, SP54/10, 84.
14. www.lochiel.net/archives/arch173.html.
15. Scott, *Memoirs*, p. 298.
16. HMC, *Calendar of the Stuart Papers*, Vol. 1, London, 1902, II, p. 169.
17. HMC, *Mar and Kellie*, p. 515.
18. TNA, SP54/10, 74b.
19. TNA, SP54/10, 84, 86a.
20. HMC, *Townshend*, p. 179.

21. Ibid., pp. 130, 133, 139; https://www.british-history.ac.uk/lords-jrnl/vol20.
22. TNA, SP54/10, 140; Keith, *Fragment*, p. 24.
23. Patten, *History*, p. 184.
24. TNA, SP54/11/7a.
25. TNA, SP54/11, 2a, 19.
26. BC, Atholl Papers, Bundle 45, 12/97.
27. TNA, SP54/11, 30b-c, 39b.
28. HMC, *Stuart Papers*, I, p. 502.
29. Ibid., pp. 490, 492, 504; TNA, SP78/160, 212.
30. Keith, *Fragment*, p. 26.

Chapter 9: The Battle of Glenshiel, 10 June 1719

1. W.K. Dickson (ed.), 'The Jacobite Attempt of 1719', *Scottish History Society* 1st series, (1895), pp. 232, 234.
2. Ibid., pp. 234–5.
3. Ibid., p. 236.
4. Ibid., pp. 237–8.
5. *The Whitehall Evening Post*, 81, 21–24 Mar. 1719.
6. *London Gazette*, 5733, 28–31 Mar. 1719.
7. *The Whitehall Evening Post*, 85, 9–11 Apr. 1719; 90, 11–14 Apr. 1719.
8. *Political State of Great Britain*, XVIII, 1719, pp. 411–12.
9. *Weekly Journal*, 18 Apr. 1719; *Daily Courant*, 5437, 25 Mar. 1719; *Political State of Great Britain*, XVIII, 1719, pp. 411–12, 625.
10. *Political State of Great Britain*, XVIII, 1719, p. 378.
11. S.D. Smith (ed.), *Joseph Symson, An Exact and Industrious Tradesman, 1711-1720*, Oxford, 2003, p. 640.
12. J.D. Oates and K. Kavickas (eds), 'Jacobites and Jacobins', *Record Society of Lancashire and Cheshire*, 2006, p. 56.
13. *Political State of Great Britain*, XVIII, 1719, pp. 399, 404.
14. Ibid., pp. 406, 408.
15. Ibid., pp. 501–2.
16. Keith, *Fragment*, pp. 46–7.
17. Ibid., pp. 47–8.
18. NRS, GD205/38/2/1.
19. Keith, *Fragment*, pp. 49–50.
20. NRS, GD205/38/2/1.
21. *Political State of Great Britain*, XVIII, 1719, pp. 498–9.
22. *Pue's Occurrences*, 5 and 9 May 1719.
23. *Political State of Great Britain*, XVIII, 1719, pp. 494–6.
24. *Pue's Occurences*, 5 May, 13 Jun. 1719.
25. *Political State of Great Britain*, XVIII, 1719, p. 500.
26. Ibid., pp. 500–1.
27. Ibid., p. 502.
28. Ibid., p. 622.
29. Dickson, 'Jacobite Attempt', p. 296.
30. Keith, *Fragment*, pp. 50–1.

31. *Pue's Occurences*, 6 and 16 Jun. 1719.
32. Ibid., 6 Jun. 1719.
33. Dickson, 'Jacobite Attempt', p. 270; NRS, GD24/5/162/4.
34. Keith, *Fragment*, p. 51; *London Gazette*, 5757, 20–23 Jun. 1719; NRS, GD24/5/78.
35. Dickson, 'Jacobite Attempt', p. 292.
36. Keith, *Fragment*, p. 51.
37. *Weekly Journal*, 27 Jun. 1719.
38. TNA, WO116/1-3.
39. NRS, GD24/5/78.
40. Dickson, 'Jacobite Attempt', p. 270.
41. Keith, *Fragment*, p. 51.
42. Dickson, 'Jacobite Attempt', p. 270.
43. Ibid.
44. *London Gazette*, 5757, 20–23 Jun. 1719.
45. Ibid.
46. Ibid., 5756, 16–20 Jun. 1719.
47. Dickson, 'Jacobite Attempt', p. 270.
48. *London Gazette*, 5757, 20–23 Jun. 1719.
49. Dickson, 'Jacobite Attempt', pp. 270-1.
50. Keith, *Fragment*, p. 51.
51. *London Gazette*, 5756, 16–20 Jun. 1719.
52. Ibid.
53. Dickson, 'Jacobite Attempt', p. 271.
54. Ibid.
55. NRS, GD24/5/162/4.
56. Ibid., GD24/5/78.
57. Dickson. 'Jacobite Attempt', p. 271.
58. NRS, GD24/5/78.
59. Ibid., GD24/5/162/4.
60. Keith, *Fragment*, p. 51.
61. *London Gazette*, 5757, 20–23 Jun. 1719.
62. Dickson, 'Jacobite Attempt', p. 271.
63. Ibid.
64. Ibid., unnumbered, map.
65. *London Gazette*, 5757, 20–23 Jun. 1719.
66. Dickson, 'Jacobite Attempt', unnumbered.
67. Ibid., p. 272.
68. NRS, GD24/5/78/.
69. Dickson, 'Jacobite Attempt', p. 272.
70. Ibid.
71. NRS, GD24/5/162/4.
72. *London Gazette*, 5757, 20–23 Jun. 1719.
73. NRS, GD24/5/78.
74. Keith, *Fragment*, p. 52.
75. Dickson, 'Jacobite Attempt', p. 272.
76. Ibid., pp. 272-3.

77. Ibid., p. 273.
78. NRS, GD24/5/162/4.
79. Keith, *Fragment*, p. 52; *London Gazette*, 5756, 16–20 Jun. 1719.
80. NRS, GD24/5/78.
81. *London Gazette*, 5757, 20–23 Jun. 1719.
82. Dickson, 'Jacobite Attempt', p. 273.
83. *Pue's Occurrences*, 7 Jul. 1719.
84. *Political State of Great Britain*, XVIII, 1719, p. 626.
85. Dickson, 'Jacobite Attempt', pp. 275–8.
86. Ibid., p. 275.
87. Ibid., pp. 273, 283, 285, 296.
88. *Pue's Occurrences*, 7 Jul. 1719.
89. *London Gazette*, 5756, 16–20 Jun. 1719.
90. NRS, GD24/5/78.
91. *Weekly Journal*, 4 Jul. 1719; TNA, SP54/13/78b.
92. TNA, WO116/1-3.
93. *London Gazette*, 5756, 16–20 Jun. 1719.
94. *London Gazette*, 5757, 20–23 Jun. 1719.
95. NRS, GD24/5/162/4.
96. NRS, GD24/5/78.
97. Ibid.

Chapter 10: New Life for the Jacobite Cause, 1720–1745

1. Elcho, *Short Account*, p. 234.
2. Alastair and Henrietta Tayler (eds), *1745 and After*, 1938, p. 45.
3. Ibid., p. 53.
4. Ibid., p. 56.
5. Ibid., p. 60.
6. TNA, SP54/25, f.38.
7. TNA, SP54/27, f.74a.
8. British Library (BL) Add.Mss 32705, f113r, 131r.
9. *Gentleman's Magazine*, 15, 1745, pp. 518–19.
10. TNA, SP54/25, f.106d.
11. TNA, SP36/69, f.207v; BL. Add.Mss, 33004, ff83r-84v.
12. Elcho, *Short Account*, p. 255.
13. Ibid., p. 257.

Chapter 11: The Battle of Prestonpans, 21 September 1745

1. Walter Biggar Blaikie (ed.), 'Origins of the Forty-Five, 1737-1746', *Scottish History Society*, 2nd series, 2 (1916), p. 406, F. Douglas, *History of the rebellion in 1745 and 1746*, Aberdeen, 1755, p. 19; John Home, *History of the rebellion in the year 1745*, London, 1802, pp. 103–5.
2. James Ray, *A Complete History of the rebellion*, London, 1754, p. 35.
3. Duncan Forbes (ed.), *Culloden Papers*, London, 1815, p. 224; Andrew Henderson, *History of the Rebellion,* London, 1748, pp. 27–8; TNA, SP54/26/29.
4. TNA, SP55/13/258.

5. Home, *History*, pp. 105–6.
6. BL. Add. Mss. 63592, f.62r.
7. W.A.S. Hewins, *The Whitefoord Papers*, Oxford, 1898, p. 93.
8. G.E.C. Hepburne-Scott (ed.), 'Marchmont Papers', Miscellany, *Scottish History Society*, 3rd series, 17, (1933), p. 320.
9. NRS, GD51/16/103/2/499.
10. P.C. Yorke (ed.), *Life of Lord Chancellor Hardwicke*, I, Cambridge, 1913, p. 456.
11. T.J. McCann (ed.), *Correspondence of the Dukes of Richmond and Newcastle, 1724-1750*, Sussex Record Society, (1983), p. 183.
12. Home, *History*, p. 121n.
13. James Kimsley (ed.), *Anecdotes and Characters of the Times*, Oxford, 1973, pp. 68–9.
14. Home, *History*, pp. 106–7; George Wade, *A Report of the Proceedings and Opinions*, Dublin, 1749, p. 37; Douglas, *History*, pp. 19–20.
15. James Allardyce, *Historical Papers of the Jacobite Period*, 1, Aberdeen, 1895, p. 279.
16. Douglas, *History*, pp. 19–20.
17. Allardyce, *Historical Papers*, p. 280.
18. *Stamford Mercury*, 10 Oct. 1745.
19. Elcho, *Short Account*, pp. 265–6; R.F. Bell (ed.), 'Memorials of John Murray of Broughton, 1740-1747', *Scottish History Society*, Vol. 27, 1897, p. 198.
20. B. Rawson (ed.), *Memoirs of the Chevalier de Johnstone*, London, 1958, p. 34.
21. Home, *History*, pp. 108–9.
22. Tayler and Tayler, *1745*, p. 75.
23. Home, *History*, p. 109.
24. Elcho, *Short Account*, pp. 266–7.
25. Blaikie, 'Origins', p. 405.
26. Tayler and Tayler, *1745*, p. 77.
27. Blaikie, 'Origins', pp. 405–6.
28. Rawson (ed.), *Memoirs of Johnstone*, p. 35.
29. RA, CP9/152.
30. Blaikie, 'Origins', p. 406.
31. RA, CP5/163; Allardyce, *Historical Papers*, p. 280.
32. Elcho, *Short Account*, p. 267; Robert Forbes, *Jacobite Memoirs*, Edinburgh, 1834, p. 37.
33. Allardyce, *Historical Papers*, p. 280.
34. Robert Forbes, *Jacobite Memoirs*, p. 38.
35. RA, CP9/152.
36. Allardyce, *Historical Papers*, p. 280.
37. Douglas, *History*, p. 20.
38. Blaikie, 'Origins', p. 406.
39. Tayler and Tayler, *1745*, pp. 78–9.
40. Robert Forbes, *Jacobite Memoirs*, pp. 38–9.
41. Bell (ed.), 'Memorials of John Murray of Broughton', p. 201.
42. Home, *History*, p. 114–15.
43. Bell (ed.), 'Memorials of John Murray of Broughton', p. 201.
44. Blaikie, 'Origins', p. 407; W.D. Blaikie (ed.). 'Itinerary of Prince Charles Edward Stuart', *Scottish History Society*, 1st series, vol. 23, 1898, p. 115; James Maxwell,

     Narrative of Charles, Prince of Wales' Expedition to Scotland in the year 1745, Edinburgh, 1841, p. 39; Elcho, *Short Account*, pp. 269–70.

45. Blaikie, 'Origins', p. 407.
46. Maxwell, *Narrative*, p. 39; Elcho, *Short Account*, pp. 269–70.
47. Henderson, *History*, pp. 29–30.
48. Elcho, *Short Account*, p. 253.
49. Donald Nicholas, 'An Account of the Proceedings from Prince Charles' landing to Prestonpans', *SHS Miscellany*, 10 (1958), p. 216.
50. Elcho, *Short Account*, pp. 253, 257.
51. Home, *History*, p. 104.
52. Rawson (ed.), *Memoirs of Johnstone*, p. 36.
53. Anon, *Woodhouselea Manuscripts*, London, 1907, p. 26.
54. Home, *History*, p. 104.
55. Anon, *Woodhouselea Manuscripts*, pp. 27, 33.
56. Kimsley, *Anecdotes*, p. 76.
57. Douglas, *History*, pp. 27–8; RA, CP5/318.
58. TNA, WO116/4.
59. Tony Pollard, *Culloden: The History and Archaeology of the Last Clan Battle*, Barnsley, 2009, p. 88.
60. Kimsley, *Anecdotes*, p. 68.
61. Anon, *Woodhouselea Manuscripts*, p. 29.
62. Home, *History*, p. 118n.
63. Wade, *Proceedings*, p. 54.
64. Ibid., p. 87.
65. RA, CP5/318.
66. Blaikie, 'Origins', p. 407; Home, *History*, pp. 115–16.
67. Blaikie, 'Origins', p. 407.
68. Tayler and Tayler, *1745*, p. 79.
69. Home, *History*, pp. 112–13.
70. Hewins, *Whitefoord*, p. 89. Douglas, *History*, p. 21; Wade, *Proceedings*, p. 39; Henderson, *History*, p. 30.
71. Home, *History*, p. 118.
72. Kimsley, *Anecdotes*, p. 71.
73. NRS, GD1440/3/5.
74. Maxwell, *Narrative*, p. 41.
75. Blaikie, 'Origins', pp. 407–8.
76. Maxwell, *Narrative*, p. 41.
77. Douglas, *History*, pp. 21, 23.
78. Henderson, *History*, p. 30.
79. Elcho, *Short Account*, p. 272.
80. Douglas, *History*, pp. 24, 27–8.
81. Hewins, *Whitefoord Papers*, p. 58.
82. *Gentleman's Magazine*, 15, 1745, p. 638.
83. Wade, *Proceedings*, p. 40.
84. Allardyce, *Historical Papers*, p. 281.
85. RA, CP9/152.

86. Home, *History*, p. 117.
87. Wade, *Proceedings*, p. 40.
88. Hewins, *Whitefoord Papers*, p. xviii.
89. RA, CP5/163.
90. Ibid.
91. Blaikie, 'Origins', p. 408.
92. Douglas, *History*, p. 21.
93. RA, CP5/163.
94. John Marchant, *History of the Present Rebellion*, London, 1746, p. 63.
95. Maxwell, *History*, p. 41.
96. TNA, WO116/4.
97. Blaikie, 'Origins', p. 408.
98. TNA, WO116/4.
99. NRS, GD26/9/486.
100. Duncan Forbes, *Culloden Papers*, p. 224.
101. Tayler and Tayler, *1745*, p. 82n.
102. RA, CP6/111.
103. Ibid.
104. Bell (ed.), 'Memorials of John Murray of Broughton', p. 203.
105. Douglas, *History*, p. 22; NRS, GD26/9/486.
106. Henderson, *History*, p. 30.
107. Rawson (ed.), *Memoirs of Johnstone*, p. 37.
108. RA, CP9/152.
109. Ibid; NRS, GD26/9/486.
110. Wade, *Proceedings*, p. 61.
111. G.C. Mounsey, *Carlisle in 1745*, Carlisle, 1846, p. 26.
112. Maxwell, *Narrative*, p. 41.
113. Elcho, *Short Account*, p. 274.
114. A.G. Seton and J.S. Arnot, 'Prisoners of the '45', *Scottish History Society*, Series 3, Vol. II, 1929, pp. 83, 85, 93.
115. Blaikie, 'Origins', p. 408.
116. Marchant, *History*, p. 98; NRS, GD1440/3/5.
117. Bell (ed.), 'Memorials of John Murray of Broughton', p. 203.
118. Tayler and Tayler, *1745*, p. 81.
119. *Caledonian Mercury*, 25 Sep. 1745.
120. Tayler and Tayler, *1745*, p. 81.
121. Douglas, *History*, p. 25.
122. Kimsley, *Anecdotes*, p. 74.
123. Douglas, *History*, p. 22.
124. RA, CP5/163.
125. RA, CP6/111.
126. Rawson (ed.), *Memoirs of Johnstone*, p. 40.
127. Anon, *Woodhouselea Manuscripts*, p. 36.
128. Hepburne-Scott, 'Marchmont Papers', p. 322.
129. Duncan Forbes, *Culloden Papers*, p. 224; Henderson, *History*, p. 30.
130. NRS, GD1440/3/5.

131. Rawson (ed.), *Memoirs of Johnstone*, p. 40.
132. Allardyce, *Historical Papers*, p. 281.
133. Wade, *Proceedings*, p. 41.
134. Ibid., p. 56.
135. Douglas, *History*, p. 22.
136. Elcho, *Short Account*, p. 273.
137. Douglas, *History*, p. 22.
138. Ibid., p. 23.
139. Ray, *History*, p. 36.
140. Kimsey, *Anecdotes*, p. 74.
141. NRS, GD26/9/486.
142. Blaikie, 'Origins', p. 408; Henderson, *History*, p. 30.
143. Tayler and Tayler, *1745*, p. 82n.
144. Iain Brown and Hugh Cheape, *Witness to Rebellion: John Mclean's Journal of the Forty-Five and the Penicuik Drawings*, Edinburgh, 1996, p. 22.
145. *Newcastle Courant*, 19 Oct. 1745.
146. Ray, *History*, p. 39.
147. Bell (ed.), 'Memorials of John Murray of Broughton', p. 204.
148. NRS, GD26/9/486.
149. Henderson, *History*, p. 31.
150. Home, *History*, pp. 121–2.
151. Bell (ed.), 'Memorials of John Murray of Broughton', p. 204.
152. David Nicholas, *Intercepted Post 1745*, London, 1956, pp. 138–9.
153. Robert Forbes, *Jacobite Memoirs*, p. 40; NRS, GD26/9/486.
154. RA, CP6/111.
155. Tayler and Tayler, *1745*, p. 82n.
156. RA, CP6/111.
157. Robert Forbes, *Jacobite Memoirs*, p. 41.
158. Kimsley, *Anecdotes*, p. 74.
159. Tayler and Tayler, *1745*, pp. 81–2.
160. Henderson, *History*, p. 30–1.
161. Bell (ed.), 'Memorials of John Murray of Broughton', p. 205.
162. Rawson (ed.), *Memoirs of Johnstone*, p. 41.
163. Kimsley, *Anecdotes*, p. 77.
164. Blaikie, 'Origins', p. 408.
165. Bell (ed.), 'Memorials of John Murray of Broughton', p. 204.
166. Blaikie, 'Origins', p. 409.
167. Henderson, *History*, p. 32.
168. Bell (ed.), 'Memorials of John Murray of Broughton', p. 205.
169. Kimsley, *Anecdotes*, p. 75.
170. Blaikie, 'Origins', p. 409.
171. *Muster Roll of Prince Charles Stuart's Army*, 1984, pp. 12, 33, 67, 147, 162.
172. Tayler and Tayler, *1745*, p. 84.
173. *Stamford Mercury*, 10 Oct. 1745; *Scots Magazine*, 4 Oct. 1745; Bell (ed.), 'Memorials of John Murray of Broughton', p. 205.
174. Ray, *History*, p. 40.

175. Elcho, *Short Account*, p. 275; Home, *History*, p. 120, *Gentleman's Magazine*, 15, 1745, p. 518.
176. Ray, *History*, p. 39.
177. TNA, WO116/4.
178. Henderson, *History*, p. 31.
179. Elcho, *Short Account*, p. 274.
180. Blaikie, 'Origins', p. 408; Tayler and Tayler, *1745*, p. 84.
181. Tayler and Tayler, *1745*, p. 84.
182. Robert Forbes, *Jacobite Memoirs*, p. 43.
183. NRS, GD51/16/103/2/449.
184. Robert Forbes, *Jacobite Memoirs*, p. 31.
185. TNA, SP54/26/54.
186. Blaikie, 'Origins', p. 103.
187. Tayler and Tayler, *1745*, p. 84; Home, *History*, p. 120n; TNA, SP36/71, f271r; Henry Paton (ed.), 'The Lyon in Mourning', I, *Scottish History Society*, 1st series, 19 (1895), p. 215.
188. NRS, GD51/16/73.
189. Nicholas, *Intercepted Post*, p. 139.
190. *Caledonian Mercury*, 27 Sept. 1745; *Scots Magazine*, 4 Oct. 1745; *Stamford Mercury*, 10 Oct. 1745.
191. Paton (ed.), 'Lyon', I, p. 215.
192. Robert Forbes, *Jacobite Memoirs*, pp. 42–3.
193. *Scots Magazine*, 4 Oct. 1745.
194. Henderson, *History*, pp. 32–3; TNA, SP42/29/122.
195. Douglas, *History*, p. 23.
196. Michael Hughes, *A Plain Narrative*, London, 1746, p. 10.
197. TNA, SP36/68, ff.209r, 239b.
198. TNA, SP36/68, f.239b.
199. Henderson, *History*, p. 32.
200. TNA, SP54/26/35.
201. RA, CP5/163.
202. Duncan Forbes, *Culloden Papers*, p. 224.
203. NRS, GD498/1/26.
204. TNA, SP54/26/35.
205. Paton, 'Lyon', I, p. 214.
206. Blaikie, 'Origins', p. 409.
207. Maxwell, *Narrative*, p. 42.
208. Anon, *Woodhouselea Manuscripts*, p. 39.
209. McCann, *Correspondence of Richmond and Newcastle*, p. 183.
210. W.S. Lewis, *Letters of Horace Walpole*, Vol. 19, Yale, 1955, p. 117; Alan Saville (ed.), 'Secret Comment: The Diaries of Gertrude Saville, 1721-1757', *Thoroton Society*, 41 (1995), p. 260.
211. Ibid.
212. Lewis, *Letters of Horace Walpole*, 19, p. 117.
213. Kimsley, *Anecdotes*, p. 76.
214. Marchant, *History*, p. 103.

215. Henderson, *History*, pp. 32–3.
216. Ibid., p. 31.
217. Bell (ed.), 'Memorials of John Murray of Broughton', pp. 206–9.
218. Elcho, *Short Account*, pp. 276–7, 302.
219. Kimsley, *Anecdotes*, p. 76.
220. Paton, 'Lyon', I, p. 211.

Chapter 12: The Jacobite High Tide, 1745–1746
1. BL Add. Mss, 33004, f.86r-87r; Marchant, *History*, pp. 71, 150, 186.
2. *The Newcastle Gazette*, 76, 27 Nov. 1745; TNA, SP36/70, f.215r, 76, f.167r; 77, f.238r; Sheffield Archives, WWM1/357; *The General Advertiser*, 3579, 17 Apr. 1746.
3. Elcho, *Short Account*, pp. 324–5.
4. Ibid., p. 331.
5. Richard Lodge (ed.), *Private Correspondence of Chesterfield and Newcastle, 1744-6*, London, 1930, p. 87.
6. TNA, SP36/73, f.326r, 75, ff. 131r, 201r; SP 44/133, p. 2, Ray, *History*, p. 138.
7. Elcho, *Short Account*, p. 337.
8. Ibid., p. 340.
9. Blaikie, 'Origins', p. 177.
10. RA, CP7/236.
11. Henderson, *History*, p. 96.

Chapter 13: The Battle of Falkirk, 1746
1. Lewis, *Letters of Horace Walpole*, 19, p. 193.
2. Lodge (ed.), *Private Correspondence of Chesterfield and Newcastle*, pp. 94, 100.
3. Elcho, *Short Account*, pp. 370–1; Tayler and Tayler, *1745*, p. 115n.
4. Elcho, *Short Account*, p. 371.
5. Maxwell, *Narrative*, p. 98.
6. Duncan Forbes, *Culloden Papers*, p. 270; Douglas, *History*, pp. 113, 116; HMC, *Report on the Manuscripts of the Earl of Eglington*, London, 1885, p. 440.
7. HMC, *Eglington*, p. 440.
8. TNA, SP54/27/18a, RA, CP9/66, 81, 134.
9. Elcho, *Short Account*, p. 372.
10. TNA, SP54/27/32D.
11. Tayler and Tayler, *1745*, p. 115n.
12. Robert Forbes, *Jacobite Memoirs*, p. 91.
13. Rawson (ed.), *Memoirs of Johnstone*, pp. 85–6.
14. Robert Forbes, *Jacobite Memoirs*, p. 80; Tayler and Tayler, *1745*, p. 116.
15. Tayler and Tayler, *1745*, p. 116.
16. Elcho, *Short Account*, p. 372.
17. Maxwell, *Narrative*, p. 99.
18. Robert Forbes, *Jacobite Memoirs*, p. 80.
19. Blaikie, 'Origins', p. 194.
20. Maxwell, *Narrative*, p. 99.
21. Tayler and Tayler, *1745*, p. 116.
22. Paton (ed.), 'Lyon', II, pp. 196–7.

23. Robert Forbes, *Jacobite Memoirs*, pp. 80–1, 92.
24. Ibid., pp. 81–2.
25. Blaikie, 'Origins', p. 194.
26. Henderson, *History*, p. 91.
27. Blaikie, 'Origins', p. 194
28. Douglas, *History*, p. 115.
29. Duncan Forbes, *Culloden Papers*, p. 271.
30. HMC, *Eglington*, p. 440.
31. RA, HT, 7411-24-101-1, p. 24.
32. Elcho, *Short Account*, p. 373.
33. Douglas, *History*, pp. 114, 116.
34. Henderson, *History*, p. 91.
35. Home, *History*, pp. 166–7.
36. RA, HT, 7411-24-101-1, p. 25.
37. Home, *History*, p. 167.
38. Duncan Forbes, *Culloden Papers*, p. 271.
39. Ibid; HMC, *Eglington*, p. 440.
40. Duncan Forbes, *Culloden Papers*, p. 271.
41. Robert Forbes, *Jacobite Memoirs*, p. 83.
42. Tayler and Tayler, *1745*, p. 117.
43. Anon, *Lettre d'un Officier du Regiment Royal Eccossais*, Stirling, 1746, pp. 4–5.
44. Elcho, *Short Account*, p. 373; TNA, SP54/27/32C.
45. Maxwell, *Narrative*, p. 99.
46. Ibid., p. 100.
47. TNA, SP54/27/32C, 38B.
48. Ibid., 22A.
49. RA, CP9/91.
50. TNA, SP54/27/22A.
51. Ibid.
52. Blaikie, 'Origins', p. 362.
53. RA, CP9/81.
54. RA, HT, 7411-101-11-1, p. 24.
55. TNA, WO116/4-5.
56. Elcho, *Short Account*, pp. 459–60.
57. Maxwell, *Narrative*, p. 100.
58. Elcho, *Short Account*, pp. 374–5.
59. Robert Forbes, *Jacobite Memoirs*, p. 84.
60. Ibid., pp. 84–5.
61. TNA, SP54/27/55B.
62. Robert Forbes, *Jacobite Memoirs*, pp. 83–4.
63. Home, *History*, p. 171n.
64. RA, HT, 7411-101-11-1, p. 25.
65. Blaikie, 'Origins', p. 411.
66. Elcho, *Short Account*, p. 375.
67. Blaikie, 'Origins', p. 195.
68. RA, HT, 7411-101-11-1, p. 25.

69. Elcho, *Short Account*, p. 375.
70. Rawson (ed.), *Memoirs of Johnstone*, p. 87.
71. TNA, SP54/27/38a.
72. Duncan Forbes, *Culloden Papers*, p. 271.
73. TNA, SP54/27/55b.
74. RA, HT, 7411-101-11-1, p. 25.
75. Ray, *History*, p. 242.
76. Henderson, *History*, p. 94.
77. Ibid., pp. 92, 94.
78. Blaikie, 'Origins', p. 411.
79. Elcho, *Short Account*, p. 375.
80. Paton (ed.), 'Lyon', II, pp. 727–8.
81. Robert Forbes, *Jacobite Memoirs*, p. 94n.
82. Henderson, *History*, p. 94.
83. Robert Forbes, *Jacobite Memoirs*, p. 85.
84. Tayler and Tayler, *1745*, p. 118.
85. Blaikie, 'Origins', p. 433; William Thornton, *The Counterpoise*, London, 1754, p. 40.
86. Blaikie, 'Origins', p. 411.
87. William Fraser, *The Earls of Cromartie*, 2, London, 1876, p. 392.
88. Blaikie, 'Origins', p. 195.
89. Duncan Forbes, *Culloden Papers*, pp. 271–2.
90. Douglas, *History*, p. 114.
91. HMC, *Eglington*, p. 441.
92. RA, HT, 7411-101-11-1, p. 25.
93. Douglas, *History*, p. 116.
94. Maxwell, *Narrative*, p. 102.
95. Elcho, *Short Account*, pp. 375–6.
96. Tayler and Tayler, *1745*, p. 118.
97. RA, CP9/110.
98. HMC, *Eglington*, p. 441.
99. RA, CP9/99.
100. *Gentleman's Magazine*, 16, 1746, pp. 41–2; Gray, 'Memoirs of Clerk of Penicuik', p. 195; RA, CP9/141.
101. RA, CP9/110.
102. Duncan Forbes, *Culloden Papers*, pp. 267–8.
103. Blaikie, 'Origins', p. 198.
104. Henderson, *History*, p. 95.
105. Ray, *History*, p. 249.
106. Elcho, *Short Account*, p. 376.
107. Henderson, *History*, p. 93.
108. HMC, *Eglington*, p. 441.
109. Ibid.
110. Ibid.
111. Douglas, *History*, pp. 117, 124.
112. *Penny London Post*, 25–27 Jan. 1746.
113. RA, CP9/102; *Penny London Post*, 25–27 Jan. 1746.

114. Rawson (ed.), *Memoirs of Johnstone*, p. 88.
115. Fraser, *Earls of Cromartie*, 2, p. 392.
116. Ray, *History*, p. 247.
117. Henderson, *History*, p. 94.
118. Home, *History*, pp. 174n–175n.
119. Robert Forbes, *Jacobite Memoirs*, p. 86.
120. Tayler and Tayler, *1745*, p. 118.
121. Home, *History*, p. 175n.
122. Tayler and Tayler, *1745*, p. 115n.
123. Robert Forbes, *Jacobite Memoirs*, p. 91.
124. Ibid., pp. 86, 88.
125. Blaikie, 'Origins', p. 196.
126. Fraser, *Earls of Cromartie*, 2, p. 392.
127. Duncan Forbes, *Culloden Papers*, p. 272.
128. Elcho, *Short Account*, p. 376.
129. Alastair and Henrietta Tayler (eds), *Jacobite Miscellany*, Oxford, 1958, p. 156.
130. Forbes, *Jacobite Memoirs*, p. 87.
131. Henderson, *History*, p. 94.
132. Rawson (ed.), *Memoirs of Johnstone*, p. 88.
133. Blaikie, 'Origins', p. 412.
134. Elcho, *Short Account*, p. 376.
135. RA, HT, 7411-101-11-1, p. 25.
136. Ibid.; Douglas, *History*, p. 117.
137. Blaikie, 'Origins', p. 362.
138. Forbes, *Jacobite Memoirs*, p. 87.
139. Blaikie, 'Origins', pp. 412–13; Forbes, *Jacobite Memoirs*, p. 88.
140. Blaikie, 'Origins', pp. 196–7.
141. Robert Forbes, *Jacobite Memoirs*, p. 88.
142. Tayler and Tayler, *1745*, pp. 119–20.
143. Blaikie, 'Origins', p. 197.
144. Ibid., p. 413; Elcho, *Short Account*, p. 378.
145. Elcho, *Short Account*, p. 379.
146. Robert Forbes, *Jacobite Memoirs*, pp. 89–90.
147. Ibid., p. 93.
148. Rawson (ed.), *Memoirs of Johnstone*, p. 93.
149. Blaikie, 'Origins', p. 413.
150. Rawson (ed.), *Memoirs of Johnstone*, p. 95.
151. Tayler and Tayler, *1745*, p. 120.
152. Elcho, *Short Account*, p. 380.
153. Blaikie, 'Origins', pp. 198–9.
154. Rawson (ed.), *Memoirs of Johnstone*, p. 89.
155. Blaikie, 'Origins'. p. 197.
156. Ibid., p. 411.
157. Elcho, *Short Account*, p. 379.
158. Henderson, *History*, p. 95.
159. Rawson (ed.), *Memoirs of Johnstone*, p. 92; Elcho, *Short Account*, p. 378; Maxwell, *Narrative*, p. 105.

160. TNA, SP54/27/55C.
161. Ray, *History*, p. 249.
162. TNA, SP54/27/22D.
163. Ray, *History*, p. 248.
164. Blaikie, 'Origins', p. 433.
165. Ray, *History*, p. 250; *Glasgow Courant*, 3 Feb. 1746.
166. Henderson, *History*, p. 95.
167. *Glasgow Courant*, 3 Feb. 1746; *Stamford Mercury*, 20 Feb. 1746.
168. Blaikie, 'Origins', p. 411.
169. RA, CP9/134.
170. Lewis, *Letters of Horace Walpole*, 19, p. 203.
171. RA, CP, 14/385.
172. HMC, *Report on the Manuscripts of the late Reginald Hastings*, London, 1928, p. 54.
173. Duncan Forbes, *Culloden Papers*, p. 267.
174. Hughes, *Plain Narrative*, pp. 17–18.
175. Douglas, *History*, p. 155.
176. Lewis, *Letters of Horace Walpole*, 19, pp. 217, 214.
177. RA, CP9/99.
178. TNA, SP54/27/40.
179. Saville, 'Secret Comment', p. 266.
180. Reid, *1745*, p. 100.
181. B. Wilson, *Life and Letters of James Wolfe*, London, 1909, pp. 56–7.
182. *Penny London Post*, 25–27 Jan. 1746.
183. *Stamford Mercury*, 6 Feb. 1746; *Glasgow Courant*, 27 Jan. 1746; Douglas, *History*, p. 153.
184. Home, *History*, p. 351.
185. Douglas, *History*, p. 128.
186. *Letter d'un Officier*.

Chapter 14: Endgame in the Highlands
1. Buckinghamshire Record Office, Bundle 54, Jan.–Feb. 1746, Trevor Papers.
2. Elcho, *Short Account*, pp. 384–5.
3. TNA, SP54/28/1a.
4. Ibid., 28/9.
5. RA, CP11/82.
6. NLS, 3734, f.430r.
7. *Gentleman's Magazine*, 16, 1746, pp. 235–6.
8. TNA, SP54/29, f.32a.
9. Henderson, *History*, p. 102.
10. Maxwell, *Narrative*, p. 119.
11. Ibid., p. 130.
12. Henderson, *History*, p. 116.
13. TNA, SP54/30/16.
14. Elcho, *Short Account*, pp. 415, 413.
15. Hughes, *Plain Narrative*, p. 31.

Chapter 15: The Battle of Culloden, 16 April 1746

1. Lewis, *Letters of Horace Walpole*, 19, p. 239.
2. Home, *History*, p. 228n.
3. Robert Forbes, *Jacobite Memoirs*, p. 287; NRS, GD1/53/81/1.
4. Home, *History*, p. 361.
5. Robert Forbes, *Jacobite Memoirs*, pp. 286–7.
6. Ibid., p. 121.
7. NRS, GD1/53/81/1.
8. Tayler and Tayler, *1745*, p. 150.
9. Blaikie, 'Origins', p. 415.
10. Hughes, *Plain Narrative*, p. 35.
11. Elcho, *Short Account*, pp. 426–7.
12. Home, *History*, p. 363.
13. NRS, GD16/35/60.
14. Hughes, *Plain Narrative*, p. 30.
15. Blaikie, 'Origins', p. 211.
16. Robert Forbes, *Jacobite Memoirs*, p. 138.
17. Tayler and Tayler, *1745*, p. 116.
18. Home, *History*, pp. 363–4.
19. Blaikie, 'Origins', p. 210.
20. Tayler and Tayler, *1745*, p. 116.
21. Home, *History*, p. 367.
22. Allardyce, *Historical Papers*, II, p. 608.
23. Maxwell, *Narrative*, p. 146.
24. Elcho, *Short Account*, pp. 438–9.
25. James Dennistoun, *Memoirs of Sir Robert Strange*, I, London, 1855, p. 60.
26. Tayler and Tayler, *1745*, p. 155.
27. RA, CP14/58.
28. Yorke, *Hardwicke*, I, p. 521.
29. Hughes, *Plain Narrative*, p. 24.
30. Anon, 'The Battle of Culloden', *Journal of the Society for Army Historical Research*, 36 , 1957, p. 184.
31. W. H. Anderson, 'The Battle of Culloden', *Journal of the Society for Army Historical Research*, 1 , 1921, p. 24.
32. A.N.C. McLachlan, *A Sketch of Cumberland's Military Life*, London, 1876, p. 287; Hewin, *Whitefoord Papers*, p. 76
33. Ilchester, Earl of, *Letters to Henry Fox, Lord Holland*, London, 1895, p. 10.
34. Robert Forbes, *Jacobite Memoirs*, p. 290.
35. Blaikie, 'Origins', p. 212.
36. Tayler and Tayler, *Jacobite Miscellany*, p. 162.
37. Paton (ed.), 'Lyon', I, p. 261.
38. Elcho, *Short Account*, pp. 429–31.
39. Rawson (ed.), *Memoirs of Johnstone*, p. 119.
40. Robert Forbes, *Jacobite Memoirs*, p. 290.
41. Dennistoun, *Memoirs*, p. 61.
42. Blaikie, 'Origins', pp. lxix–lxx.

43. NRS, GD1/53/86/2.
44. Home, *History*, pp. 33–4.
45. Henderson, *Duke of Cumberland*, London, 1766, p. 251.
46. Rawson (ed.), *Memoirs of Johnstone*, pp. 119–20.
47. Tayler and Tayler, *Jacobite Miscellany*, p. 80.
48. Yorke, *Hardwicke* I, p. 522.
49. Anon, 'The Battle of Culloden', p. 184.
50. NRS, GD1/53/81/1.
51. Hughes, *Plain Narrative*, p. 24.
52. Anderson, 'The Battle of Culloden', p. 22.
53. Blaikie, 'Origins', p. 418.
54. NLS, MS 3735, 290.
55. Ray, *History*, p. 345; RA, CP14/7 WO 116/4–6.
56. Ray, *History*, pp. 333–4; Hewins, *Whitefoord Papers*, p. 77.
57. Elcho, *Short Account*, pp. 423–4, 430; BL Stowe, Mss 158, f.214r.
58. Henderson, *History*, p. 114.
59. Elcho, *Short Account*, unnumbered pages between pp. 432 and 433.
60. Ray *History*, p. 333; *Gentleman's Magazine*, 16, 1746, p. 210.
61. Maxwell, *Narrative*, p. 150; Blaikie, 'Origins', p. 213.
62. RA, HT, 7411-101-11-1, p. 27.
63. Tayler and Tayler, *1745*, pp. 161–3.
64. Wilson, *Life and Letters of Wolfe*, p. 65.
65. Rawson (ed.), *Memoirs of Johnstone*, p. 119.
66. Blaikie, 'Itinerary', pp. 120–1.
67. Ibid., p. 213.
68. Maxwell, *Narrative*, p. 149.
69. Hughes, *Plain Narrative*, p. 31.
70. Henderson, *Cumberland*, p. 253.
71. Hughes, *Plain Narrative*, p. 40.
72. Marchant, *History*, p. 399.
73. Home, *History*, p. 167; Historical Manuscripts Commission Report Vol. 10, London, 1885, p. 443.
74. NRS, GD61/115, 5.
75. NLS, MS. 3735, 190.
76. Robert Forbes, *Jacobite Memoirs*, p. 291, Blaikie, 'Origins', pp. 212–14.
77. Maxwell, *Narrative*, p. 150.
78. Tayler and Tayler, *1745*, p. 160.
79. Hughes, Plain Narrative, p. 29.
80. Home, *History*, p. 166.
81. Ray, *History*, p. 334.
82. Anderson (ed.), 'The Battle of Culloden', p. 24.
83. RA, HT, 7411-101-11-1, p. 28.
84. Ibid.
85. Ray, *History*, p. 334.
86. Henderson, *History*, p. 115.
87. Maxwell, *Narrative*, p. 150.

88. HMC, *Report on the Manuscripts in Various Collections*, London, 1913, VIII, p. 167.
89. NRS, GD61/115, 5.
90. Ibid.
91. Allardyce, *Historical Papers*, II, p. 610.
92. Hughes, *Plain Narrative*, p. 25.
93. Ibid.
94. Wilson, *Life and Letters of Wolfe*, p. 62.
95. TNA, SP54/30/21A.
96. Hughes, *Plain Narrative*, p. 26.
97. Robert Forbes, *Jacobite Memoirs*, p. 142.
98. Elcho, *Short Account*, p. 431.
99. Robert Forbes, *Jacobite Memoirs*, p. 292.
100. Ray, *History*, p. 334.
101. Blaikie, 'Origins', p. 214; Yorke, *Hardwicke*, I, p. 523; Wilson, *Life and Letters of Wolfe*, p. 65 (NLS, MS. 3735, 290).
102. Robert Forbes, *Jacobite Memoirs*, p. 142; NAM, 7411-101-11-1, p. 28.
103. Rawson (ed.), *Memoirs of Johnstone*, p. 123.
104. Elcho, *Short Account*, p. 432.
105. NAM, 7411-101-11-1, p. 28.
106. Paton (ed.), 'Lyon', I, pp. 67, 86, 87.
107. Maxwell, *Narrative*, pp. 151–2.
108. TNA, SP54/30/21A.
109. Paton (ed.), 'Lyon', I, p. 5.
110. TNA, SP54/27/55a.
111. Anderson, 'Culloden', p. 22; Anon, 'The Battle of Culloden', *Journal of the Society for Army Historical Research*, 36, 1957, p. 24.
112. Blaikie, 'Origins', p. 215.
113. Tayler and Tayler, *1745*, p. 164.
114. Anderson, 'Culloden', p. 22.
115. Maxwell, *Narrative*, p. 152.
116. NLS, MS 3735, 288.
117. Hughes, *Plain Narrative*, p. 26.
118. Wilson, *Life and Letters of Wolfe*, p. 65.
119. Robert Forbes, *Jacobite Memoirs*, p. 142.
120. Elcho, *Short Account*, p. 433.
121. Pollard, *Culloden*, p. 143.
122. Maxwell, *Narrative*, p. 152.
123. Yorke, *Hardwicke*, p. 523.
124. Henderson, *History*, p. 115.
125. Ray, *History*, pp. 334, 335.
126. Anon, 'Culloden', p. 24.
127. Anderson, 'Culloden', p. 22.
128. Hughes, *Plain Narrative*, p. 26.
129. Marchant, *History*, pp. 400–1.
130. Henderson, *History*, p. 115.
131. Hughes, *Plain Narrative*, p. 26.

132. NRS, GD1/53/81/1.
133. Wilson, *Life and Letters of Wolfe*, p. 62.
134. Douglas, *History*, p. 197.
135. Yorke, *Hardwicke*, I, p. 523.
136. TNA, WO116/4.
137. Pollard, *Culloden*, p. 145.
138. Yorke, *Hardwicke*, I, pp. 523–4.
139. *Gentleman's Magazine*, 16, 1746, p. 220.
140. NLS, MS 3735, 288.
141. *Newcastle Courant*, 19–26 Apr. 1746.
142. Douglas, *History*, p. 197.
143. *The Oxford Gazette or Reading Mercury*, 28 Apr. 1746.
144. Elcho, *Short Account*, p. 433–4.
145. Douglas, *History*, p. 199.
146. Ibid.
147. Henderson, *History*, p. 117.
148. Wilson, *Life and Letters of Wolfe*, p. 63.
149. RA, CP14/11.
150. Paton (ed.), 'Lyon', II, p. 262.
151. Wilson, *Life and Letters of Wolfe*, p. 63.
152. Henderson, *History*, p. 116.
153. Robert Forbes, *Jacobite Memoirs*, p. 124.
154. HMC, *Hastings*, pp. 55–6.
155. LMA, WJ/SP/1746/06/15.
156. Ray, *History*, p. 335.
157. D.W. Kemp (ed.), 'Bishop Pococke's Tours of Scotland, 1747-1760', *Scottish History Society*, series 1, I, 1887, p. 105.
158. RA, CP14/10-11.
159. Paton (ed.), 'Lyon', I, p. 87.
160. RA, CP14/58.
161. Blaikie, 'Origins', p. 214.
162. Rawson (ed.), *Memoirs of Johnstone*, p. 123.
163. Henderson, *History*, p. 116.
164. Wilson, *Life and Letters of Wolfe*, p. 65.
165. Rawson (ed.), *Memoirs of Johnstone*, pp. 135–6.
166. RA, CP14/422.
167. Anderson, 'Culloden', p. 22.
168. Pollard, *Culloden*, p. 148.
169. Yorke, *Hardwicke*, I, p. 524; Blaikie, 'Origins', pp. 214–15.
170. Elcho, *Short Account*, p. 433.
171. Tayler and Tayler, *1745*, p. 165.
172. Paton, 'Lyon', II, p. 262.
173. RA, HT, 7411-101-11-1, p. 28.
174. Elcho, *Short Account*, p. 434.
175. Rawson (ed.), *Memoirs of Johnstone*, p. 124.
176. Tayler and Tayler, *1745*, p. 164.

177. Robert Forbes, *Jacobite Memoirs*, p. 143.
178. NLS, MS. 3735, 290.
179. NRS, GD45/1/229.
180. RA, HT, 7411-101-11-1, p. 28.
181. Tayler and Tayler, *1745*, p. 165.
182. Marchant, *History*, p. 400.
183. Wilson, *Life and Letters of Wolfe*, p. 63.
184. NRS, GD45/1/229.
185. TNA, SP54/30/21a.
186. Marchant, *History*, p. 393.
187. Ray, *History*, p. 337.
188. *Caledonian Mercury*, 29 Sep. 1746.
189. Yorke, *Hardwicke*, I, p. 514.
190. Rawson (ed.), *Memoirs of Johnstone*, p. 126.
191. RA, HT, 7411-101-11-1, p. 28.
192. *Newcastle Courant*, 26 Apr. 1746.
193. RA, HT, 7411-101-11-1, p. 28.
194. TNA, SP54/30/21A.
195. RA, HT, 7411-101-11-1, p. 28.
196. TNA, SP54/30/21A.
197. Marchant, *History*, p. 401.
198. *The London Gazette*, 26 Apr. 1746.
199. Marchant, *History*, p. 395, 401.
200. *Caledonian Mercury*, 10 Jun. 1746.
201. Kemp, 'Pococke's Tours', p. 108.
202. Paton (ed.), 'Lyon', II, p. 4.
203. NRS, GD18/3260.
204. TNA, SP54/30/21A.
205. Anderson, 'Culloden', p. 24.
206. HMC, *Laing*, II, p. 367.
207. NLS, MS. 3735, 190.
208. *Gentleman's Magazine*, 16, 1746, p. 219.
209. Henderson, *Cumberland*, p. 118.
210. LMA, WJ/SP/1746/06/15.
211. NRS, GD18/3260.
212. HMC, *Laing*, II, p. 367.
213. Historical Manuscripts Commission Report Vol. 10, London, 1885, p. 445.
214. Allardyce, *Historical Papers*, II, p. 610.
215. Lewis, *Letters of Horace Walpole*, 19, p. 249
216. McCann, *Correspondence of Richmond and Newcastle*, p. 211.
217. Ray, *History*, p. 341.
218. Henderson, *Cumberland*, p. 118.
219. Douglas, *History*, p. 198.
220. Henderson, *Cumberland*, pp. 118–19.
221. *Gentleman's Magazine*, 16, 1746, pp. 239–40; TNA, SP54/29/32d; WO10/30.
222. Blaikie, 'Origins', pp. 432–4.

223. Anderson, 'Culloden', p. 23.
224. *Caledonian Mercury*, 10 Jun. 1746.
225. *Gentleman's Magazine*, 16, 1746, p. 235.
226. RA, CP14/385.
227. Anderson, 'Culloden', p. 22.
228. Lewis, *Letters of Horace Walpole*, 19, p. 247
229. Henderson, *Cumberland*, p. 121.
230. Elcho, *Short Account*, p. 434.
231. Henderson, *History*, p. 116.
232. Yorke, *Hardwicke*, I, p. 514.
233. *Stamford Mercury*, 4 Sep. 1746.
234. Henderson, *History*, p. 117.
235. Hughes, *Plain Narrative*, p. 44.
236. Rawson (ed.), *Memoirs of Johnstone*, p. 126.
237. Yorke, *Hardwicke*, I, p. 553.
238. Tony Pollard and Neil Oliver, *Two Men in a Trench*, London, 2002, pp. 263, 285.
239. Ray, *History*, pp. 343–4.
240. *Newcastle Courant*, 26 Apr. 1746.
241. Paton (ed.), 'Lyon', I, pp. 32–3.
242. Lewis, *Letters of Horace Walpole*, 19, p. 299.
243. Elcho, *Short Account*, pp. 461–2.
244. Bell (ed.), 'Memorials of John Murray of Broughton', p. 335.
245. Hughes, *Plain Narrative*, pp. 31–2.
246. Paton (ed.), 'Lyon', II, p. 4.
247. Ibid., I, p. 218.
248. Anderson, 'Culloden', p. 23.
249. NRS, GD139/535.
250. NLS, MS. 3735, 290.
251. TNA, SP54/30/21A.
252. Yorke, *Hardwicke*, I, p. 528.
253. NRO/ZRI/27/4/66.
254. RA, CP13/385.
255. Anon, 'The Battle of Culloden', pp. 184–5.
256. Henderson, *History*, p. 119.
257. Rawson (ed.), *Memoirs of Johnstone*, p. 132.
258. Maxwell, *Narrative*, p. 156.
259. Henderson, *History*, pp. 119–120.
260. Saville, 'Secret Comment, p. 271.
261. Bell, 'Memorials', p. 220n.
262. Gray, 'Memoirs', p. 202.

Chapter 16: The End of the Jacobite Campaigns
  1. Blaikie, 'Origins', p. 216.
  2. Elcho, *Short Account*, p. 436.
  3. Rawson (ed.), *Memoirs of Johnstone*, p. 127.
  4. Maxwell, *Narrative*, pp. 158–9.

5. TNA, SPS, 54/30/21a.
6. RA, CP14/123.
7. Wilson, *Life and Letters of Wolfe*, p. 68.
8. S. Boyse, *An Impartial History of the Late Rebellion in 1745*, Dublin, 1746, p. 154; Ilchester, *Letters*, p. 10.
9. Anderson, 'Culloden', p. 24.
10. McLachlan, *Sketch*, p. 308.
11. RA, CP14/233
12. Wilson, *Life and Letters of Wolfe*, p. 68.
13. Ray, *History* p. 348.
14. TNA, SP54/31, 17.
15. RA, CP14/233.
16. BL.Add. Mss, 32707, ff.128.
17. RA, CP14/354.
18. TNA, SP54/31/9a.
19. Douglas, *History*, p. 235.
20. *Gentleman's Magazine*, 16, 1746, p. 274.
21. *General Advertiser*, 3620, 3 Jun. 1746.
22. Douglas, *History*, pp. 231–2.
23. RA, CP15/302.
24. TNA, SP54/32/2B.
25. RA, CP15/384.
26. TNA, SP54/32/4A.
27. Douglas, *History*, p. 230.
28. Ibid., pp. 237–8.
29. Ibid., p. 232.
30. McLachlan, *Sketch*, p. 323.
31. RA, CP16/74
32. Paton (ed.), 'Lyon', III, p. 72.
33. RA, CP16/59.
34. Paton (ed.), 'Lyon', II, pp. 79–80, 253.
35. McLachlan, *Sketch*, pp. 322, 325.
36. TNA, SPS, 54/30/21a.
37. RA, CP14/292.
38. TNA, SP36/85, f232r-233v.
39. Arnot and Seton, 'Prisoners', I, pp. 152–3.

Conclusion
1. Home, *History*, p. 2.

Bibliography

Primary Sources
Manuscript
    Blair Castle
    Atholl Papers, 45/12/77.

    British Library
    Additional Manuscripts, 32707, 63592, 33004, 63592.
    Stowe, 158.

    Edinburgh University Library Special Collections
    Laing MSS, 11, 89/388.

    Lancashire Record Office
    QSP 1091/8.
    DDX2244/1.
    DDX1788/1.

    London Metropolitan Archives
    WJ/SP/1746/06/15.

    National Archives
    Forfeited Estates Commission 1/246-250.
    State Papers Domestic 35 and 36.
    State Papers Entry Books, SP44.
    State Papers Scotland, 54/9-11, 13, 26-32.
    SP55/13/258.

    War Office
    WO4/17, WO5/5, 20, WO116/1-5.
    KB8/66.

National Records of Scotland
CH12/12/1717.
E100/13.
GD1/53/86/2.
GD24/1/872/1/3.
GD24/5/162/4.
GD24/5/78.
GD26/8/71.
GD26/9/229, 486.
GD51/16/73.
GD51/16/103/2/449.
GD77/189.
GD112/39/145/11.
GD124/15/808.
GD200/5/787a.
GD205/38/2/1.
GD220/5/601.
GD220/5/817.
GD220/5/489.
GD406/1/3065, 3608, 3609.
GD498/1/26.
GD1440/3/5.
RH15/14/149.

National Library of Scotland
MS 3738, 3740.
MS 542.
MS 1498.
MS 7012.
MS 975.

Royal Archives
Cumberland Papers, 9-16.
Hawley-Tuovey Papers, 7411-24-101-1

Northumberland Record Office
ZRI/27/4/66.
QS44/51.

Tyne and Wear Archive Service
CP3/22.

West Yorkshire Archive Service: Wakefield Archives
QS10/13.

Printed

Addy, Peter and McNiven, Peter (eds), 'Diary of Henry Prescott', II, *Record Society of Lancashire and Cheshire*, CXXXII, 1992.

Allardyce, James, *Historical Papers relating to the Jacobite Period, 1699-1750*, 1 Aberdeen, 1895.

Anderson, W.H. (ed.), 'The Battle of Culloden', *Journal of the Society for Army Historical Research*, I, 1921.

Anon, *Annals of the Reign of George I*, London, 1716.

Anon, *An Account of the Battel of Dunblain in a Letter from a Gentleman at Stirling to his Friend in Edinburgh*, 1715.

Anon, 'The Battle of Culloden', *Journal of the Society for Army Historical Research*, 36, 1957.

Anon, *Memoir of Lord Dundee, by an Officer in the Army*, London, 1711.

Anon, *Exact Narrative of the conflict at Dunkeld*, Edinburgh, 1689.

Anon, *The Life of the Late Right Honourable George, Lord Carpenter*, London, 1736.

Anon, *Woodhouselea Manuscripts*, London, 1907.

Anon, *A True and Real account of the Defeat of General Buchan and Brigadier Cannon*, London, 1690.

Anon, *Great News from Scotland and Ireland*, 1690.

Anon, *A Letter about the Occurrences from and at Preston*, Edinburgh, 1718.

Atholl, John, *Chronicles of the Atholl and Tullibardine Families*, 5 vols, Edinburgh, 1908.

Balfour-Maitland, Evan Whyte Melville (ed.), 'Estate Proceedings, An Account of the Proceedings of the Estates of Scotland, 1689-1690', *Scottish History Society*, series 4, vols 46–47 , 1954.

Bell, R.F. (ed.), 'Memorials of John Murray of Broughton, 1740-1747', *Scottish History Society*, series 1, vol. 27, 1897.

Blaikie, Walter Biggar (ed.), 'Itinerary of Prince Charles Edward Stuart', *Scottish History Society*, 1st series, vol.23, 1898

_____, 'Origins of the Forty-Five, 1737-1746', *Scottish History Society*, Series 2, Vol. 2, 1916.

Boyse, S., *An Impartial History of the Late Rebellion in 1745*, Dublin, 1746.

Brown Iain, and Hugh Cheape, *Witness to Rebellion: John Mclean's Journal of the Forty-Five and the Penicuik Drawings*, Edinburgh, 1996.

Calendar of Treasury Books, XXXII, 1716, Part 1.

Campbell, Robert, *The Life of the Most Illustrious Prince, John Duke of Argyle and Greenwich*, Edinburgh, 1745.

Carleton, George, *The Military Memoirs of an English Officer*, London, 1728.

Cowper, Spencer (ed.), *Diary of Lady Mary Cowper,*, London, 1865.

Creighton, John, *Memoirs*, London, 1731.

Dalton, Charles, *English Army Lists, 1660-1714*, 6 vols, London, 1892–1904.

_____, *Army of George I*, London, 1930.

Dennistoun, James, *Memoirs of Sir Robert Strange*, I, London, 1855.

Dickson, W.K., 'The Jacobite Attempt of 1719. Letters of James, second Duke of Ormonde', *Scottish History Society*, Vol. 191, 1895.

Doddridge, Phillip, *Some Remarkable Passages in the Life of the Hon. Colonel James Gardiner*, Hedley, 1812.

Douglas, F., *History of the rebellion in 1745 and 1746*, Aberdeen, 1755.

Dundee Letters: Letters of John Graham of Claverhouse, Viscount Dundee, Edinburgh, 1826.

Elcho, Lord, *Short Account of the Affairs of Scotland, 1744-1746,* Edinburgh, 1907.

Ellis, Joyce (ed.), 'The Letters of Henry Liddell to William Cotesworth', *Surtees Society,* 197, 1987.

Fitzjames, James (ed.), *Memoirs of the Duke of Berwick,* II, London, 1798.

Forbes, Duncan (ed.), *Culloden Papers,* London, 1815.

Forbes, Robert, *Jacobite Memoirs,* Edinburgh, 1834.

Fraser, William, *Melvilles Earls of Melville and the Leslies Earls of Leven,* III, Edinburgh, 1890.

_____, *The Earls of Cromartie,* 2, London, 1876.

Graham, James (ed.), 'The Grameid', *Scottish History Society,* Series 1, Vol. 2, 1886.

Gray, John (ed.), 'Memoirs of Sir John Clark of Penicuik', Hughes, Matthew, *Plain Narrative,* London, 1746.

Hearne, Thomas, *The Remains of Thomas Hearne,* ed. John Buchanan-Brown, London, 1966.

Henderson, Andrew, *History of the Rebellion,* London, 1748.

_____, *Duke of Cumberland,* London, 1766.

Hepburne-Scott, G.E.C. (ed.), 'Marchmont Papers', *Scottish History Society Miscellany,* 3rd series, 17 (1933).

Hewins, W.A.S., *The Whiteford Papers Papers,* Oxford, 1898.

Hibbert-Ware, Samuel (ed.), 'Lancashire Memorials of 1715', *Chetham Society,* V (1845)

Historical Manuscripts Commission, *Calendar of the Stuart Papers,* Vol. 1, London, 1902.

_____, *Manuscripts of the Marquess of Townshend,* London, 1887.

_____, *Manuscripts of S.H. Le Fleming Esq. of Rydal Hall,* London, 1896.

_____, *Report on the Laing Manuscripts preserved in the University of Edinburgh,* London, 1925.

_____, *Report on the Manuscripts of the Earl of Eglington,* London, 1885,

_____, *Report on the Manuscripts of the Earl of Mar and Kellie preserved at Alloa House,* London, 1904.

_____, *Report on the Manuscripts of the late Reginald Hastings,* London, 1928.

_____, *Report on the Manuscripts in Various Collections,* II, London, 1903.

_____, *The Manuscripts of the Duke of Athole and the Earl of Home,* London, 1891.

Home, John, *History of the rebellion in the year 1745,* London, 1802.

Hughes, Matthew, *A Plain Narrative,* London, 1746.

Ilchester, Lord, *Letters to Henry Fox, Lord Holland,* London, 1895.

Kane, R., *The Campaigns of King William and Queen Anne,* London, 1745.

Keith, James, *A Fragment of a Memoir of Field Marshal Joseph Keith,* London, 1845.

Kemp, D.W. (ed.), 'Bishop Pococke's Tours of Scotland, 1747-1760', *Scottish History Society,* Series 1, Vol. 1, 1887.

Kimsley, James (ed.), *Anecdotes and Characters of the Times,* Oxford, 1973.

Kington-Oliphant, T.K. (ed.), *Jacobite Lairds of Gask*, London, 1870.

Kirkconnel, James, *Narrative of the Campaign of Prince Charles' Expedition to Scotland*, Edinburgh, 1841.

Lewis, W.S. (ed.), *Letters of Horace Walpole*, Vol. 19, Yale, 1955.

Lodge, Richard (ed.), *Private Correspondence of Chesterfield and Newcastle, 1744-6*, London, 1930.

Mackay, Hugh, *Memoirs of the War carried on in Scotland and Ireland, 1689-1691*, Edinburgh, 1833.

MacKnight J. (ed.), *Memoirs of Lochiel*, Glasgow, 1842.

MacPherson, James (ed.), *Original Papers, containing the Secret history of Great Britain*, London, 1775.

Marchant, John, *History of the Present Rebellion*, London, 1746.

Matthews, William (ed.), *The Diary of Dudley Ryder, 1715-1716*, London: Methuen, 1939.

Maxwell, James, *Narrative of Charles, Prince of Wales' Expedition to Scotland in the year 1745*, Edinburgh, 1841.

McBane, Donald, *The Expert Sword-Man's Companion*, Glasgow, 2015.

McCann, T.J. (ed.), *Correspondence of the Dukes of Richmond and Newcastle, 1724-1750*, Sussex Record Society, 1983.

McKnight, J. (ed.), *Memoirs of Sir Ewen Cameron*, Edinburgh, 1841

McLachlan, A.N.C., *A Sketch of Cumberland's Military Life*, London, 1876.

Miller, A.H. (ed.), 'Eyewitness Account of Killiecrankie', *Scottish History Review*, III, 1905.

Napier, Mark, *Memorials and Letters of Dundee*, 3 vols, Edinburgh and London, 1862.

Neil, G. (ed.), 'Journal of a Soldier in the Earl of Eglington's Troop of Horse', *Transactions of the Glasgow Archaeological Society*, I, 1868.

Newton, Lady (ed.), *Lyme Letters 1660-1760*, London, 1936.

Nicholas, Donald, 'An Account of the Proceedings from Prince Charles' landing to Prestonpans', *Scottish History Society Miscellany*, Series 4, Vol. 10, 1958.

—————————, *Intercepted Post 1745*, London, 1954.

Oates, J.D., and Kavickas, K. (eds), 'Jacobites and Jacobins', *Record Society of Lancashire and Cheshire*, 2006.

Paton, Henry (ed.), 'Lyon in Mourning', *Scottish History Society*, 20-21, 1895.

—————————, 'Journal of the Several Occurrences', *Scottish History Society Miscellany*, I, 1893.

Patten, Robert, *History of the Late Rebellion*, London, 1745.

Radcliffe, Charles, *A Genuine and Impartial Account*, London, 1747.

Rae, Peter, *History of the Late Rebellion*, Dumfries, 1746.

Rawson, B. (ed.), *Memoirs of the Chevalier de Johnstone*, London, 1958.

Ray, James, *A Complete History of the rebellion*, London, 1754.

Registers of the Privy Council of Scotland, 13–15, 1689–1691.

Robinson, J.O. (ed.), 'Military Memoirs of Lieutenant General the Hon, Charles Colville', *Journal of the Society for Army Historical Research*, XXV, 1947.

Saville, Alan (ed.), 'Secret Comment: The Diaries of Gertrude Saville, 1721-1757', *Thoroton Society*, 41 (1995).

Scott, Andrew Murray (ed.), 'Letters of John Graham of Claverhouse', *Scottish History Society*, Series 5, Vol. 3, Miscellany II, 1989.

Scott, Walter (ed.), *Memoirs of the Insurrection in Scotland in 1715*, Edinburgh, 1845.

Slezar, John, *Theatrum Scotiae*, 1693.
Smith, S.D. (ed.), *Joseph Symson, An Exact and Industrious Tradesman, 1711-1720*, Oxford, 2003.
Tayler, Alastair and Henrietta (ed.), *1745 and After*, London, 1938.
_____, *Jacobite Miscellany*, Oxford, 1958.
Thomson, T., *Acts of the Parliament of Scotland*, 1814–1875.
Thornton, William, *The Counterpoise*, London, 1754.
Wade, George, *A Report of the Proceedings and Opinions*, Dublin, 1749.
Wilson, B., *Life and Letters of James Wolfe*, London, 1909.
Yorke, P.C. (ed.), *Life of Lord Chancellor Hardwicke*, I, Cambridge, 1913.

Newspapers
Caledonian Mercury, 1745–1746.
Daily Courant, 1715–1716, 1719.
Evening Post, 1715.
Flying Post, 1715.
General Advertiser, 1746.
Gentleman's Magazine, 1745–1746
Glasgow Courant, 1746
London Gazette, 1689, 1715, 1719, 1746.
Newcastle Courant, 1746.
Newcastle Gazette, 1745.
Oxford Gazette or Reading Mercury, 1746.
Penny London Post, 1746.
Political State of Great Britain, 1715, 1716, 1719.
Pue's Occurrences, 1719.
St. James' Evening Post, 1715.
St. James' Post, 1715.
Stamford Mercury, 1745–1746.
Weekly Journal, 1715, 1716, 1719.
Whitehall Evening Post, 1719

Secondary Sources
Anon, 'The Battle of Culloden', *Journal of the Society for Army Historical Research*, 36, 1957.
Anon, *The Battle of Sheriffmuir*, Stirling, 1898.
A9 Dualling Programme: Killiecrankie to Pitagowan – Archaeological Metal detecting Survey at the battlefield, 2015.
Anderson, W.H., 'The Battle of Culloden', *Journal of the Society for Army Historical Research*, 1, 1921.
Bailey, Geoff, *Falkirk or Paradise: The Battle of Falkirk Muir, January 1746*, Edinburgh, 1996.
Barthorp, Michael, *The Jacobite Rebellions, 1689-1745*, London, 1982.
Baynes, John, *The Jacobite Rising of 1715*, London, 1970.
Blackmore, David, *Destructive and Formidable: British Infantry Firepower, 1642-1765*, London, 2014.
Duffy, Christopher, *Fight for a Throne, The Untold Story of the Last Jacobite Rising*, Solihull. 2015.

_____, *The Military Experience in the Age of Reason*, London, 1987.
Hardwicke, Charles, *The History of the Borough of Preston*, Preston, 1857.
Harrington, P., *Culloden 1746: The Highlanders' Last Charge* Oxford, 1991.
Hopkins, Paul, *Glencoe and the End of the Highland War*, Edinburgh, 1989.
Inglis, William, *The Battle of Sheriffmuir*, Stirling, 2005.
Johnston, Arran, *On Gladsmuir shall the battle be: The battle of Prestonpans, 1745*, Solihull, 2017.
Lenman, Bruce *The Jacobite Risings in Britain, 1689-1746*, London, 1980.
Linkwater, Magnus, and Christian Hesketh, *John Graham of Claverhouse, Bonnie Dundee: For King and Conscience*, Edinburgh, 1989.
Marguiles, M., *The Battle of Prestonpans*, Stroud, 2007.
Nicholas, David, *Intercepted Post 1745*, London, 1956
Oates, Jonathan, *Battle of Killiecrankie and the first Jacobite Campaign*, Solihull, 2018.
_____, *The Last Battle on English Soil: Preston, 1715*, London, 2015.
_____, *The Crucible of the Fifteen: Sheriffmuir*, Solihull, 2017.
Oxford Dictionary of National Biography, 2004.
Page, William (ed.), *Victoria County Histories Lancashire*, VII, London, 1911.
Petrie, Charles, *The Jacobite Movement*, London, 1932.
Pittock, Murray, *Culloden*, Oxford, 2016.
Pollard, Tony (ed.), *Culloden: The History and Archaeology of the Last Clan Battle*, Barnsley, 2009.
Pollard, Tony, and Neil Oliver, *Two Men in a Trench*, London, 2002.
_____, *Two Men in a Trench II*, London, 2003.
Prebble, John, *Culloden*, London, 1963.
Reid, Stuart, *1745: A Military History of the Last Jacobite Rising*, Staplehurst, 1996.
_____, *Sheriffmuir: 1715*, London, 2014.
_____, *Like Hungry Wolves: Culloden Moor, 16 April 1746*, London, 1994.
_____, *Culloden*, Barnsley, 2005.
_____, *Killiecrankie*, Leigh on Sea, 1989.
_____, and G. Embleton, *Culloden Moor, 1746*, Oxford, 2002.
Roberts, John, *The Jacobite Wars: Scotland and the Military Campaigns of 1715 and 1745*, Edinburgh, 2002.
Scott, Andrew, *Bonnie Dundee*, Edinburgh, 2000.
Seton, A.G., and J.S. Arnot, 'Prisoners of the '45', *Scottish History Society*, Series 3, Vol, II, 1929.
Sked P., and S. Horrocks, *Culloden*, Edinburgh, 1997.
Stewart, D. and J., *The Stewarts of Appin*, Edinburgh, 1880.
Szechi, Daniel, *1715: The Great Jacobite Rising*, New Haven, 2006.
_____, *The Jacobites: Britain and Europe, 1688-1788*, Manchester, 1994.
_____, *Britain's Lost Revolution? Jacobite Scotland and French Grand Strategy, 1701-1708*, Manchester, 2015.
Tayler, Alastair and Henrietta, *John Claverhouse*, London, 1938.
Terry, Charles Stanford, *John Graham of Claverhouse, Viscount Dundee*, London, 1905.
Tomasson, Kathleen, and Frances Buist, *Battles of the Forty-Five*, London, 1962.
Worton, Jonathan, *The Battle of Glenshiel: The Jacobite Rising of 1719*, Solihull, 2018.

Index